CW01262735

THE GREAT MOUNTAIN CRAGS OF SCOTLAND

A CELEBRATION OF SCOTTISH MOUNTAINEERING
Compiled by Guy Robertson & Adrian Crofton

Published by Vertebrate Publishing, Sheffield.
www.v-publishing.co.uk

THE GREAT MOUNTAIN CRAGS OF SCOTLAND

First published in 2014 by Vertebrate Publishing.

Vertebrate Publishing. Crescent House, 228 Psalter Lane, Sheffield S11 8UT.

Copyright © Guy Robertson, Adrian Crofton and individual authors 2014.

Foreword copyright © Andy Cave 2014.

The authors have asserted their rights under the Copyright, Designs and Patents Act 1988 to be identified as authors of this work.

The authors have stated to the publishers that, except in such minor respects not affecting the substantial accuracy of the work, the contents of the book are true.

A CIP catalogue record for this book is available from the British Library.

ISBN: 978-1-906148-89-8 (Hardback)

10 9 8 7 6 5 4 3 2 1

Front cover: Dave MacLeod climbing *Dalriada* (E7) on The Cobbler.
Photo: Dave Cuthbertson.

Back cover: Mainreachan Buttress, Fuar Tholl.
Photo: Colin Threlfall.

All rights reserved. No part of this work covered by the copyright hereon may be reproduced or used in any form or by any means – graphic, electronic, or mechanised, including photocopying, recording, taping or information storage and retrieval systems – without the written permission of the publisher.

Every effort has been made to obtain the necessary permissions with reference to copyright material, both illustrative and quoted. We apologise for any omissions in this respect and will be pleased to make the appropriate acknowledgements in any future edition.

Designed & produced by Nathan Ryder – www.v-graphics.co.uk

Printed and bound in China by Latitude Press Ltd.

MIX
Paper from responsible sources
FSC® C010256

Contents

Acknowledgements by Guy Robertson & Adrian Crofton … 7
Foreword by Andy Cave … 9
Introduction by Guy Robertson & Adrian Crofton … 10
Ecological Notes by Gareth Marshall … 12

The South West Highlands

Poem: *South West Highlands* by Stuart B. Campbell … 17
Introduction to the South West Highlands by Simon Richardson … 18
The Cobbler by Dave MacLeod … 23
Slime Wall, Buachaille Etive Mor by Guy Robertson, story by Mark McGowan … 31
North Face, Aonach Dubh by Blair Fyffe … 39
Church Door Buttress, Bidean nam Bian by Ian Taylor … 47
Orion and Minus Face, Ben Nevis by Viv Scott … 55
Carn Dearg Buttress, Ben Nevis by Adrian Crofton, story by Guy Robertson … 65
Number Three Gully Buttress, Ben Nevis by Blair Fyffe … 75

The North West Highlands

Poem: *North West Highlands* by Stuart B. Campbell … 85
Introduction to the North West Highlands by Jason Currie … 86
Giant's Wall, Beinn Bhan by Martin Moran … 91
Mainreachan Buttress, Fuar Tholl by Andy Nisbet … 99
West Central Wall, Beinn Eighe by Jason Currie … 105
Far East Wall, Beinn Eighe by Andy Nisbet … 115
Atlantic Wall, Slioch by Roger Webb … 123
Cárn Mór by Graham Tyldesley … 131
Coire Ghranda Upper Cliff, Beinn Dearg by Guy Robertson … 139
The Fhidhleir's Nose, Ben Mor Coigach by Simon Richardson … 145
West Buttress, Stac Pollaidh by Ian Taylor … 153
Barrel Buttress, Quinag by Roger Webb … 163
First Dionard Buttress, Foinaven by Rick Campbell … 171
Lord Reay's Seat, Foinaven by Malcolm Bass … 177
Sgor a' Chleiridh, Ben Loyal by Keith Milne … 183

The Islands

Poem: *Islands* by Stuart B. Campbell	**195**
Introduction to the Islands by Blair Fyffe	**196**
Cir Mhor, Arran by John Watson	**199**
The Bastion, Cioch na h-Oighe, Arran by Kevin Howett	**207**
The Great Prow, Bla Bheinn, Skye by Grant Farquhar	**213**
Sgurr Mhic Choinnich North Face, Skye by Mike Lates	**223**
East Buttress, Sròn na Ciche, Skye by Kevin Howett	**229**
Sròn Uladail, Harris by Tony Stone	**237**
Creag Dhubh Diobadail, Lewis by Tony Stone	**245**

▲ Coire Mhic Fhearchair from the top of the Triple Buttress, Beinn Eighe, Torridon. Photo: *Colin Threlfall.*

The Cairngorms & Central Highlands

Poem: *Cairngorms* by Stuart B. Campbell	**255**
Introduction to the Cairngorms & Central Highlands by Adrian Crofton	**256**
Pinnacle Buttress, Creag Meagaidh by Es Tressider	**263**
Shelter Stone Crag by Guy Robertson, story by Rick Campbell	**271**
Central Gully Wall, Creag an Dubh Loch by Julian Lines	**279**
Tough-Brown Face, Lochnagar by Brian Davison	**287**
Black Spout Pinnacle, Lochnagar by Guy Robertson & Nick Bullock	**295**
Mitre Ridge West Face, Beinn a' Bhùird by Adrian Crofton	**303**
Further Reading	**312**

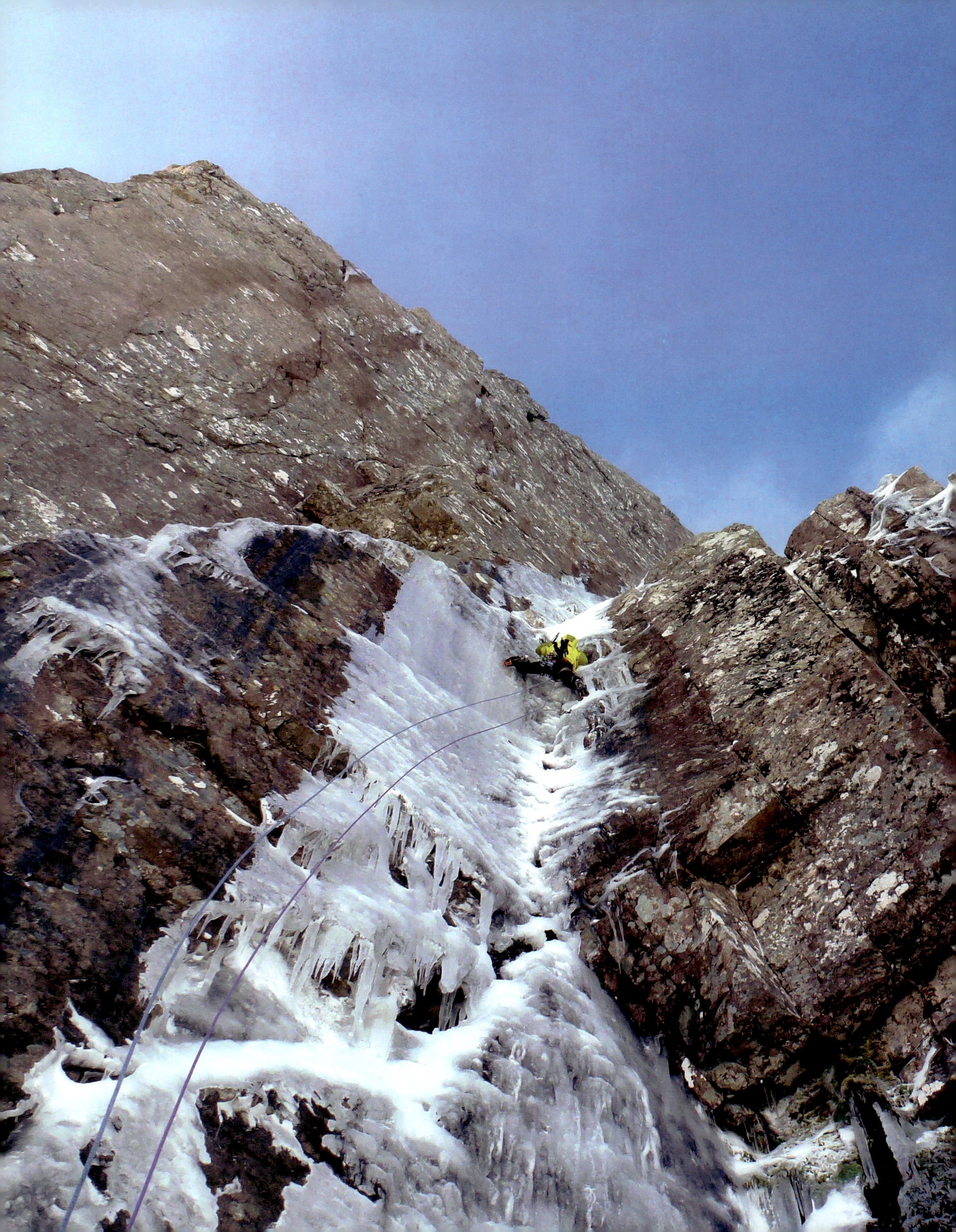

Acknowledgements

To all the writers who have generously contributed original pieces to this book we owe a huge debt of gratitude; for believing in the project and for their shared love of these mountains and the traditions of Scottish climbing. They are, in no particular order: Graham Tyldesley, Andy Nisbet, Gareth Marshall, Blair Fyffe, Tony Stone, Jason Currie, Dave MacLeod, Kev Howett, Malcolm Bass, Grant Farquhar, Keith Milne, Mark McGowan, Julian Lines, Simon Richardson, Brian Davison, Viv Scott, Es Tressider, Martin Moran, Rick Campbell, Roger Webb, Nick Bullock, Ian Taylor and Mike Lates. Stuart B. Campbell's rich verse provides the perfect lyrical glue for the book, and each of his four pieces draws on and adds to the texts that follow. Our thanks for these four perfect gifts.

Whilst a few of the photographs here are our own, most have been kindly donated by others – in this respect the climbing community has been more than generous in its response to our pleas. For the photographic content, however, we are particularly indebted to Colin Threlfall of Armadale, on Skye. His obvious and quite unique talents were first spotted hidden away beneath the headlines on UKClimbing. We were immediately impressed. We were even more impressed when he agreed to commit his valuable time to a number of very successful 'photo shoots', often in remote places and at short notice. Colin also freely provided many other tremendous images which stand out from the pages of the book. Above all, we will always be truly grateful to Colin for his quiet, yet clear and unstinting enthusiasm and belief, for and in the book, which came at a critical juncture bringing renewed energy and direction.

Among the other photographic contributors, we owe a big thank you to Dave 'Cubby' Cuthbertson for giving up a day to carefully go through his considerable collection, and for letting us use so many of his stunning images. Cubby's talents behind the lens are well known, and it is a privilege for us to be able to present them here alongside some equally fine and inspired words.

Thanks to everyone who sent us their images to consider, including Gary Latter, Simon Yearsley, Pete Benson, Neil Morrison, Dave Cowan, Dave Ogden, Ross Hewitt, Andy Inglis, Rob Durran, Dave Redpath, Paul Tattersall, Dan Moore, Stuart Walker, Robert Mott, Murdoch Jamieson, Robin Clothier, Doug Hawthorn, Adam Russell, Ian Hey, Greg Boswell, Fionn McArthur, Jim Higgins, Patrick Roman, Ewan Lyons, Paul Diffley, R. McMurray, Dan Moore, Ali Coull, Gerry Neely and Neil Adams. Apologies if anyone has been left out here.

Our heartfelt thanks to Blair Fyffe who very kindly scrutinised the factual and technical content of the book, and to Angus Dunn for painstakingly proofreading the entire text. Any remaining errors are those of the two authors. Tony Stone also deserves a special mention, offering general advice and encouragement during the early stages of the book's development, when others were perhaps less optimistic. John Watson of Stone Country Press was involved closely at the start of the project, and gave generously of his expert advice and time throughout, as well as contributing to the text. Thanks to Roddy Read in Stornoway for the loan of his camera and tripod. Big Ian Nicolson at the Kings House Hotel kindly provided both of us with gainful employment at a stage in our lives when we might best have been described as feckless, thereby introducing us to a host of characters who in turn made us party to the tradition that is Scottish mountaineering. And thanks to Patey, Smith, Bell, Raeburn, MacInnes, Murray and all the other great Scottish pioneers who went before us, whose writings have and will continue to inspire those with the time, freedom and inclination to continue creating the great routes and tales without which this book would not exist.

Thanks to Jon Barton and John Coefield of Vertebrate Publishing for their immediate enthusiasm for the book, which had up to that point failed to find a publisher north of the border.

A great number of other climbers accompanied us on adventures that have fed into the book. They include Helen Rennard, Gordon Lennox, Alistair Robertson, Tim Whitaker, Pete McPherson, Andy Inglis, Charlie Henderson, Ritchie Biggar, Mark Garthwaite, Matt Halls, Pete Benson, Tim Rankin and others. Once again, our sincere apologies to any whose names our ailing memories have failed to recall here.

Finally we need to give humble thanks to our families; to our partners, Susan and Rachelle, and to our children Eilidh, Alasdair, Finn and Jess. They have put up with a lot to allow us to complete this book, and we have valued their opinion throughout. We hope they are pleased with it.

◀ Nick Bullock on *The Shield Direct* (VII,7), Carn Dearg, Ben Nevis.
Photo: *Guy Robertson*.

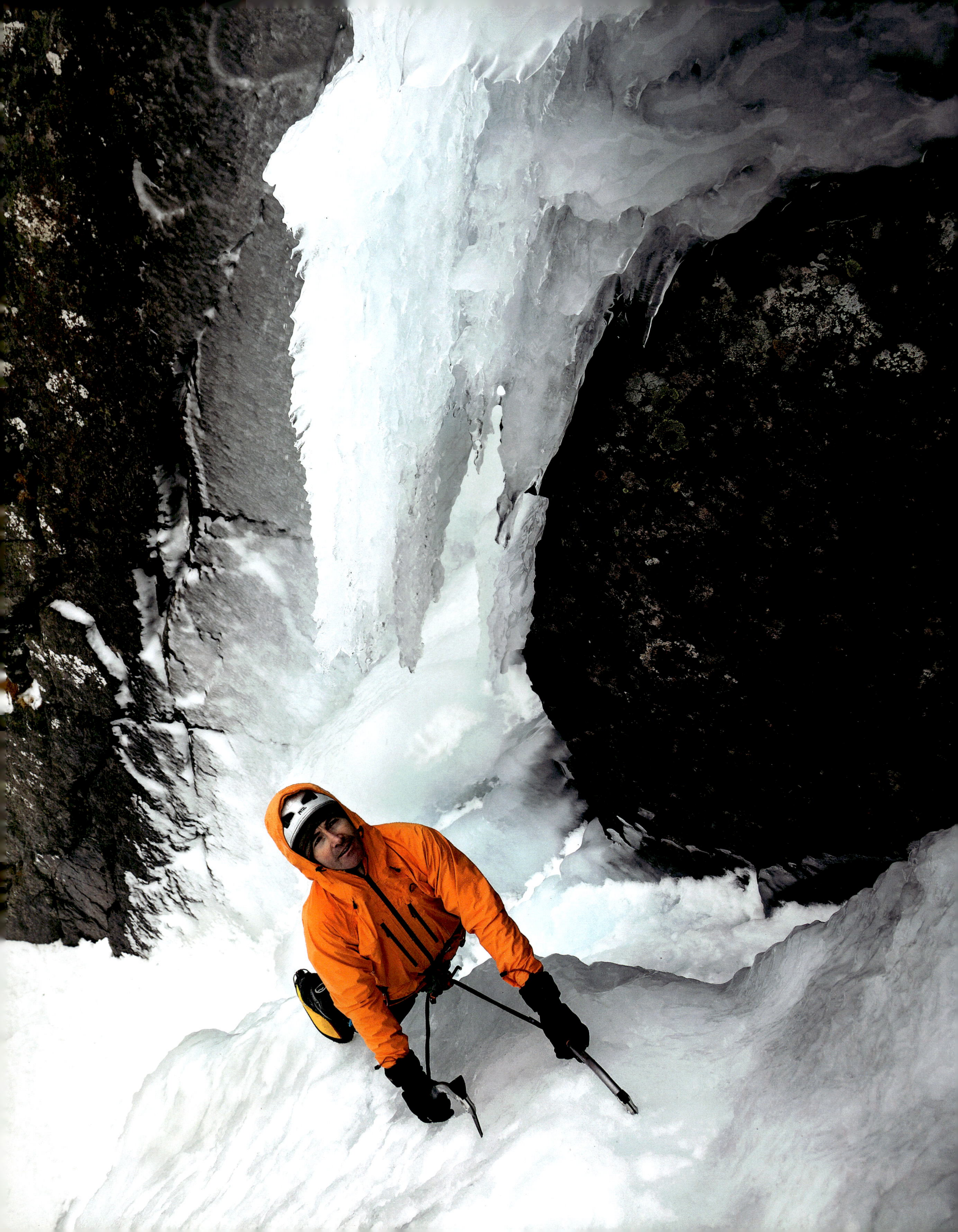

FOREWORD

Sometimes parts of Britain feel crowded. At night from the air, car lights stream between packed glowing cities. On the ground, the light pollution robs us of the night sky. Sometimes our lives seem crowded too – commuting, chatting, texting – a constant to-ing and fro-ing. For some, what keeps them going are the memories of glorious days on rock and ice and the promise of more to come.

Most of Britain's biggest and best cliffs are in Scotland, and these empty unspoilt places still excite me. The adventure is first rate, the challenge unlimited, the beauty unparalleled. For me, a few days up north, sharing a couple of classic climbs with a friend, still ranks as a highlight in the climbing year.

Coffee table books form an important part of climbing literature and over the years some have achieved classic status, fuelling the imagination of climbers of all abilities and experience. *Cold Climbs*, *Hard Rock*, *Extreme Rock* and Gaston Rébuffat's *100 Finest Climbs in the Mont Blanc Massif*, which was something of a bible for climbers in the 1980s. As a young climber, I was utterly absorbed reading these classics, and today, despite all the information available online, I still get excited when I open them.

In *The Great Mountain Crags of Scotland*, the quality of the photography alone raises the bar for the genre. The action shots perfectly capture the commitment required to negotiate these grand cliffs, be it in summer or winter. On one page, tiny red figures cling to a thinly iced *Centurion*, on another a climber wanders, seemingly lost in an impeccably smooth, blank groove. In this book, however, it is often the cliffs themselves that take centre stage, and even if we don't feel able to tackle all of the suggested climbs, we are sufficiently inspired to visit many of the venues. The sheer variety of locations, captured in such differing moods of light, is breathtaking and a reminder that – from ocean to summit – these are some of the most unspoilt places in the world.

Landscape is central in the writing too, and the various authors share their intimate knowledge and passion for the high crags, be it the famous walls of Ben Nevis or lesser known cliffs, such as Beinn Dearg's Coire Ghranda. Many of the writers, like Nisbet and Richardson, have dedicated years developing Scottish climbing, and contained within their wonderful recollections are valuable nuggets that might help us succeed in our adventures. Development of new areas combined with a surge in climbing standards has drawn interest to Scotland, nationally and internationally. It is a treat to get a glimpse of this exploration via original, first-hand accounts, such as the heart-racing piece *Steep Frowning Glories* by Robertson and Bullock. Sometimes the biggest climbing prizes have been the result of season after season of effort, Brian Davison's excellent piece about the first winter ascent of *Mort* on Lochnagar is testament to that and forms a unique historical record. I admire the hard work in the drawing together of so many new stories that are set down here.

I found Stuart B. Campbell's wonderful poetry arresting, quirky and seemingly knowing of the climber's mind and these beautiful, inhospitable places. I feel his lines both question and celebrate our antics and form a perfect bridge between the images and the longer narrative.

Some large format books become lists to be worked through over the years, but this work is much more than that. Yes, it is a celebration of magnificent climbs, but it is also a meditation on a very special relationship between people and place. Marvel at the images, savour the mystery of the great cliffs and dream of great days past and future.

Andy Cave
April 2014

◀ Andy Cave on *Waterfall Gully* (IV,4), Carn Dearg, Ben Nevis.
Photo: *Paul Diffley*, Hot Aches Productions.

Introduction

In Kevin MacNeil's novel, *The Stornoway Way*, the hero protests that the remote Outer Hebrides, far from being the back of beyond, are in fact the heart of beyond. The great Highland poets Norman MacCaig and Sorley MacLean – who wandered and fished regularly amongst the lonely Scottish hill lochs – also reflected this attitude in their work: that this is an environment beyond valuation, far more than mere recreational resource, and infinitely more precious than real estate. The value of what people now call mindfulness, of being here in the present, truly alive to the place where they are, resounds in this phrase; and there is no place we can conceive of more apposite to this state of mind than the great high crags of the Scottish Highlands.

This idea of Scotland's wild places being at the centre of things is a pivotal theme of this book. A desperate crux, a complex pitch, a spectacular traverse, or a comfortable belay – in each case, the depth of the experience is hugely enriched by dramatic surroundings, a sense of solitude, of close communion with the natural world, and of the self-sufficiency that Scottish traditional climbing requires. But always there is the place in and of itself, where we can feel simultaneously liberated and terrified by our microscopic insignificance, by the durance and the beauty of this seemingly infinite land of adventure.

The concept of this book germinated from the seeds of careless banter over a few beers and days on the hill, now well over five years ago. Why, we wondered, had there never been a major book dedicated solely to the celebration of Scotland's great crags, and the exploits and experiences of more than two generations of Scotland's leading mountaineers among them? Why does an ever-larger climbing populace appear to climb at fewer and fewer places? Of course, there are the invaluable historical accounts in the SMC journals, the compilations from Ken Wilson, and, of course, the inspired writing of Murray, Bell, Patey and others. But none of them combine historical, informative, literary and dramatic visual elements in one place, under the unifying theme of the great cliffs themselves. This then would be the book we would have loved to have had in our hands when we first started our mountaineering apprenticeship.

From the outset, there were certain things that we wanted to achieve. Fundamentally, we wanted to share the intimate knowledge, connection and passion of the writers with a wider climbing audience. All the individual climbers who have contributed to the text are seasoned specialists in the traditional climbing art. In many cases they have enjoyed extended love affairs with the cliffs they describe, and in so doing have developed a deep understanding on the style, conditions and idiosyncrasies of these great crags. This in itself is a wonderful resource. To give each author the freedom to express this knowledge with passion and vigour provides a richness and colour to the subject matter that no guidebook could contain. Add to this a magnificent selection of large format photographs, and we have hopefully achieved our aim of inspiring and equipping a new generation of climbers in Scotland, whilst sharing the attitudes and philosophy that we value from the tradition of our climbing culture. We hope that this free and heartfelt expression breathes life into the scale and atmosphere of the great cliffs and climbs, and inspires others to go and explore, developing the same sense of pride and custodianship that will ultimately help to ensure these places are cherished and protected:

> *'Like the true philosopher, the true mountaineer can look forward with rejoicing to an eternity of endeavour: to realisation without end ... I know that my position at the close of my span will be the same as it is now, and the same as that happy day when I first set foot on a hill – the Scottish Highlands will spread out before me, an unknown land.'*
> **W. H. Murray, *Undiscovered Scotland***

On a practical level, the informative elements of the book should help the reader to use their time more constructively – formulating effective strategies for success based on hard won experience. Read closely, between the lines even, and you will find some of the key ingredients that underpinned many of the great ascents of recent times. You would also be well advised to note the detail in some of the failures!

By focusing primarily on cliffs, rather than routes, we hope by default to engender an open-minded, adventurous approach. It's good to be focused, to have a plan, but it's also good to just go somewhere you've never been before and get a feel for what fires you up. In winter, especially, the ability to change your plans according to conditions as you find them, rather than as you will them, usually pays dividends. It will also undoubtedly help to keep you alive.

One of the most exciting aspects of this book is that it contains debut writing from a number of great Scottish climbers. As such there is a clear element of historical narrative, particularly in The Story that forms the main part of each cliff chapter. It is gratifying to know that, since putting pen to paper for these pages, many of the contributors have gone on to write further material for climbing journals.

Bear in mind, of course, that this is, by necessity, a selective book. Of course there are other great cliffs that should probably have been included. Many of the Cuillin cliffs, for example, and some of the other walls in the Cairngorms and Glen Coe, would in many climbers' eyes rank alongside or even eclipse some of those we decided to include. But as well as seeking to provide good geographical coverage of all the main mountain regions, we sought to concentrate on those cliffs which have been largely developed in the last few decades. We will be content to know that the book has thereby stimulated debate and discussion around the great mountain cliffs.

In this book the cliffs — rather than the climbs — take centre stage. The great majority are several pitches long, always in a high mountain environment, always a good walk from the roadside. The routes selected are always on leader-placed protection, and only those that have received at least one known 'ground-up' ascent have been included. They are not described in any detail but instead are there to draw some attention to either the most aesthetic features, notable ascents or simply the best climbing to be found on each cliff. Again, the wealth of experience of the authors lends substantial authority to each route's inclusion — or omission.

We hope you enjoy reading this book. Use it for inspiration, for ideas, or just for pleasure. Let the photos tell the story as much as the text itself. Indeed, look closely and you will no doubt find some interesting gaps. •

Guy Robertson and Adrian Crofton
Aberdeen, February 2014

Ecological Notes

I'll never forget the day I climbed *Eagle Ridge*, following a mountain hare's fresh trail over the col and into Lochnagar, the cold silence punctuated only by the rasp of ptarmigan. Or the way the peregrine falcons circled and dived above us on the day we climbed Carn Etchachan's *Route Major*, shrieking silhouettes against a watery winter sky.

The magic of climbing in Scotland's high places is more than the rock, the lines and the aesthetics of movement. A day spent on the mountain crags is more than just another day's climbing. The landscape in which we play our game is just as much a part of the experience – summer's green slopes blending into autumn's gold and winter's white; the sweet scent of crowberry crushed underfoot; the echo of red deer roaring in the rut. Exploring the great Scottish mountain crags affords us the opportunity to connect with some of the last untamed places in Europe.

Scotland's mountain crags lie far from civilisation, across windswept bogs, bleak plateaux and blasted heaths, tucked away in the quiet corries of the high hills. Unlike the low altitude world from which we start our approach – a world of gentle weather, a landscape we have chopped and changed, farmed, built on, and on which we live out our lives in comfort and plenty – these are different places; undeveloped and undevelopable. Despite the intricate effects of location, aspect and geology that make each summit or cliff unique, altitude is the primary factor that sets them apart from the world below. The climate is severe: colder, wetter, windier and cloudier. We know this from our own experiences as climbers: numbing, spindrift-drowning winter belays and joyous summer days when the cool of the mountains becomes a welcome retreat during heatwaves. This summer, perched high on a shady belay on Beinn Eighe's Eastern Ramparts I watched as red deer grazed in the crag's shadow, staying out of the baking heat beyond, just like us.

A glimpse back in time sets the scene: when the mighty glaciers of the last Ice Age started to retreat around 11,500 years ago, they revealed the long-hidden mountains and glens that they had been secretly sculpting beneath. Buried under ice for thousands of years, the Scottish landscape would have been a soil-less, scoured blank canvas, ready for the plants of the non-glacial south to colonise once again. The mild damp Atlantic climate of the lower altitudes provided perfect conditions for plants to grow and spread, adding nutrients as they died, transforming the rock-strewn wastes into magnificent forests over thousands of years. As more time passed, oscillations in the climate brought wetter and cooler conditions, saturating the soil so that dead plant matter only partially decayed thus forming peat. Slowly, the vast tracts of peat bog and heath that characterise much of Scotland today developed, smothering the forests. Bog pines – ancient Scots pine preserved in deep peat – bear testimony to this and are often seen exposed in peat hags when heading into the hills.

Up in the mountains, the harsh climate and short growing season meant that the species that colonised the lower slopes couldn't spread any higher, leaving a space for specially adapted plants to fill – plants that tolerate extreme conditions and long periods under snow. The changes in climate which affected the lower altitudes were too subtle to have much discernable effect on the high tops, and with very little accumulation of plant matter as soil, fertility never improved. Succession continued on the lower slopes, a constantly changing combination of pressures influencing survival. Conditions on the tops, however, have never really changed. Our high mountains are our only refuge for the habitats we find in them, mostly unchanged for thousands of years, where Arctic plants cling on at their most southerly global distribution. These are special places indeed.

Picture the approach to any mountain crag. It starts in the wooded glens where the relatively fertile soil and mild climate allow trees to grow among a ground layer of dwarf shrubs like heather (*Calluna vulgaris*) and blaeberry (*Vaccinium myrtillus*). Gaining height, the trees get smaller and less dense, and eventually they give way to a mosaic of grassland, heath and blanket bog, pockmarked by occasional wind-stunted trees and montane shrubs like juniper (*Juniperis communis*). Starting to move above the treeline, we see exposed areas where the heather is noticeably shorter and 'wind-clipped'. Higher still and the ground gets rockier, with a mix of grasses and sedges becoming more dominant. When we eventually reach the summits we're in the most extreme of British habitats – the alpine summit heath. Exposed to strong winds and buried under snow for much of the year, these fragile areas are dominated by swathes of the woolly-fringe moss (*Racomitrium lanuginosum*) and matt grass (*Nardus stricta*) and are dotted with stiff sedge (*Carex bigelowii*). On the very highest tops – particularly in the Cairngorms – conditions become too harsh for even these hardy species, and plant cover gives way to small patches of the three-leaved rush (*Juncus trifidus*) and huge areas of shifting gravel and rock debris.

Among these general habitats are localised areas where some of the real specialists and rarities are found. Distinct carpets of liverworts and mosses form in areas where snow lies for much of the year, and the upwelling of groundwater or snowmelt creates flushes where wet-loving mosses, sedges and rushes grow in abundance. Obviously, rocks make up a significant part of the mountain environment, from our majestic crags to areas of shattered boulders and scree. The cracks and crevices hereabouts provide a home for rare ferns, mosses, lichens and liverworts. Communities of tall shrubs and flowers grow on sheltered ledges, inaccessible to herbivores like mountain hare and deer. On the lower slopes of many Scottish hills the effect of years of high grazing pressure is even more obvious, as the only places where trees survive are rocky ledges and steep ravines that deer and sheep can't reach.

This picture is repeated across Scotland, with the distribution of habitats varying with local climate and topography, providing stark contrast to a day's climbing on different mountain crags. One can enjoy moving swiftly and freely across the springy dry heath of the eastern Cairngorms, then find one's self cursing and sweating up wet grassy approaches to the great cliffs in the west. The chemistry of the underlying rock affects what can grow too, with the general rule that the more acidic the rock the less fertile it is. For this reason, turfy mixed climbing on southern Highland schist is very different to snowed-up rock climbing on Cairngorm granite.

Our mountains are home to a diverse array of animals too. Even a fleeting glimpse or distant call enriches any day in the hills: the chuckle of red grouse as you cross heather moorland, the trill of snow bunting song floating across a coire at dawn, or a snatched glimpse of a golden eagle soaring high above a distant summit. Each summer, wading birds like golden plover and greenshank return to breed on the high bogs and moorlands, filling the air with their plaintive calls. The first time I ever saw a dotterel, one of Britain's rarest breeding birds, I was racing over the Cairngorm plateau thinking about a route I'd been trying on the short slabs below Hell's Lum. It shot out from behind a rock a few feet ahead and burst me out of my self-obsessed bubble – a reminder that we're nothing but fleeting visitors in their realm.

Despite appearing to be ancient resilient environments, robustly withstanding their extreme conditions, mountain ecosystems can be very fragile. Their height, shape and climate protect them from much disturbance but it only takes a small change for the balance to shift. With an increasing population, a changing global climate and improved transport making mountain access easier for all, this delicate balance becomes ever more precarious. At a small scale, through our actions as climbers, this could lead to footpath erosion, nest disturbance or damage to vegetation. At a larger scale, the impacts of climate change will no doubt affect the distribution of mountain habitats, with arctic species at the edges of their global distribution pushed north and perhaps even ultimately lost forever from Scotland. Pollutants such as nitrogen oxides are dissolved in rain and can act as a fertiliser, enriching naturally nutrient-poor soils and thus altering the mix of species that can survive.

To try to keep our impacts low, climbers should follow the advice provided by the **Mountaineering Council of Scotland** and the **Scottish Outdoor Access Code**. Stay on footpaths where they exist, and try not to cause undue ground disturbance. Follow advice on the location and timing of nesting birds. If winter routes rely on turf then make sure it is fully frozen before committing to the climb. Avoid unnecessary 'heavy gardening' if pre-cleaning mountain rock routes. As climbers, for whom the mountain environment is a vital resource, we must be mindful of our actions and be aware that all our choices, from the way we travel to the crag or the conditions we decide to climb in, to the products we buy and the way we consume energy, may all have far-reaching effects that reach to the very summits of our high mountains.

Gareth Marshall
March 2014

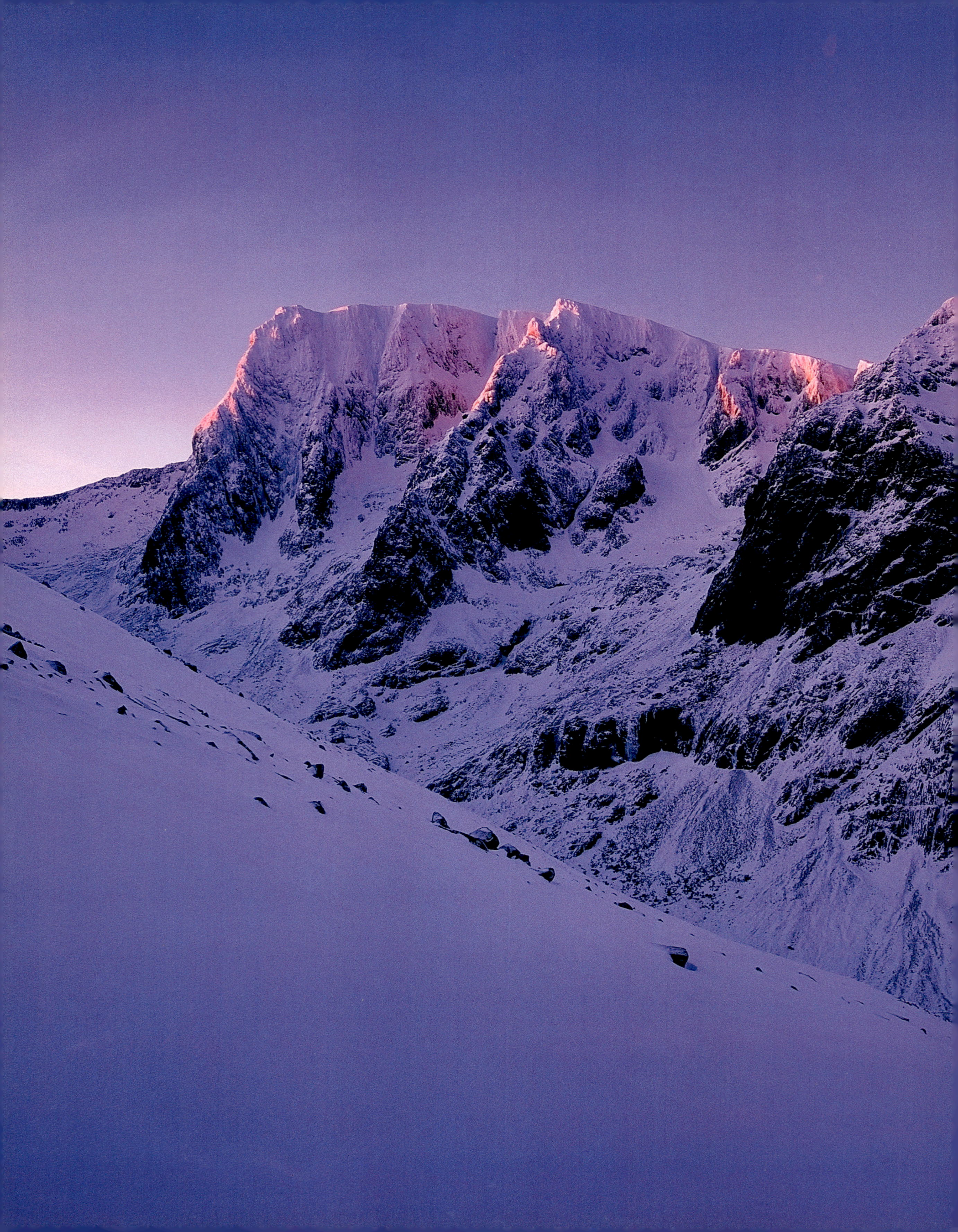

THE SOUTH WEST HIGHLANDS

The North East Face of Ben Nevis.
Photo: *Dave Cuthbertson*.

Iain Small on *Agrippa* (E5), Carn Dearg, Ben Nevis.
Photo: Colin Threlfall.

South West Highlands
by Stuart B. Campbell

*Failte! Welcome, to Bargain Land
where you'll always get more
than what you reckoned for.
Aye, ye'll pey fur it;
you'll pay for it, alright, but
it won't be all right; you'll pay for it
with the small change of
frozen-stiff fingers; bivis to die in;
midge-infested nostrils.*

*— and not just once; get this,
it's on the never-never, this is the life
-long never ever paid off mortgage;
it's the Faustian pact for a fantasy route.*

*This might be your account:
a whole rack dropped; on Minus One:
a friend lost, a relationship terminated
forever when you were on The Edge
of Insanity; your steely resolve smelted
on The Forge; self-confident banter
breaking down to incoherence on Shibboleth;
paranoid navigation, somewhere
between Orion and god knows where*

*— but maybe, just maybe, once,
with the route below you,
it will all pay off; you will be rewarded
with the miracle of a sunset;
feel you are treading on air,
walking like a demigod, attuned
to the silent music of the mountains;
will be abnormally alive.*

Introduction to the South West Highlands – *By Simon Richardson*

Driving west along the A86, the pulse quickens. The rounded mass of the Cairngorms is left behind and the hills become angular, more rugged and mountainous. At first the cliffs are hidden away – the great walls of Creag Meagaidh are shielded by the curve of the Allt Coire Ardair and the rock climbing on Binnein Shuas is hidden behind the rounded bulk of the mountain. But descending towards Roy Bridge, the long friendly cliffs of Aonach Mor become visible on the horizon with Aonach Beag suggestive of sterner fare behind. The true splendour of the area is reached just before Fort William where the great North East Face of Ben Nevis dominates the eastern skyline. Continuing south, the seascape of Loch Linnhe opens up to the west, with tantalising views of the rugged peaks of Ardgour behind, before reaching a crescendo as the A82 winds through the deep cleft of Glen Coe heading south towards Arrochar. There are so many mountains here that it is difficult to know where to look first. This is the true Scottish Highlands – an intoxicating mix of mountain and sea, heather and rock, all entwined with over a century of mountaineering history and tradition.

Although it is fair to say that Scottish mountaineering had its genesis in the Cuillin of Skye, it is here, on the great peaks of Glen Coe and Ben Nevis, that it came of age. The Victorian pioneers were quick to unravel the great structural puzzles of the area, such as Church Door Buttress on Bidean and Buachaille Etive Mor's North Buttress, but it was on Ben Nevis where events unfolded at pace. Venturing on to the great Nevis ridges showed extraordinary confidence and ability, and winter ascents of *Tower Ridge* and *North East Buttress* before the turn of the 20th century stand out as truly extraordinary.

One man dominates the history of this period – Harold Raeburn. His ascent of *Green Gully* in 1906, cutting steps up near vertical ice with a single long-handled alpenstock, set a standard that was not equalled for over 30 years. 100 years on, few climbers would have the requisite skills to climb this chute of tumbling ice with a single axe, and for most it is a fulfilling outing with the full armoury of modern ice climbing equipment. The area has inevitably attracted the pioneers from each generation and all have left their mark, with a series of revolutionary routes that have stretched the boundaries of the possible. The list is a long one, but Bill Murray's visionary winter ascent of *Garrick's Shelf*, Jim Bell's aptly named *Long Climb* on Ben Nevis, Robin Smith's artistry on *Shibboleth*, Jimmy Marshall's step-cutting 'tour de force' on *Minus Two Gully*, Dave Cuthbertson's bold technicality on *Revengeance* and, more recently, Dave MacLeod's futuristic winter ascent of *Anubis*, would be sure to feature on any such list.

As the highest mountain in the land, with the tallest mountain cliffs, it is appropriate that Ben Nevis has a special place in Scottish mountaineering. There is a weather dimension too, because its proximity to the western seaboard exposes it to the full severity of the Atlantic weather systems, with significant precipitation and rapid temperature changes. The consequence is some of the finest winter climbing in the country, and when conditions are good, the ensuing snow and ice conditions are unique across the world. As a result the mountain can take on a cosmopolitan air, and in peak season you are as likely to encounter a climber from Spain or Slovenia on the summit plateau, as you are one from Manchester or Macclesfield.

Ben Nevis is a huge lump of a mountain where everything is on a larger scale than anywhere else in Scotland. The cliffs are higher and more extensive than any other venue, and the complexity of the mountain's structure has meant that successive generations have been kept busy unravelling the mountain's mysteries. Winter climbing on Ben Nevis has progressed from ridges to gullies through to thinly-iced face routes and mixed climbing on the walls between. Multiple generations have pushed the limit of the possible with the technology of the day, most notably Robin Smith and Jimmy Marshall. In February 1960, they spent a week on the mountain and step-cut their way up six demanding ice climbs, culminating in the first ascent of *Orion Direct*. This is the archetypical Scottish winter climb, combining sustained difficulty with alpine scale and exposure, and it was the forerunner for the dozens of outstanding thin face routes that became possible with the front point revolution in the late 1970s.

For a couple of decades it was thought that ever steeper and more precarious thin face routes would provide the ultimate winter challenges on the mountain. As a result, future development of Ben Nevis winter climbing was dependent on exceptional weather conditions to coat the remaining unclimbed grooves and faces with ice, but all this changed in the late 1990s when the mixed potential of the mountain was discovered. It was quickly realised that rock in Coire na Ciste was more featured and cracked, and offered better opportunities for hooking and protection than the smooth-sided walls of Observatory Gully that had previously attracted the bulk of the attention from the thin face aficionados. Leashless tools extended the technical envelope, creating yet more possibilities, and during the course of the last 15 years over 100 new mixed climbs, many of the highest quality, have been added to a mountain that was considered worked out. As a bonus, many of these new mixed routes have become easier with more ascents, as pick placements have become more established and the protection cracks cleared. Routes like *Darth Vader*, *Babylon* and *Sioux Wall* have now become modern classics and are accessible to many climbers.

Although Ben Nevis is primarily known as a winter venue, its rock climbing rates with the best in the country. Some consider Carn Dearg Buttress, with its superbly defined corners and roofs of beautifully firm andesite, the finest mountain cliff in the land. The great classic routes such as *Centurion*, *Torro*, *The Bat* and *Titan's Wall* quite rightly attract regular ascents, and Gary Latter and Rick Campbell's more recent additions of *The Wicked* and *Trajan's Column* hint at more untapped potential to come.

Until the early 1930s, the West Highland Railway meant that Ben Nevis was far more accessible than Glen Coe. With no motorable road across Rannoch Moor, the Glen Coe pioneers either had to approach on foot from Ballachulish, take a boat up Glen Etive or endure an uncomfortable horse and cart ride from Tyndrum. One can only marvel at the splendour of Buachaille Etive Mor with no road at its foot. The Buachaille is Glen Coe's mountain 'par excellence', and the achievements on its flanks of clean rhyolite have not only defined the history of rock climbing in Glen Coe, but of Scotland itself. The first ascent of *Crowberry Ridge Direct* by George Abraham in 1900 was hailed as the most difficult climb in Scotland, if not the world, at the time, and with delicate unprotected Severe-grade climbing from a non-existent belay, it is easy to see why.

Glen Coe has a high mountain feel. The tops of the peaks are austere and barren and the flanks are typically steep, rocky and raked by scree. The mountains are often shrouded by mist, and even when the sky is clear, there is that ever-present feeling that the weather may turn, adding just a touch of excitement and a little urgency to the day. Whilst rock is abundant, the steepest and most continuous cliffs are not always prominent. Rannoch Wall and Slime Wall are good examples. They offer some of the finest climbing in the glen, yet at first glance they are almost hidden away either side of North Buttress, the great structural feature that immediately draws the eye.

Rannoch Wall displays Glen Coe rhyolite at its best – rough and bubbly and a delight to climb – but it does not always run to good protection. Glen Coe rock climbs are often exposed and run out, demanding a steady approach. Route finding can be perplexing, even on routes of apparently moderate difficulty such as Iain Ogilvy and Esme Speakman's *Red Slab* and *Satan's Slit*. Climbed on the same day, way back in September 1939, they still provide VS leaders with a stern test of skill and commitment. After the Second World War, standards in Glen Coe rocketed when the Creagh Dhu came to prominence. John Cunningham was the most prominent of an outstanding group of climbers, and *Gallows Route* on North Buttress of the Buachaille (Scotland's first mountain Extreme), followed by *Guerdon Grooves* with Bill Smith (the first route on Slime Wall), set new standards for difficulty and seriousness.

Since then rock climbing in Glen Coe has been synonymous with advancing standards across the British Isles: *Bloody Crack* (Pat Walsh, 1956), *Trapeze* (Jimmy Marshall, 1958), *Shibboleth* (Robin Smith, 1958), *Carnivore* (Cunningham and Noon, 1958) all rate with the hardest climbs of their day. This trend has continued with *The Risk Business* (Whillance, 1980), the first E5 in Glen Coe, through to *Symbiosis* (Cuthbertson and Thorburn, 1995), Scotland's first E8.

Warmer winters have meant that winter climbing in Glen Coe is now often confined to the highest coires, and the outstanding routes on the lower cliffs are rarely in condition. But fortunately Glen Coe has Stob Coire nan Lochan, which, being high and exposed, comes into condition quickly and has a superb collection of routes. Whether you climb Grade II or Grade IX, there are quality routes here to suit all climbers. When conditions are good however, Glen Coe can provide the finest winter climbing in the country. Perhaps the best recent example of this was in January 2012 when Guy Robertson climbed three Grade IXs – *Guerdon Grooves*, *The Duel* and *Satyr* – on consecutive days.

Arrochar is different to Glen Coe. The landscape is not as harsh, the environment is less austere and the atmosphere is friendlier. The wide-open hillsides are grassy and dotted with sheep and convey a feeling of expansiveness rather than the compressed desolation of Glen Coe or Ben Nevis. In a similar way to Glen Coe however, Arrochar's mica schist demands a confident and calm approach. The routes are typically steep and difficult to protect and there is always a degree of unpredictability as to what lies ahead. Poise and balance are the watchwords here rather than speed and brute strength.

The area's showpiece mountain – The Cobbler – has a distinctive profile that literally juts out of the landscape. Impossible to ignore, it always demands a second look. The mountain's proximity to Glasgow has meant that its early history has been more associated with working class climbers, rather than the pre-war middle class elite that developed Glen Coe and Ben Nevis. Jock Nimlin, a crane driver from the Clyde shipyards, added 11 new climbs to the mountain in the 1930s including the classic *Recess Route* on the north peak. The Creagh Dhu pushed standards considerably after the war with Cunningham, Walsh, Smith and Hamish MacInnes adding the majority of today's most climbed classics such as *Whither Whether*, *Punster's Crack*, *Gladiator's Groove* and *Club Crack*. Dave Cuthbertson took up the mantle in the late 1970s with a trio of superb additions including *Wild Country*, Scotland's first mountain E6, and a forerunner for the hard on-sight climbs put up across Scotland in the 1980s. The mountain's test piece is *Dalriada*, the spectacular undercut prow directly under the summit of the north peak, put up by Gary Latter in redpoint style in 1995.

Ben Nevis and Glen Coe have always been, and will always be, areas that are vitally important to British climbing. Accessible and iconic, they are central to any Scottish climber's itinerary. The Ben has a stature out of proportion to its size and scale on the world stage and has been at the forefront of climbing development on several occasions. But whilst Ben Nevis has benefited from advancing technology and is deservedly popular for the quality of its ice and mixed routes, high standard technical climbing on The Cobbler and Glen Coe is unlikely to become commonplace. Away from a few dozen well-known routes, these areas will never be overrun by climbers because technological advances have not tamed the nature of the rock. As always, significant challenges remain for the visionary, the talented and the bold. ●

Buachaille Etive Mòr.
Photo: *Dave Cuthbertson*.

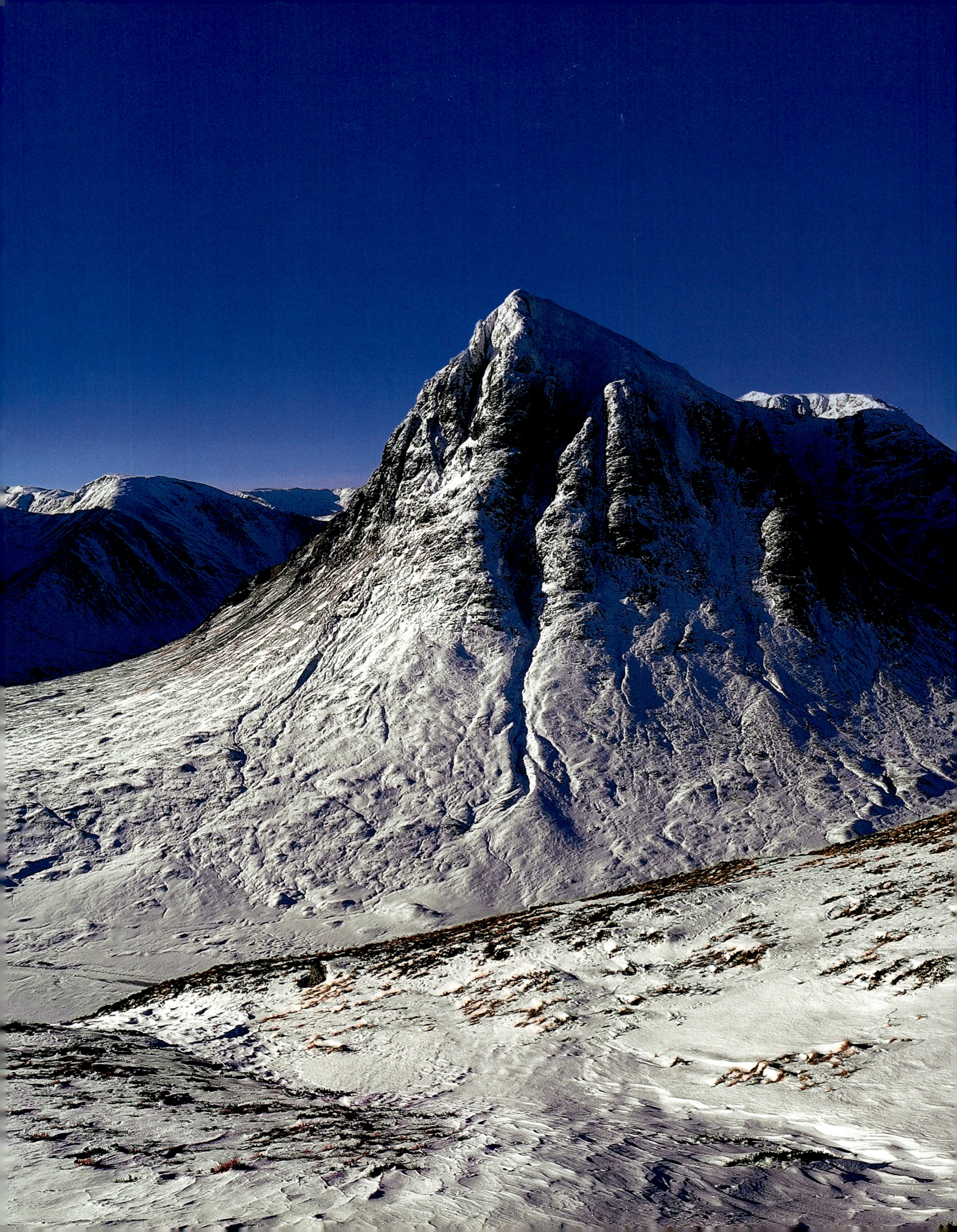

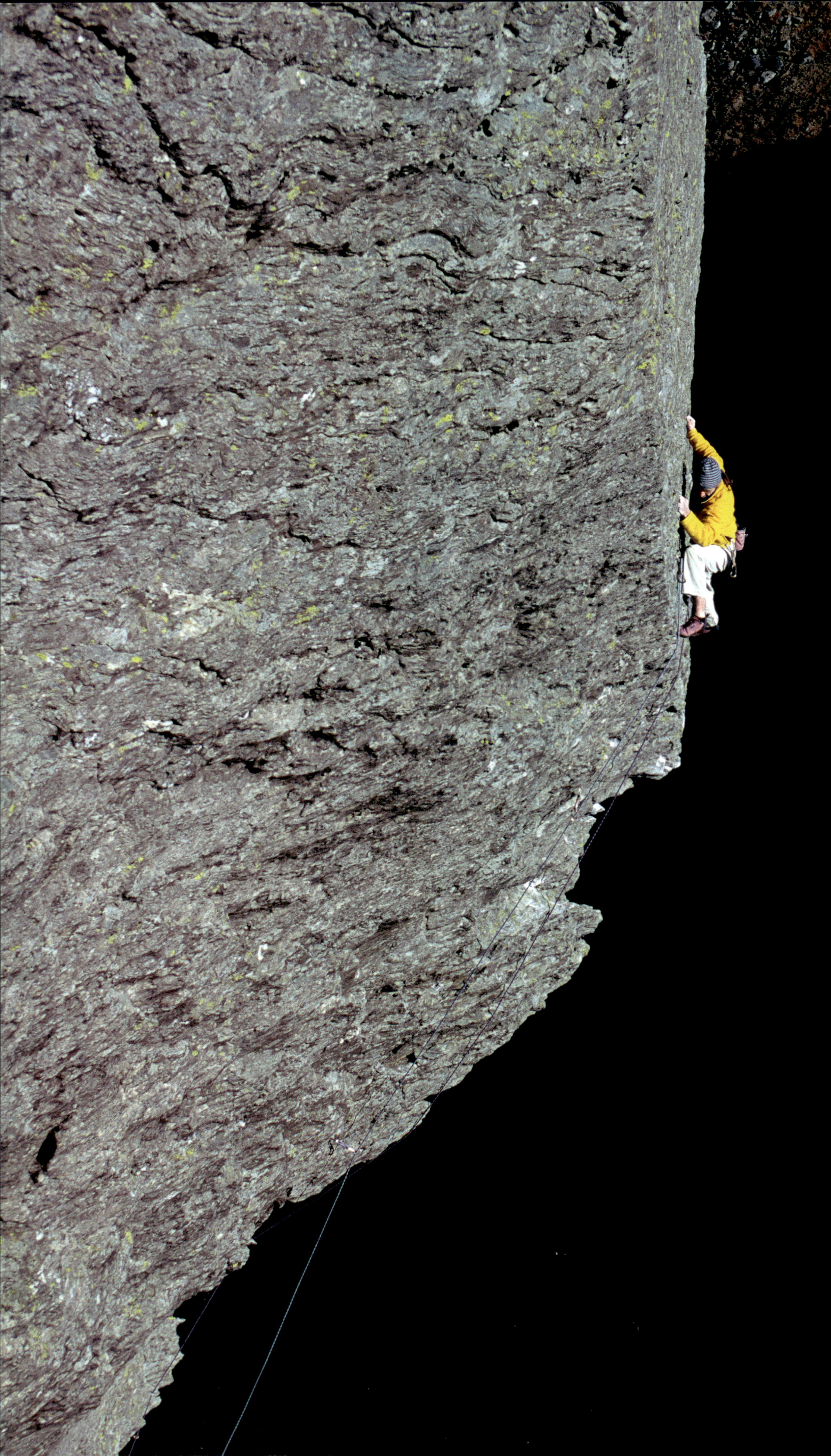

THE COBBLER – *by Dave MacLeod*

THE PLACE
If you wanted to design and sculpt a miniature alpine climbing playground within spitting distance of Glasgow, it would be hard to do a better job than the glaciers of the Lomond re-advance at the end of the last Ice Age. Although it is surrounded by rugged and higher neighbouring hills, the jagged, unmistakeable outline of The Cobbler's three peaks grab your attention as you ride up the West Highland line from Glasgow.

Contained within that tiny cirque of spiky buttresses is a small world of adventures. The situations and the rock architecture couldn't be more dramatic. Yet the scale of the mountain is small enough that you can enjoy them with a lighthearted approach, free from the logistical awkwardness of the bigger mountain cliffs in the Highlands.

And a playground it is. The peaks reverberate with Glaswegian banter on a sunny weekend, summer or winter. Underneath the climbers pinned to huge overhangs of schist, day trippers from Glasgow shuffle and sweat up the path below. 'Iss hill's pure murder-polis man!' Someone always brings a small radio strapped to a rucksack, blaring out the progress of the Old Firm match back down the road. As they crane their necks upwards and spot the climbers, they are dumfounded. Waving an outstretched arm clutching a bottle of Irn Bru, they shout 'You boyz are pure mental!'

THE CLIFFS
Because of The Cobbler's super-compact nature, it makes more sense to describe the whole mountain rather than any one facet. The mountain forms a cirque of three small peaks which are really just large spiky buttresses about 100–120 metres high.

The majority of the climbing is on the south and north peaks. Viewed from the main approach path, the south peak presents an imposing and shady north face, with turfy ramps and steep vegetated grooves and cracks above. The upper part of the face is split by a great corner, taken by *North Wall Groove*. Its shelter from the sun, and the abundance of vegetation, make it home to the mountain's finest winter routes. The clean and sunny south face is less easily viewed from any approach and is comparatively neglected as a result. The most striking feature of the centre peak is the 'eye of the needle' pinnacle which forms the summit of the mountain; a nice short scramble through a hole in the pinnacle leading to the top. The north peak holds the most spectacular features. Its summit is formed by two hugely impressive overhanging ship's prows.

◀ Dave MacLeod on *Dalriada* (E7).
Photo: *Dave Cuthbertson.*

These are taken by *Wild at Heart* and *Dalriada*. They loom over the approach path and demand any climber's attention. Below and right of these is a large sprawling buttress with numerous corner and chimney lines, holding many of the best lower-grade routes on the mountain.

THE CLIMBING
The Cobbler's rippled mica schist lends itself to a great variety of climbing. The cliffs have been sculpted by glacial plucking and since the rock is not quite as hard and compact as granite or rhyolite, the formations are about as dramatic as you can get. Huge flying arêtes protrude between deep cracks and chimneys and great corners.

The wavy ripples of schist also mean that virtually all the faces can be climbed at a reasonable or sometimes remarkably amenable standard, although they can be bold outings. The perfect example of this is the great blade-like prow of *Dalriada*, which leans out over the approach path to the north peak. *Dalriada* takes the steep side of the prow with some wild swinging around over the roofs at E6 6b. The easier angled side of the blade is poorly protected, but the face is covered in good holds and it seems almost unbelievable that it goes at VS by the route *Whither Whether*.

The rock on the north peak is very clean and generally free from vegetation compared to the south peak. There is rock on all sides though, and the south face is bathed in sunshine and has several classic lines from HVS to E4.

To climb the routes here is to experience the progression in Glaswegian climbing since the 1930s. From the huge cavernous chimneys and corners that always seem to go at VDiff, right through to the well known modern desperates such as *Dalriada* and *The Cathedral*. Fortunately, the easier routes have every bit as much airy scenery as the hard extremes. However, it's perhaps the mid-grade routes, at around HVS to E2, of the 1950s Creagh Dhu Club era that carry the greatest richness of climbing history. In this period, The Cobbler was the hangout of the likes of Hamish MacInnes, Dougal Haston, John Cunningham, Robin Smith, John MacLean, Elly Moriarty and other steely figures. Their legacy of crack climbs wasn't properly superseded until 1979. But Dave Cuthbertson moved things on in style with the very futuristic *Wild Country* (E6), boldly taking on the

24 THE GREAT MOUNTAIN CRAGS OF SCOTLAND

great overhangs of the north peak. He arrived with chalk, better equipment and training behind him. The route is still the hardest rock climb on The Cobbler! Gary Latter climbed the two great overhanging arêtes of the north peak, adding *Wild at Heart* and *Dalriada* (both E7), with lots of pegs for protection; a sport climbing feel with spectacular exposure. For the last 20 years, development has focused more on winter mixed possibilities, with increasingly harder rock routes on the vegetated south peak being climbed in winter. Rab Anderson and Rob Milne showed a passion for The Cobbler in winter with routes like *Deadman's Groove* (VI,7). This catalysed Mark Garthwaite to explore the thinner open slabs like *Viva Glas Vegas* (VIII,7), and later I tackled some of the summer extremes, like *MacLean's Folly* (summer E2 and winter VIII,8).

SELECTED ROUTES

North Wall Groove (VII,7)
A gobsmacking winter line. Aesthetic, interesting and varied climbing in a great situation.

Punster's Crack (Severe)
Three contrasting pitches among the best of The Cobbler's rock scenery. The superb finishing slab above an airy belay is pure joy.

Dalriada (E7)
The modern sought-after classic of the grade in the area, if not the country. Fairly amenable climbing and well protected by plenty of pegs to keep you pushing on, but wild exposure and an athletic crux.

◀ The south peak of The Cobbler from the north peak.
Photo: *Dave MacLeod.*

▲ Unknown climbers on *Punster's Crack* (Severe). Photo: *Dave Cuthbertson*.

THE STORY

I was schooled in winter climbing on Cobbler mica schist and frozen turf. By the time I was 21 and had been winter climbing five years, I still wasn't great, or fast at the actual climbing, but I felt the mountain had given me a good apprenticeship in the art of keeping a good head on the lead. My first Cobbler mixed climb as a 15-year-old was *MacLay's Crack* (III,4).

It was quite steep but with plenty of turf. Unfortunately, I couldn't make much use of it since I only had hill walking boots with no crampons, and one walking axe. There were plenty of cracks for gear too, but not much for my rack, which totalled two karabiners and one sling. Belay anchors consisted of whatever way I could invent to jam the walking axe in a crack. The fingers of my right hand were raw from clawing into the frozen turf as best I could while moving the ice axe. On that route, with the lip of my boots balanced on ice-smeared rock, I learned a lot about keeping my feet still and moving gingerly on delicate mixed ground.

The following year, I learned of the chance to borrow some crampons and a pair of 'Vertige' mixed climbing axes from a friend the next Saturday. I hatched a plan from my guidebook, read under the table in Chemistry class, to go for *North Wall Traverse* for my first IV,5. My usual partner was away, so solo it would have to be. Standing underneath the looming pinnacle of the south peak, rimed up like a cake, the line looked so inviting that I don't remember feeling scared to start climbing up it without a rope. However, halfway up the crux pitch, moving out across a smooth wall with axes shuffling in a lonely

26 THE GREAT MOUNTAIN CRAGS OF SCOTLAND

▲ Tim Newton on *Club Crack* (E2). Photo: *Adam Russell*.

moustache of turf, I had the feeling of being totally alone and self-reliant for the first time in my climbing. I must've stayed there for ages, going back and forth, unable to commit to the mantel using little hooks above. I peered around at the overhangs above my head. Rab Anderson had climbed that overhanging wall in winter via *Deadman's Groove*. Crazy! I was psyched out and backed off. I walked back down the path utterly dejected. It was four hours until the 8 p.m. train home to Glasgow and I couldn't face shivering on the platform in my wet clothes so I figured I'd see if I could get into a pub in Arrochar. I managed to get the barman to serve me a pint of beer in the deserted and freezing pub. I sipped it to last the full four hours, since I didn't have money for another. After two hours the barman walked over and put another down in front of me, smiled and walked off. I must have looked fed up.

I boiled inside for the entirety of the following week at school. I couldn't stop thinking about how amazing it felt to be on that big wall of frozen rock totally by myself and how crap it felt to down climb and retrace my steps in the snow from the bottom of the wall. Almost automatically, the following Saturday I got the train back to Arrochar, walked back up and climbed with total commitment past the crux mantel and onto the turfy ramps above. On another stellar day of ice, rime and sunshine, I climbed to the top of the south peak on a wave of sheer joy. Standing on top of its sharp peak, it was the top of the world as far as I was concerned.

A few years later, I'd ticked off several of the established classic mixed lines and was just about feeling confident about my progress. But an article in *On The Edge* magazine on the cutting edge of Scottish winter climbing was a revelation to me, and suddenly I saw where I wanted to go next with my hobby of spending the winter weekends on the Cobbler. One picture stood out. Mark 'Dr Death' Garthwaite on a new Grade VIII on the Cobbler's south peak – *Viva Glas Vegas*. Everything about this climb sounded horrendously scary. According to the description it basically climbed an open smooth wall on tiny rock edges, with a huge runout above two sole 'warthog' drive-ins in frozen turf. This was exactly the type of terrain that we wondered if the best climbers could climb. Even the grade of VIII,7 was 'nu-school' at the time. I imagined teetering about on scrabbly hooks with ropes dangling uselessly below. It churned my stomach but filled me with curiosity at the same time. Dr Death certainly looked hard as nails in the picture, but what would it really take to be comfortable in that situation?

It was probably the following season when I found myself standing below the frozen south peak staring up at it with a friend. We had no fixed plan of which route to climb, but I walked straight up to the foot of it, to get a close look at the route I'd wondered so much about. I'm not sure which one of us suggested that I go for a 'quick look at the start' just to settle the question of whether the initial wall was as thin as it looked. Perhaps that wasn't a good idea. Inevitably, as soon as I balanced off across the wall on tiny but positive quartz crystals, I entered a state of total concentration. Straight away I got an insight into how this sort of climbing worked. For the first time, I could feel the precision placement and analytical breakdown of the unfolding sequence was working just as it did for me in my more familiar surroundings of the boulders of Dumbarton Rock. Testing each placement and remembering to keep the angle of pull the same through the whole move, all too soon I found myself balanced on the thin 'warthog' ledge, staring up at the crux wall.

It did indeed look long and smooth, and free from any sanctuary to aim for. What was I going to do? Just go down like on *North Wall Traverse*? At least I could try the first move off the ledge before judging it out of my league? Or the second move? But what does that next edge feel like?

There was a vague plan in my mind not to go any higher if I didn't feel I could reverse the move. 20 feet out from the ledge, with my tools hooked sideways on quartz crimps I probably couldn't hang in summer with my fingers, I suddenly felt my plan had gone out of the window. I could feel my throat going dry, but the only thing keeping my head cool was lingering curiosity about just how hard these moves would get. So I followed that thought, and stood up again and again on the edges.

My partner below went quiet, but I could hear my heart thumping, and with my face leant in tight against the rock I could feel forcefully expired air warm my face. Its comfort almost melted my composure. I had reached a tiny cluster of moss patches, probably resting on ripples of schist underneath. I struggled to get a stick that would hold even a portion of my weight. But once established, I could see that better turf was suddenly only one more move away. One more move. I'd done so many that were sketchy up to here, I could surely do just one more. I had a good discussion with myself and clarified my options. Going down would probably be worse. So committing should be easy? Hesitation on this disintegrating dry frozen moss would clearly be the very worst option.

Hesitation followed, I made my placements worse by trying to make them seat better. I wanted to go back to five minutes ago when at least one axe felt solid enough to pull on. My eyes scanned the rock over and over, and automatically I saw what to do. A cross through to hook a chickenhead quartz crystal would allow me to kick a foot up high and rock over to within reach of easy ground. Twice I crossed through and came back, too scared to fully hang on the quartz. Had I learned anything from my apprenticeship on previous routes here? I was still asking myself what the hell I was doing hesitating, when I held my breath and fully committed to the quartz and the welcome turf beyond. With that whack into solid turf, it was over. All that was left was an easy climb to that spectacular summit.

Like all climbs on small mountains, what Cobbler climbs lack in scale they make up for in intensity. To this day, I look forward to a winter climb on The Cobbler with more excitement than perhaps any other Scottish mountain.

Trevor Wood and A. N. Other on *Wild at Heart* (E7).
Photo: *Adam Russell*.

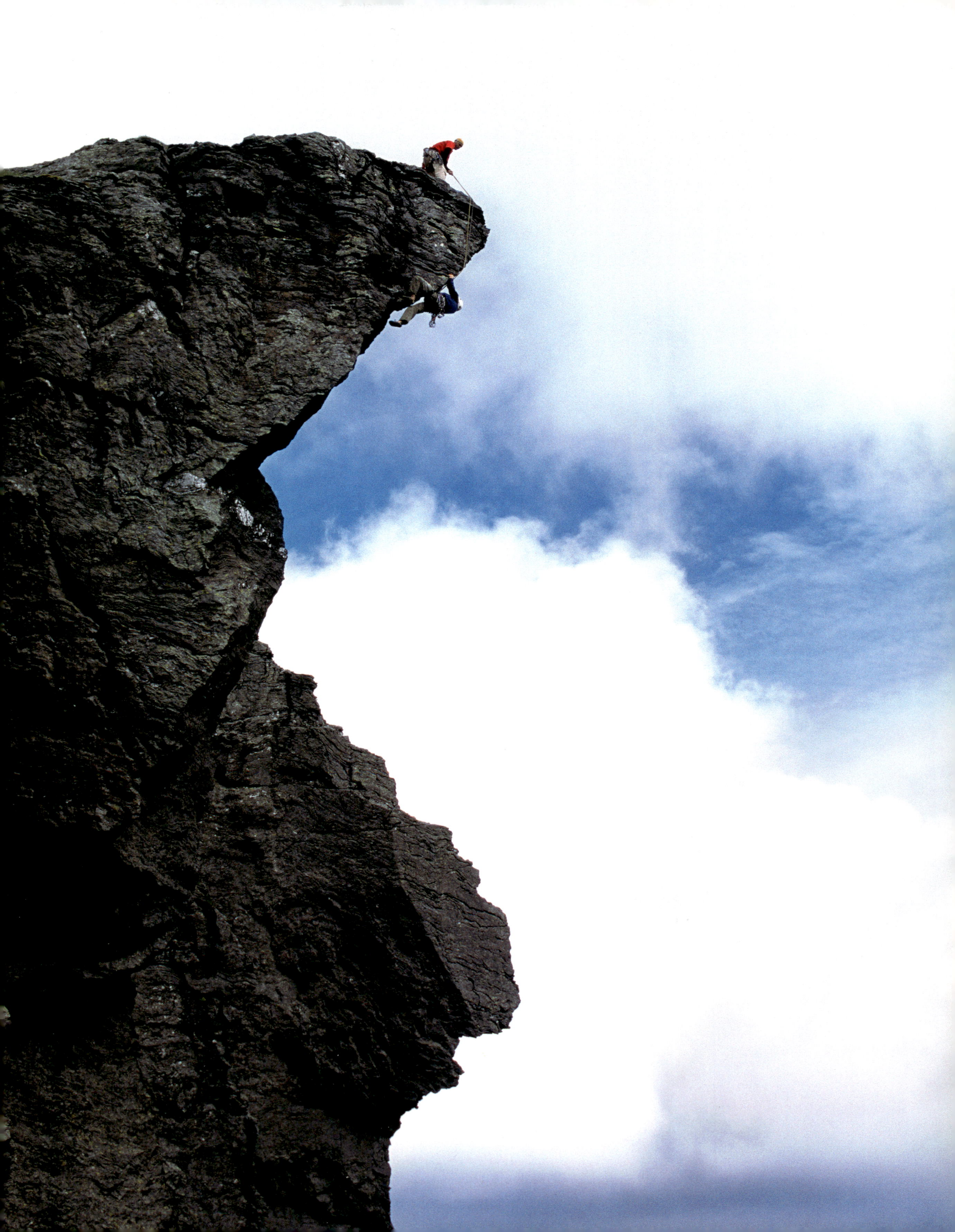

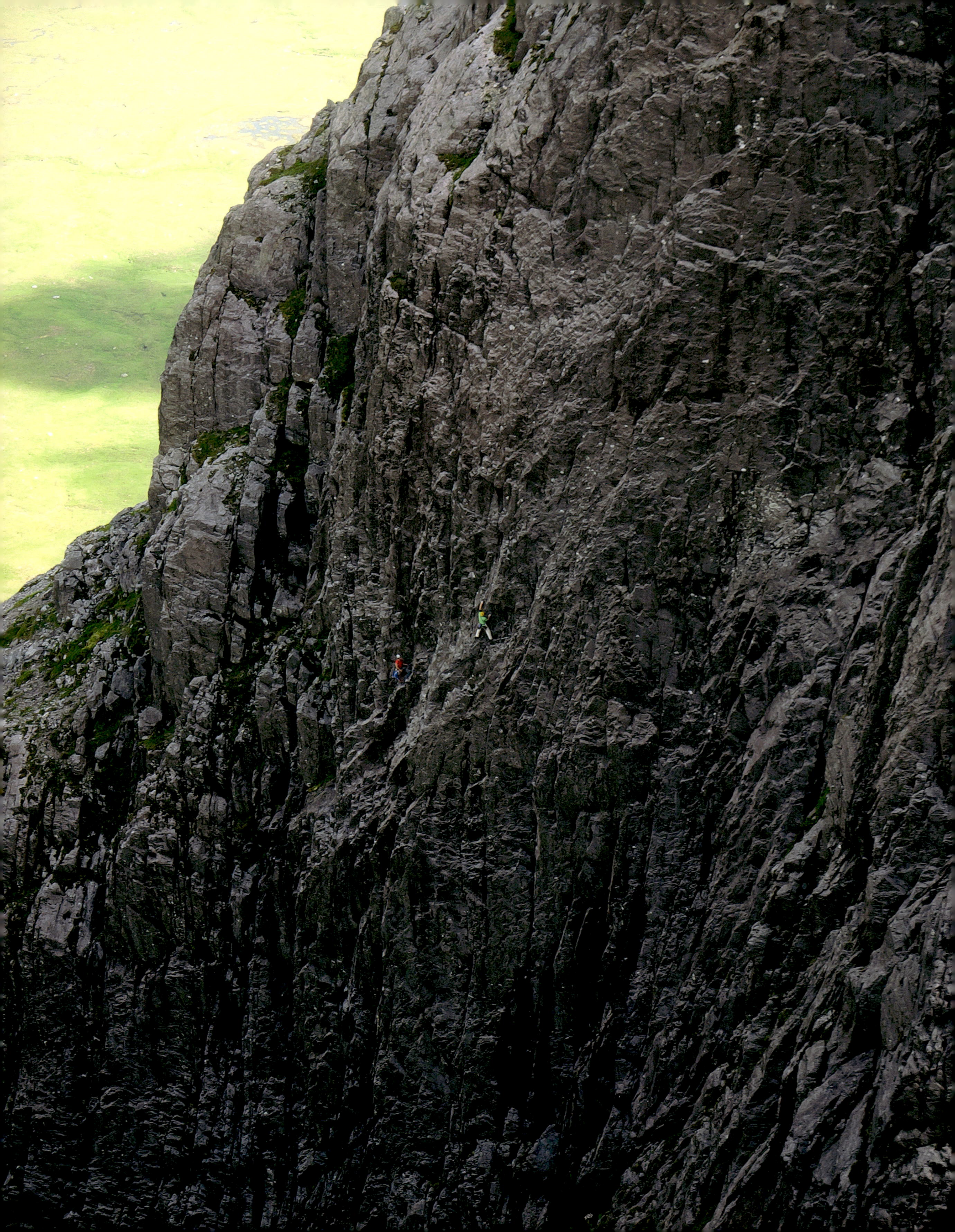

Slime Wall, Buachaille Etive Mor –

by Guy Robertson, story by Mark McGowan

THE PLACE

There are surely few Scottish mountain crags quite as intimidating as Slime Wall. The approach is relatively quick and straightforward, cutting gently up eastwards from the SMC hut at Lagangarbh.

However, the approaching climber is soon awoken from a sleepy start as Great Gully abruptly calls upon both hands and feet for a series of steepening, slippery rock steps on its eroded left bank. A descent in the dark is unappealing, and even on reaching the dubious sanctuary of a sloping perch at the base of the wall, care is needed to avoid dropped helmets and other vital apparel from taking off down the hill. Like the beating heart of Glen Coe itself, the sound of dripping water never stops here, and an apparent dimensional shift pulls one's centre of gravity away across the breast of the crag and out into space. And this before the climbing starts.

THE CLIFF

Slime Wall is a fortuitous geological extension of the left wall of Raven's Gully. Presenting around 600 feet of continuous near-vertical rock at its highest point, the geology is confusing, the crag tapering considerably to both top right and bottom left.

This of course creates an alarming exposure that sucks immediately at the climber's heels upon contact with the rock, the gully underneath dropping suddenly down to the glen below. The penetrating rent of Raven's marks the cliff's right-most extremity, festooned with gargantuan chockstones all cloaked in hideous greenery; a classic post-war lesson in extreme chasm-ing if ever there was one. To the left of this, the main bulk of the wall is seamed by a complex array of shallow, right-slanting grooves and arêtes, occasionally interrupted only by worrying blankness in between. Out towards the left skyline the stature of the wall diminishes somewhat, but here the air seems to deepen as the crag turns sharply round toward the vast expanse of Rannoch Moor. The routes here get shorter but they begin to feel bigger. When the full expanse of the wall is viewed from the other side of Great Gully, the only readily definable feature as such is the huge black hole of the Great Cave, high up on the top right-hand side, oozing slime onto the walls below. It is at once a most repulsive and alluring sight.

Atmosphere is everything here – rarified and giddying – to be savoured at its best after a long dry spell on a hot summer evening with the sun kissing the upper ramparts. The final pitches are a bit steeper on some of the harder routes, but the protection helpfully improves, providing some of the most exhilarating climaxes to mountain rock climbs anywhere in the UK.

◀ Adrian Crofton and Helen Rennard on *Bludger's Revelation* (HVS).
Photo: *Colin Threlfall*.

THE CLIMBING

Fortunately, the climbing resolutely refuses to live up to the crag's name. This is the jewel in the crown of the monarch of Scotland's rock climbing glens. In the main the rock is solid, clean and very rough to the touch. This is a great mountain cliff, providing a series of mostly long, two-to six-pitch routes with complex, delicate and sometimes quite 'cerebral' climbing.

The routes out on the left are shorter, but pack an extreme exposure punch that is guaranteed to make most climbers hold on tighter and yearn for more protection. The physical style of climbing is something of a Scottish mountain delicacy; never too strenuous or brutal, but with a paucity of incut holds where it matters most. Protection is good when it arrives, but can be difficult to locate. Slime Wall is a place to be comfortable running it out gently on small sloping edges and sidepulls, rather than powering up steep cracks – the 'eagle's lilt' of Slime Wall, one old-timer once called it.

There is no real secret to protecting the climbs here – just carry as much as you can, with perhaps a little more in the way of micro-cams and wires. If you should find yourself standing at the base of the crag in acceptable winter condition, give yourself a pat on the back for guessing right and make sure you've taken a healthy supply of knifeblades and hooks before you set off. Although the low altitude and smooth, clean nature of the rock mean this will never be a premier winter climbing venue, a colourful history and sense of enigma have meant that a winter ascent has become something of a holy grail.

▲ Slime Wall and Raven's Gully (right) in winter condition. Photo: *Colin Threlfall.*

THE ROUTES

Bludger's Revelation (HVS)
Fine sustained and clean climbing with more protection than most climbs on this wall. A superb introduction, with a spectacular link section.

Shibboleth (E2)
Totemic. First climbed by a teenager in big boots. Screw on your bold head and don't miss out on the direct finish.

▲ Nick Bullock on the second winter ascent of *Guerdon Grooves* (IX,8). Photo: *Colin Threlfall*.

The New Testament (E4)
Cuthbertson's development of Ian Nicolson's bold 1970s adventure, *Apocalypse*, is the ultimate Slime Wall route – big sustained pitches that are thin and technical with just enough protection, but more than enough exposure.

Guerdon Grooves (HVS, IX)
The only winter route on the wall and something of a holy grail, with a huge reputation and only one repeat.

THE SOUTH WEST HIGHLANDS | SLIME WALL, BUACHAILLE ETIVE MOR | 33

THE STORY — *by Mark McGowan*

For a brief period in the 1970s, solo free climbing almost became fashionable. Climbers like Jimmy Jewell in North Wales and Ian Nicolson in Scotland pushed the limits by solo climbing very close to the technical limits of the day. However, soloing is never likely to be a mainstream form of climbing, and seems increasingly rare in the modern era.

I had always wanted to try and do something special with *Shibboleth*, and it had never been soloed before. It had a particular reputation for quality and boldness, and it was steeped in tradition. It makes its way through some extremely impressive and intimidating rock scenery on a huge cliff situated near the top of one of Scotland's most iconic mountains — the mighty Buachaille Etive Mor. For me at the time, everything about it felt perfect.

The line is usually climbed in six pitches, the second and fourth forming the meat of the difficulties. The first crux is steep, intricate and often damp. The second is in a very precarious setting — some 400 feet up the wall — and provides unusually delicate face climbing on holds that slope consistently the wrong way. At this critical point there would be only fresh air and the distant noises of cars inching their way along the road 2,000 feet below. Perfect.

Stephen and I hitched up from Balloch after work and dumped our kit at the Ville. It wasn't long before we were rushing up excitedly to the base of Slime Wall. I had been contemplating the ascent for some time previously and had therefore visualised the climbing, pitch by pitch inside my head. I was training aggressively as a sport and competition climber, and I had reached a technical standard and fitness that made a solo ascent viable.

The challenges involved in soloing a climb like *Shibboleth* are many and varied, physical and psychological. Firstly, there is the style of climbing — it isn't really a route that grows tamer with time through improvements to training and fitness, or innovations in technology. It requires a steady, cautious and light touch, depending more on good footwork and technique than sheer physical strength. Secondly, and historically, the route has rightly become the stuff of legend on the back of Robin Smith's audacious first ascent. Climbed way back in the fifties — wearing big boots and carrying little more than a handful of pegs — it is as near to E3 as E2 gets, and was undoubtedly a contender for Britain's hardest lead at the time. History can be heavy at times — heavy enough to weigh you down. And finally, there's the location — in the huge, dank, north-facing recess of a great mountain. If atmosphere is what you want then you've come to the right place. *Shibboleth* to me was a raw scare factory that presented a unique opportunity. Its ingredients combined to make the prospect of a solo ascent intoxicating and irresistible.

For bold routes with big reputations there is something rather disarming about a solo ascent. Tied onto a rope, the boldness of a poorly protected route often masks its lack of technical difficulty. Everything seems harder where there is potential for big leader falls with serious or even fatal consequences. However, once you commit to a solo ascent, the climbing becomes very clear, and movement is usually seamless and flowing. If it isn't, then something is wrong. Pan bread. Tea's out.

Stephen was there to record my ascent on film and the plan was he would climb an easy neighbouring route to get a prime view from across the gully. We sat at the bottom while I squeaked the soles of my boots, taking a minute to look up and investigate the first crux. Stephen left and started up his climb to gain some height. Then there was silence, only the moist air and steady dripping of water down the gully. When you stand alone beneath the great wall of *Shibboleth* with no ropes, you realise you haven't even been born.

Inside, I felt relaxed and ultimately sure that this was going to be a fantastic climbing experience beyond any before. Fingertip moves 400 feet above the floor, high on the most majestic of mountains. I remember soaking up the magnificent setting — a great bulging mass of rock soaring up into the heavens. Nobody in the entire world had done this before me. I didn't pause to consider failure — the route belonged to me. I had completed my climbing apprenticeship here, and this moment was its culmination.

Mark McGowan on a solo ascent of *Shibboleth* (E2).
Photo: *Steve Yates*.

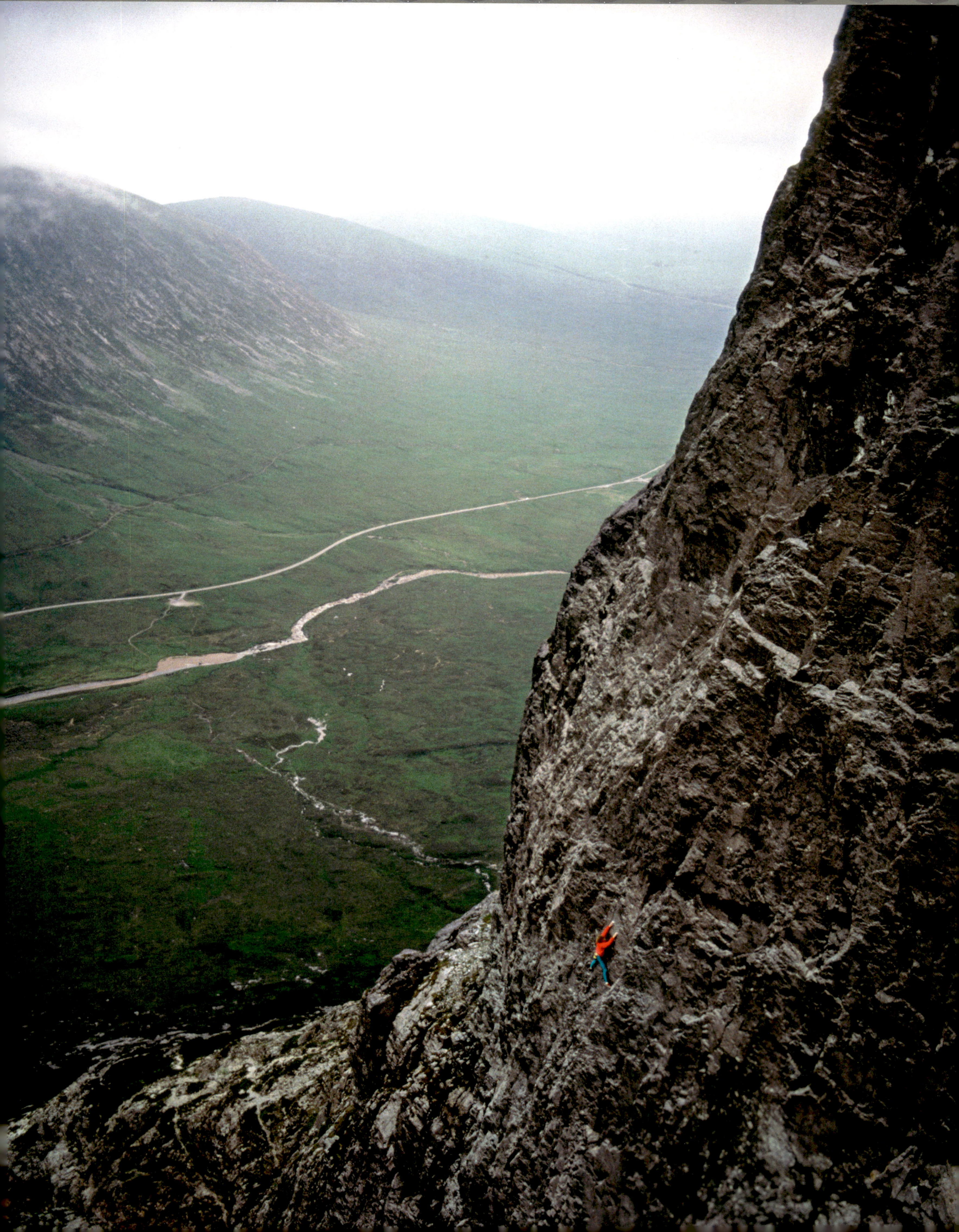

I set off up the first easy VS pitch to the base of the first crux. I was cautious of dampness as this section is renowned for a wet streak in precisely the wrong place. However, I felt a familiar intimacy with the roughness of the rock and the feeling of vertigo it induces. The first pitch went without incident and I recall pulling confidently across the steep traverse of the first crux and up onto the ledge below the next pitch. I climbed swiftly and without thought. However, as I stood at the usual belay point below the second crux pitch I became increasingly tense. Normally one would clip into a belay and relax and lean back on the rope to enjoy the airy exposure, but not so on this occasion. Now I was preparing for perhaps the most intense moment of my life – the infamous '50 foot pitch to the hidden jug'.

There was no bullshit, only pure hard rock, myself and, of course, the weather. This was no playground – every move, every thought, every moment would matter. I took a deep breath. It felt good. I was soloing *Shibboleth*, and I was loving it! I began the sequence away from the belay flake, moving slowly up and out, further and further until I reached a point where I remember gently curling my fingers carefully on an awkward sloping ledge. The rock seemed to have unusually good friction, but then each finger was individually monitoring the friction levels – intense beyond my wildest dreams and still vivid to this day.

I dared to look down at this point, initially at my foothold placements, my toes placed carefully on sloping holds about one inch in depth. That view could have burst my brain cells. The exposure was outrageous. I pictured myself, a fly on that great sweeping wall, the gully below, the mountain, the hut and the glen below. I could imagine seeing myself there. There is such great strength in smallness. I began to relax again, climbing on to the next belay and taking a breather to ask Stephen if he had got any good pictures.

And then my nightmare scenario – it began to sprinkle a light smear of rain. The threat of failure or worse became very real, as I waited, held fast. I was 500 feet up a vertical wall wearing nothing but my rock boots, a chalk bag, a pair of climbing tights and a fleece jumper. If it began to rain heavily there was nowhere for me to go, nothing to be done, nobody to help within a time frame that would prevent my exposed hands numbing up in the cold. Would I be able to hang on long enough for a technical rope rescue, possibly hours later? I ask myself this question now but daren't have even thought about it at the time.

But the rain slowly receded. I waited for the rock to dry. Relaxing once more, I looked across at Stephen who was climbing higher again in order to get a shot looking down. I was climbing faster than he was, partly due to the steep nature of the wall I was on, but also because he was just climbing slowly, as bloody usual. This really annoyed me.

I remember this early backpacking trip we did where we walked from his Gran's house in Milngavie to Drymen, camped there and walked in to the Queen's Forest round the back of Ben Lomond in the pissing rain. We eventually dragged our wet and sorry arses over the shoulder of the hill and down onto the road – he was behind me the whole way except when we hatched a plan to plead for a lift back to safety. I had been the driving force of that experience. In reality we were suffering from exposure, soaked and wading through flooding rivers and becoming weaker and weaker. He was behind me all the time – it did my head in; I always felt as though I was mentally pulling us both forward. I remember the plan was I was supposed to act extra ill and he would ask for the lift. I was so affronted at this – he was the one lagging behind most of the way!

Once he was up and in position I continued on up to a small overlap. Perhaps I was just starting to get cocky, posing for photos. My foot slipped a little, my heart skipped a beat. Fortunately for me, I was on good handholds. I refocused on reality and told myself everything was cool. Before long Stephen and I were united on top of the wall, all smiles and banter and relaxed retrospective.

Back at the pub Ian Nicolson grinned and shook my hand. He's a harsh judge and one of the greatest exponents of Scottish solo climbing, summer and winter. He congratulated me only twice in my life – once for this, and on a previous occasion for climbing the North Wall of the Eiger. He understood the significance of the day. So there it was; a handshake from the man himself – it seemed a fitting end to one of the best days of my life.

Shauna Clarke on *Shibboleth* (E2).
Photo: *Dan Moore.*

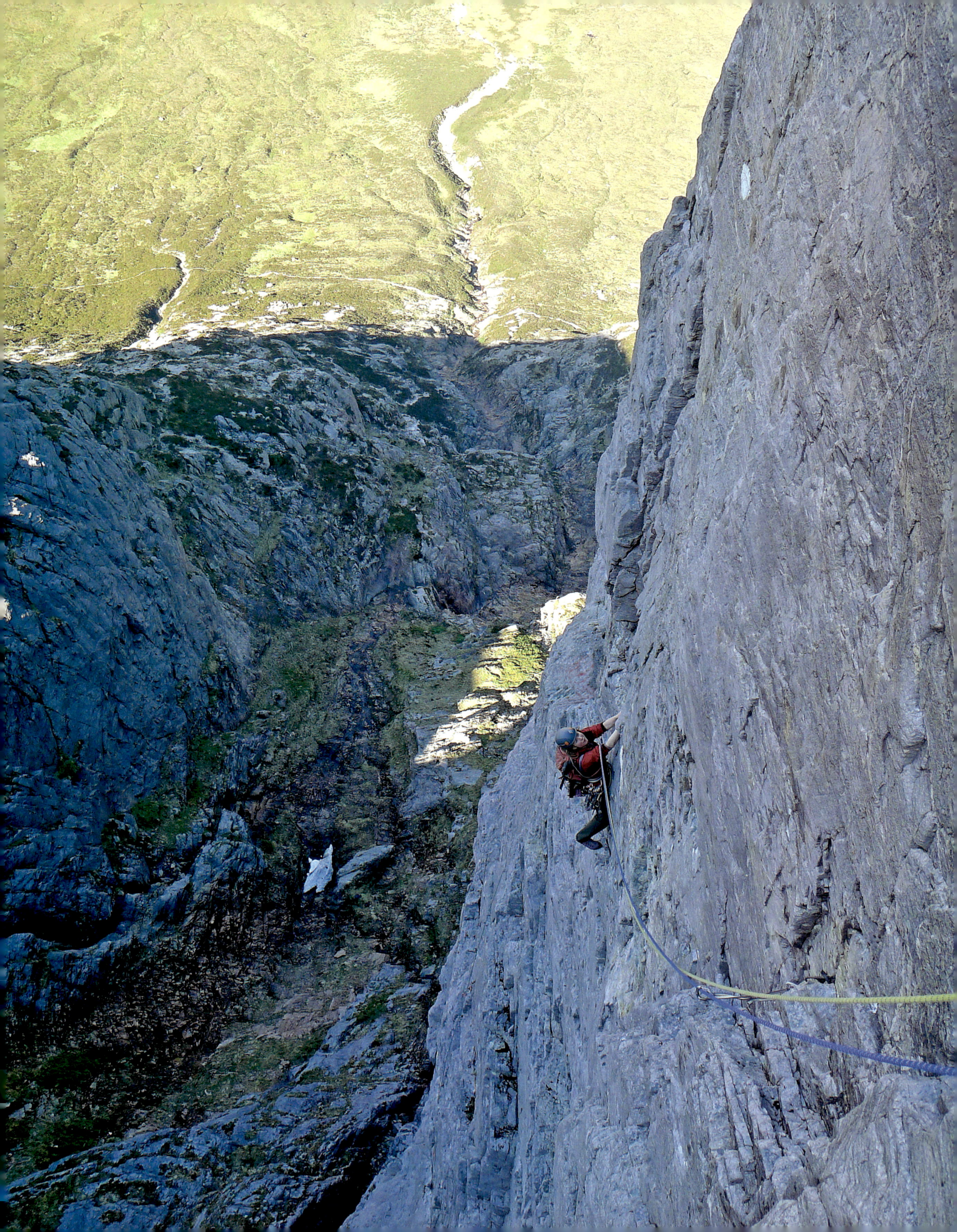

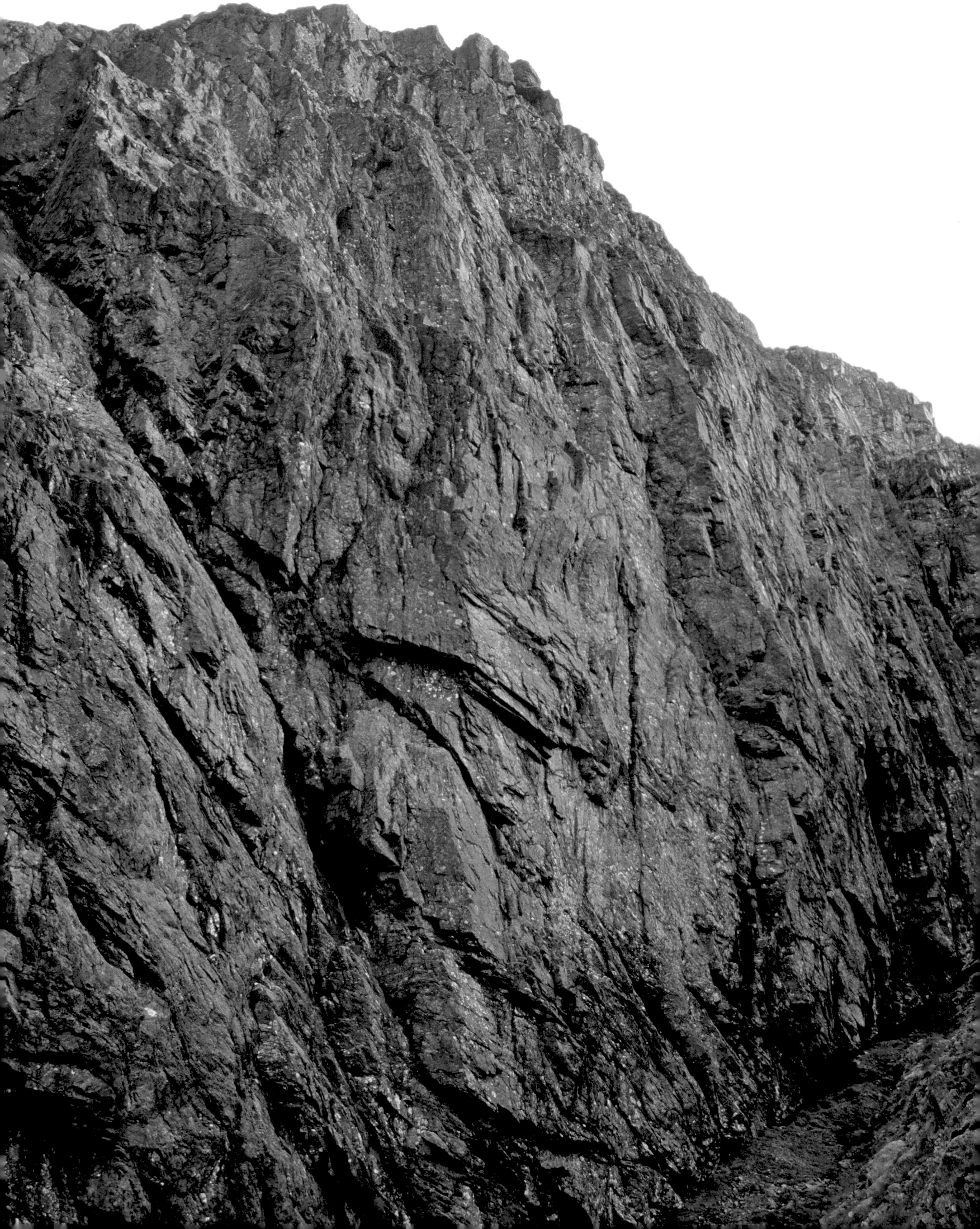

NORTH FACE, AONACH DUBH – *by Blair Fyffe*

THE PLACE
When passing through Glen Coe, my eyes are often drawn up to the great dark slot of Ossian's cave high on the North Face of Aonach Dubh. Up there, above the steep and vegetated face, the crags have a commanding view across the glen.

A natural ramp rising diagonally across the hillside provides access, gradually narrowing and becoming increasingly exposed high up where it merges into the Sloping Shelf. The approach to the Shelf is complex terrain where man and deer have been forced to take the same route, forming only a slight path in places. Once the base of the crag is reached, the atmosphere is tremendous. Sloping Shelf drops off steeply into the dripping depths below, while overhead the crag creates a real Nordwand impression. And it's a serious place too – a slip here could be catastrophic. However, time it right, and on a clear summer evening the setting sun will bathe your route in a beautiful golden light.

THE CLIFF
The main cliff is defined on its left by the huge slot of Ossian's Cave. Immediately right the wall is split by two parallel vertical faults. Although not quite of the same botanical value as the route into the cave, the rock here is still somewhat vegetated for good modern rock climbing. However, these great faults provide two fantastic and much sought-after winter routes.

Further right the wall becomes much more clean, sheer and continuous, forming a superb 100-metre high wall of perfect mountain rhyolite. The strongest feature here is the soaring open book corner of *Yo-Yo*, which stretches the whole height of the wall. There are other grooves and some cracks but these are generally less continuous. The terrain in between these features is often smooth and compact, lending an intimidating and uncertain air to the majority of routes.

THE CLIMBING
One of the first rock climbs in Britain, *Ossian's Ladder*, is found here, created when in 1868 a local shepherd boldly climbed up into the cave. I think it is fair to say this is not one of Glen Coe's finest. Fortunately the crag right of the cave provides something infinitely more appealing to the modern climber.

In summer the character of the routes varies substantially depending on the route and the particular features being followed. There are sections of bold face climbing with long run-outs on crimps and edges, but there are also long, strenuous and well protected cracks and grooves. In general the crag dries out relatively quickly after rain, and is one of the first in Glen Coe to offer dry rock after winter. Protection is sound where available, and there is little in-situ, so a good-sized rack will pay dividends in summer and winter.

This is a difficult cliff to catch in good winter condition – a very wet autumn, lots of snow and at least a week of freezing temperatures appear to be required. However, the requirement for a plastering of snow to bring the smooth, sheer walls into an acceptable state for winter ascents means that avalanches on the approach are often a serious objective hazard. At least one party has come to grief here, although fortunately without fatality.

◀ The North Face of Aonach Dubh.
Photo: *Ian Taylor.*

▲ Tony Stone on *Repossessed* (E5). Photo: *Adam Russell*.

THE ROUTES

Against All Odds (VII,8)

The name says it all. Not often in condition, it was finally climbed into the night after an earlier attempt saw the pioneers avalanched off Sloping Shelf. Steep, very exposed and very turfy, with the novelty value of a bendy tree to bridge up.

Yo-Yo (E1)

The first route to tackle the steep and clean right-hand section of the face. Although it can seep a bit at the start, it is often a lot drier than the black rock makes it appear from a distance. Three excellent sustained pitches of corner and groove climbing up the strongest line on the face.

▲ Iain Small on the second ascent of *Eragon* (E6).
Photo: *Murdoch Jamieson*.

The Clearances (E4)

The obvious hanging crack left of *Yo-Yo*. Bold face climbing is required to reach the crack, followed by strenuous but better-protected crack climbing. The second pitch gives good groove climbing and a bulge above.

THE STORY

It has to be said, my first attempt to climb on the North Face of Aonach Dubh was less than successful. I had been in Glen Coe for a few days, ticking various routes on Slime Wall and Church Door Buttress. The *Hard Rock* classic *Yo-Yo* was on the list. Unfortunately, I made a bit of a route-finding error on the approach, and ended up on a smaller shelf below Sloping Shelf, among a world of steep, loose choss. A retreat was called for.

Eight years later my second trip up there was a bit more successful, even if it did not turn out quite the way we had planned. I had intended to do *The Clearances* with Guy Robertson, who had been up there before and thus would know the way. Unfortunately the mountain crags were not very dry, and when we arrived we found the route to be wet. Wandering around the Sloping Shelf below the wall, wondering what to do, Guy pointed to the large area of un-climbed and generally dry looking rock to the right of *Yo-Yo*. He suggested we did the first pitch of *Yo-Yo* and then quest out rightwards.

The first pitch of *Yo-Yo* provided a fine warm up. From there our proposed line broke out right across an undercut wall and then upwards, somewhere, somehow. I gingerly stepped out of the *Yo-Yo* corner: there were just enough holds and runners to tempt me cautiously onwards, the exposure growing with every move. I found some sanctuary in a small right-facing corner. Above, the angle of the wall reared up. I got a high runner and shuffled right to have a wee peek around the arête. There was nothing very useful around there and, disappointed, I retreated to the corner. The wall above, it would have to be.

I climbed up, got a decent runner in, and climbed back down. I repeated the process of shuffling up, then retreating to shake out in the little corner. Each time I was getting a bit higher, a bit further from my gear, but working out the moves and getting closer to the sanctuary of a small ledge I could see above. However, we were climbing totally on sight, and having hurt myself once before when a hold snapped, I was a little wary, testing things before yarding on them. Finally I got to a point when my body seemed to decide for itself that it was easier to go for the ledge above, than to shuffle all the way back to the sanctuary of the corner. A couple of stiff pulls and I was up. Above, the angle eased a bit and some relatively amenable climbing up a shallow corner brought me to a long flat ledge, a perfect belay spot. With the benefit of chalked holds and a top rope, Guy cruised up what I had been huffing and puffing on.

While belaying him I enjoyed the atmospheric situation, and relaxed in the knowledge that it was Guy's turn to embrace the unknown above. A short steep wall above the belay didn't look too difficult to climb, but blocked our view of the rest of the cliff. However, it didn't seem to put Guy off. He grabbed the rack and was soon out of sight above. Although I could not see him, the whooping noises suggested that he was having fun, and from the rope I could feel that he was making steady progress. He was soon safe, and then after some faff so that he could haul the one camera we had between us, it was my turn to climb. When that was all sorted, I discovered what all the fuss was about. Above the short wall, which had blocked my view, a sustained crack ran up a superb exposed wall of clean mountain rhyolite.

After that, a final short pitch took us to Pleasant Terrace. The guidebook suggests that this is an ironic name, but it was nowhere near as bad as I was expecting. From the end of this, a quick abseil took us back down to the Sloping Shelf, and the long winding path back down to the floor of the glen.

A few weeks later I returned with Guy and we climbed *The Clearances*. It was a great route, but somehow did not have the satisfaction of what we had gained on the previous trip, on our little voyage into the unknown.

Blair Fyffe on the first ascent of *Bunjee* (E4).
Photo: *Guy Robertson*.

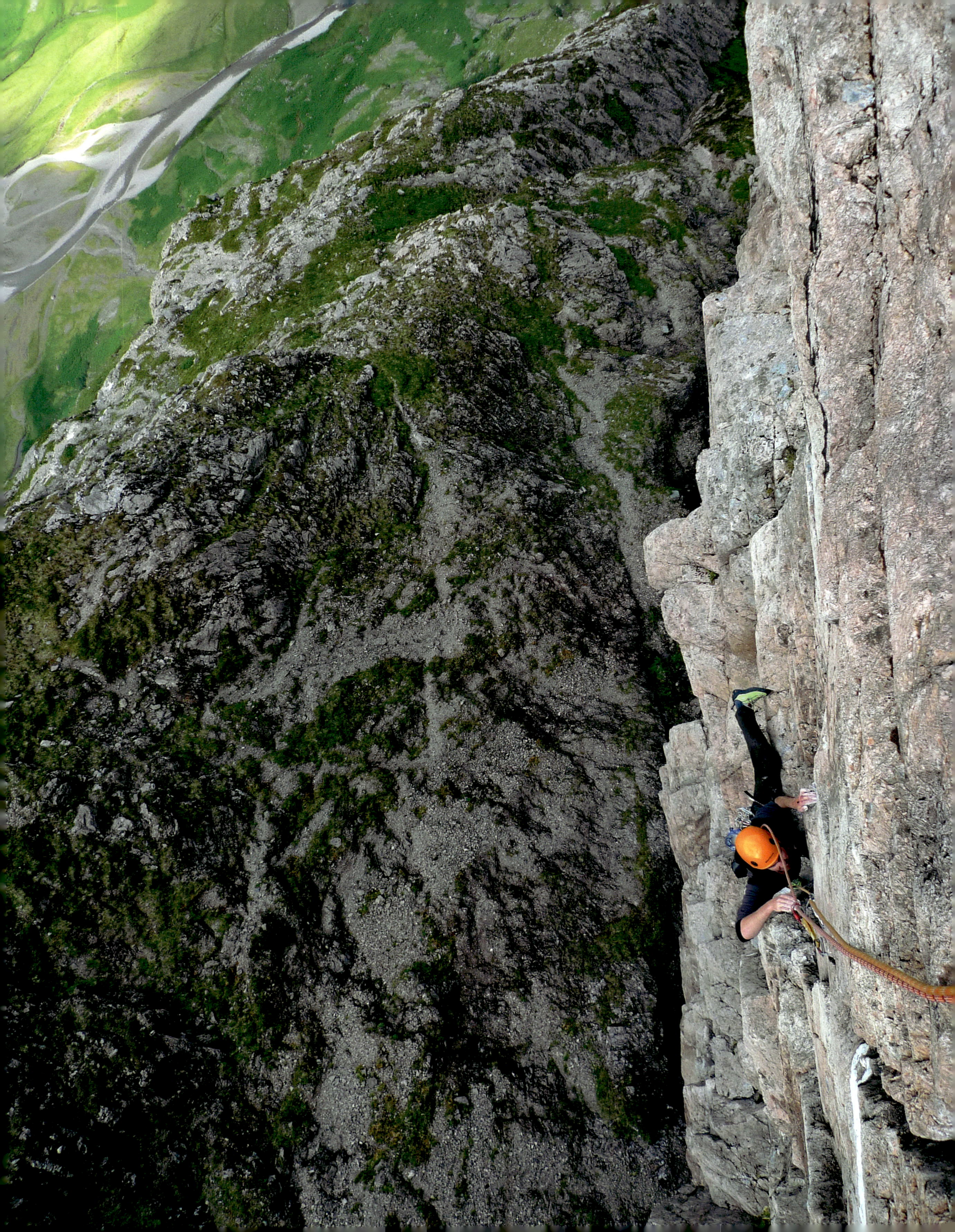

Guy Robertson and Tim Rankin on *Eldorado* (E5), Aonach Dubh North Face. Photo: *Dave Cuthbertson*

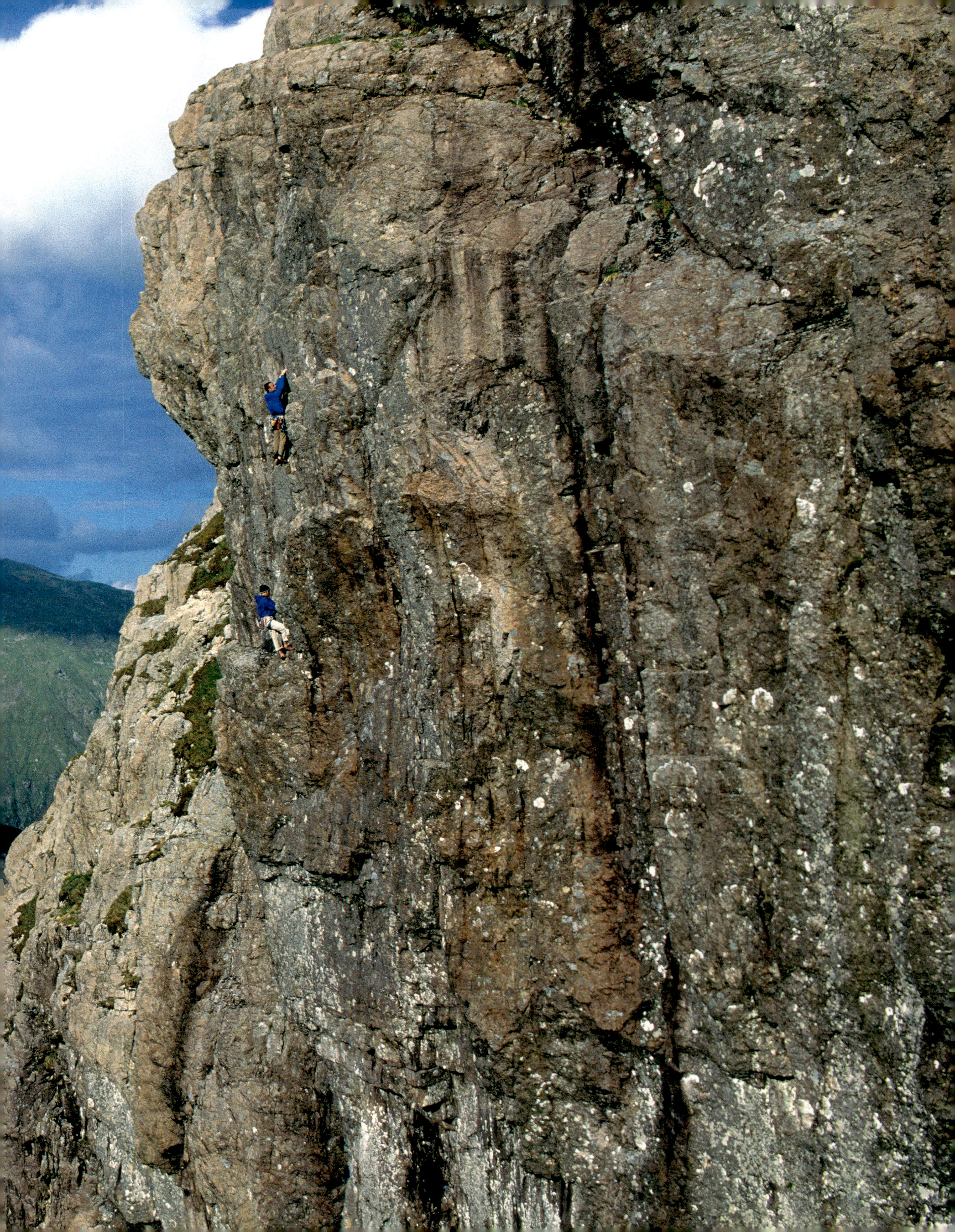

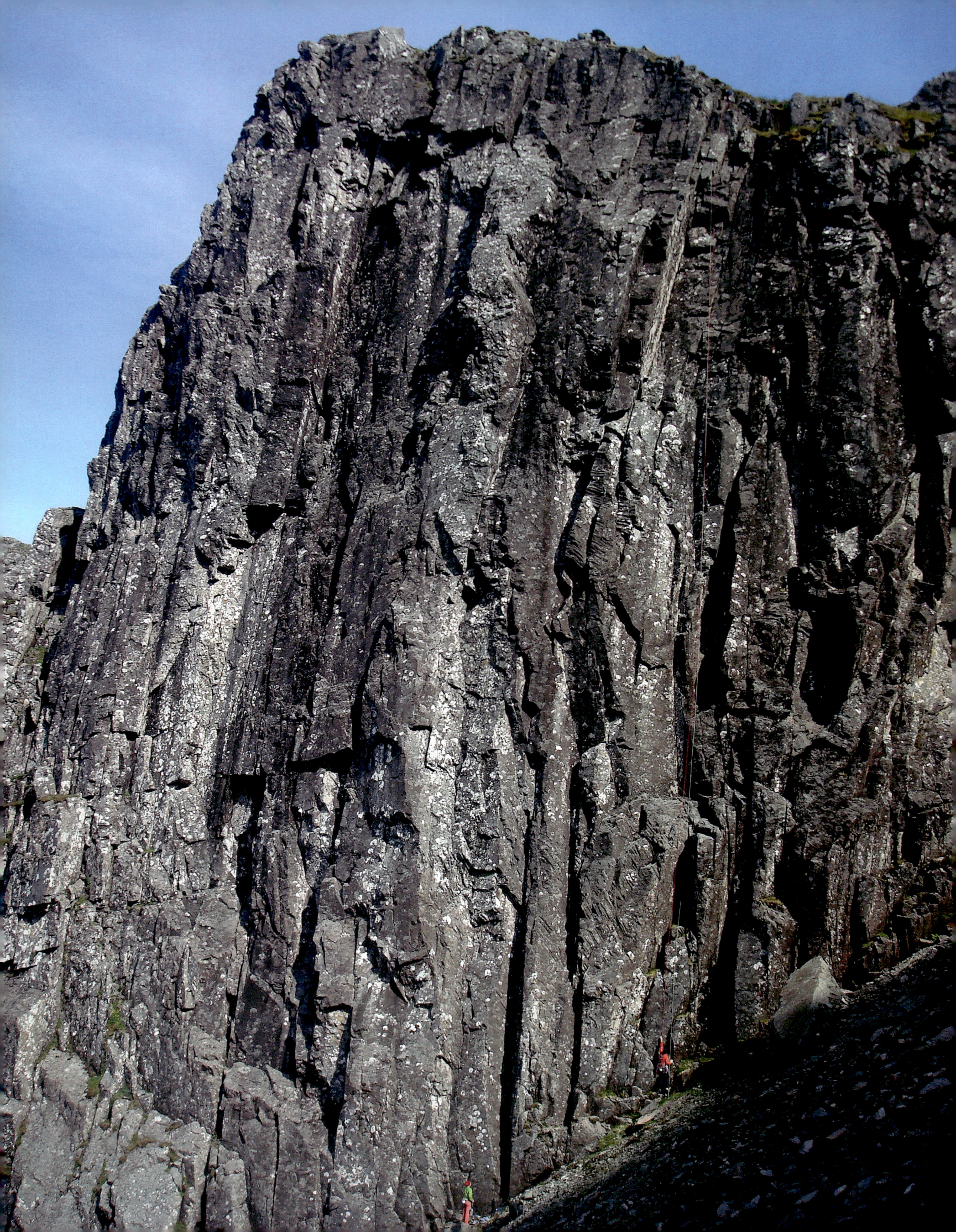

Church Door Buttress, Bidean nam Bian – *by Ian Taylor*

THE PLACE

The first guidebook I ever bought was Hamish MacInnes' *Scottish Climbs*. This magnificent tome, with its strangely coded route descriptions, was stuffed full of gritty black and white photos of dreadful looking cliffs.

In this book the sun never shone. There was one particular photo of Church Door Buttress in all its Gothic glory, completely plastered in snow and rime. I naively assumed it was at such an altitude that it was always like that and I was very nearly right. A school hill walk revealed it in its normal summer condition. Dropping down from the summit of Bidean in the lashing rain, a saturated cliff loomed through the mist. Between dripping walls, water cascaded down grooves and corners and poured over roofs. I couldn't believe people climbed there; they must surely have webbed feet or be superhuman.

THE CLIFF

Here is a wildness you don't find on the other crags of Glen Coe, almost totally hidden from the sight and sound of the road, with a stunning view westward out across Ardgour. Cast your eye past the east face, badly constructed of tottering blocks and pillars, to the west face – Church Door Buttress – rammed full of solid, tempting looking grooves and cracks. There'll be a raven, of course. It'll cruise past, laughing as you stretch for some far hold, caw, flip on its back then just drop out of sight in a freefall dive.

The cliff, dark grey with black lined grooves, sits under a large mossy sponge which continues to seep long after most crags are parched. The name of the crag broadly describes its shape – a broad, arch-shaped buttress of Gothic proportions. A well-defined chimney slants up left from the centre of the face, right of which the rock is uniformly steep and unbroken save for a confusing array of grooves, cracks and pillars. This area is the preserve of the Extreme rock climber only (to date, at least). Left of the chimney, the crag sports a huge detached rock arch in its upper reaches, a number of routes heading for and squeezing under this, providing unusual and dramatic rock scenery – when you can see the light, that is! The chimney itself (West Chimney) and this area to the left provide a number of excellent winter routes.

◀ Church Door Buttress.
Photo: *Ian Taylor*.

THE CLIMBING

In summer, the climbing has an old school feel. Technical rather than powerful sequences requiring a quota of traditional techniques not easily learned at the climbing wall. Lots of holds seem to face the wrong way and progress is often head-scratchingly slow. The rock when clean is really rather wonderful: lovely edges full of friction and rough smears for the feet. Starting at 950 metres, here are some of the highest Extremes in Britain and inevitably the altitude enforces a slow drying regime. The sun reluctantly comes onto the face around 3 p.m., but it soon dips behind Stob Coire nam Beith.

In winter, the crag also provides superb climbing, coming into condition with the first snows and a good freeze. Snowed-up rock is the order of the day, with the climbs following good strong natural lines with solid protection.

The buttress was named Church Door by early SMC stalwart William Tough, and although there is an ecclesiastical resemblance, you certainly have to squint a bit. It was the original last great problem. Waves of the leading climbers of the day threw themselves at it in all weathers until Harold Raeburn cracked the crux chimney in 1898 and led a team to the top. In 1920, Morley Wood, John Wilding and Fred Pigott, from Manchester's Rucksack Club, made a quiet ascent of *Crypt Route*, tunnelling through the darkness to pop out below *Raeburn's Chimney*.

Fast forward to 1968 when local climbers John Hardie and Will Thomson pulled out all the stops with *Kingpin*, the first route to tackle the futuristic west face. Their handful of aid pegs later freed by Dave Cuthbertson and Dougie Mullin. In the eighties, Lakeland raider Pete Whillance snatched the first of the pre-cleaned modern routes, with the soaring grooveline of *The Lost Ark* (E5) – solving the problematic lower section by skirting around it using the left arête. Since then the Scots have had it all their own way: Murray Hamilton, Rab Anderson and Graham Livingstone plucked the classic groove and exposed stepped corner of *Temple of Doom* (E3), then Gary Latter and various partners added *The Lost Arrow* (E3), *The Holy Grail* (E5) and *The Fundamentalists* (E4), all taking strong natural lines through hostile ground.

THE ROUTES

West Chimney (V,6)
Classic climbing up a classic line, well worth the long approach and very often in condition.

Kingpin (E3)
The classic *Extreme Rock* tick, taking a grand natural line up the left side of the central pillar on the steepest section of the crag.

The Lost Ark (E5)
The superb white-speckled groove right of the central pillar.

Dave MacLeod on *West Chimney* (V,6).
Photo: *Dave Cuthbertson.*

THE SOUTH WEST HIGHLANDS | **CHURCH DOOR BUTTRESS, BIDEAN NAM BIAN**

▲ Church Door Buttress from the approach. Photo: *Ian Taylor*.   Joanna George and Blair Fyffe on Church Door Buttress. Photo: *Dave Cuthbertson*. ▶

THE STORY

As the years went by all my plans for getting up to Church Door came to naught. Indeed, it wasn't till 2003 that I got my chance. It was a brilliant dry summer and Tess Fryer and I had been making the most of it. But after a day on Stac Pollaidh and two wind-frazzling days on the Ben, we were knackered. Just when we needed a rest the forecast promised one more dry day, and the opportunity was too good to miss. At the pace of an underachieving sloth we staggered up the 900 metres of gruelling ascent.

It was warm and sweaty as I started up *Kingpin*. An easy crack and slab led all too quickly into a nasty steep and shallow groove. Thin, committing bridging, with little in the way of comforting handholds or protection, landed me at an awkward stance in a niche. The difficulties were short, but it was definitely not a pitch to fall off. About ten metres above the belay was a short hanging chimney. Obviously unaware of the ongoing drought, water seeped out the base of the chimney and trickled down a black groove. It looked like a good pitch to second and after a tentative look, Tess came to the same conclusion, cleverly playing the 'this route was your idea anyway' card. Switching into mountaineering mode I managed a horrible mantelshelf onto a ledge below the chimney,

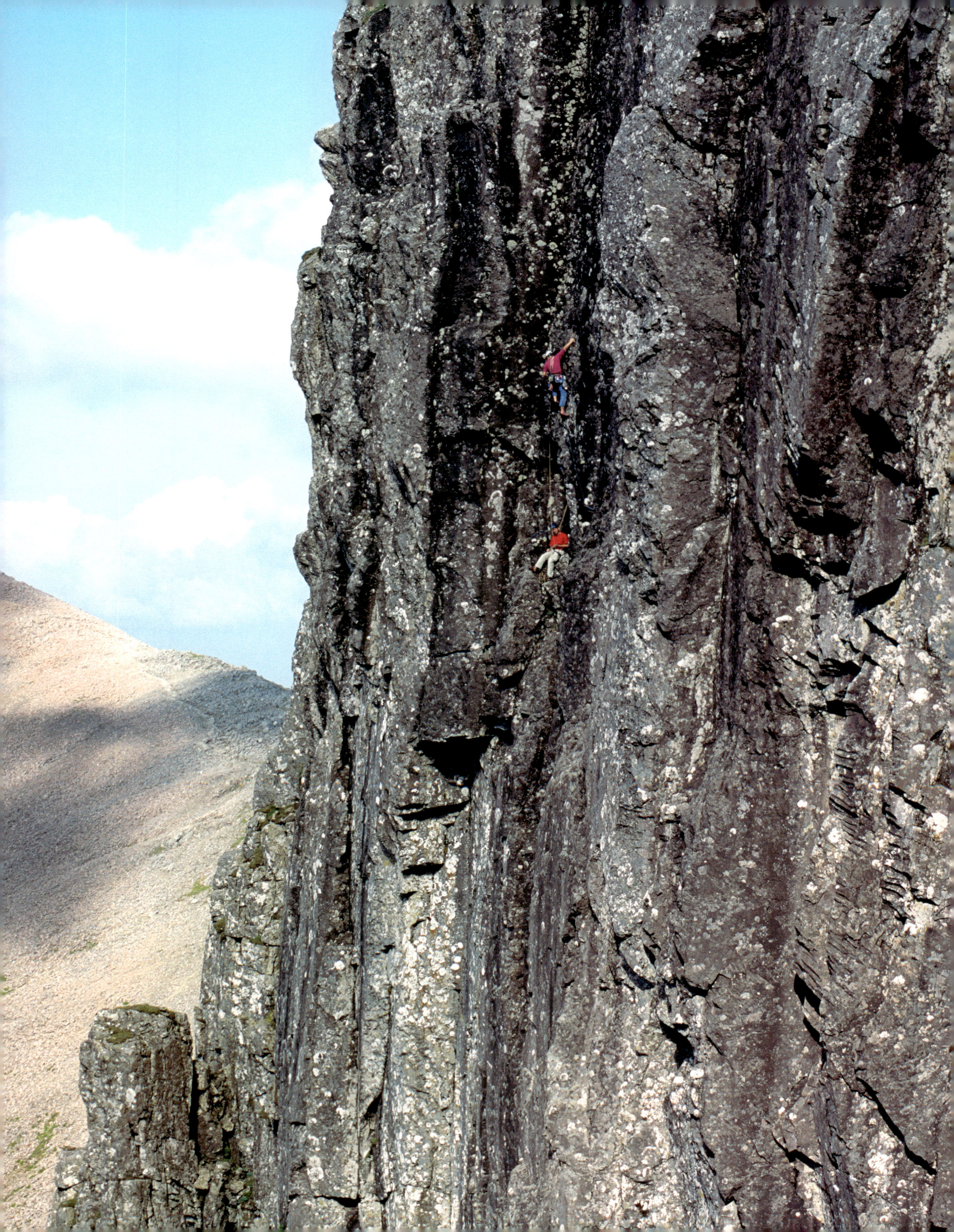

foot placed luckily on the only dry patch. The rest of the pitch was drier and I was soon swinging left to a tidy wee stance. The next pitch was the best on the route. Tess trended rightwards up a fine exposed ramp which led to a recess, out of which some steep moves led without incident to the belay. By now the morning's blue skies had gradually been replaced with darkening clouds and a threatening rumble of thunder echoed around the coire. The clock was definitely ticking. A groove, a roof and a footless swing right passed in a blur to a ledge on the edge, followed by an excellent wall that I was in too much of a rush to enjoy. Amazingly, apart from a few fat drops, the rain held off as we half-ran, half-stumbled down the never-ending path. One nil to us.

Four years later we were back, and having done *Spacewalk* the day before, we thought we'd take a gamble on the higher crags. It was another hot, humid day by the time we got to the cliff. Conditions looked far from ideal and there was a lot of dampness about, but *The Lost Ark* looked the driest, so we went for that. The speckled groove was nice and steady, and the moves up the arête, though committing, just seemed to click, and soon I was feeling smug on good holds. Out right across the top of the groove, then up to a peg, said the description, but out right was mossy, wet and looked rather bold. I went back and forth a few times, clearing moss and dabbing damp bits with a chalk ball until, in growing desperation, I crimped some tiny wet edges and found myself high above my gear, eyeballing a useless rotten peg. With a rush of blood to the head I sprinted for the sanctuary of the ledge above, but it had been a bit too close for comfort. The raven drifted by, smirking and giving me the eye, as Tess made short work of the traditional grovelling groove above. As we headed down, perhaps in retaliation for escaping dry last time, we were soaked to the skin in a sudden deluge. Let's call it two nil, but it could have gone either way.

2011 hadn't been a great summer for the high hills, but a week of drying northerlies in July, followed by a warm and sunny weekend, tempted us up for another visit. It had to be *Temple of Doom* this time. Tess made slow, but steady progress up a well featured groove, heading for a blanker leaning corner above. Although the corner was well protected, the fingerlocks seeped badly and the footholds were few and far apart. On reaching the top of the corner she tried to move left, but again the footholds were all in the wrong place. With a massive move she grabbed a wet sloping hold and shouted 'take' as she slipped off, but her momentum took her to a better, drier part of the hold and on up to belay. Seconding, I had a similar 'I'm off, no I'm still on' experience and feeling lucky I headed up the next pitch. Being complacent I hadn't bothered to bring the description, as I thought it just went up that big obvious corner. After some enjoyable climbing I moved right to below the corner, which looked surprisingly dirty and had a big nasty loose block guarding entry. I managed to do a careful loop around the block, but ended up standing on it anyway. I hadn't been wrong; the corner was dirty and incredibly sustained. I worked hard for the moves and protection and began to run out of gear. Eventually, tiring rapidly, I pulled gratefully over a bulge to a ledge, and easy climbing led to the top. I felt beaten up. Back at the sacks and the guidebook reveals all. I should have moved left to a hanging stepped corner. What an idiot. Tess suggests calling it *Temple of Dumb*. There was no sign of our friend the raven, but I'm sure I heard a faint caw, caw, echoing round the rocks.

At my current rate and with plenty more routes to do, I'll be ancient by the time I'm king of the crag, and then there's a heap of new lines. It's going to take a long time for sure. Fortunately the dampness, moss and the long approach fade quickly from my memory and I just remember the fantastic rock and situations. •

Es Tressider on *Un Poco Loco* (VII,7).
Photo: *Dave Cuthbertson*.

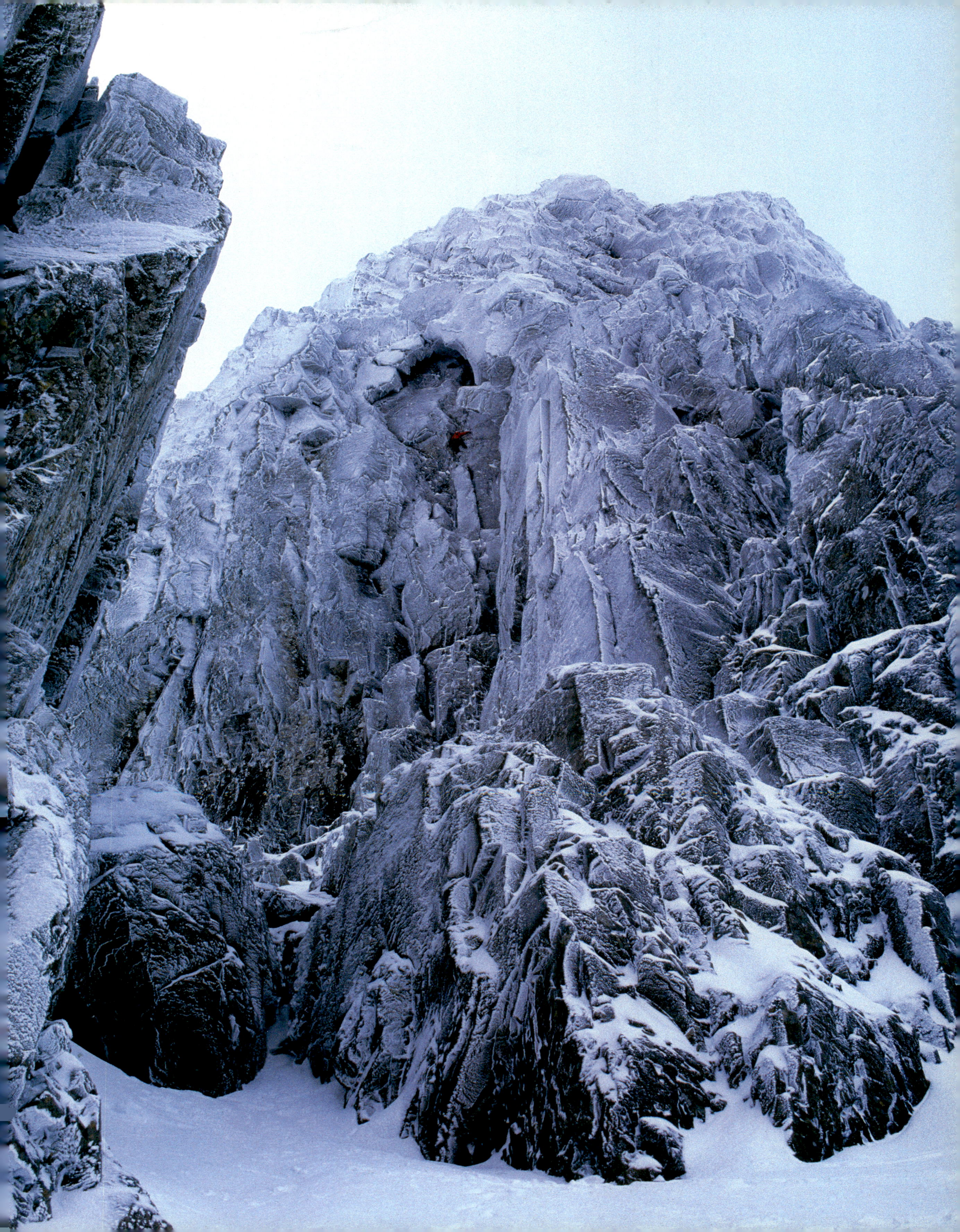

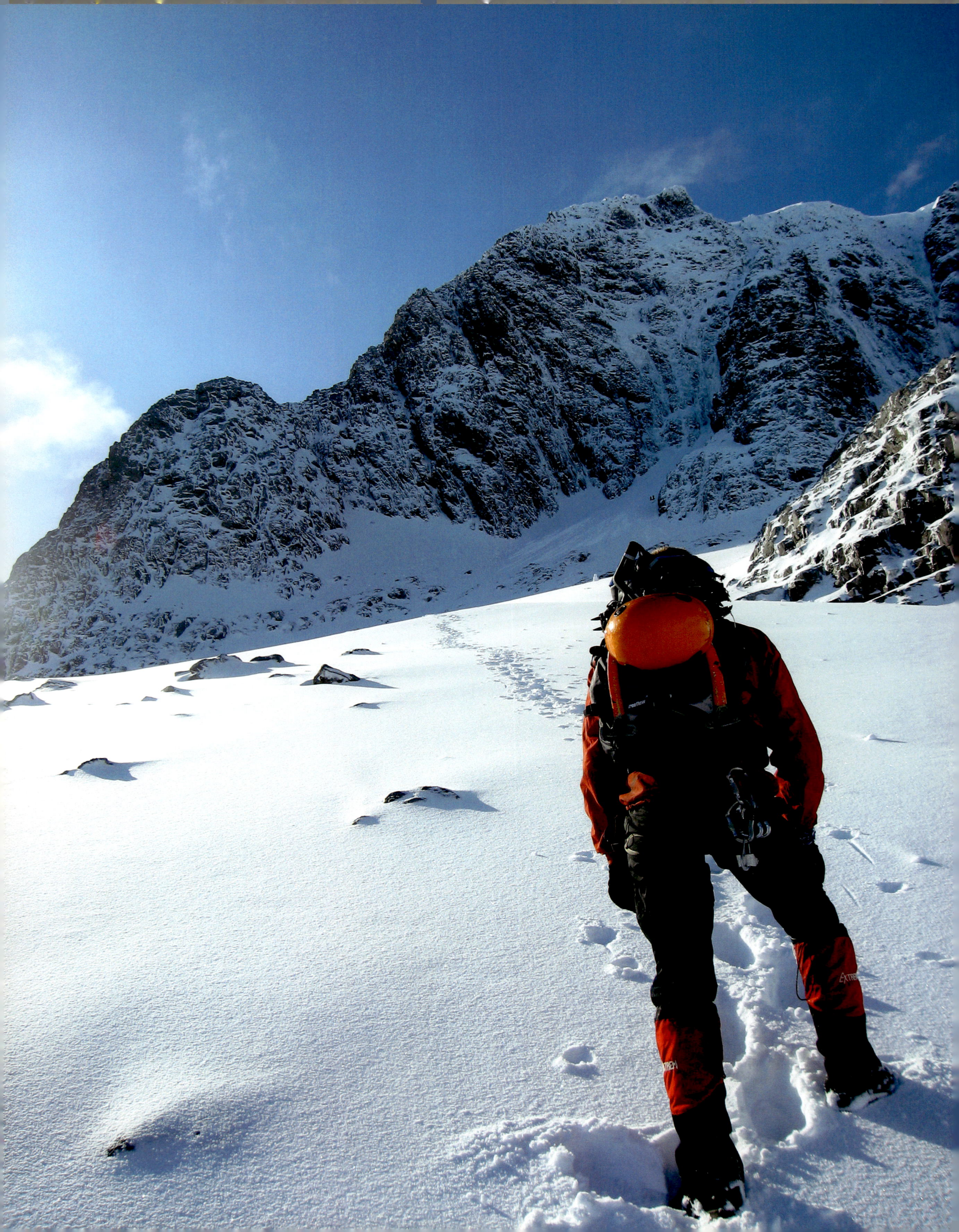

ORION AND MINUS FACE, BEN NEVIS – *by Viv Scott*

THE PLACE
There's an appropriate symmetry in the fact that Scotland's highest mountain also hosts its greatest cirque of cliffs. Sweeping down from the summit plateau of Ben Nevis, great castellated ridges and buttresses frame the showpiece which, when veined with winter's coat, draws every climber's eye – the vast concave wall of the Orion and Minus Face.

Their allure lies in more than the name, this really is an alpine world among the stars, standing proud above the lesser hills, glens and lochs below. As spring strips Scotland's cliffs of snow, these mighty north walls – poking their nose that bit higher into the sky – keep winter alive for a few more precious moments of magic.

THE CLIFF
Seen from the approach up the Allt a' Mhuilinn, the face hangs high behind the crest of Tower Ridge. Its far right hand side lies hidden behind Observatory Buttress, terminating in the deeply recessed groove of Zero Gully. In summer the face appears chaotic, the lower slabs leading to an apparent jumble of broken grooves above.

The rock climber's eye is drawn leftwards to the cleaner parallel ribs of the Minus Face which, although perhaps not as attractive a challenge technically as nearby Carn Dearg, nonetheless contains some of the best and longest mild Extremes anywhere in Britain. However, when summer ends and moist Atlantic storms alternate with cold eastern highs, both faces become deeply plastered with snow and rime ice. It is arguably during these colder winter months that the cliff's true character is revealed. Sitting squarely in the centre, the great snowfield of the Basin provides a focal point connecting sweeping slabs and grooves below to the icy smears fanning out above – Scotland's very own (little) 'White Spider'. To its left, the endless skyline of North East Buttress drops away, its flanking wall a series of great soaring ribs, gullies and grooves – the Minus Face.

THE CLIMBING
On the Orion and Minus Face, the andesite forms compact sweeping slabs frequently devoid of helpful cracks – many a winter climber has dug frantically at the back of a promising corner only to be repelled by a blind seam.

Summer routes pick their way up the cleaner rock, teetering across slabs to connect viable cracks, while away from the principal drainage lines of the major gullies and grooves the winter lines follow icy smears which may or may not connect depending on the whims of the weather gods. These are the largest and most complex walls found anywhere in Scotland, and although there are no desperate climbs by modern standards, there are none especially easy. Any ascent, summer or winter, combines length, sustained climbing and route-finding interest rarely matched anywhere else.

Despite its obvious prominence, the Orion Face presented few chinks in its armour to early pioneers who preferred the relative security of neighbouring chimneys, ridges and arêtes. Only in 1940 was the challenge of the Orion Face matched – Bell and Wilson picking their way up the intricate and serious *Long Climb* (VS). On the neighbouring Minus Face, the extraordinary talent of Kellet, prospecting solo, was first to explore its sweeping buttresses, but the greatest of these – *Minus One Buttress* (E1), fell to raiding Sassenachs led by Downes. In its straightened form this route remains among the best and most sought-after of classic mountain Extremes.

◀ The Orion and Minus Face of Ben Nevis.
Photo: *Viv Scott Collection.*

Winter exploration awaited the enigmatic Robin Smith, who, eschewing the siege tactics of the time, step cut his way into the unknown – *Smith-Holt Route* (V,5), *Minus Three Gully* (IV,5) and the crowning glory of Smith and Marshall's legendary week – *Orion Direct* (V,5). Like the iconic routes of the great Alpine faces, *Orion Direct* unlocks the face by a route-finding tour-de-force. Picking an intricate line through the mountain's defences it remains perhaps the greatest winter route on the mountain. Front-pointing opened new possibilities; the final conquest of the much attempted *Minus One Gully* (VI,6), and ventures onto the exposed icefalls and smears that drool tantalisingly down the Orion: *Slav Route* (VI,5), *Astral Highway* (VI,5) and *Journey into Space* (VII,5). Seeking cerebral challenges, today's mixed pioneers have been tempted onto the steeper ribs; thinly-iced slabs giving access to *Integration* (VIII,8) by Richardson and Small, and *Minus One Direct* (VIII,8) giving Benson, Bullock and Robertson 'possibly the best winter climb ever'.

THE ROUTES

Orion Direct (V,5)
Arguably Scotland's most iconic winter route, and without doubt one of the very best, providing a truly alpine scale experience with first class ice and mixed climbing. A variety of starts are possible, all gaining the central snowfield of the Basin, before sneaking out right into the upper grooves by some delicate mixed climbing.

Minus One Direct (E1, VIII,8)
A scintillating line up the front crest of Minus One Buttress, the longest and best defined of the flanking ribs on North East Buttress. In either season it provides a tremendous, long and sustained route among the top five of its grade anywhere in Scotland.

Minus One Gully (VI,6)
The last of the Nevis gullies to fall, so perhaps not surprisingly the hardest. It takes the narrow iced groove bounding the right side of Minus One Buttress. The difficulties are concentrated on an icy overhang low down, but the climbing is sustained and it isn't over once North East Buttress is reached!

Murdoch Jamieson on *Minus One Gully* (VI,6).
Photo: *Adam Booth*.

56   THE GREAT MOUNTAIN CRAGS OF SCOTLAND

THE SOUTH WEST HIGHLANDS | ORION AND MINUS FACE, BEN NEVIS

THE STORY

Arriving for university in Edinburgh, fresh from a summer season in the Alps, I was keen to make amends for my previous and essentially abortive Scottish winter trips from London.

An at times over-enthusiastic apprenticeship in the weird world of Scottish winter climbing ensued, including the long, heavily-laden soggy slog up to camp beneath the holy grail of the Ben's north face. Routes came and went, but a combination of often poor conditions and fear induced by guidebook descriptions of long, tenuous run-outs between poor belays steered my focus towards the Ben's less intimidating snowed-up rock and mixed options.

Fortunately, the long high pressure that brought the 2007 season to a close was impossible to ignore – framed by cloudless skies, white veins of ice ran through dry rock picking out every line on the mountain. Following a tough day repeating our friends Blair Fyffe and Es Tresidder's superb route *Rhyme of the Ancient Mariner*, the lure of the Orion Face was too much to ignore. Far from the chilling descriptions that had lodged in my brain, the reality of *Astral Highway* – a variation on *Orion Direct* that breaks leftwards from the Basin via steep ice smears – proved a light-hearted experience. Perfect ice allowed us to move together, stopping only to recover gear, swap grins and heckle friends on adjacent routes.

The following April, a late snowfall followed by a perfect forecast once again summoned attention to Scotland's only alpine wall. While our companions headed for Minus One Gully, Guy Robertson and I had sterner fish to fry. His ever roving eye for new adventures had lit upon the description of a lesser-known summer E1 on Minus Two Buttress:

'Subtraction, a neglected route with a fierce reputation, although recent ascents suggest this may not be justified.'

▶ The Orion and Minus Face in summer; to the right are Observatory Ridge and the Douglas Boulder of Tower Ridge. Photo: *Dave Cuthbertson*.

THE GREAT MOUNTAIN CRAGS OF SCOTLAND

THE SOUTH WEST HIGHLANDS | **ORION AND MINUS FACE, BEN NEVIS**

For Guy, uncertainty and unknown are an elixir like no other – the description may as well have read 'red-rag – bull wanted'. Quickly skimming the description, I elected for the first pitch: 'well-defined groove, 4c' which seemed less ominous than the second: 'surmount the overhang, 5a'. Gearing up beneath the line reinforced the impression – a relatively innocuous looking lower and upper groove split by a small ledge, both grooves sporting thin trickles of ice and leading to a niche below the overlap.

While somewhat steeper than it looked from below, the ice proved helpful at first, and a bit of digging even yielded a runner or two to calm the nerves. Pulling up from the small ledge, the groove steepened, its sidewall veering inwards. A few feet up, a tough dig yielded only a poor bulldog half tapped into the blind seam backing the groove. Above, a patch of snow on the sidewall offered a possible crack, so I stemmed upwards, teetering on small nicks in the slab, probing above for that 'sinker hook' that sometimes rewards the brave. Nothing doing on this occasion. Some frantic clearing revealed a tiny incut hold – insecure with a tool, but udging upwards I closed my fingers onto it. 'I've got a jug!' I yelled at Guy, who had been gently heckling my performance from below.

Now for some gear – but five minutes of increasingly frantic clearing offered nothing. Shifting weight to relieve cramping calves, another five minutes of scraping produced no result other than a cold trickle of sweat starting to form down my spine. 'Jugs make good footholds,' offered Guy critically from below, bringing a wry grin to my predicament as I remained frozen in place contemplating my future. Then fate intervened … with a sickening shift the ice in the groove supporting my right foot gave way. Desperately scrabbling, the fingers of my right hand uncurling I seized on a tiny nubbin on the slab above to my right. Desperately hooking it I yarded without testing – managing to mantel my right hand just as the pick popped. Reliant more on momentum than connection I scrabbled upwards, vision blurred through the sweat of panic to find myself front points teetering on the nubbin with axes in nothing. Calves bursting I sought redemption – the snow packed into the niche beneath the overhang taunting just out of reach above. With nothing else left to give, I yelled a hopeful 'Watch me!', and hooking a poor seam in the groove lunged all-out for the snow. The axe bit, poorly, but just enough to fling its partner in alongside. Feet and knees scrabbled behind, seeking purchase on the edge of the niche. The snow shifted, pulled loose by my flailing, but with a final yelp of desperation I grabbed at the rock in the back and willed a frontpoint onto an edge and into balance.

Half an hour later, firmly tied into an assortment of mediocre gear in the shattered back of the niche I looked down on Guy's growing expression of mischief as he followed in a much less frantic fashion.

Guy's pitch began straight off the belay – the bare rock under the overlap inviting a gloves-off crimping approach followed by some urgent pulls onto a hanging, icy slab. My onset of belay stupor was rudely interrupted by an irritable squawk from above the overlap … Guy paying the ultimate price for the leashless revolution as one of his tools clattered past his heels and described a lazy arc to land on the snow below. Some belay re-arrangement allowed the passing up of a replacement, and Guy forged onwards through a secondary overlap into the unknown above. All too soon, a shout of 'safe' required action, some combined hooking, crimping and 'watch me' antics just allowing me to second with one tool. Above Guy's belay, an easier ice-choked crack and groove beckoned, but the Nevis gods hadn't quite finished their fun. A few feet up, the handle of my leashless axe fell apart, and lacking any method to repair I carried on with a 'half-tool'. A couple of steep but thankfully well-protected corners lead to easier ground overlooking Minus Two Gully.

Across the gully, the upper corner of *Subtraction* was bare of ice or snow, so Guy continued upwards before joining the final steep ice pitch of *Minus Two* to the easy ground of North East Buttress – an entertaining second with only one axe. A quick series of abseils down the gully gained the bags and errant axe at the bottom and we headed for the hut to rendezvous with friends.

Strolling out under the gathering gloom, bright stars congregating high in the black above the Orion Face, our conversation turned to summer.

Subtraction marked a turning point for me. Unwilling to stretch that far again, or to engage in the increasingly physical, if safer, draw of the new wave of super-steep winter lines, I instead turned back to my running and scrambling roots – seeking the gentler adrenaline-drip of the flow of unbroken movement on moderate ground. It is in this guise that I finally followed in the footsteps of Marshall and Smith, watching the dawn break from a perch high on their fifties masterpiece, the impeccable *Orion Direct*. Who could possibly ask for more than that?

Top: Pete Benson on the first winter ascent of *Minus One Direct* (VIII,8).
Photo: *Guy Robertson.*
Bottom: Steve Ashworth on *Orion Face Direct* (VI,5).
Photo: *Viv Scott.*

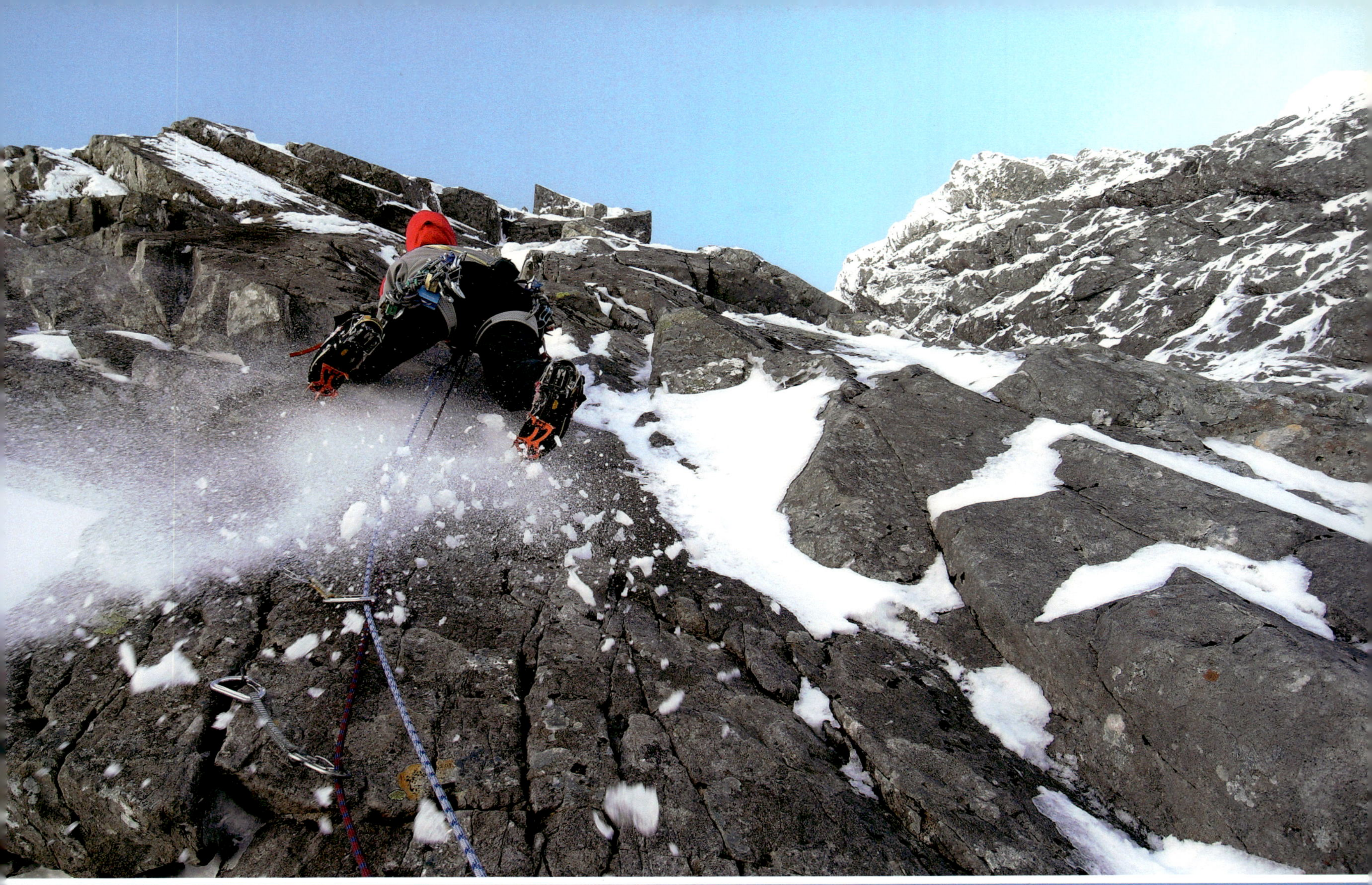

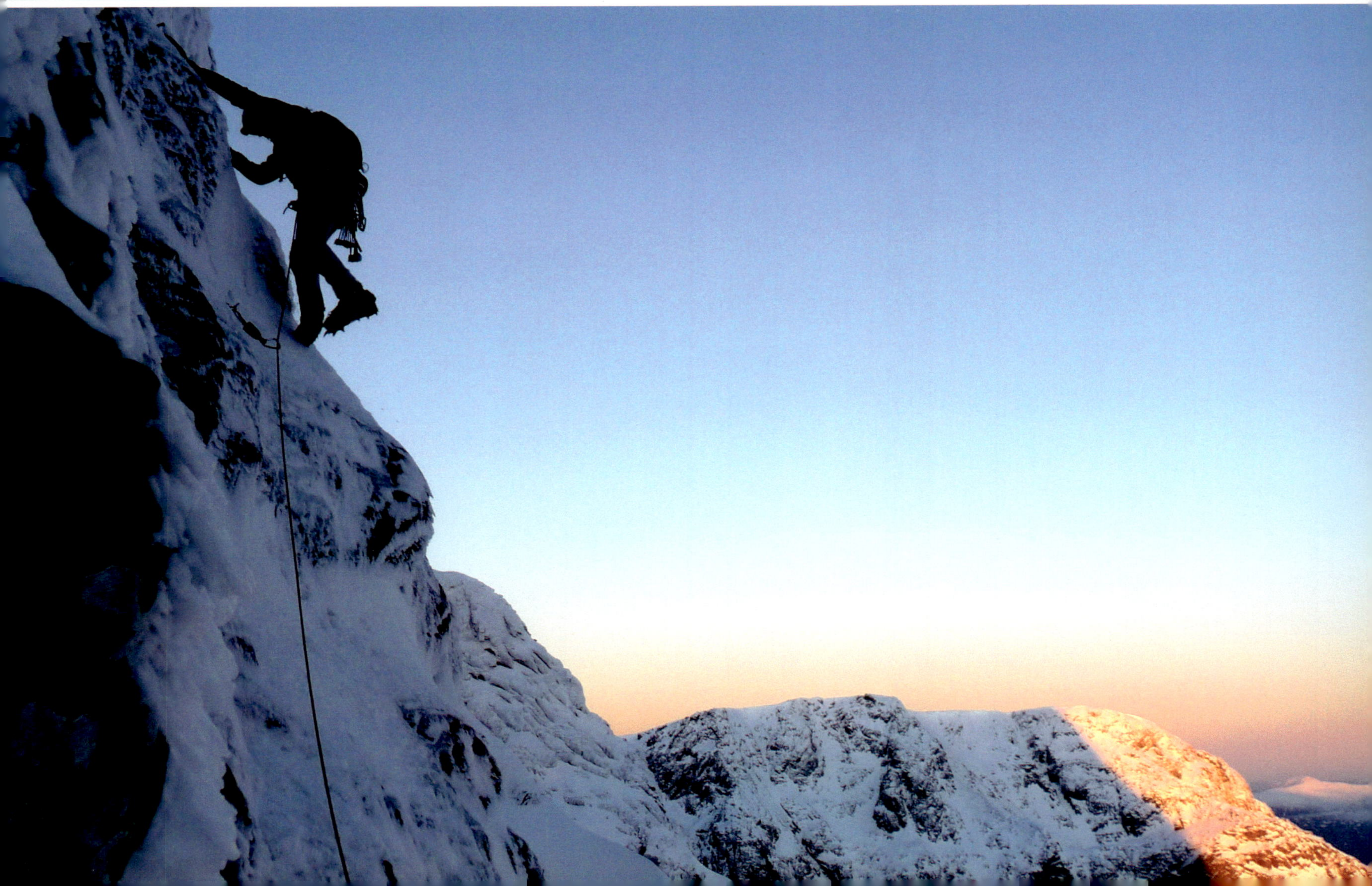

Unknown climbers on *Minus One Gully* (VI,6).
Photo: *Laurence Monkton.*

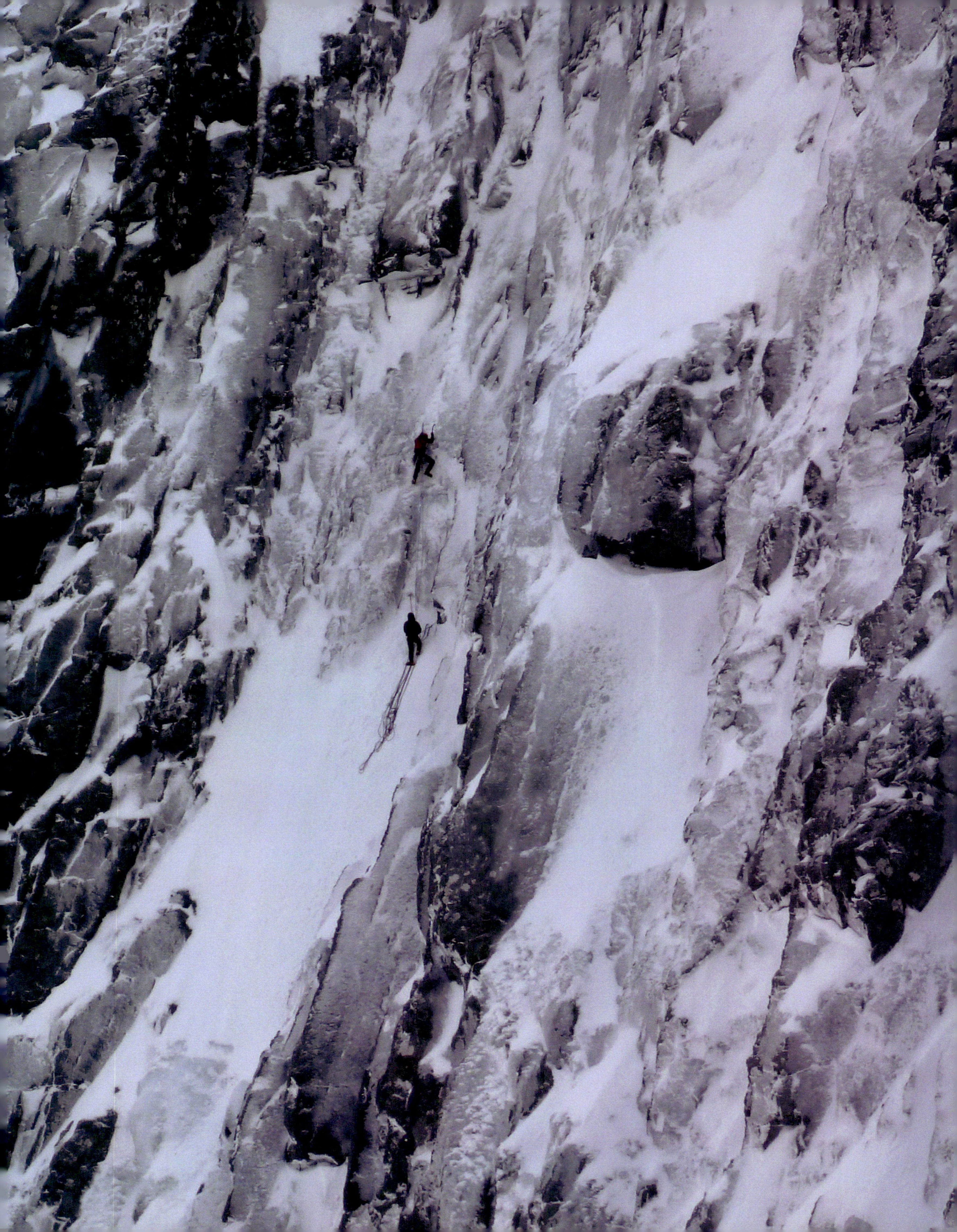

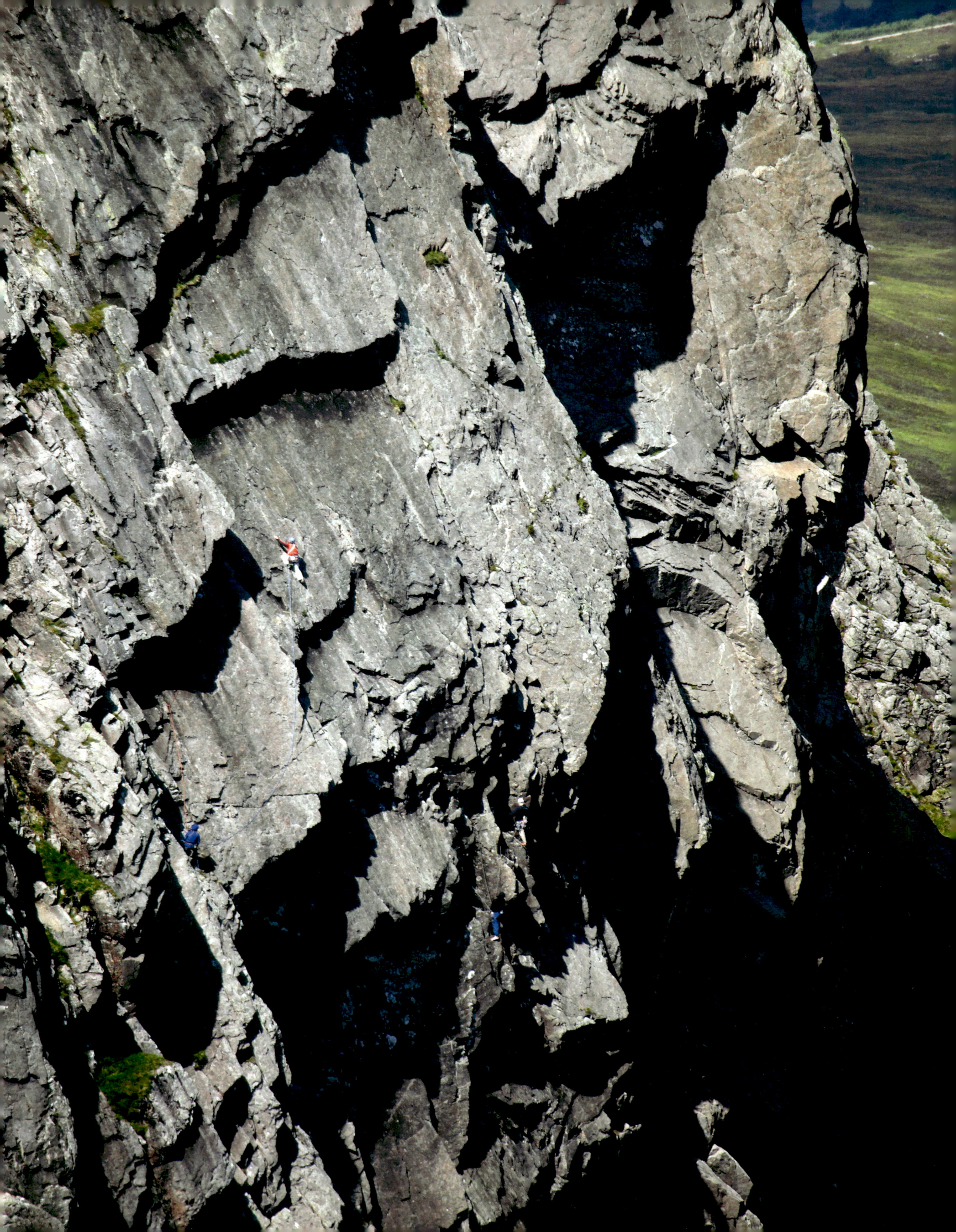

CARN DEARG, BEN NEVIS – *by Adrian Crofton, story by Guy Robertson*

THE PLACE

In midsummer on a hot weekend, the Ben is a very popular place. Busloads of sponsored walkers, corporate team-builders, runners, Italian tourists, young offenders, Duke of Edinburgh's groups, old couples, families with young kids – all humanity is there on the tourist track. But take the left fork over the halfway lochan and you descend to a very different scene, below the great cliffs of the North East Face.

Here you will often be alone, even in midsummer – especially midweek. The scale of the cliffs is so much greater than almost anything else in Scotland, the atmosphere more alpine. It is peaceful and spacious. There are so many tempting destinations on the mountain, so many facets, that it can be difficult to choose where to go and what to climb. Yet one of the first features you pass is the great hulk of Carn Dearg. If you pass it. Most likely you will be trapped by its gravity, drawn upwards from the CIC hut, over slabs and past great boulders, unable to resist its allure, until you are standing at its base, sweating in the morning sun, the arc of Carn Mor Dearg's silhouette at your back. I have always found this a very relaxing place. More often than not, the base of a mountain cliff is cold, steep, loose and inhospitable. But here you sit on flat dry grass, gazing up at the bright clean features, full of anticipation and excitement.

THE CLIFF

Carn Dearg is the most handsome crag in the British Isles. Broad-chested, with sharp clean lines, and beautiful fawn-coloured rock. A veritable drill sergeant: imposing and orderly, standing proud from the otherwise untidy chaos of the Ben's summer cliffs. You can see him waking early every morning and brushing himself down, puffing out his chest in the sun: 'Come and climb me if you're up to it.'

The routes start huddled fairly close together, yet after a pitch or two spread across the cliff, increasingly convex and expansive, diverging and finding their individual territories, eventually losing their distinctiveness much higher up, where the cliff seems to ascend endlessly to the summit of Carn Dearg. Most climbers, however, descend long before this point down a convenient slanting shelf above the end of the steepness. It is a big cliff, so on an initial visit it pays to familiarise oneself with the topography from a distance and pay close attention to route finding.

THE CLIMBING

Rhyolite and andesite are as variable as any rock, but there are places throughout the British Isles where their quality is delectable: East Buttress on Scafell, the East Face of Aonach Dubh, the Cromlech. It is only fitting, then, that the highest peak in the country is blessed with the best of all. The andesite here tends towards the rougher end of the spectrum, with better friction than is usual, and is generally well featured. Even away from the corners there is a reasonable amount of protection available on most routes.

The name of the most famous route here was inspired by the dominant theme of the cliff – successive undercut slabs of smooth appearance, interlocked as the plates of a centurion's armour. The famous early direct routes (*The Bat*, *Sassenach*, *Centurion*) exploit great corner lines which cut through the overlaps, whilst other early climbs took a more lateral approach, shuffling sideways along the armour plating, and sneaking up from one plate to the next (*Bullroar*, *Route Two*). Later routes, like *Torro* and *King Kong*, took more sophisticated lines, which interlaced all these ingredients to provide more subtle but very satisfying climbing. Ultimately the bold arêtes were tested and succumbed, first to Pete Whillance (*Agrippa*), and later to Campbell and Latter (*Trajan's*). Frightening but exquisite expressions of the trad climber's art.

◂ Gary Latter on the traverse of *Bullroar* (HVS).
Photo: *Colin Threlfall*.

▲ Carn Dearg Buttress. Photo: *Adrian Crofton*.

THE ROUTES

Route Two (Severe, VI,6)
The entry grade route, for both summer and winter – a fantastic voyage from bottom left to top right.

Torro (E2)
Freed by Ian Nicolson in 1971, this is a contender for the best E2 in the British Isles. With four great varied pitches on perfect rock, and a total of eight, it has length, variety and quality.

▲ Dave MacLeod and Donald King on *The Wicked* (E6). Photo: *Dave Cuthbertson*.

Centurion (HVS, VIII,8)

The great book corner is a popular summer classic and often climbed. Whillans' canny route through the upper overhangs gives a superb finale, and in winter, when it occasionally ices, strong parties can look forward to a very long and very hard, sustained climb.

Trajan's Column (E6)

There are a number of quality hard rock routes on Carn Dearg that would be hands-down winners anywhere else, but this route has bowled over all ascencionists to date. So allow me one last superlative – Britain's best E6?

THE STORY — *by Guy Robertson*

Winter climbing is arguably the most ephemeral form of our art. Close your eyes for a second and all your dreams can melt away in the march of a warm Atlantic front. Conversely, on rare and precious occasions, open your eyes again and hey presto – the stars have mystically aligned to create something magical for your eyes only.

I can't recall precisely when it all kicked off, but it must have been just after I'd seconded the fourth pitch. Things always go a bit fuzzy in the strange, lonely stupor of climbing into the night. Pete had faltered a bit on that pitch, though not unduly, given the difficulty. But soon enough he pulled the rope tight, as I stretched left to the arête, feet cutting loose and swinging down before being thrown away up high onto the only lonely foothold. The last glimpses of daylight were dissolving over my shoulders, and flutters of snow were becoming more frequent. I don't think we noticed that the wind was gathering strength.

Half an hour later, ten metres into the fifth pitch, it was dark. It was now snowing hard, and the wind was gale force. We'd been on the route for about nine hours at this point, with the most technical climbing behind us, but a growing awareness of the scale of the challenge ahead quickly eliminated any thoughts of celebration. To make matters worse, an easing of angle meant there was now two feet of snow obliterating the rock. Stupidly, I had left my head torch in the belay jacket below. I couldn't find any protection, and verbal contact was severely curtailed. This was the first of our three 'easy' exit pitches, and here I was, screaming, utterly desperate.

'Tie! ... it! ... on! ... to! ... the! ... blue! ... rope!' Again and again I screamed the instructions into the murk, my shouts becoming softer as my throat dried out. Each time, nothing. Pete either disagreed, or misunderstood my request. I couldn't move without that bloody torch, and right now I felt like jumping on his head, stupid bastard. Eventually I deciphered a muffled 'OK!' and started yanking the blue line, praying the axe in my other hand would hold. The torch appeared on a knot in the rope. Jesus, was that so difficult?

With the torch on, protection was forthcoming, but, typical of such predicaments, it wasn't particularly inspiring. I remember a limp hex, rocking alarmingly, but too deep in its seating to be hammered into place. I was stuck fast between two parallel grooves, clinging to a sort of bulging rib between them, with one axe placed in either side, holding a koala-like pose. It was precisely the kind of inefficient and precarious lodgement one attains when climbing frantically without thought. I kicked myself inside, furious with my carelessness. Very gingerly, I crossed first right foot then right axe over into the left hand groove, quickly stamping my left foot out onto some deep snow to stabilise my position. Wiping the memory of the hex from my mind I continued, battle-frenzied now, hacking and mantling into the driving sleet, my feet up by my axes. A few more feet and a little stance afforded a belay. I tugged at Pete to follow on the rope.

We weighed up the options, or so we pretended. In reality, there were two – abseil off, or keep going into the thick of it. We were already battle-weary, and with at least two roped pitches to go the climbing was far from finished. A deafening storm raged about us, huddled fast in our nook, nibbling energy bars and searching for inspiration.

'Listen, I've been here before. It's not difficult, we might as well keep going!' Pete screamed at me assertively. 'I'm pretty keen to bag this little beggar after all that effort!'

I mumbled in agreement, though in truth I wasn't convinced. It seemed to contradict my instincts to climb wittingly up into the teeth of a blizzard, knowing full well that even once we got to the top our descent would be highly dangerous.

The rope had been static for about half an hour when I switched the torch back on. Shuffling round and trying to look up between gusts, I could just make out the dancing shadows from Pete's torch. He had gained maybe ten metres in an hour and a half. The storm was still gathering force, and the temperature was rising. I slumped back again, only this time I felt water running down my chest, across my belly and down inside my shorts. It couldn't get any worse. Then Pete was shouting from above, but I struggled to interpret him, until after ten minutes or so I gathered he was proposing I used a back rope. He could clearly see a hard traverse right without the promise of protection, and was looking out for me on the blunt end. Perhaps he sensed my apathy crawling up the rope. Whatever, in my frozen penance it was a kind, warm thought.

▲ Pete Benson on the second winter ascent of *Centurion* (VIII,8). Photo: *Guy Robertson*.

I think we would have reached the junction with *Ledge Route* at around 11 p.m., but the chaos and darkness combined with such ferocity that we couldn't identify it. By that time the thaw had well and truly set in, and what we previously knew to be a perilous avalanche risk all of a sudden had worsened. The situation was grim. Every tired step created giant sludge balls on the base of our crampons, slowing us up further and threatening to skitter us off the mountain. Descending on this side wasn't an option – even if we could have found the way – as the snow was in such condition now as to release at the faintest trigger. Resigned to our fate, but not comfortable with it, we trudged on and untied. Memories of the hard climbing were remote up there, and I giggled inwardly at the insanity of this compulsive desire, sensing the descent was near and allowing a fleeting moment of humour. Then Pete fired down his shot from above, 'Guy, have you got a compass?!'.

His words arrested me, igniting a sudden panic like that of a bride jilted at the altar. A compass. A little piece of magnetised plastic that helps you get down safely. One of those bits of kit that very rarely gets used but in certain situations separates life from death. Of course, I didn't have one, or at least I was pretty sure of it, remembering it had lived in the map pocket of my old shell jacket. I'd given the jacket away, but hadn't replaced the compass. In a rather desperate and futile bid to restore order I asked the same question in return. No he didn't have one, why on earth would he have asked.

We sat fixed to the summit cairn, exhausted and vulnerable, the freezing rain building thick rime across the lee of our sodden bodies. Visibility was zero, but our eyes were clamped shut. We couldn't hear beyond the howl of the wind, but didn't care to listen. In total whiteout, with creeping damp, and no firm grip of what might come next, the cairn was soon our only reference in a swirl of impossibilities. Beside me, something barked loudly, awakening my fuzzy head. I turned to see Pete kneeling, head hung low, shouting at the rock, pounding an axe in frustration. This shouldn't have happened, that was it and we both knew it.

Our first attempt failed in blind panic, the steady descent we were praying for ending abruptly where the rocks underfoot disappeared, replaced instead by nothingness, just pure white space. More than 20 hours in, with empty tanks and dying limbs, our imaginations needed no catalyst to have us wandering terminally off into the abyss. We were lucky to regain the cairn, our footprints painted out behind us within seconds of each step.

On the second attempt we stayed further left, embracing the consensus that a long walk out from Glen Nevis was daunting, but safe. 20 minutes down and it happened – we were spared. The clouds parted below us. Ahead and to our right the soft lights of Fort William beckoned, their ochre twinkle shooting warmth into our souls. The mouth of the Red Burn was immediately below us, full of nice soft snow – we were home and dry at last. Two hours or whatever still to go, through drenched bog, raging torrents, and away off down the forestry track – I'd have happily run the lot, down and back, if that's what was needed. We had reached salvation, and would have given anything for it.

Just beyond the halfway lochan, we stopped and festered, drank a bit, and dozed. It was 3 a.m. I noticed Pete was talking on his mobile phone, but thought nothing of it, my brain melted through an overdose of relief. Flushed of emotion, I couldn't think. Throwing a glance over my shoulder, back up the Allt a' Mhuilinn and on to the crags where we had climbed, I could make out the bottom of Carn Dearg below a quilt of mist. It was stripped bare, jet black and no doubt running with water. Snaps of the route flickered through me – the white and the cold, sticky ice. The anticipation of walking in, the excitement of our first glimpse, and then all the relieved bravado of climbing surely through the crux pitches. It was still there, just overshadowed temporarily. But gone was the route, washed away, quite literally, and within the space of a single day. It might wait for another 20 years, or even more. I ponder this thought quite deliciously now, in the knowledge that something amazing had been gifted to us. Something exciting and totally unique, that had stretched us beyond reason. For our eyes only. ●

Pete Benson and Guy Robertson on the second winter ascent of *Centurion* (VIII,8).
Photo: *Viv Scott*.

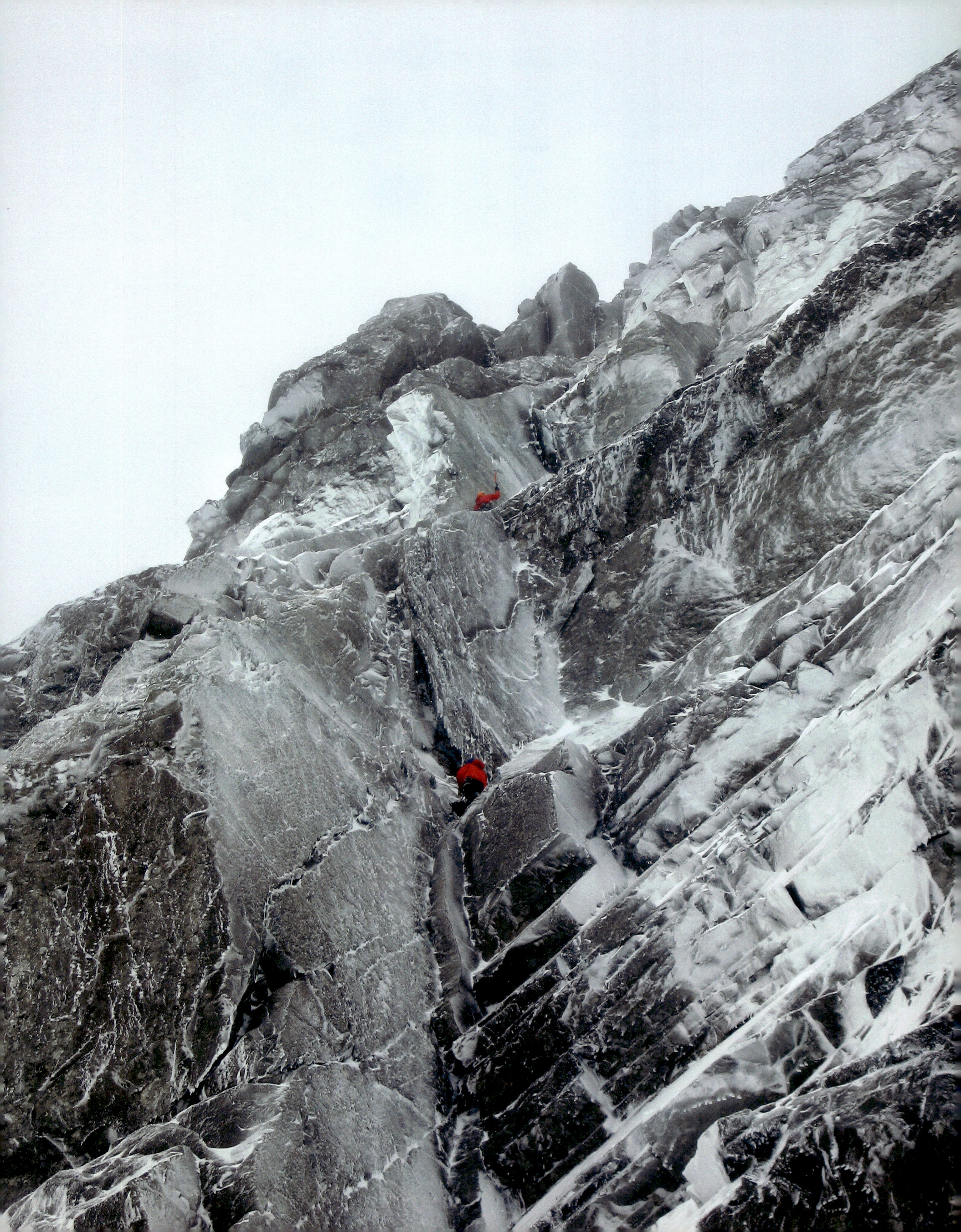

Carn Dearg Buttress (right) and Coire na Ciste.
Photo: *Dave Cuthbertson*

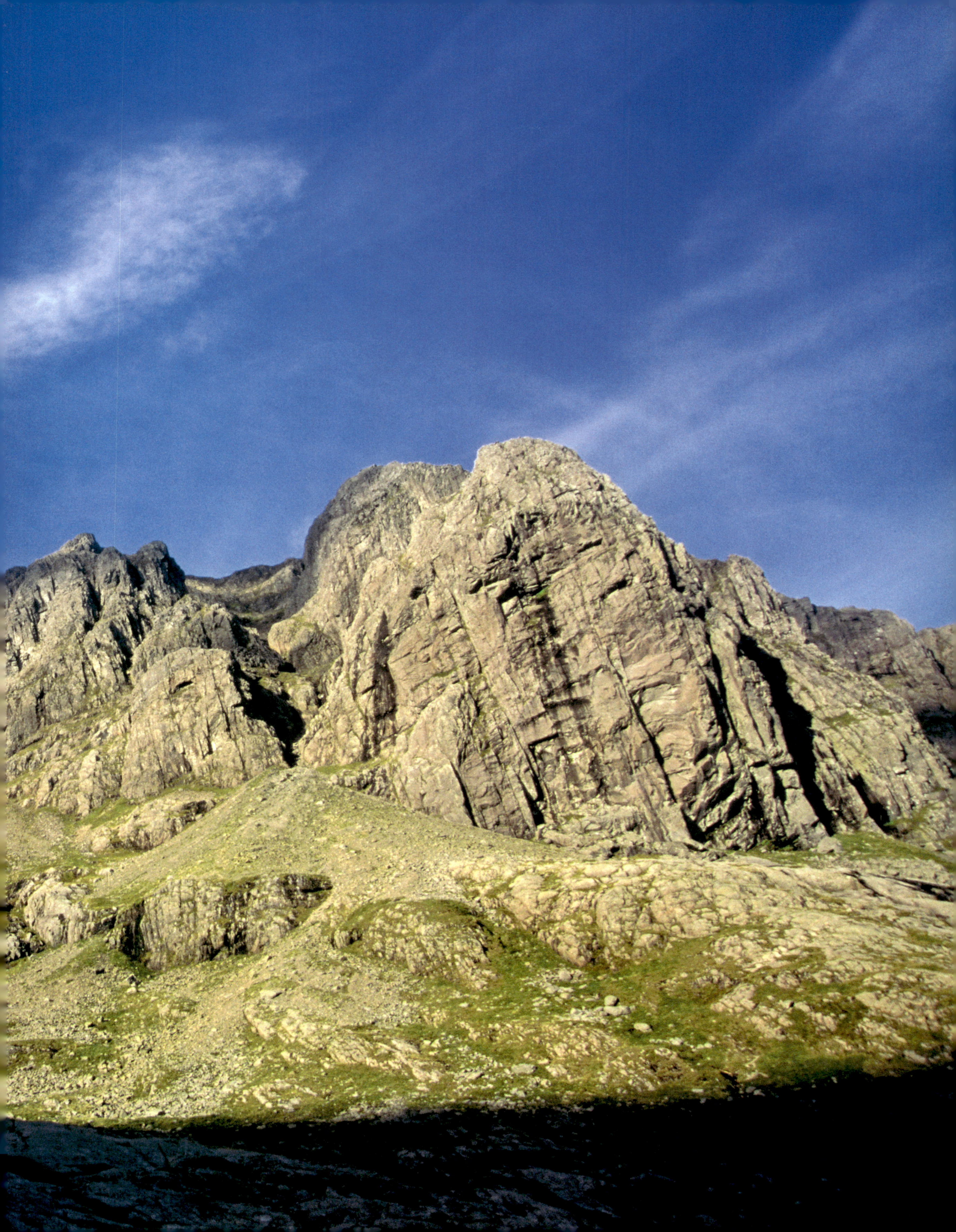

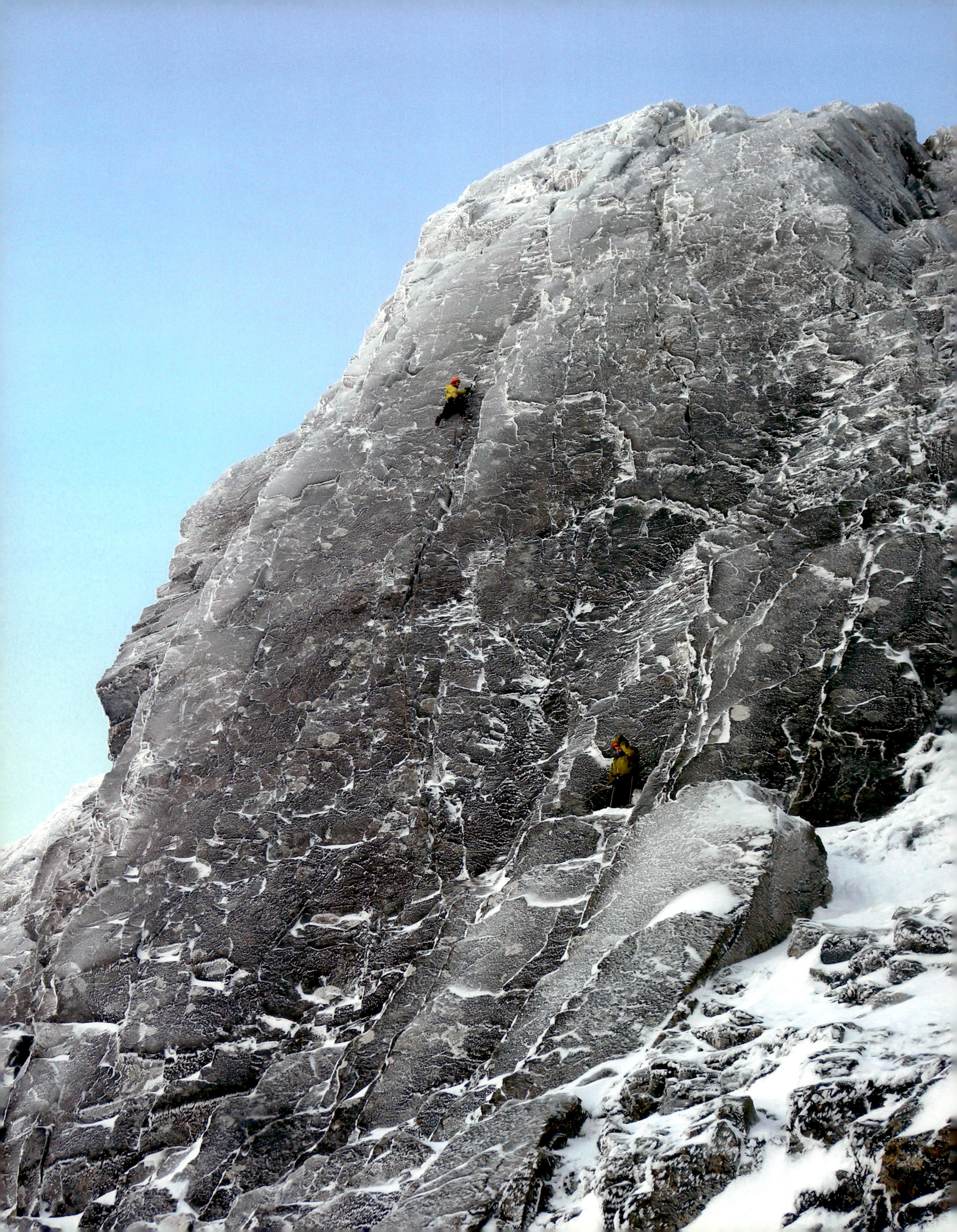

Number Three Gully Buttress, Ben Nevis – *by Blair Fyffe*

THE PLACE
Away up at the back of Coire na Ciste, a good hour's walk beyond the CIC hut, the snowy passage of Number Three Gully cuts through a very steep band of crags guarding the plateau.

Once the preserve of those in search of classic grade IV and V ice, these relatively short but viciously sheer walls have recently emerged as a forcing ground for modern 'snowed-up' rock climbing. It's an impressive location – at the heart of Britain's capital mountain – but its popularity is now such that on a fine winter day you'll need to get up early and be quick to get on your route first.

THE CLIFF
As the gully bed has crumbled away, the tougher surrounding rock has so far resisted erosion, leaving forbiddingly steep and intimidating sidewalls. Strictly speaking, Number Three Gully Buttress describes the extensive area of crag between Green Gully on the left through to Number Three Gully itself on the right. The left-hand side is slabby and ill-defined, but as the crag swings round to form the sidewall of the gully it rears up to an impressive 100-metre thrust of vertical and seemingly blank rock. This is the area of interest to modern climbers, providing some of the finest modern mixed winter routes anywhere.

The standout feature is the great central groove of *Knuckleduster* – a massive soaring corner bisecting the crag almost its entire height. A glance at the verdant colours decorating the walls around the big overhang at half height will be enough to persuade most suitors to wait for a winter coating before attempting an ascent. Immediately right of this lies a superb smooth wall adorned with slight grooves and cracks of varying width, while right again the crag bends right into the more amenable fault of *Thompson's Route* (IV,4). To the left of *Knuckleduster* the crag is at first more broken and complex, though still very steep, before the angle leans back substantially and the routes fill out readily with snow and ice.

◀ Harry Holmes (leading) and Helen Rennard on *Sioux Wall* (VII,8).
Photo: *Andy Inglis*.

THE CLIMBING
In common with other parts of the Ben, Number Three Gully Buttress contains some good ice climbs. However these lack the stature of those nearby on the Orion Face, nor are they as committing as the thinly iced slabs of Indicator Wall. The rock climbing is good – mostly in the middle grades – but is very rarely travelled and therefore suffers from lichen and some loose rock. However, the crag boasts the highest concentration of quality hard mixed winter routes anywhere on the mountain, rivalling any venue in Scotland.

The rock is well suited to modern mixed climbing techniques and being high on the mountain the routes come readily into condition. The lines are uniformly steep and on first appearance appear hard, if not impossible. The trick here is not to be too intimidated; keep the faith and believe in your abilities. The rock is volcanic breccias, and, in contrast to the andestic lavas which produce the blank slabs and shallow seams of the Minus and Orion Faces, it tends to be blocky and fractured. This means the cracks are deep, offering good axe placements and runners, while any edges tend to be positive – ideal for hooking and balancing on crampon points.

The crag doesn't support much in the way of vegetation. In contrast to the grasses and sedges that cover the ledges of the Cairngorms and Northern Highlands, little more than moss grows here. Therefore the climbs rely almost exclusively on hooking and torquing on snowed-up rock, with only occasional use of snow and dribbles of ice.

The reliability of conditions on this part of the Ben was a major factor in the crag's development. It was during a poor ice season that Simon Richardson and Chris Cartwright started exploring the mixed climbing possibilities hereabouts in 1996. They began on the other side of Number Three Gully with an ascent of the now classic *Cornucopia* (VII,8). Eventually others started to tap the obvious potential and in 2004 Bruce Poll and Tony Shepherd were the first to make a winter ascent of the central bastion of Number Three Gully Buttress via the summer line of *Arthur* (HVS in summer). Over the next few seasons most of the remaining summer lines fell, to produce a trio of hard and sustained grade VIIIs as good as any the country over.

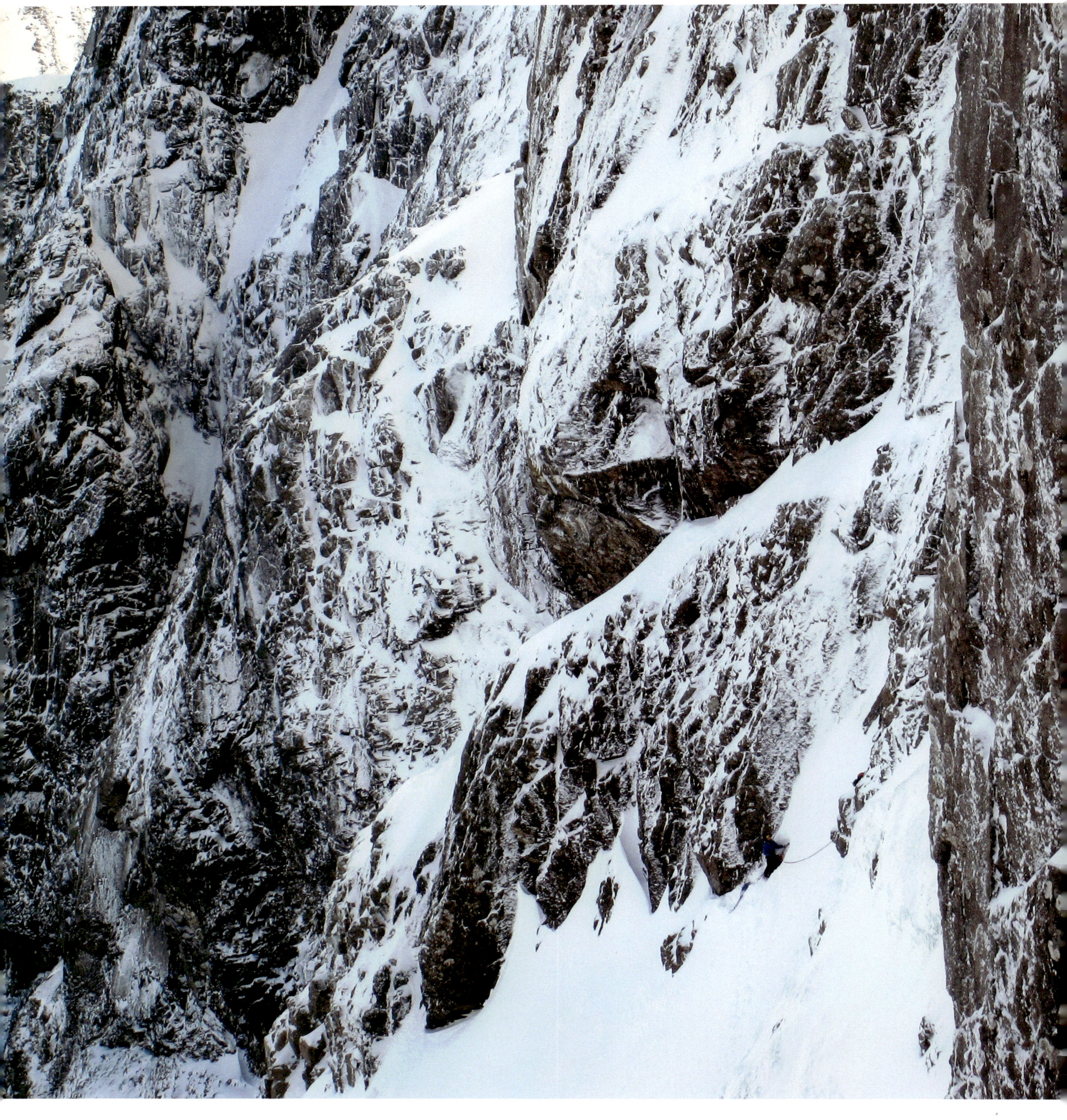

THE ROUTES

Gargoyle Wall (VI,6)
Climbed in the dying days of 1977, this demanding mixed route was well ahead of its time – an indicator of trends 20 years later. Named after a projecting block high up, clearly visible from the gully, the route takes a devious line through some steep ground on the right flank of the central bastion.

Sioux Wall (HVS, VII,8)
An imposing route blasting straight up a line of shallow grooves in the right centre of the compact buttress. Good cracks and positive edges make it much more amenable than its fearsome appearance suggests.

Knuckleduster (HVS, VIII,8)
A truly awe-inspiring line, plundering the striking groove in the heart of the steepest section of crag, and visible from the CIC hut. The intimidation factor is amplified by the knowledge that an early attempt ended in the local hospital with numerous broken bones!

THE STORY

I readily associate Ben Nevis with storms. The wind howls and the precipitation beats down with a fury and suddenness not often seen elsewhere. It is these wild conditions that make the Ben such a unique winter climbing destination. It was one such stormy day in early February 2007 that eventually led to my successful first ascent of the *Knuckleduster* groove.

I'd been out on the hill, but had sacked it off due to storm force winds. However, frustrated and over-keen after an unsuccessful trip to the Alps, Lakeland raiders Steve Ashworth and partner were in amongst it, despite the weather conditions. Although their ascent of *Two Step Corner* went OK, a vicious gust while descending hurled Steve's partner off his feet, resulting in a painful wrist and bashed face. The facial injury was quickly cleaned up, but a trip to hospital next morning confirmed the wrist was broken.

◀ Andy Inglis on *Apache* (VIII,8).
Photo: *Neil Adams*.

THE SOUTH WEST HIGHLANDS | **NUMBER THREE GULLY BUTTRESS, BEN NEVIS**

Rob Jarvis on *Gargoyle Wall* (VI,6).
Photo: *Nick Carter.*

Steve was soon on the hunt for a stand-in. All his friends were busy, so I got the phone call late that evening.

'Hi Blair, Steve Ashworth here. I met you last year when we were dossing at Owen's, fancy going climbing tomorrow?'
'Can't, I'm working.'
'How about the next day then?'
'Er ... yeah, OK then. What do you want to climb?'
'Knuckleduster.'

In the warmth of my house, it seemed a good idea. A couple of days later we found ourselves below the route, the butterflies beginning to flutter and the usual uncertainties slowly emerging. I peered up the towering groove, ever-steepening as it reared alarmingly into the mist. It was definitely in condition. Some higher power had decided for us – it was plastered. We had no choice but to have a go.

Looking at the summer description, I saw the second and third pitches presented the meat of the route. The second was only 15 metres long while the third pitch was a daunting 35 metres. Intimidated by either prospect, a short hard pitch seemed preferable, so I blagged it and Steve soon set off up the first pitch. This proved to be a perfect warm up – sustained but not too difficult. Arriving at his belay, however, the prospects for my pitch were grim. The continuation was barred by overhangs which looked hard – very hard. A more amenable looking option was to make a few moves up the groove, then head diagonally rightwards across the wall, then optimistically over a nasty bulge. Starting up the groove, I was vaguely aware of Steve having a conversation with some friends who had spotted us from below.

'How's it going up there?' they shouted.
'Quite serious,' was Steve's reply.
'Looks like it is about to get a lot more serious above,' came the none-too-helpful response.

After passing an old snapped wire, some tricky moves led out to the arête where the angle steepened abruptly. I managed to get in a good runner, and figured that even if I did blow it higher up, there was not much below to crash into! A committing move allowed me to grab an obvious flake. It creaked and groaned under my weight, but it held. Steep and progressively more flustered moves allowed me to get my axes into a small ledge. With the last runner now a long way below, and the wall above overhanging with few hooks, an inelegant and desperate struggle ensued. Axes, crampons, hands, knees and various other body parts were indelicately exploited to allow a precarious lodgement on the ledge. Despite only gaining a mere 15 metres in height, I was exhausted, and belayed immediately.

The guide informed us that a traverse led back into the main groove, but in winter this looked impossibly hard. However a series of smaller grooves in the edge of the arête appeared to lead upwards, providing an alternative. Steve led off, but his pace soon slowed; mutterings floated down about poor placements and protection. Suddenly he was hurtling backwards towards me. As the ropes came tight, he swung in, smashing his thigh on a ledge. Amazingly, he kept a grip of his leashless axes, and after a few painful moans pulled back on and started climbing again. This time he took a slightly different line, and slowly edged past his high point. The pitch was long, sustained and with protection not too evident. Eventually, with daylight fading, he announced that he was safe. I seconded as quickly as possible, but daylight had all but gone by the time I reached his stance. We could just make out easier ground above, but a blank-looking wall blocked access. It looked testing and I was spent.

'Fancy leading this pitch?' I offered.
'No!' was the emphatic response.

I couldn't escape my duties, so with my head torch on I shuffled off rightwards towards a groove; the only feasible looking option. Once established there, a hidden crack appeared and for the first time I allowed myself a fleeting thought of success. Although not that technical, in the darkness the climbing here felt as extreme as any other part of the route. I battled on over a bulge to an easing in the angle. A few more moves and I was wallowing in snow, the big platform marking the end of the difficulties. One more long pitch moving together in silence and we were up on the summit plateau.

The night was cold, clear and calm, the plateau deadly silent. The ice encrusting our jackets sparkled brightly in the torchlight. Down below, the lights of the Fort twinkled as we wandered toward the gully and the start of a long descent.

The next day a mild south-westerly came howling in and the rain hammered down. The route was soon stripped of its winter coating. Such is the nature of Scottish winter conditions. Not that Ben Nevis, that dark, hunched and brooding mountain, cares about the weather, nor the successes and failures of those who appear every winter to tussle with its frozen delights. •

THE GREAT MOUNTAIN CRAGS OF SCOTLAND

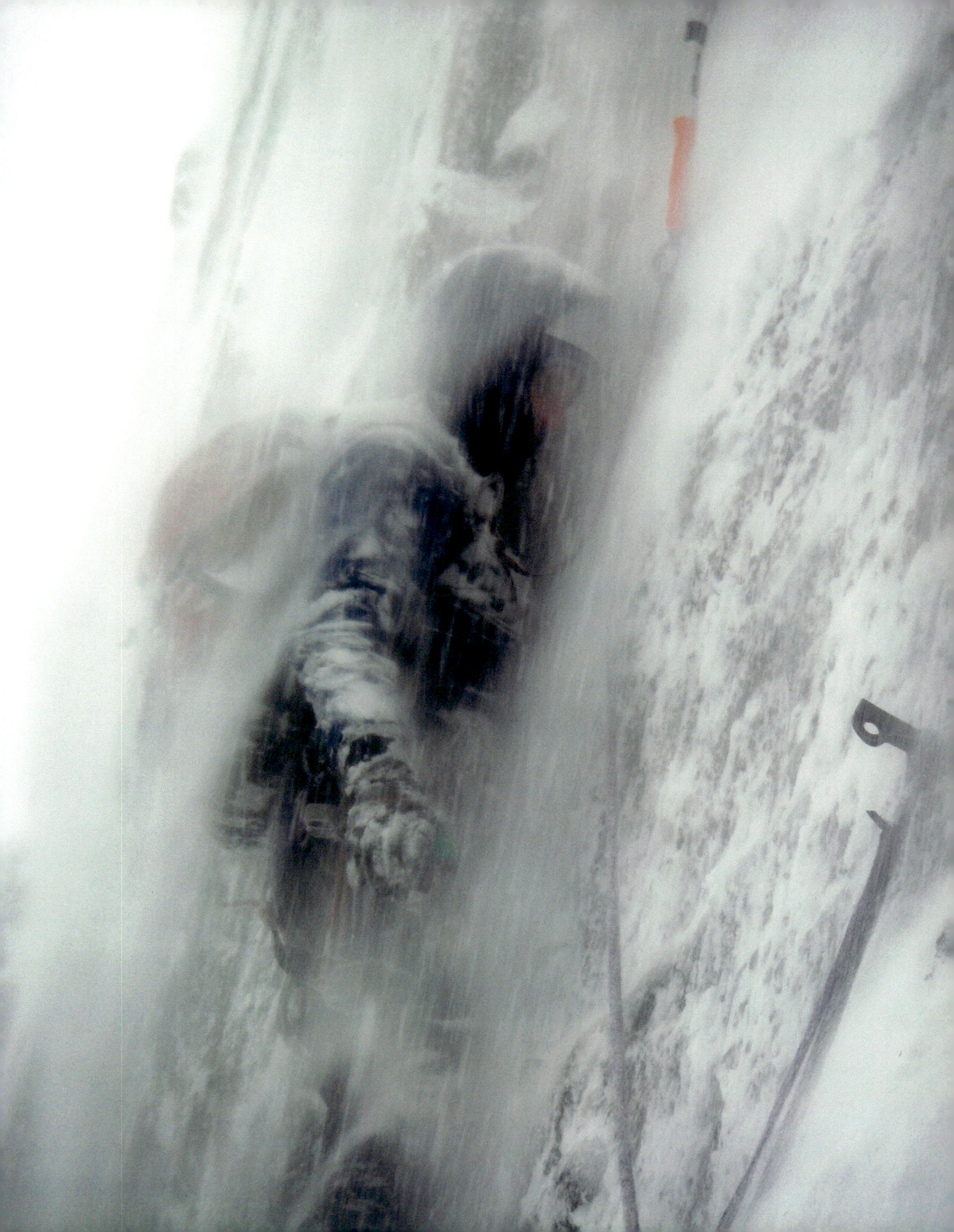

The North East Face of Ben Nevis in summer.
Photo: Dave Cuthbertson.

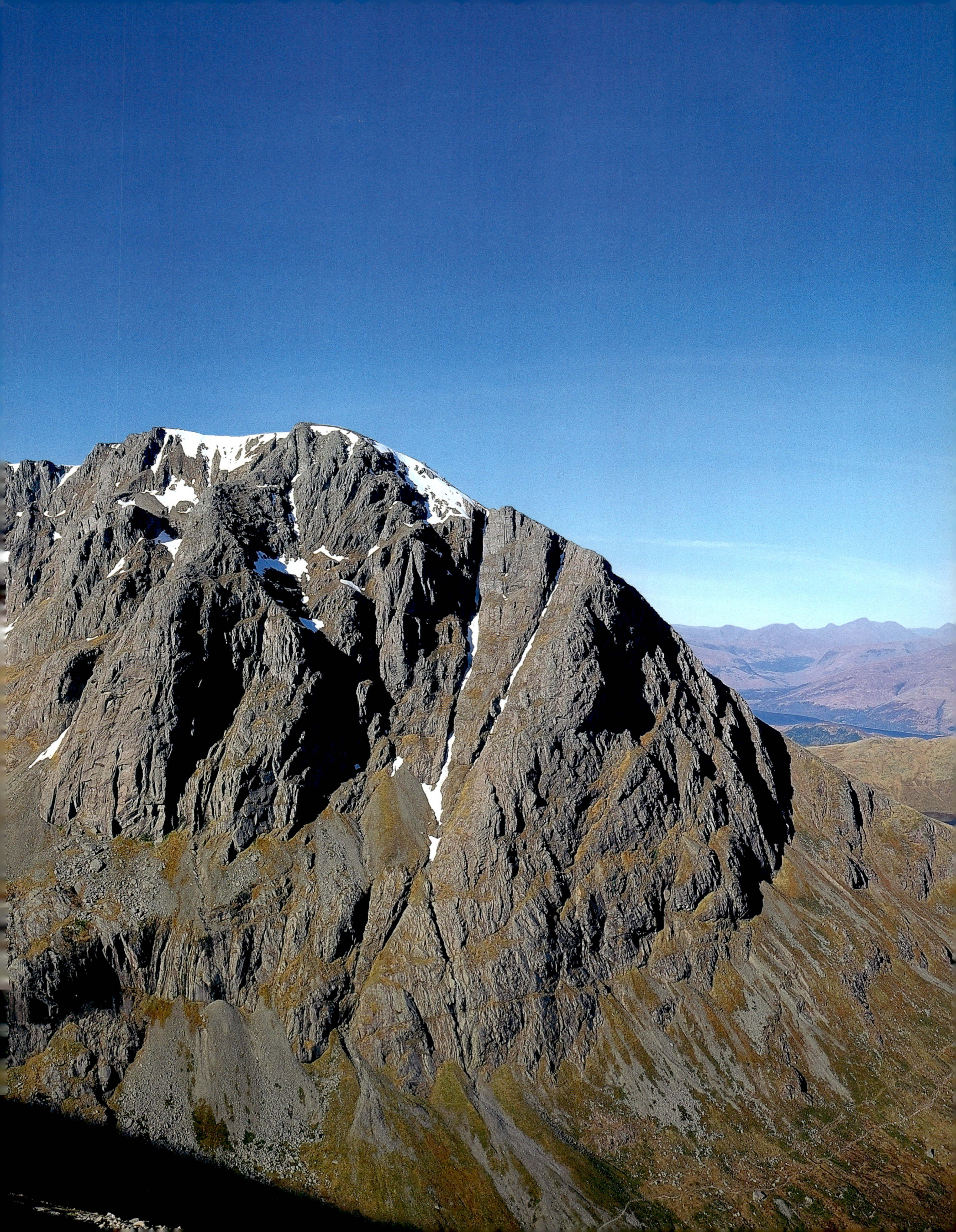

THE NORTH WEST HIGHLANDS

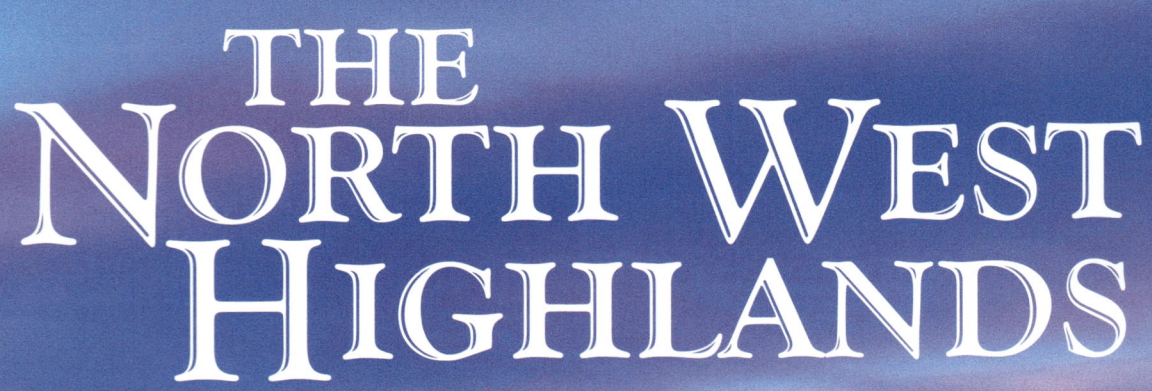

Mountains of Coigach, from left to right: Cùl Mòr, Cùl Beag and Stac Pollaidh. Photo: *Dave Cuthbertson*.

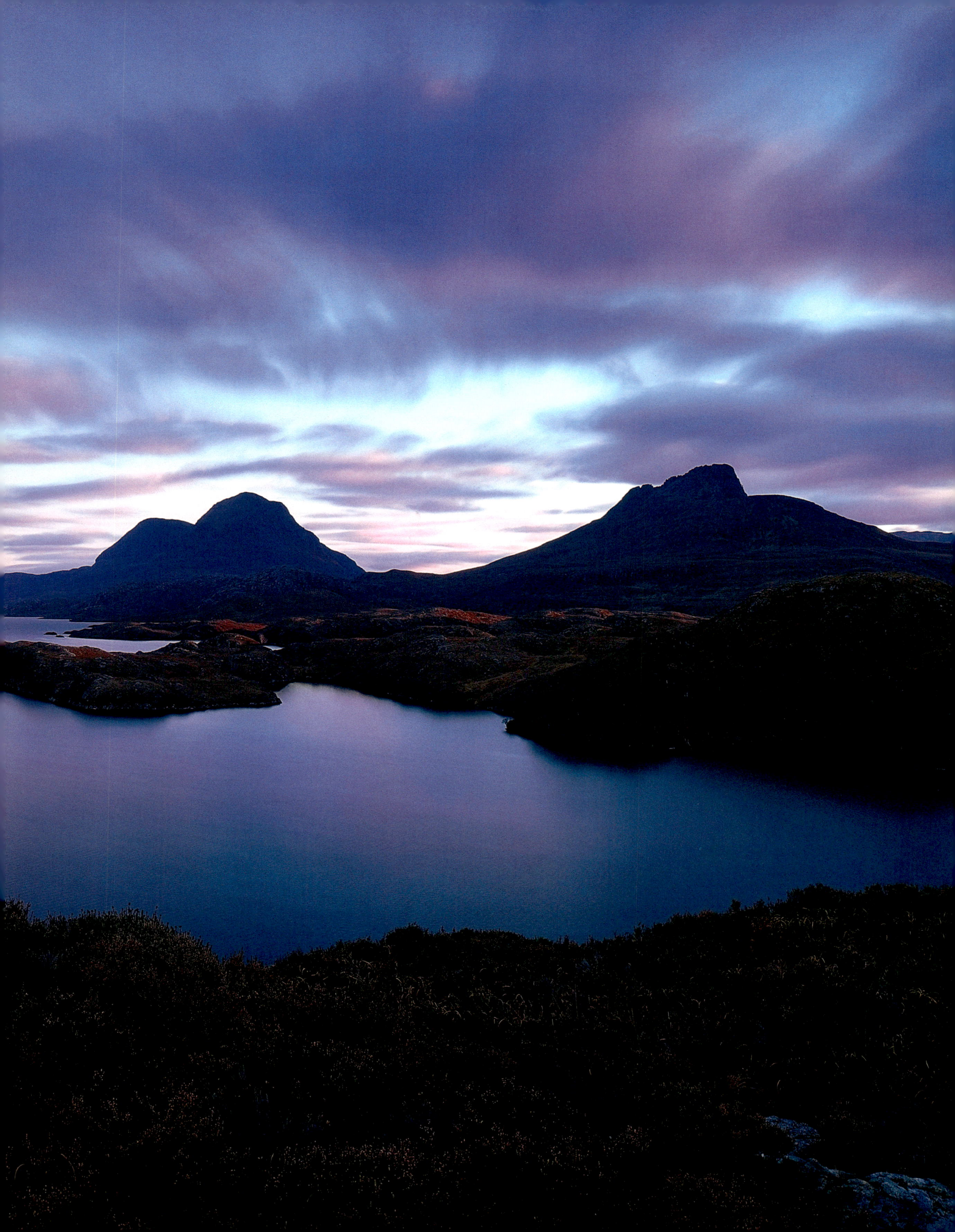

Sunset from the slopes of Ben Mor Coigach.
Climbers: Martin Moran and Guy Robertson.
Photo: *Pete Macpherson.*

North West Highlands
by Stuart B. Campbell

*A frozen snotter dreeps down
off the Fhidhleir's Nose;
you're face to face with Fear
of the Dark: rounded holds
of old red sandstone (friends could be useful),
the quartzite capping it all.*

*Where does this route, this ascent, begin, man?
    Below a prominent chimney line...
    up the right side of a wide crack... or
somewhere south of the tropic of Capricorn, an island
surfacing off the west coast
of Africa, 1,000 million years ago or more.*

*Your amphibian ancestors dragged themselves
from their dubby bivouac, then,
man, you hauled yourself upright out of a howff;
steadying yourself on two feet,
wondered what your next move might be.*

*1988: Prentice, Dinwoodie. Trace their line
back: Whillance, Cunningham, Weir, Collie,
Aonghas Mór of the Eggs ... and there's
a hairy hand's pinch-grip fossilised in a flange.*

*With the Wall of Flame behind you, look
over the moor and rising mist, a summer's sun
descends to Tir nan Òg. Beinn Eighe, Torridon;
this is about as far away as you can get
and maybe that, Fairytale
Groove, will be as far as you'll ever go.
Fear and wonder
run in that daisy-chain of your DNA.*

This is climbing history.

Introduction to the North West Highlands – *By Jason Currie*

We tumbled out of the pub, having stretched the goodwill of the bar staff well past closing. The day had been spent sulking along the cliffs of Stoer in the grip of an Atlantic gale that battered us with frequent showers from a sullen sky. Our bird's eye view of the Old Man had compounded frustrations that the long drive north had been fruitless. What a surprise then, to find that the depression had blown through and a full moon sailed a calm, star-flecked sky.

A combination of drink-fuelled exuberance, youthful enthusiasm and enforced abstinence from mountains can lead in many directions. On this occasion, I remember, it led boldly to Suilven, the thrust of sandstone that lies like an upturned boat on the broad foreshore of moorland stretching inland behind Lochinver.

The walk-in began well, no doubt buoyed up by the evening's recreation. Head torches were unnecessary in the moonlight, even when the map was consulted. As we left the landrover track behind, the hangover began to kick in. We picked our way over the soaking hinterland. The steep ascent to Bealach Mor pinched our dehydrated heads and enthusiasm was all but gone as a blanket of mist settled on the hill.

Trudging along the narrow ridge to the top of Caisteal Liath, breakfast was taken on the summit whilst waiting in vain for a view to appear. But there we were anyway, and so it was agreed that we continue with our original plan to traverse the ridge in its entirety. A section of steep scrambling over a band of cliffs came as something of a surprise but this was nothing compared to the elation we felt as the mist finally cleared. Laid out before us in the flash of an eye, the peaks of Inverpollaidh and Coigach sculpted on a plinth of bejewelled gneiss. Cùl Mòr and Cùl Beag, Stac Pollaidh and the complex of hills around Ben Mor Coigach stood like silent sentinels of the western seaboard. The hills further north remained shrouded, serving only to heighten the sense of mystery and wonder that a place of such outstanding and singular beauty could ever exist. Immediately I wanted to be atop each of those wonderful summits. I yearned to leap over the intervening moor in a single bound and learn of their secrets.

There is an overwhelming feeling of age and permanence about the North West Highlands, despite the ravages of the last Ice Age and the marks of human activity. Nowhere else in Scotland does the interplay of loch, moor and mountain, of mist, snow and sea leave such an indelible mark on the mountaineer's psyche.

The geology of the area plays no small part in creating this sense of a land that time forgot. The thin skin of soil cannot hide the past; it seeps up from the rocks beneath, some of which are among the oldest in Europe. The foundations are built from Lewisian gneiss; an ancient stone baring the scars of its metamorphoses in the colourful and convoluted crystalline walls and outcrops that are so much in vogue with the modern day rock climber. The pockets, slots and twisted spikes it offers provide delightful variety – from steep jug-hauling up impending walls to delicate cranking on slabs scattered with small edges.

All across the region a plethora of small but notable crags pepper the moorland, but the undisputed overlord – at least in terms of summer rock – is Cárn Mór Crag. This superb cliff lies on the side of Beinn a'Chaisgein Mor above the Fionn Loch in the heart of the Fisherfield wilderness. Amazingly it took until the 1950s for a route to be opened on this great cliff, but it wasn't until the 1970s and 1980s that Cárn Mór really came of age, the crag now boasting a string of fine, hard and very remote summer routes. Drying quickly after rain, climbing is possible here when the higher and more typically north-facing crags are out of bounds. The routes are intimidatingly steep, and tremendous exposure sucks at the feet of the climber; a vulnerability amplified by the long, lonely miles back to civilisation. As the essence of wild Scottish mountain rock, you would struggle to match this place.

Atop the gneiss is a layer of deep crimson rock known as Torridonian red sandstone. Formed from sediments deposited by a primeval river delta flowing before life on earth had evolved beyond single-celled organisms, this has somehow managed to remain unaltered in the intervening 1,000 million years. The great age it exudes is palpable. The cliffs of Applecross, Coulin, Torridon and Coigach bear witness to the improbable fortune that has been bestowed upon Torridonian red, and by extension to us as climbers. Their vast, vertical ampitheatres and impending buttresses all exhibit a characteristic terracing that highlights the rock's sedimentary origins. Between these ledges are walls of unremitting steepness often traced by lines of pebbles that mark out flash floods which happened almost 1,000 million years ago.

On the sandstone, with the exception of the deep gullies, there are few powerful lines offering easy route finding. Ascending these laminated fortresses is more akin to safe-cracking – twisting and turning relentlessly back and forth to seek out the next line of weakness. Even the obvious challenge of the *Nose Route Direct* on Sgurr an Fhidhleir has a particular sequence that must be discovered before its perfect crescendo is revealed.

The early pioneers like Raeburn seem to have taken delight in such intricacies, including an audacious attempt by Ling on the Fhidhleir Nose itself in 1907. After a long period of quiet the cliffs enjoyed something of a renaissance in the sixties, with visits by such luminaries as Patey and MacInnes amongst others. To the modern rock climber, however, many of the north-facing buttresses simply hold too much vegetation. In winter, on the other hand, it is this turf, together with drools of steep ice down often holdless walls, that provide the keys to a treasure trove of adventurous riches, arguably surpassing anywhere else in the country. Modern technology and attitudes have allowed access to hideously steep ground formerly considered out of bounds. Lines like *Snoopy* (Mainreachan Buttress) and *The God Delusion* (Beinn Bhan) typify this aggressive style. Today's activists have become highly adept at unlocking the many secrets compressed into the sickening verticality of these great banded cliffs.

Daring to be different, there is Stac Pollaidh: with its compact walls and jumbled pinnacles, it bristles bold as brass above the road out to Reiff. With an attitude completely at odds with its altitude, it is not the place for climbers brought up on a diet of resin at climbing walls. A quiet Sunday on Stac Pollaidh soon develops into a full blown fist fight, and those without the requisite jamming skills will struggle. For those prepared to rumble, the West Buttress is the place.

Very fortunately for today's climbers, a protective cover of quartzite formed on top of the sandstone and gneiss whilst the north west of Scotland still lay, somewhat improbably, under water and near the South Pole. This capping rock forms the distinctive screes of Beinn Eighe and the upper portions of its emblamatic Triple Buttress in Coire Mhic Fhearchair. With the Far East Wall in attendance, these huge towers project out into the mountain fastness to form a simple symmetry of unparalleled beauty. Each has a longer north-easterly aspect: the long, columnar Eastern Ramparts, the Central Wall and the giddying heights of the West Central Wall. The abrupt change from sandstone to quartzite comes as something of a shock to the system, offering the climber a unique two-for-the-price-of-one opportunity. From the rounded breaks, vegetated ledges and deceptively hard walls of the sandstone a sudden transition occurs to the positive, but relentlessly steep, blocky quartzite. Split by angular cracks and carrying large, flat holds, the upper band of rock is surprisingly amenable, and climbs of awesome steepness have been completed.

Another quartzite mountain that is far less frequented but certainly no poor relative is Foinaven. It too hides its light under a bushel: its great climbing cliffs, Creag Urbhard, the Dionard Buttresses and Lord Reay's Seat, are all well hidden from the road. They offer the same blocky climbing on impressively steep ground, although there is more loose material to contend with on some lines. A previous lack of detailed information regarding routes, coupled with the mountain's remoteness continues to deter visitors, but this surely is the essence of the place, which still holds a bounty of splendid hidden treasures.

Further inland, away from the coastal hills, the mountains are charecterised by a more familiar rock. As a result of the great, heaving push of the Moine Thrust, an older schist now lies on top of the younger rocks. This forms the enigmatic cliffs of the Fannaichs and Beinn Dearg. Once again, although too vegetated to ever become good modern summer venues, they provide a wealth of stunning winter climbs when the abundant turf freezes and sinuous lines of ice form. With access eased by cycling, the little known but massive cliffs of An Coileachan have played host to a number of regular visitors in recent winters, but the more challenging approach to the Coire Ghranda cliffs has enforced a slower pace of development. Alternatively, the spaced protection and biblical exposure of the Upper Cliff may have been more of a deterrent than the long walk in?

Finally, sat overlooking a long and desolate sea loch, away up on the far north coast, Ben Loyal is the only mountain of igneous origin in the north west. It is a complex hulk, with altogether four craggy tops. In keeping with its remote and isolated position there have been few suitors to this 'Queen of Highland Mountains'. It is the huge westerly sweep of Sgor a'Chleirich that holds most interest for the hard climber – a 250-metre barrelled bastion of strange and gnarled syenite, providing a style and situation that is simply like no other. Martin Boysen passed by here, leaving one of his 'desert island routes', but vague descriptions and rumours of steep, verdant walls have put off most people until recent times. Indeed it wasn't until as late as the turn of the recent millenium that some stunning summer potential was literally unearthed, and a winter ascent of the central issue of Marathon Corner became a superb and challenging modern reality. Like many of the mountains in this region though, Ben Loyal is still an open book.

We returned to the Bealach Mor, descending in the sunshine to the Fionn Loch. An intermittent path led along the shore to its outlet. Progress was slow, and yes, we were tiring, but it was the view back to our hill, the afternoon sun picking out its subtle hues of rock and heather, that drew our gaze back behind us again and again, causing us to tarry by the loch's sandy beaches. The River Kirkaig, cascading over powerful falls, led us to the sea. Wearily we stumbled along the coast road and back to Lochinver. As we neared the village, with fatigue fostering aural hallucinations from the voice of a nearby stream, we caught our final glimpse of the hill. A monolithic dome rising improbably and without warning over a low ridge, a delicate green lochan nestled in the foreground. One hill, so many facets – the essence of the North West Highlands.

Tim Rankin approaching the Upper Cliff of Coire Ghranda.
Photo: *Guy Robertson*.

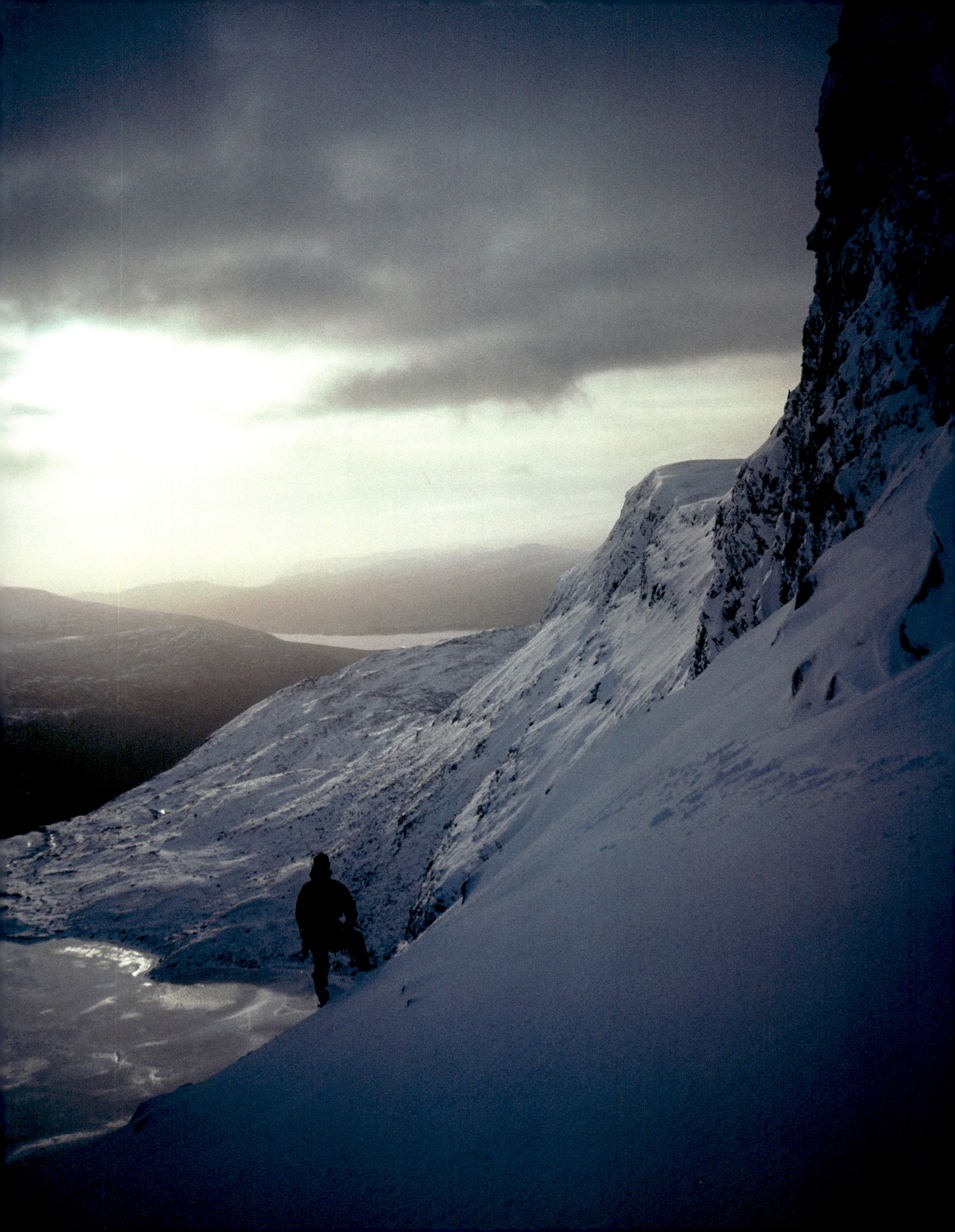

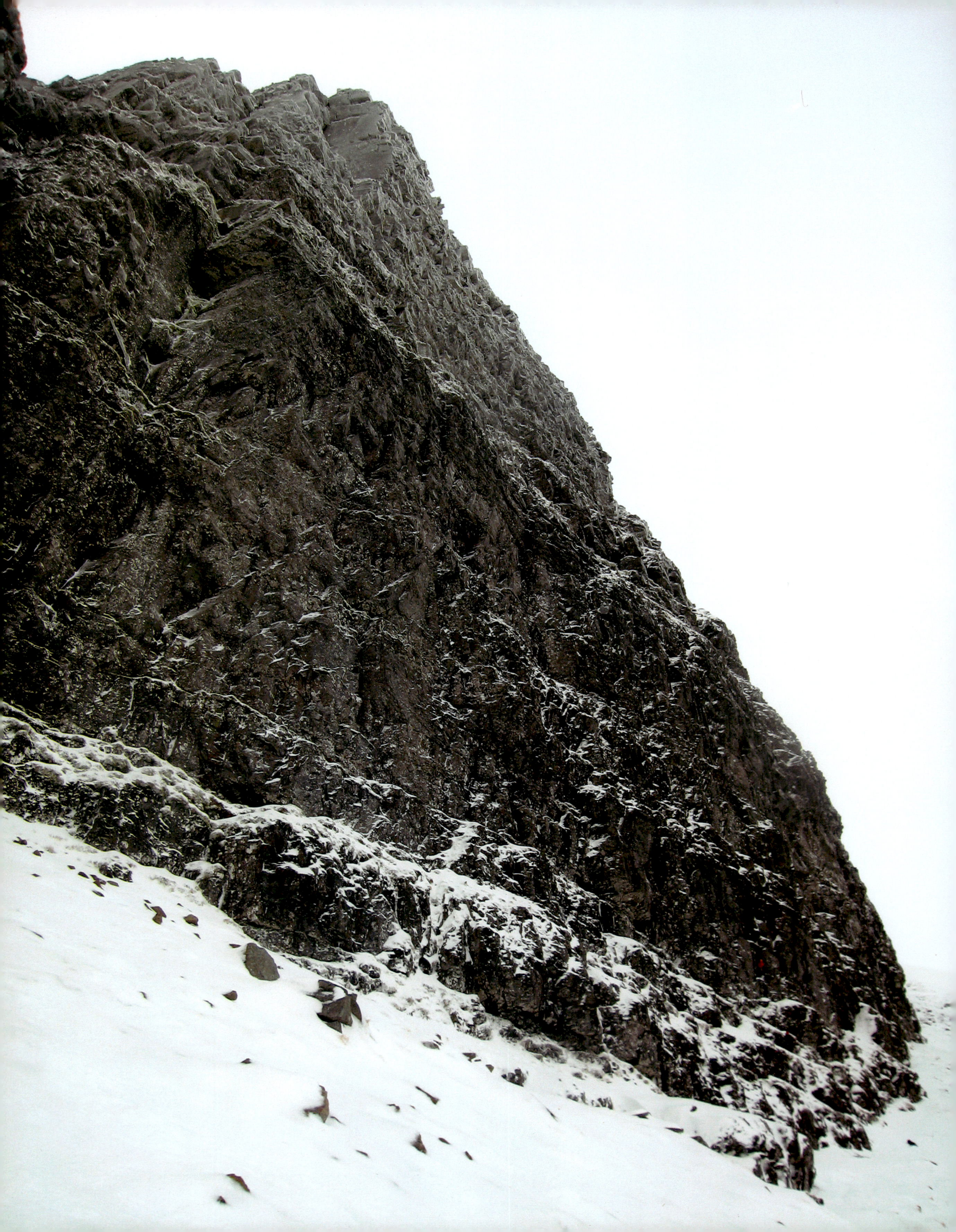

Giant's Wall, Beinn Bhan – by Martin Moran

THE PLACE
Scotland's north-west wilderness begins with the Applecross peninsula, the Torridonian geology making its first appearance there. Massive beds of sandstone rise from the shores of the Inner Sound and sweep gently upwards to a bleak plateau. Beinn Bhan is the culminating point, and is home to arguably the finest coire grouping in all of Scotland. The plummeting topography on the eastern side of the mountain creates a sense of scale out of all proportion to the modest altitude.

There are many impressive cliffs here, but most impressive of all is the Giant's Wall of Coire an Fhamhair (The Giant's Coire). Hidden away at first appearance behind the huge tower of A' Phoit, this place was well named by the shepherds and hunters of centuries past; it is etched on a scale simply beyond human grasp.

THE CLIFF
The Giant's Wall describes the long and very steep terraced wall on the back left of Coire an Fhamhair. The cliffs rise in an ugly succession of bare lichenous overhangs and dizzy ledges fringed by turf. The beauty is in the scale and the dramatic contrast. The level rim of the summit plateau fringes the sky a thousand feet overhead, providing a perfect take-off for the golden eagle.

Three striking vertical clefts spilt the face. From the left, the first is a vile corner, overhanging some 12 metres, which is defended by huge blank overhangs and broken only by perched ledges choked with moss and exotic grasses. This is the improbable line of *Genesis*. Right of this a series of narrow terraces criss-cross the open face, providing the masterly *Die Reisenwand* (Giant's Wall) – Scotland's equivalent to the Eiger North Face. The face ends in a soaring arête which bounds the central cleft, a cavernous shaft that disappears into the dark bowels of the mountain. This is the *Gully of the Gods*. The square-cut prow, right again, provides the steepest facet of the coire, 200 metres sheer, cut by a traversing terrace at two-thirds height, and marked by an eye-catching corner cutting through its upper tiers. The third and final big cleft cuts the right side of this face to provide *Great Overhanging Gully*, a truly compelling chimney and one of the great lines on Torridonian sandstone. Beyond, the face finally peters out into scree.

THE CLIMBING
Needless to say, no worthwhile rock climbing is found on this dank, slimy wall. In winter, however, it is without doubt one of the finest. The cliffs lie at a relatively low altitude – between 550 and 850 metres – which, combined with the prevailing steepness of the wall, means that full winter conditions are rare. This only serves to enhance the prestige of the climbs – only a few bold souls venture here, even fewer return successful.

For all the climbs the turf must be solidly frozen. A spell of north-westerly winds produces the ideal mix of humidity and regular sticky snowfall to bank up the terraces. A subsequent period of freeze-thaw can allow the rapid growth of ice smears from a steady supply of groundwater oozing from the horizontal breaks.

The climbing itself is invariably steep and strenuous, although below the midway terrace some of the existing routes use devious ramps and traverses to outflank the bulges. On the upper wall, however, there is no escaping continuous overhanging terrain. Protection, fortuitously, is typically good, with nuts, hexes, Friends, pegs and turf gear all likely to prove useful at some stage in the proceedings. Frozen turf often provides sanctuary above the steepest bulges, to some extent defining the style. An ability to heel hook and mantel onto grassy ledges buried in snow will certainly provide an advantage.

The cliffs of Beinn Bhan languished long in obscurity, remaining largely untouched until the arrival of Tom Patey in the 1960s. The Giant's Wall itself waited longer still. Predictably, it was Andy Nisbet (with Brian Sprunt) who worked out a tenuous route linking sweeping snow terraces, vertical grass walls, ice smears and giddy rock gangways up the left side of the great terraced central wall to give *Die Reisenwand* (VII,6) in 1980. They were so impressed by the scale of the place that they carried bivouac equipment on the first ascent.

◀ The Godfather area of the Giant's Wall with climber bottom right.
Photo: *Guy Robertson.*

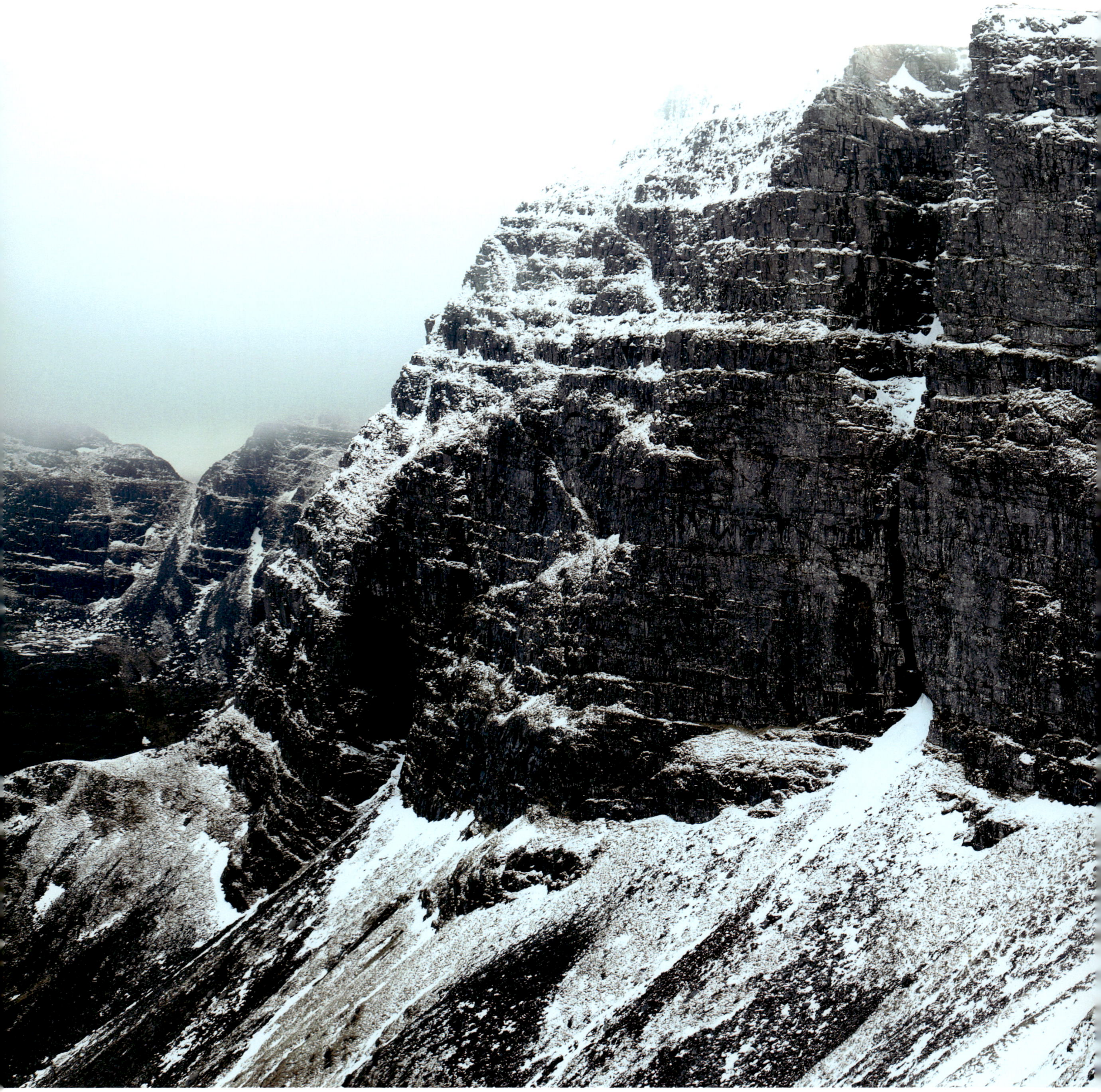

In the eighties the cliff came under sustained assault by the irrepressible Mick Fowler. He claimed the much-prized central line of *Gully of the Gods* (VI,6) in 1983 and in 1984 he returned with Phil Butler for *Great Overhanging Gully* (VI,7). Andy Cave and Dave Heselden scooped the remaining left-hand fault line with the awesome *Genesis* (VII,7) in 2000, leaving the vast prow right of *Gully of the Gods* as the obvious remaining 'gap'. Martin Moran fixed this in 2004 – *The Godfather* was the first grade VIII on the mountain and remains one of the great mixed climbs anywhere in the North West Highlands. Even more difficult routes have been added in recent years, and there can be no doubt that the Giant's Wall has cemented its place centre stage in hard exploratory climbing on long, winter-only routes.

◀ The Giant's Wall in winter condition.
Photo: *Colin Threlfall.*

THE ROUTES

Genesis (VII,7)
The left-hand fault becomes climbable when the turf is hard frozen and an ice streak develops down the culminating chimney. Impeccable mixed climbing on turf, rock and ice, which is much easier than it looks.

Die Reisenwand (VII,6)
The original route and a bewildering line starting just right of *Genesis* and gaining the zigzag ledges. The lower pitches are easier when thickly iced, but more usually involve delicate and bold interplay of iced and mixed moves. A direct ice route above the cave has also been done – *Divine Retribution* (VII,6).

Gully of the Gods (VI,6)
There must be a liberal coating of ice on the left wall of the central chimney. Another superb route providing very steep and intimidating climbing with an 'other-worldly' feel.

The Godfather (VIII,8)
The easiest line on the great prow right of *Gully of the Gods*. The route ascends the lower walls by the right-hand of two diagonal ramps, then works back left to enter the big corner in the upper tiers. The crux is right at the top!

THE STORY

I'd first looked at that cliff on Coire an Fhamhair in 1972 as a 17-year-old Scout. We camped on the beach by Lochan Coire na Poite and walked up the side of the cliff to the plateau. Even then I noticed that big corner because I remember drawing a fantasy crag diagram a couple of years later with 'my' routes all over it, including the corner! In those days I naively thought it would be a mecca for summer rock.

In more realistic days, living locally, I was aware of the possibility of the corner, but didn't think that the lower cliff could reasonably be climbed. The cliff is so shaded that it is difficult to get a clear view of it at any time of year, and from below it looks really blank, all the tufty bits and rock cracks being hidden. I traversed across the halfway ledge on my Beinn Bhan girdle in 1989 and kept the idea of a winter ascent of the corner in mind, but the combination of good conditions, time off work and the right partner never arose.

By October 2001 I was getting frustrated. Having built up the frightening mental picture that this was a sheer flake corner guarded by big overhangs at its base (the sort of line that would be E2 or E3 in summer) I thought I should abseil into it to check the feasibility, so took the dog for a walk and gave it a look. I was surprised how big and incut the corner was, with a prevalence of grass and ledges. Concluding that it was obviously climbable I neglected to check out the features in any detail.

A week off work in early March coincided with splendid conditions and the right partner. Paul Tattersall is a redoubtably strong rock climber, now resident near Gairloch. Whilst not known as a winter activist he had made a solo ascent of Beinn Eighe's Central Buttress. So here was a man on whom I could rely when the going got really steep.

We left the car at 6.30 a.m. on a cold clear morning of exceptional brilliance. On reaching the coire the sun was casting oblique light across the headwall, illuminating the right wall of the big corner. Conditions were immaculate. We inspected all possible lines on the lower wall and chose the right-hand of two slim ramps. Reaching the ramp was a game of trial and error. I traversed a long way right to a broken corner, which offered positive progress to a narrow ledge under the ramp. Paul led the ramp, which gave a long, complex pitch that offered just sufficient protection. By the time we gained an exposed balcony ten metres below the girdle ledge, five hours had passed.

Pete Benson on the first ascent of *Godzilla* (IX,8).
Photo: *Guy Robertson*.

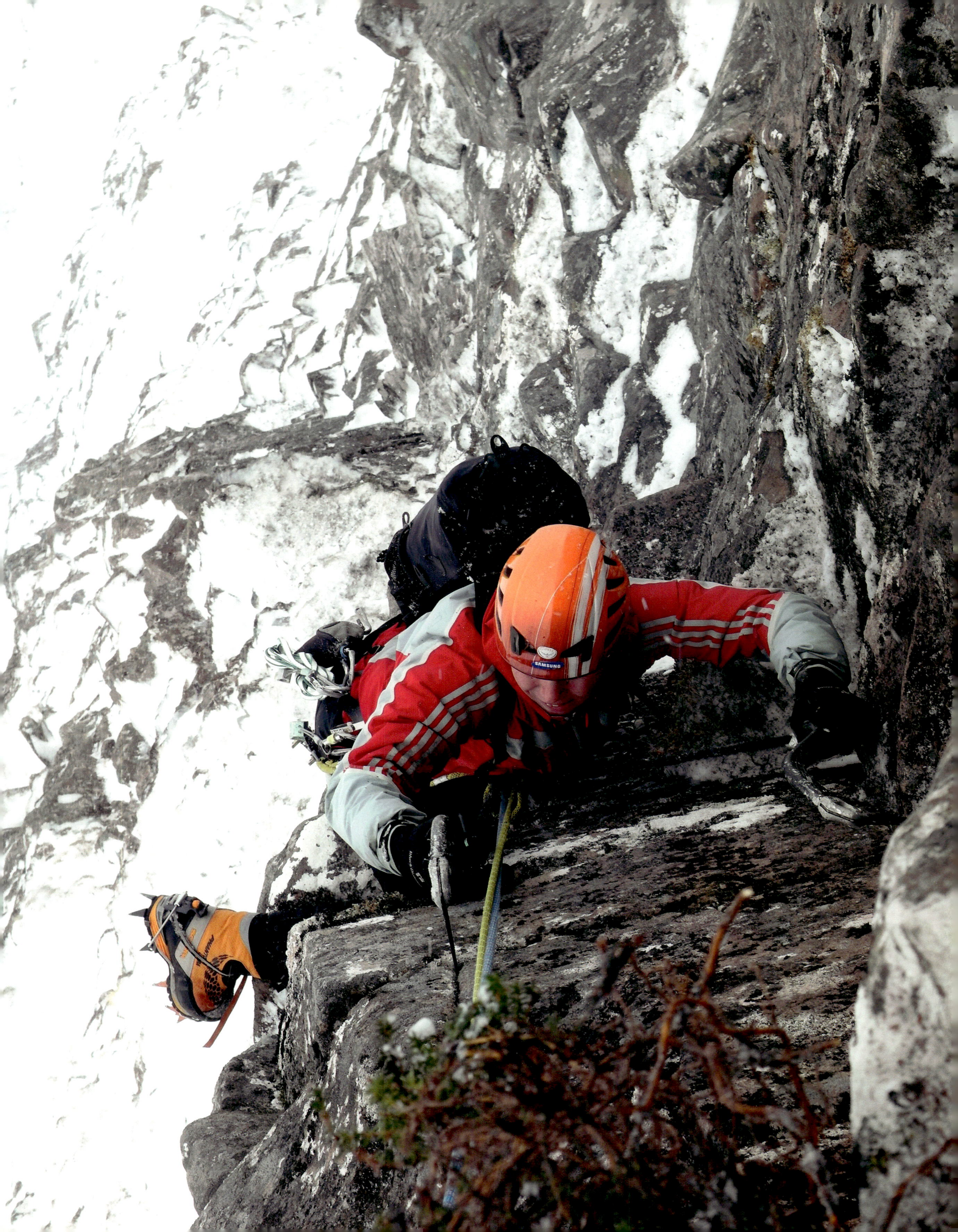
SAMSUNG

After another short and unexpectedly strenuous pitch, we traversed to a point under the corner at dusk. Paul led a committing pitch into the corner itself by which time it was dark. I was shocked to realise that the scale and angle of everything was greater than I remembered. Looking up, I realised that what had started as a grade VI and had graduated to a sustained grade VII was now moving into unknown and even harder territory. The first section of corner was desperate. Luckily, I was able to find a crack on its left to climb, but the angle still bulged and had I not found a good thread runner my courage might have failed. The pitch debouched on to a lovely little ledge where I thought I could sit snug as Paul led through. Paul arrived puffing and, having already led two big pitches, declared himself too knackered to lead on.

Peering up the main corner, my heart sank. I was dismayed to see a roof that overhung by a metre just where the right wall was devoid of edges. As I approached the bulge my fingers, forearms and shoulder muscles were cramping badly. On reaching the roof, after much nervous flickering, my torch failed completely. Why had I not checked the batteries or brought spares? I dropped a loop of rope and pulled up Paul's torch.

Above me reared a gently impending corner crack with a depressingly smooth right wall. After failed attempts on the left wall, I arranged some decent protection, calmed my nerves and prepared for a 'do or die' effort on the corner direct, fully prepared for a long fall. A flurry of crossed picks, ripping tools and blind torques took me to the exit. The second I planted my axes in tufts over the top my feet came off. Not being strong enough to do a straight pull-up into a mantelshelf, I hooked my heel up into a rock crevice above my head and squirmed my way to freedom. Almost at once Paul's torch failed completely.

There was zero moonlight. Couldoran's salmon hatchery was the brightest object in the universe. I had to make the belay by feeling for the cracks. Paul started to prusik the pitch in darkness. He seemed to be getting nowhere, dropping an axe and several bits of gear. It was past midnight and deeply freezing. In desperation I tried the torch again and found that after a few minutes warming in my pocket it would glow dimly for about 20 seconds. So with an occasional lighthouse beam from above, Paul somehow disentangled himself from the ropes and got up the pitch.

The next pitch was the exit and looked three grades easier but was choked with powder snow. After swimming through the cornice I emerged on a windless silent plateau at 2.30 a.m. I quickly lowered the torch to Paul who joined me just as the battery finally died.

We groped our way back to the sack, stumbled down the screes then thrashed an ungainly retreat over the moor, skidding on every patch of ice and often getting dumped painfully on our backsides. We reached the stalking track at 5.15 a.m. just as light was returning to the sky.

Our wives greeted our dawn return with consternation and relief. I tried to sleep for half an hour but, in truth, my excitement was too great. It was no great hardship to get up and take our labrador for a 10 a.m. appointment at the vets in Broadford. Domestic life soon regained its claim! •

Guy Robertson on the first ascent of *The God Delusion* (IX,9).
Photo: *Pete Benson.*

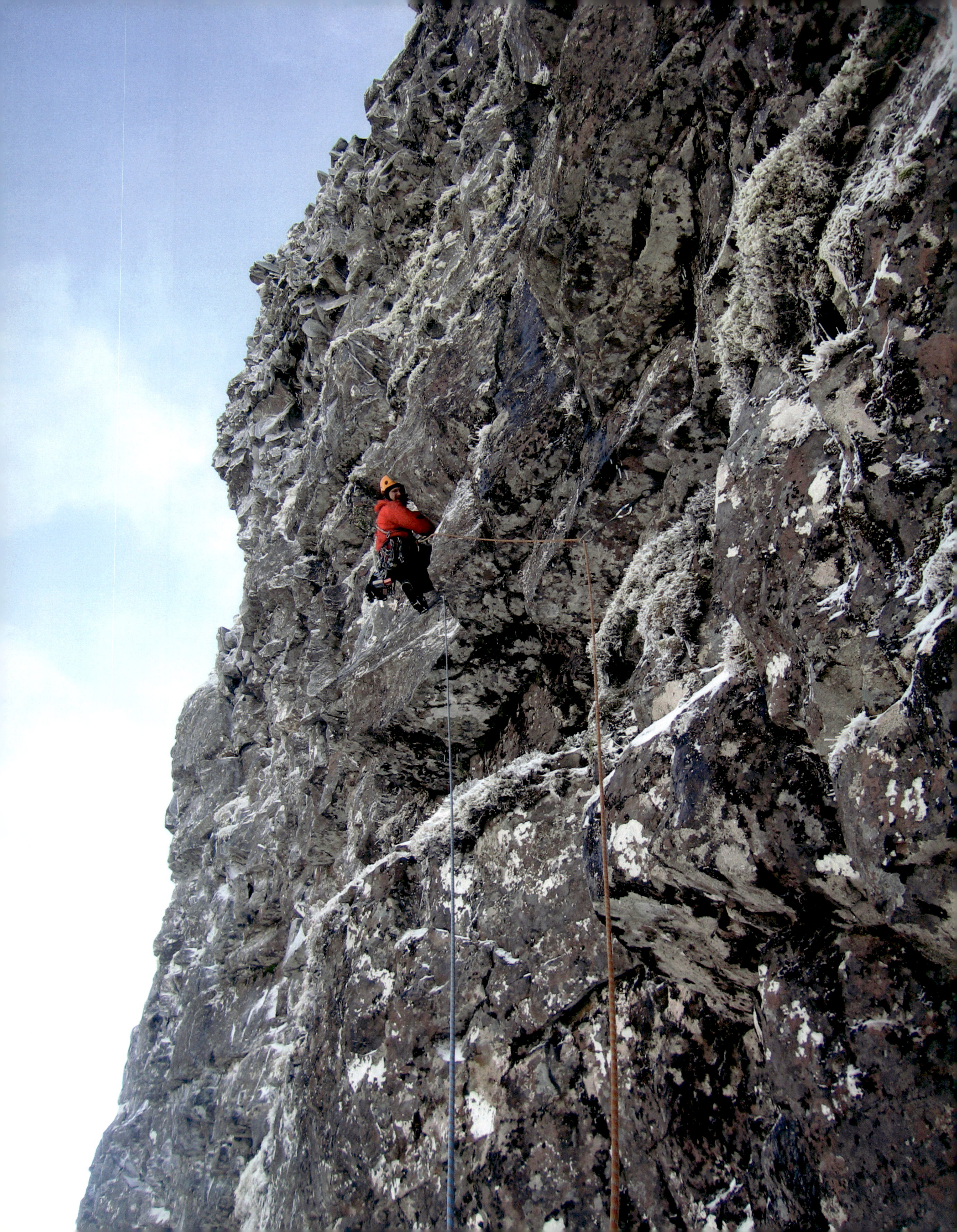

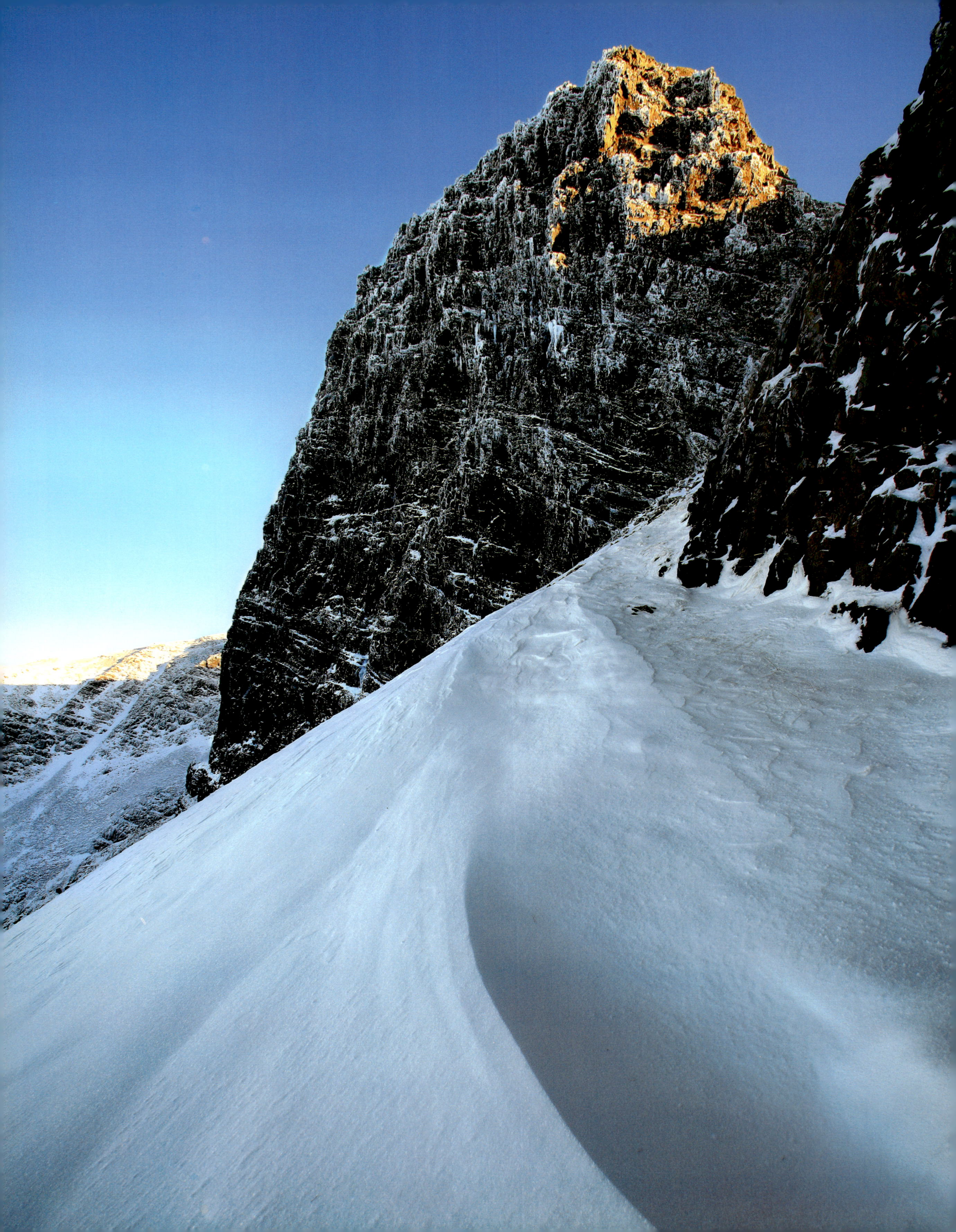

Mainreachan Buttress, Fuar Tholl – *by Andy Nisbet*

THE PLACE

Fuar Tholl sits above Glen Carron, the next valley south of Torridon, and is scenically the junior partner. Though its cliffs may be isolated, they lack nothing in stature compared to their northerly neighbours.

This lack of celebrity status is an added boon to the few who love the area. The mountain is well seen from Lochcarron, and pictures of the village often include it in the background. Viewed from this angle, villagers refer to the tip of Mainreachan Buttress as Wellington's Nose. The other slight peaks of Fuar Tholl complete the Duke's well-kent face in profile, with a curving snow patch for his mouth.

THE CLIFF

Mainreachan Buttress is up there with some of the biggest and steepest cliffs in Scotland. Few other mainland Scottish cliffs compare in the 'drop a stone and see if it touches anything' league. The cliff is rather shy, though well seen from high up on the Torridon peaks. However, from that distance you lose much of the sense of scale.

The approach is not short, but there are good paths leading from Achnashellach station up into Coire Lair. From the path it looks close, but unless you know the scale, a surprising 15 minutes is needed to reach it. Even then the angle of its right sidewall can be underestimated unless you've seen its awesome profile from the ridge above. The best clue in winter is to look for icicles, and there is one particularly big one – not that you'd reach it without wings. Now there's a challenge! The only real line of weakness is a big ramp, hopefully a white ramp, otherwise you should move swiftly on. It leads into very steep ground, but an entry ticket is better than nothing. The left sidewall is smaller and less steep but would be a major cliff anywhere else. Between the two is a wide frontal nose with even longer but marginally more amenable routes.

As a smooth sandstone cliff, the climbing can be on any or all of rock, ice or turf. There are some 'exciting' summer routes, but this is really a prime winter venue. The cliff is at mid altitude, so ice needs time to form and good conditions are not common. But half the routes don't need ice, only well frozen turf, and this should come into condition most winters, although probably not for long.

THE CLIMBING

In the 1973 guidebook, Mainreachan was described as offering '*the best sandstone climbing in Scotland, on very steep clean rock*'. Now we have to remember that most sandstone climbing is grim in summer – often north-facing, lichenous, slimy and with vegetated ledges. But this one is too steep to have many ledges and as a result the rock is quite clean, but it remains an awesomely big steep wet cliff, unattractive to the modern extreme rock climber.

I climbed several of the summer routes while checking grades for a new guidebook, and in dry conditions the climbing can be good. Good in an old-fashioned way. Sure enough the rock is clean, and there are nice moves, but it is also remarkably compact and in general the only runners are behind hollow blocks. In fact, the only holds are often hollow blocks, which is fine for an old-fashioned climber who has learnt that being hollow doesn't mean they will come off, who doesn't mind sinking his fingers into turf to gain that vital ledge. Once away from the fault lines, however, there are precious few holds.

Although the early summer lines climbed an impressive face, they never became classics. The winter ascent of *Sleuth* in 1970 was a much more important event. It was Scotland's first grade VII, and a remarkably long, steep, turfy route for pre-front pointing days. It was almost two decades before a second route appeared.

This is one of Scotland's great winter cliffs, not only huge and inspiring but requiring some planning and determination to find the right conditions, and to be there on the right day with enough good weather and daylight. The rock is compact and offers neither weakness nor much in the way of protection. But turf is always a weakness and the fault lines have just enough. The higher you get, the greater the tension and the exposure, but what a wonderful feeling to succeed here.

◀ Mainreachan Buttress in winter.
Photo: *Colin Threlfall.*

▲ Mainreachan Buttress in summer. Photo: *Rob Ferguson*.

THE ROUTES

Snoopy (VII,7)
Magnificent dribbles of ice link hanging features on the cliff without you actually having to hang anywhere. It requires good conditions but some recent ascents have had even thinner ice than the first.

Sherlock (VIII,8)
The most recent and hardest route based on the summer line. Unlike *Snoopy* this is pure snowed-up rock, so finding it in acceptably white winter condition won't be easy. Superb sustained climbing all the way.

Supersleuth (VII,8)
A direct line based on *Sleuth* taking in some steep walls which *Sleuth* sensibly avoided, continuing directly up the crest where the north face swings east.

100 THE GREAT MOUNTAIN CRAGS OF SCOTLAND

▲ Malcolm Bass on an early attempt on *Sherlock* (VIII,8). Photo: *Simon Yearsley.*

THE STORY

I had only ever spoken with Martin Moran before, when I wrote a chapter on mixed climbing in his well known 1988 book. Clearly he thought I was a worthy partner for the first winter line on the sidewall of Mainreachan, since he invited me over without telling me where we were going. We approached over the top in darkness and mist, and as we descended under fearsome smooth walls, my spirits waned. When we finally reached a ramp leading out on to the face, it felt more like a trapdoor than the key to success.

I conceded to leading the first pitch – it was clearly easy, and the weather too misty to see what I was heading towards. I soon reached a smooth ramp leading up right. The thin ice on this might have felt easier with brand new monopoints, but it took Martin three hours to lead and it's doubtful the protection would have held an Eddie the Eagle impersonator. As the consultant for torquing and snowed-up rock, I was wearing suitably blunt crampons and only seconded the pitch by the skin of my teeth, finally reaching a good spike belay ten metres up and left. I certainly wasn't going to continue up the ramp when all I could see was a looming overhanging wall, and this time neither was Martin, so he suggested we try a ledge leading out left. I think 'we' was supposed to be me, but I tied in to the belay and declined to move.

Martin disappeared for another two hours, before eventually returning in the dark saying he couldn't do it and did I want to have a try? I didn't. I scuttled off to eastern mountains with better turf and less ice.

Martin returned a few weeks later with Simon Jenkins and carried on up the ramp to the overhanging wall where, miraculously, they found a one-foot ledge leading out left. Martin then led a sustained and difficult mixed pitch, to be stopped by a typically blank wall. Another few weeks later, conditions were much better and this time the team of terriers had spotted a fine icefall down the blank wall. Their March ascent of *Reach for the Sky* (VII,6) went smoothly, yet neither of them rushed back to try the intended line which headed right from the ramp, following the summer route *Snoopy*.

During the good winter of 1994, I was busy working while others were climbing hard routes, and I began to dream about *Snoopy*. Casually at first, but the familiarity of walking past it with my clients fed a growing excitement, which eventually overcame the fear of ice-smeared hanging slabs. I could see ice forming varying distances down towards the top of the ramp, but always falling short. The occasional comment on the grapevine let me know that Simon Richardson had a route in mind on the cliff. Of course I assumed it was *Snoopy*, but I never saw enough ice on it for me to try. But that didn't stop me imagining he could still do it. The news that he and Chris Cartwright had climbed a version of the summer route *Enigma* (VII,6) in January 1997 was a relief, but galvanised me to try *Snoopy*. Their ascent has a curious story attached to it. On the approach they had seen a distress signal and good-heartedly headed past the cliff to a nearby col only to discover it was a distant lighthouse!

The warmest and wettest February on record in 1998 suddenly ended with proper winter storms. I walked down past Mainreachan as usual, but this time I spotted ice forming further down towards the ramp, almost reaching snowy ground. With a brief ridge of high pressure forecast, I decided to stay for the weekend and roped in Chris Dale for an attempt. I knew the line, so volunteered myself for the two thin ice pitches. I knew to take sharp crampons this time, but even so, the ramp pitch was much harder than expected. The ice was as thin as ever, the limited turf wasn't fully frozen and my runners were close to psychological. I remember Chris laughing as he pulled my two peg runners out by hand.

It was a clear day so Chris knew to head to the outside of the ramp and round the overhanging wall to below the ice. After a vain attempt to reach some cracks over to the right, I was forced to attack the bulge above and reach the ice direct, which was more bold than hard. The first placements were very shallow, but each move up brought thicker ice, though never enough for screws. With excellent chewy, but thin, ice, the following unprotected 20 metres were more nerve-wracking than terrifying. I was now belayed in a recess below the ice source, which flowed out of a niche to form a short fat pillar.

Chris is the total opposite of short and fat, so it proved difficult for him to gain the niche with low ice placements in the pillar, but this he did before making equally impressive blind but protected moves round a corner to avoid overhangs above. We expected easy ground now, but as ever, there was still an awkward slabby bulge barring access to salvation.

I reached the top in diminishing light and gathering cloud as the bad weather arrived. But arrive it did, and heavy overnight snow blocked the road, giving us an extra day during which to savour the route, rather than teach snowcraft to beginners.

This was my perfect route: an improbable line on an unclimbed section of a big face, hard but just within my capabilities, requiring very particular conditions for success. But I'd spotted them and timed it right. Had it been my last big route I'd have been satisfied.

Fortunately, though, it wasn't. ●

Guy Robertson on the first winter scent of *Sherlock* (VIII,8).
Photo: *Iain Small*.

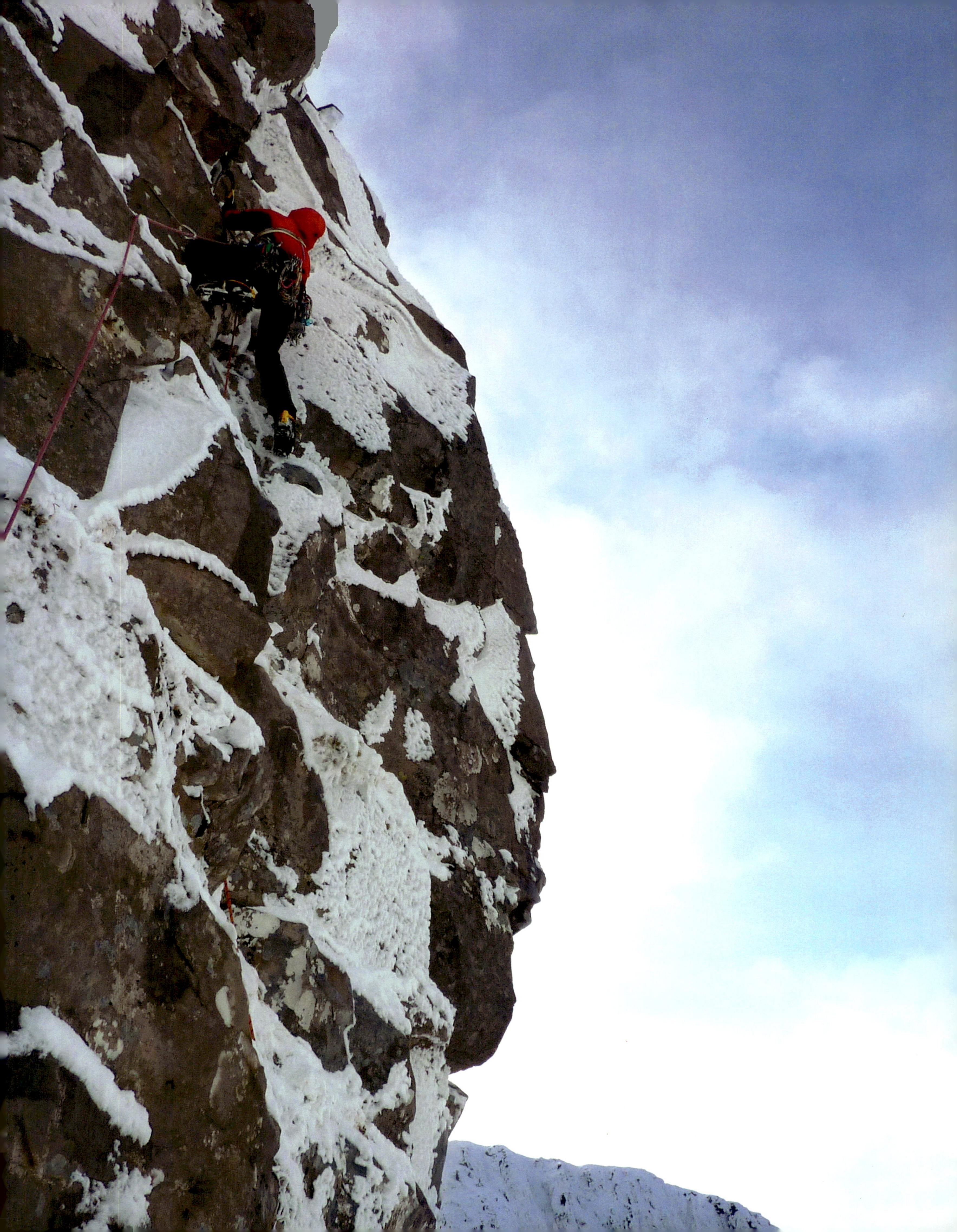

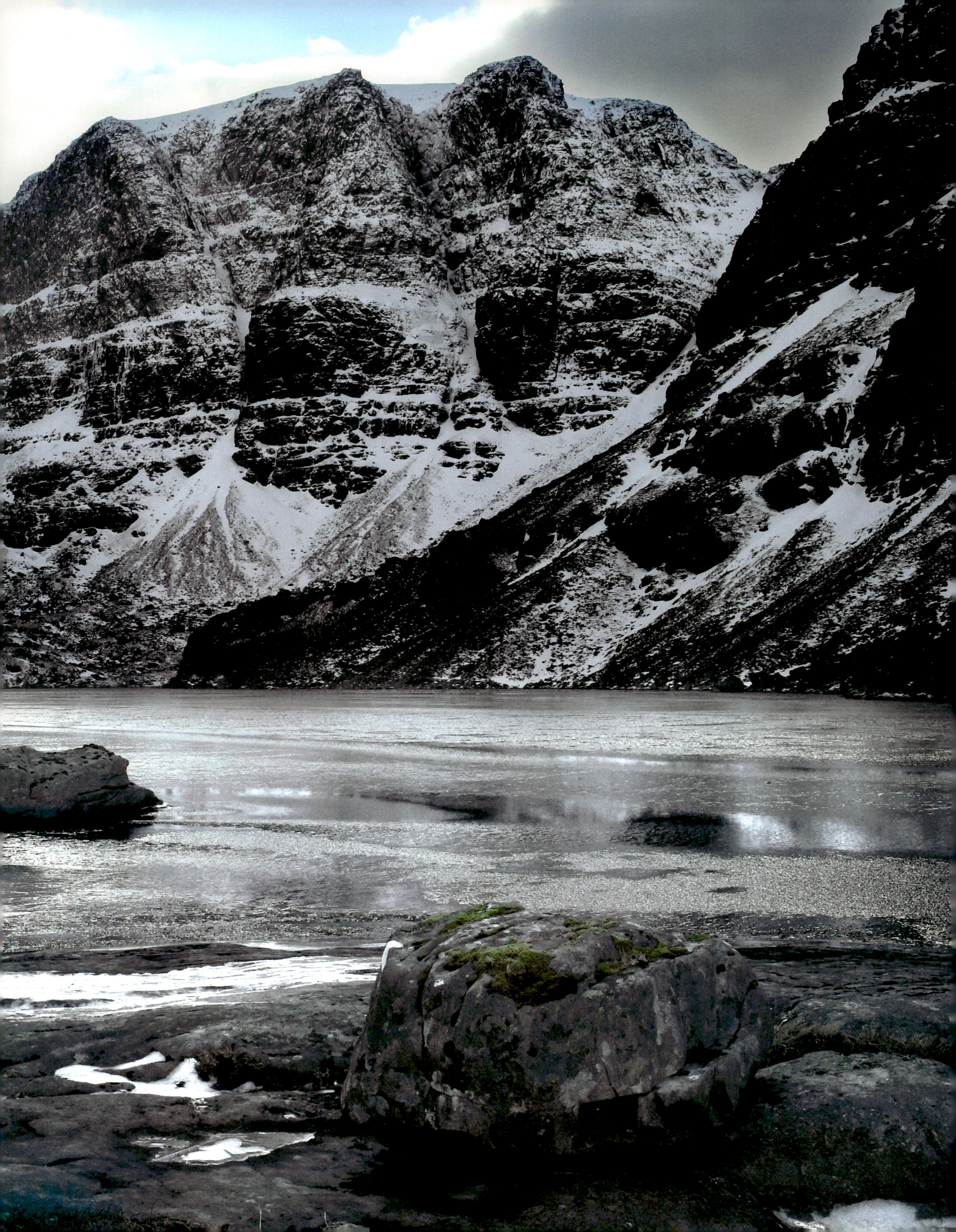

West Central Wall, Beinn Eighe — *by Jason Currie*

THE PLACE

There isn't a climber in the country that doesn't recognise Coire Mhic Fhearchair. The view of the Triple Buttress from the shores of the inky lochan below is emblematic of Torridon and the North West Highlands as a whole.

It's difficult not to be inspired by the scene as one rounds the imposing bastion of Sail Mhor and clambers up the sandstone staircase to the edge of those melancholic waters. The elegant simplicity and the awesome scale of those three great pillars! This is Scotland's very own Brouillard face. Now cast your eye high up to the impending upper right wall of the deep right-hand gully, and you'll find one of Scotland's most intimidating and atmospheric mountain walls.

THE CLIFF

West Central Wall is by some margin the steepest of all the faces on the Triple Buttress. It is as though a vast stage curtain has been drawn across the gully, its pleats and folds delineating lines of awe-inspiring steepness that thread their way through a pelmet of overhangs at the top of the cliff.

Peering gingerly across from the summit of the Central Buttress was my first experience of this wall. I was trying to direct my partner down the correct line of approach on abseil. Like a stereoscopic picture, a definite line slowly revealed itself out of the confusion of corners, grooves and roofs. Once my probe was safely belayed in the middle of nowhere he shouted my cue. I was immediately struck by the dizzying drop and at how infrequently my crampon points brushed the blocky rock. How was I supposed to stay attached to it on the way back up?

It is beside the point to try and describe vertical features of the topography on this wall — its attraction lies in its unrelenting steepness, daunting exposure and immediate commitment on account of its location. Any failure on ascent here will require a lengthy and involved descent in anything but perfect snow conditions (which are rare). The most substantial geological relief is afforded by the girdling ledges — one at the base, not far above the start of the quartzite, and another two at a third, and half height respectively. However these are not 'ledges' in the traditional sense, so don't embark on a route expecting an easy lifeline to effect an escape!

THE CLIMBING

Although summer routes have been established here, it will never be popular as a rock climbing venue. Access is complex (easiest from above) and seepage is often a problem on many of the routes. A pervasive looseness also haunts the lower reaches. However, if you can deal with all this, routes like *Shoot the Breeze* and *Force Ten*, both summer E2s, are outstanding examples of just how spectacular Scottish rock can get.

In winter however, the cliff is a mixed climber's paradise. Conditions require just a good coating of white, which is found regularly enough, although too cold may mean dry black rock. The continuous angular cracks are perfect for torquing and protection, and the numerous flat edges give good foot placements and positive hooking. Although turf is not abundant there can be a surprising amount of ice. Modern techniques and attitudes are prerequisites to success on these audacious winter lines, which follow often continuously vertical or overhanging grooves, corners and walls, snaking complex lines through the most unlikely-looking territory.

The first routes came as late as the seventies, but the great majority are the product of Andy Nisbet's explorations throughout the eighties and nineties — a one man mission that produced some of the country's finest. The impeccable grooves of *Blood, Sweat & Frozen Tears* (VIII,8) represent the very best the north-west has on offer, although Mick Fowler's legendary *West Central Gully* (Scottish VIII) from 1987 is of similarly outstanding quality. Pushed to the limit on the crux section, Fowler was forced to clip into his rucksack straps — only to lurch back into action on seeing the stitching start to rip! The turn of the century has seen many repeats and some new additions, with undoubtedly more to come. Perhaps the most audacious recent addition was Ian Parnell and Andy Turner's tour-de-force plundering a direct winter line, completely on sight, through the exceptionally steep ground above *Chop Suey's* first pitch — *Bruised Violet* (VIII,9).

◀ The Triple Buttress of Beinn Eighe in winter.
Photo: *Colin Threlfall.*

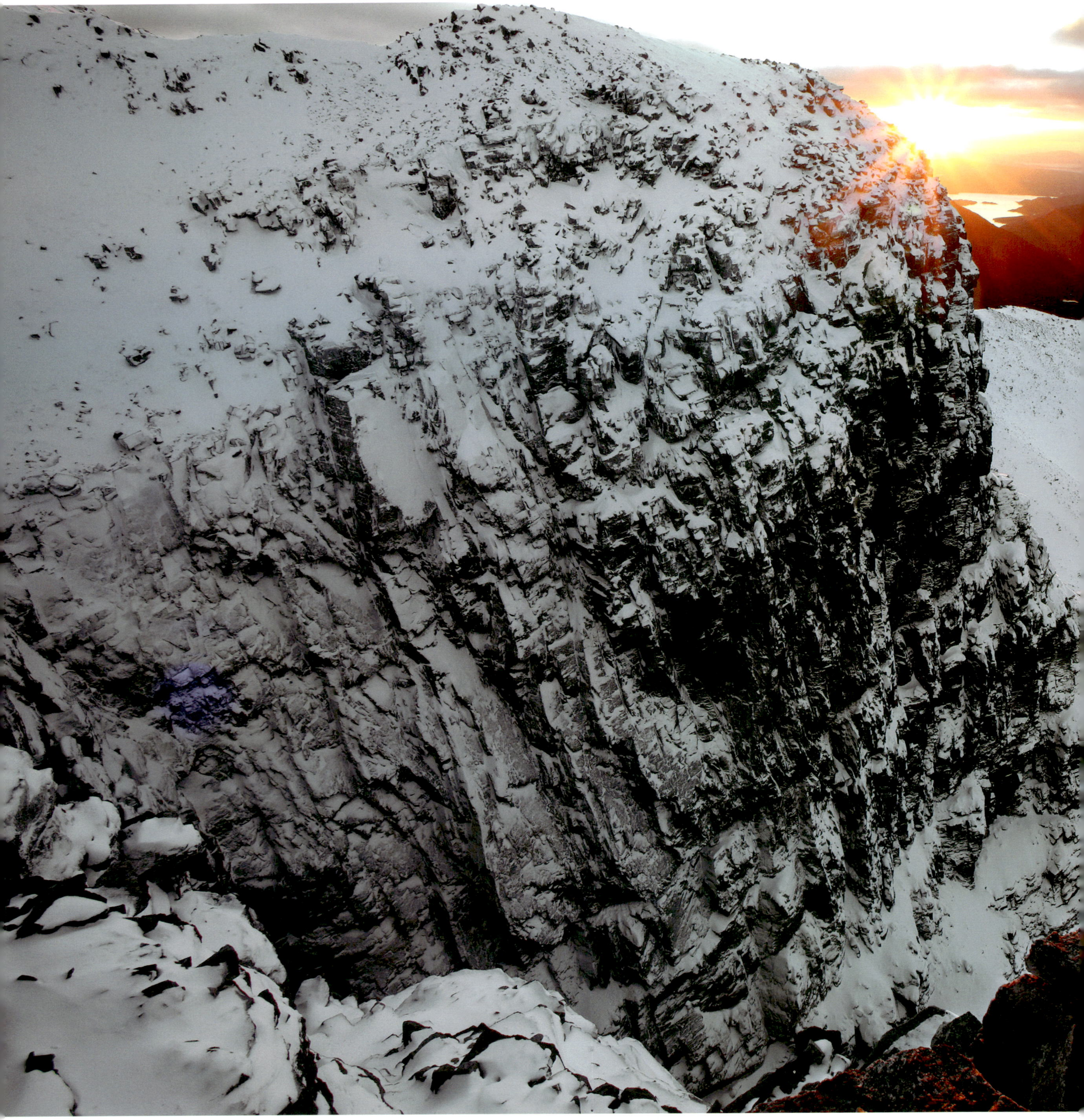

THE ROUTES

Shoot the Breeze (E2, IX,8)
An outstanding climb – the best of the summer lines, and as good, if not better, in winter. Dolomitic exposure. A corner system leads to overhangs that force moves onto an arête, which fires its way through hyperspace and past the final overhangs.

Blood, Sweat and Frozen Tears (VIII,8)
Undoubtedly the most climbed grade VIII in the Northern Highlands, and justifiably so – a modern classic and only just making the grade. A tremendous climb with snowed-up rock, turf and ice, taking a soaring winter-only line of dirty overhanging grooves.

West Central Gully (VIII)
An unparalleled route of awesome steepness; less of a gully and more of a system of roof cracks! Although it doesn't lie on the wall itself, the gully sucks in and distills all the atmosphere of the wall, and presents one of the greatest challenges on Scottish ice.

◀ West Central Wall from the top of Central Buttress.
Photo: *Colin Threlfall*.

▲ Murdoch Jamieson and Lee Roberts on *Blood, Sweat and Frozen Tears*, (VIII,8). Photo: *Andy Inglis*.

▲ Guy Robertson and Greg Boswell on the first winter ascent of *Shoot the Breeze* (IX,8). Photo: *Adam Russell*.

THE STORY

'I have a truly marvellous demonstration of this proposition which this margin is too narrow to contain ... '
Pierre de Fermat, c. 1630

This is Fermat's enigmatic reference to a proof of what became known as his Last Theorem. He never published his proof but this simple scribble sent mathematicians on searches for it that led them in diverse and surprising directions. I've never been one for annotating books myself. Commenting, underlining, highlighting, even turning the corner of a page down all seem wrong and somehow disrespectful. But it didn't stop Gavin penciling the names of new routes into my *Northern Highlands* guidebooks as reports of their ascents were published. And Ryle's scrawls continued to lead me into memorable adventures long after he left us. In particular they brought me face to face with the West Central Wall.

It was Guy who first took a serious interest in *Blood, Sweat and Frozen Tears*. We had begun to search out routes still awaiting a repeat. The quality and thrill of hard climbing and the strength of the lines we were somehow getting up were feeding a whirlpool of ambition and an ever stronger partnership.

It was a day of superb clarity that saw me at the top of Central Buttress, guidebook in hand, trying to match the right combination of grooves and roofs to the description in front of me. I happily agreed to Guy's gallant offer to abseil in first and watched amazed as he whisked through space down into the frigid air of the gully. It was with an unusually high degree of scepticism

▲ Guy Robertson and Pete Benson on *Shoot the Breeze* (E2).
Photo: *Colin Threlfall*.

that I said goodbye to the sun and went down after him. A second, equally daunting abseil, deposited us in a deep, powdery drift.

The wall to our left denied us a proper look at Fowler's legendary *West Central Gully* so our attention returned to the matter at hand. A steep groove twisting up over two roofs defined the first pitch. After quietly organising the rack, Guy set off and I was left contemplating the points of his crampons until the first protection was found. Then I settled into the familiar world of frosty rope, stamping feet and tantalising views of distant, sunny peaks.

When my turn came to follow I was struck by the balancy nature of the climbing. The groove was stupidly steep, but precise footwork on small, positive edges allowed me to bridge across it and take a lot of the weight off my arms. There were good cracks but often it was necessary to hook those same edges with the tips of my axes and twist and turn back and forth as the placements dictated. The intricacies continued right to the belay, the roofs providing moments of intense, static control. Technical and superbly sustained, it wasn't a pitch to be climbed quickly.

Guy was belayed on the lower of two girdling ledges. My pitch sounded simple enough: continue up the groove, go left across a steep slab, surmount a break in the overhang rightwards, then move up and left to belay. The groove was definitely of the winter-only kind. It was covered in a layer of dirt and moss that provided just sufficient traction when frozen but would have been repulsive ooze in summer. Protection was sparse and difficult to arrange all the way to the steep slab. And what a slab! Holds almost had to be willed into existence and even then none were bigger than a fingernail. A reassuring nut placement was unearthed at the top of the groove, from where there followed a series of tentative 'looks' as each hold was tested and weight transfers gingerly practiced. Finally a sequence was unlocked and, pressing down my fear, I teetered up. A tiny crack was found that allowed one wobbly tooth of an axe but no gear. That fear bubbled up to the surface and the retreat was sounded – but I was totally committed now, and reversing seemed sure to result in a fall. With every spare muscle locking my body rigid I stretched up to a hook and then reached beyond to the flatness of the upper girdle ledge. The other axe followed and I spent a few moments desperately trying to bury it into what looked like turf, without success. A worrying, rocky mantel and I was gasping on the ledge.

Gear was hastily arranged before I contemplated the overhang. However, the slab had exacted its mental toll and I had to will myself to continue. Roofs have never been my forte and this one was quite meaty. Locking off on a good torque on the lip, I tried many times but couldn't find a placement above it. With time against us we were forced to admit failure. We descended the gully and collected our rucksacks after a rapid ascent of Fuselage Gully.

Andy Inglis on West Central Gully (VIII,9).
Photo: *Duncan Hodgson*.

110 THE GREAT MOUNTAIN CRAGS OF SCOTLAND

THE NORTH WEST HIGHLANDS | **WEST CENTRAL WALL, BEINN EIGHE**   111

My disappointment soon turned to annoyance when Guy told me he'd been back on the route without me. Even though this had been midweek I felt cheated and was quietly pleased to find out that he'd been forced to turn back at the slab. Once again early season daylight, or rather lack of it, had stopped play. So I had another chance, and this time it was clear that I had to succeed.

The first pitch was cleanly dispatched before I was once more confronted with the poorly protected groove. Unavoidably focused on the overhangs I made the groove feel unduly difficult and fought for confidence as I turned my attention to the slab. Amazingly, this time a thick layer of snow covered the smooth, grey rock. It took a while to clear the holds and work out the sequence. Despite the arrival of mono-point crampons, I was still stubbornly sticking to my filed down classics – but here they worked to my advantage. Stepping inside my left leg I was just able to reach a tiny edge with the outside point of my right crampon, which would have been impossible with an offset single front point. The next move had to be, by definition, smooth. Rocking up, axes wobbling, I caught the tiny crack. This time I waggled a Peenut in above my axe, making the on-off moves to the girdle ledge slightly more relaxed.

Time was on our side this time, but again I struggled to find a placement over the roof and a short fall came close to breaking my resolve. After several attempts I called down to Guy saying that I might have to give up – but his look alone scolded me back into action. Locking off one final time, I cleared away more snow to reveal a sinking crack that took the whole pick of an axe. Bingo. A few scrabbling lurches and I was back in balance above the lip, heart pounding as fear threatened to burst my ribcage. Below my feet was nothing but still air all the long way down to the gully bed below. I was utterly beaming when Guy joined me at the belay, and nearly forgot that there was still another hard pitch to climb.

He teetered left and up to a huge corner, then disappeared from sight. Just as for the previous pitches, the rope inched out haltingly. But eventually, and with some relief, I got the call to climb. The moves left were precarious and I was secretly glad to be seconding, but as soon as the corner was won I began to grin uncontrollably. It was lined with streaks of steep, green, bulging ice. This was clearly going to be fun.

We called across to some friends high on Central Buttress and bade them a good night on their crux before making our way over the ridge in the gathering gloom and descending to the car.

And so it was, an old mate's short scribbled comment at the edge of a guidebook page, hinting at something elusive and special, produced a series of experiences way beyond expectation. As climbers we may be doodling in the margins, but the affirmation our passion brings to our lives is central to why we do it. ●

Greg Boswell on the first winter ascent of *Shoot the Breeze* (IX,8).
Photo: *Guy Robertson.*

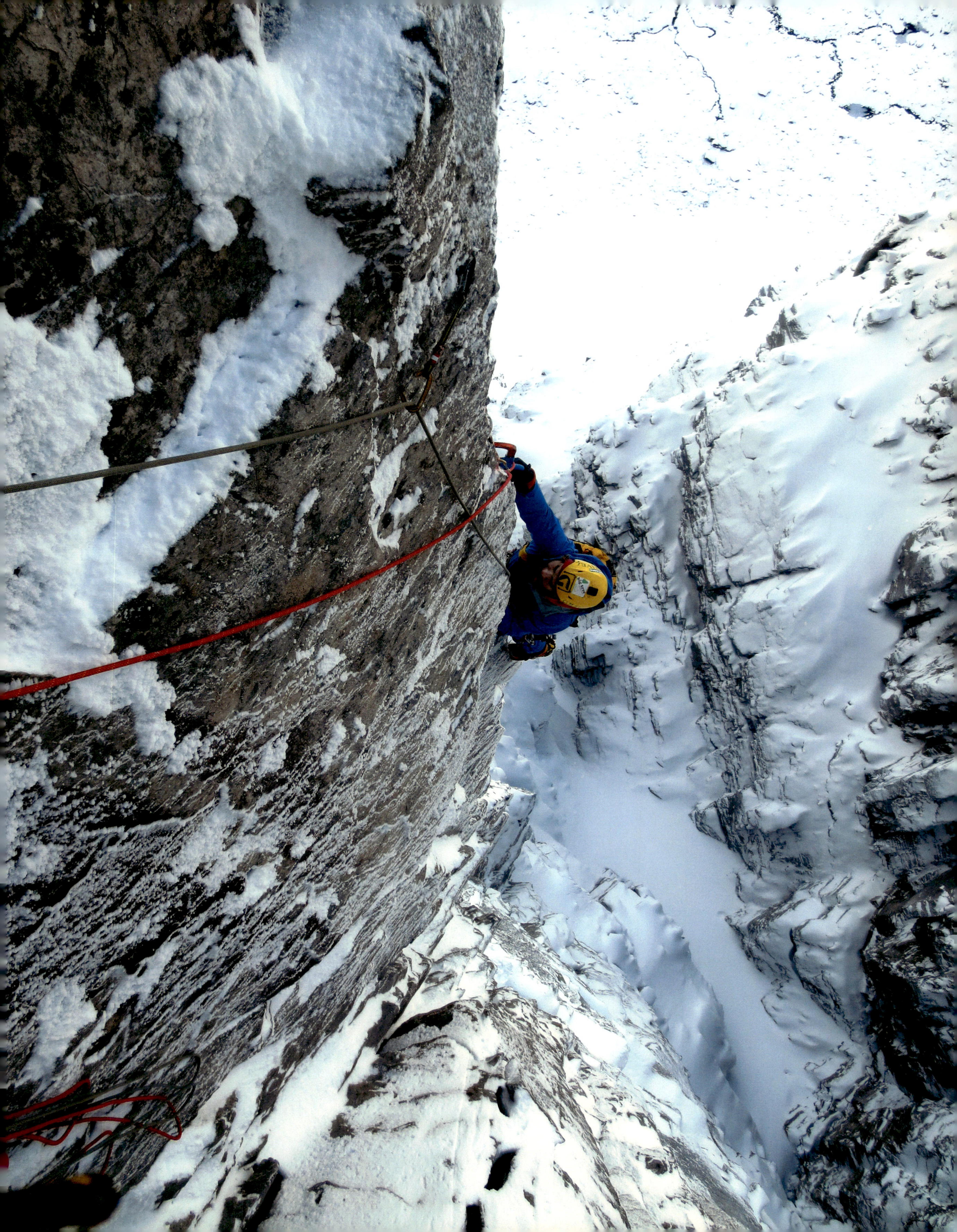

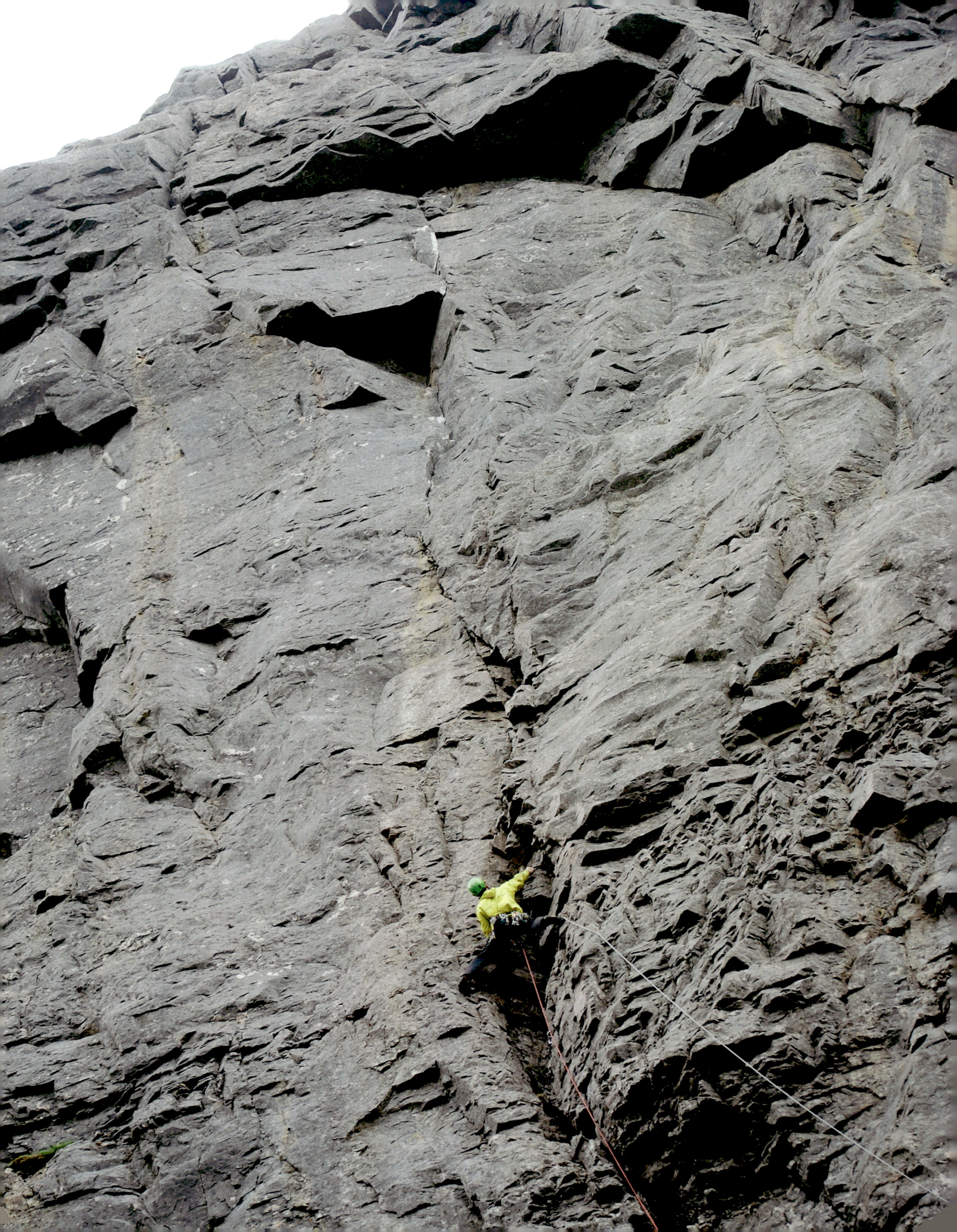

Far East Wall, Beinn Eighe – *by Andy Nisbet*

THE PLACE

Back in the early seventies, Torridon felt like a wild place in remote country. There was no Kessock Bridge and most of the roads beyond Inverness were single track. The great explorers of the early SMC had been here and written detailed notes, but really they'd only scratched the surface. My first visits followed their scratches and struggled with their notes to avoid entering unclimbed ground. There was a lot of unclimbed ground, and soon I was brave enough to go exploring this myself. Despite modern guidebooks and photographs, Torridon is still a wild place in remote country.

Torridon is famous for its magnificent three peaks – Beinn Alligin, Liathach and Beinn Eighe, together forming the north side of the glen. Coire Mhic Fhearchair is Beinn Eighe's most magnificent coire, with its classic lochan overshadowed by huge cliffs. While the Triple Buttresses are the highlight for the mountaineer, three steep walls stand out to the technical climber. These are West Central Wall – the glowering left wall of West Buttress, the Eastern Ramparts – a long and open, but deceptively steep wall attached to East Buttress, and the aloof Far East Wall – an elongated sheet of unremitting smoothness.

THE CLIFF

Far East Wall is carved out of the hillside in the top left of the coire. Plumb vertical or overhanging for most of its length, this is an arena for the modern gladiator. The pillars of clean white rock at either end offer the best rock climbing, while the big fault lines forming their inner boundaries offer the best winter routes.

Traditional winter conditions on such a steep smooth wall are hard to find. Despite modifying the rules to fit a modern cliff, you still need some snow and ice. This means quite a lot of snow, in the hope that at least a little will stick. Wet stormy weather followed by cold will provide ideal conditions.

The traditional low level approach round into the floor of the coire is slow, and even more so in snowy conditions, so the steep frontal assault is better. It's a real flog up the relentless slopes, but the great coires of Liathach are in full view all the way, and this, together with the anticipation of the wonderful climbing that awaits you, helps to dull the pain!

THE CLIMBING

While the many cliffs of Beinn Alligin and Liathach are all sandstone – usually wet and vegetated and superb for winter – Beinn Eighe is largely quartzite, an old sterile rock producing little soil and therefore producing only moss in the drainage lines, but also heavily fractured, so very helpful in both summer and winter. Exposure is the single most memorable feature of climbing on Far East Wall. Smooth walls cut in underneath you, and very few features interrupt the dizzying drop. Of course you know there really are holds down there, how else could you have got to this point?

Although the quartzite is very smooth with little friction on the vertical faces, it is rough and often knobbly on the horizontal plane. Geologists say that the knobbles are metamorphosed worm casts (Pipe Rock). There must have been a lot of worms. These rough square-cut edges are all but invisible from below, so do not be intimidated by the dauntingly smooth appearance.

In 1980, Brian Sprunt and Greg Strange climbed (and narrowly avoided) *The Reaper*, on the big smooth wall at the left end of the cliff. Brian's story of running out of strength 50 feet above his runners and resting by hooking his chin on a ledge inspired me to make multiple visits over the next ten years. Despite Brian's epic, I discovered that a more cautious approach was possible as the walls usually had both runners and holds.

◀ Graham Tyldesley on Ling Dynasty (E5).
Photo: *Julia Harker.*

The Far East Wall and the Eastern Ramparts (right).
Photo: *Colin Threlfall*.

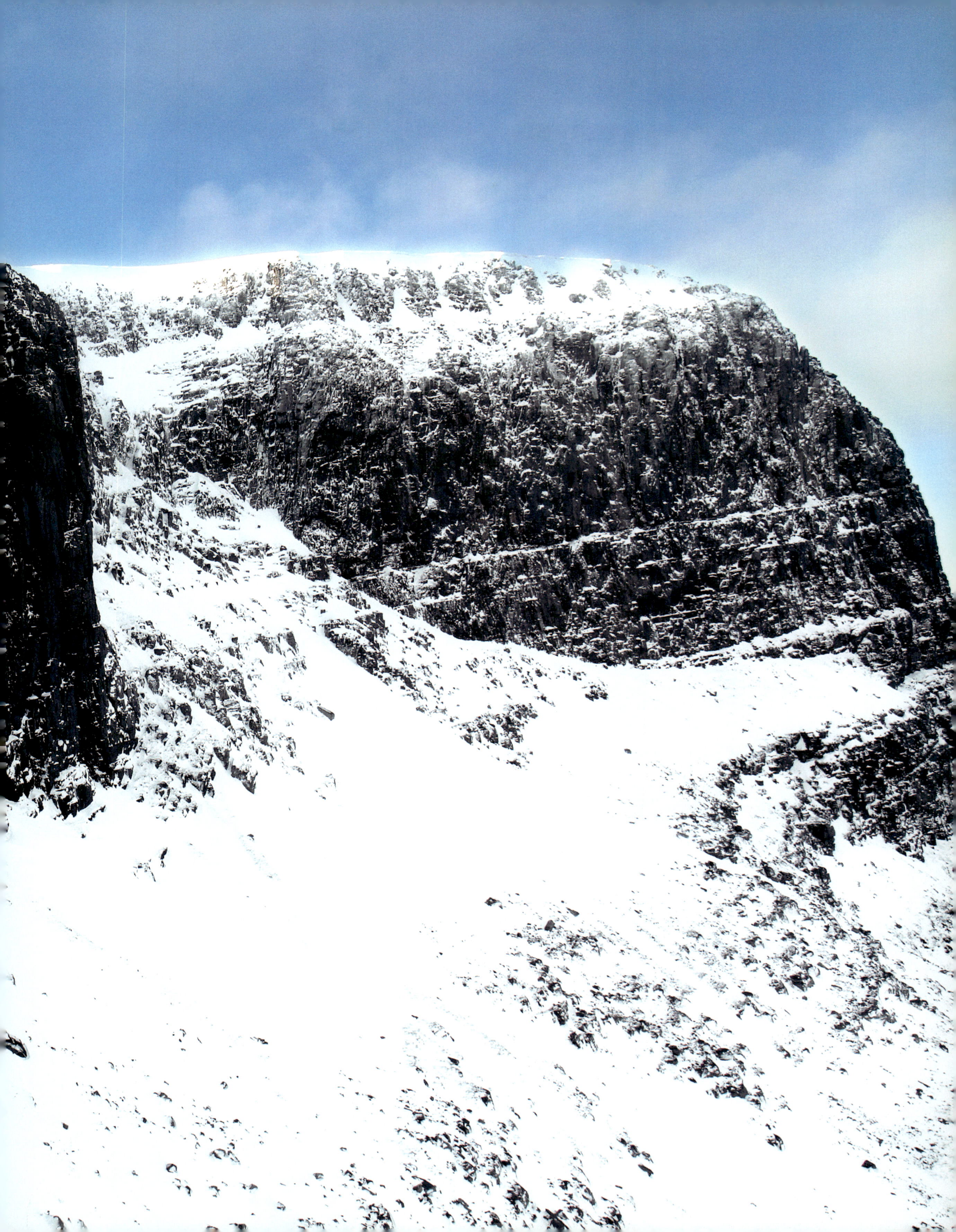

▲ Pete Macpherson on the first winter ascent of *One Step Beyond* (IX,9). Photo: *Guy Robertson*.

THE ROUTES

Ling Dynasty (E5)
A soaring crack-line, very sustained but well protected if you've the stamina to put it all in. Topped by a big roof, which adds some excitement.

Angel Face (E2)
A series of shallow ramps and hidden cracks emerge out of an outrageous wall to provide a memorable climb at an unexpectedly amenable grade.

Sundance (VIII,8)
Winter climbing on Beinn Eighe has progressed from steep to overhanging. For years Martin Moran tried to persuade me on to the huge corner line of *Sundance*, so steep that a huge icicle from its top roof never had anything to touch, but thoughts of swinging out into mid-air always put me off. Guy Robertson and Ian Parnell finally climbed it in 2008 with the icicle forming some memorably exposed moves round the lip of the overhang. It is very mossy in summer, and gave an almost unique pitch for Scotland at a 'modest' grade of VIII,8.

THE STORY

Since my first day of rock climbing on the Triple Buttress, on an Aberdeen University Lairig Club meet in 1975, I was drawn back time and again to the remote climbing amphitheatre of Coire Mhic Fhearchair. Winter climbing was my passion, and I could hardly believe how little attention these cliffs had received. Only the two easiest gullies had been climbed, plus an indirect ascent of Central Buttress. As an Aberdonian brought up on buttress climbing, it was baffling why the amenable summer grades of the two outer buttresses had attracted no winter ascents. Every last groove had been climbed in the Cairngorms, yet here were huge untouched cliffs.

A highly publicised one day ascent of Central Buttress in 1978 finally forced me into action. An early attempt on West Buttress reached the lip of the coire but here gale force winds scouring the lochan left us soaked and disheartened. I was soon back, and a successful ascent in very snowy but dry conditions introduced me to the Beinn Eighe style of steep snowy rock and good cracks. We were just in time, as it turned out, Murray Hamilton and Hamish MacInnes climbed the same route only a couple of weeks later.

In those early days, all but the left wall of Central Buttress was too steep for me, so it was to there that Pete Barrass and I were driven after a storm forced us out of Braeriach in the very cold December of 1981. Despite the relatively easy angle, the huge face was still intimidating, and we had a scary struggle up the hollow ice of *East Gully Direct*. Another tricky mixed pitch took us up to the base of the main wall just as darkness also arrived. I remembered how much I hated abseiling, so I pushed on into an expected epic, but the first two pitches were straightforward and some tricky moves near the top weren't going to stop us.

There would clearly have to be a jump in grade for any more routes, so my attention switched elsewhere. However, after Colin MacLean had torqued me up *Nymph* on Lochnagar and opened my eyes to climbing steep cracks, the huge possibilities on Beinn Eighe re-entered my imagination.

After a splurge of ice climbing in the exceptionally cold winter of 1986, at the end of which Rab Anderson and Rob Milne climbed their well-publicised *West Buttress Direttissima*, I was again galvanised into action with a winter ascent of *Pelican*, a fine chimney line, but again on the East Central Wall. This summer Severe was far from easy, but I still suspected that an even bigger chimney line on the fantastically steep Far East Wall might also be possible. *Kami-kaze* turned out to be quite amenable despite its appearance, and high on enthusiasm we found ourselves sucked into attempting an even more amazing line – the huge adjacent vegetated fault, festooned with dangling icicles. Perhaps if we'd waited longer common sense would have prevailed, but we were climbing well and decided to give it a go.

Following the entry pitch, Andy Cunningham – the ice man in our team – led on up the second. Despite being very thin, the ice still gave good enough placements. However, it was thick enough to block most of the protection cracks. Certainly I was glad to be seconding, but the overhanging key to the route was soon going to be mine.

I set off with my usual trepidation, hardly expecting to succeed but unwilling to suffer the disappointment of failure, until I met a 'stopper' move. Andy was belayed under the biggest Damoclean icicle I'd ever seen, but it hung well out behind him, the chimney angling out above us towards its source. It was outrageously steep, but since the chimney was a perfect back and foot width and my legs were particularly strong from carrying snowholing equipment round the Cairngorms, the stopper move never came and I was soon through the worst of the overhangs. With an easier angle now in prospect, a bit more determination saw a gently overhanging groove dispatched to reach a reassuring belay above a nice flat Beinn Eighe ledge.

The ground above was still steep – close to vertical – and heavily rimed, so there was no real indication of its difficulty. As the adrenaline ebbed, I was increasingly intimidated by the ground above, but Andy boldly pushed on. After a committing move up a corner he found a good runner and suddenly I began to feel we were in with a chance. Now he worked his way hooking steadily across the wall above me, always finding good footholds but needing a cool head and more faith than I could muster. Eventually he disappeared into the upper gully.

After the usual question, he announced it was fine and the rope made steady progress into what was now total darkness. In those days our axe picks were too steep for ideal hooking, but there was no option on the angular rock, and the threatening sense of exposure was lost in the darkness. I made it into the upper gully without any heart-stopping moments. Two further steep sections were overcome before we finally reached the top at 9 p.m.

We were standing on flat ground in a whiteout. Just behind us in the dark was an overhanging void of big icicles and impending chimneys, and a battle for success and survival. In front of us, just 12 hours away, was a Glenmore Lodge staff meeting and a long day teaching beginners how to climb. For a lovely moment we were in limbo, until a blast of spindrift brought us back to reality. ●

Guy Robertson on the first winter ascent of *One Step Beyond* (IX,9).
Photo: *Pete Macpherson*.

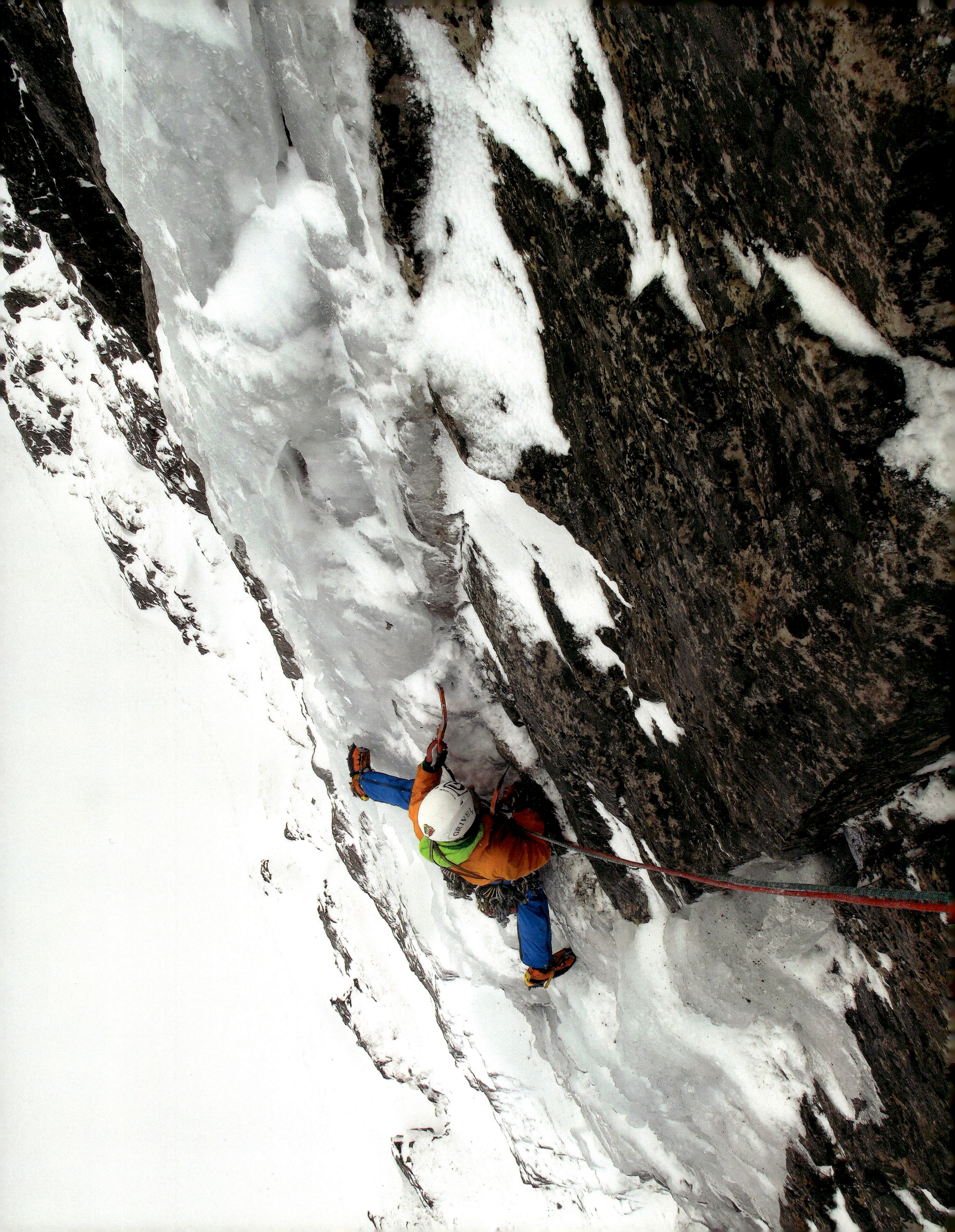
GRIVEL

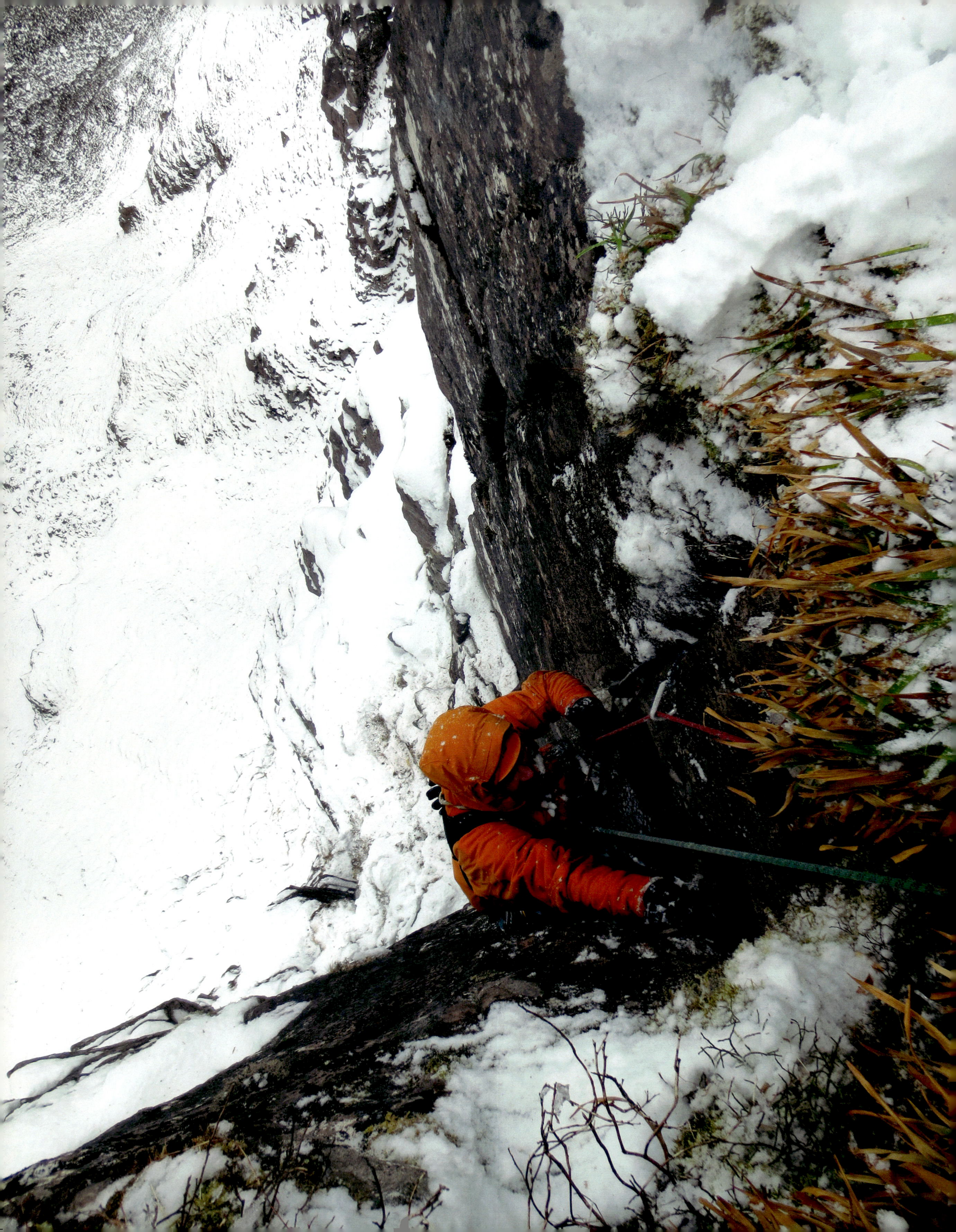

Atlantic Wall, Slioch – by Roger Webb

THE PLACE

On a November day in 1991 I crossed the col that runs south-west from Slioch's North West Face for the first time. My eye was caught by a fast moving dark object about 200 yards away. It stopped, turned and looked at me. It was a wildcat. I watched until it scurried off beneath some boulders.

Only then did I look around me and couldn't help but smile. The view was magnificent – snowy hills rolling away to the north – but that wasn't why I was smiling. I smiled because I had just had my first sight of Slioch's main buttress, the Atlantic Wall. I was in winter heaven. It might not be the biggest or the best cliff in Scotland but it is certainly one of the wildest and most beautiful.

Slioch stands above the south-eastern end of Loch Maree. Its North West Face commands the view along the length of the loch, its cliffs strikingly obvious in the afternoon sun. Despite the impressive prospect, it has a sparse climbing history, having been eclipsed by its neighbours, Beinn Eighe and Liathach. The reasons for this are not difficult to discern – the cliffs are sandstone and vegetated, offer little in the way of ice, and have approaches that put off casual visitors. Nonetheless, since 1933 there has been a determined if small trickle of willing fools, ever eager to look around the corner.

THE CLIFF

Although the climbing on Slioch is now spread out across the mountain, there is little doubt that Atlantic Wall remains the principal attraction. The approach is long at nearly four hours, starting with a pleasant walk from the public car park at Incheril along the bank of the Kinlochewe River, to the bridge across the Abhainn an Fhasaigh at the south-east corner of Loch Maree. From this point the route carries straight on north-west up Coire Smiorasair to reach a col at its head, from where the huge wall springs into view on the right.

The west-facing wall is triangular in shape, about 300 metres across its base and rising 250 metres to a distinctive apex with a flat top. This is connected to the main mass of the hill by a long and well defined ridge. Its right flank drops vertically to Easy Gully, its left more gently to Starters Gully.

The cliff is sandstone, split into four tiers by two steeply angled terraces that merge on the right-hand side of the crag and a thin girdle ledge at two-thirds height. The bottom is largely overhanging but there are breaks at its extreme right edge and about three quarters of the way towards the left. Above the bottom tier the angle eases progressively to the flat.

Being higher than any of the hills to the west, Slioch is extremely exposed to the prevailing winds. This, combined with the length of the approach and the huge scale of the climbs, leads to the cliff having a very remote feel, despite its relative proximity to the road.

THE CLIMBING

The routes here are all strong 'winter only' lines, and apart from the three gullies, depend largely on frozen turf for upwards progress. With a couple of exceptions they would be foul prospects in summer. As the face is convex, route finding is difficult, so it is worth studying the cliff from a distance before starting. The climbing is of a physical nature using a full repertoire of thrutching techniques: knees, elbows, shoulders, laybacks, jams and bridges are all required. On the bright side, the belays are generally spacious, the protection is usually good and the scenery outstanding. A full set of nuts and Friends, plus some turf gear, is recommended.

It wasn't until 1933 that the first pioneers, MacDougall, Cram and Blackwood, completed *Stepped Ridge*, a 200-metre VDiff. This is the ridge immediately left of Atlantic Wall and nowadays makes a great expedition whatever the season. More remarkable was A. Parker's solo of the unclimbed main buttress in 1952 – undoubtedly one of the more committing climbs of his era. In the early eighties, Steve Chadwick and friends explored the possibilities both in summer and winter. He and Ian Davidson did *Skyline Highway*, the first route since Parker's to breach the main buttress, naming the cliff Atlantic Wall as they did so. At this time modern mixed climbing was being developed and in the nineties a new wave of routes appeared.

By 2008 the wall was host to a total of seven routes ranging from III to VII,7, although as none have seen repeats at the time of writing the grades should be treated with caution. This should merely serve to further whet the appetites of those adventurous souls willing to commit and make the effort.

◀ Roger Webb on the first winter ascent of *Morgane* (VII,8).
Photo: *Guy Robertson*.

THE ROUTES

Skyline Highway (HVS, VI,7)

This route follows the right-hand edge of Atlantic Wall. It starts at the bottom right corner below a shallow groove containing distinctive twin cracks and continues up the crest to the top of the crag. Difficulty – but not quality – recedes as height is gained.

The Sea, The Sea (VII,7)

Works its way from the lower tier's left-hand break to gain an elegant groove that splits the centre of the face. It climbs this groove and then continues by grooves and corners.

Slioch Slim Plan (III)

This route has a lowly grade but spectacular situations in its final third. It starts up Starters Gully before breaking out right onto and away across the upper reaches of Atlantic Wall in a very exposed position to join *Skyline Highway*.

The Atlantic Wall of Slioch in winter.
Photo: *Guy Robertson*.

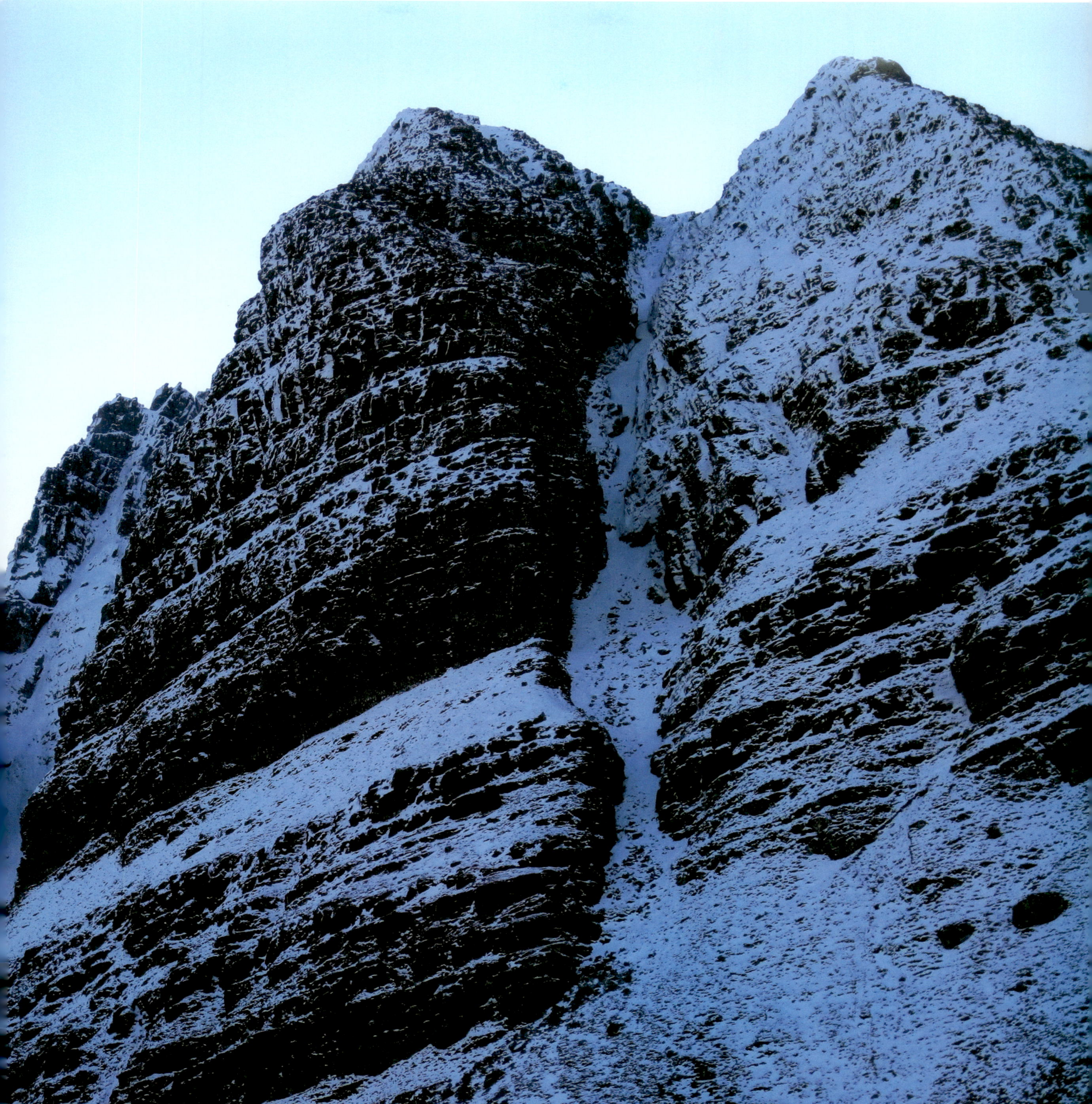

Slioch from across Loch Maree. Photo: *John Port*.

THE STORY

It was January 1993, the first time Neil Wilson and I had climbed together since 1991. That year Neil had broken his femur and I'd been blinded in one eye. In the intervening period we'd learnt nothing, so when the forecast said it would deteriorate late in the day, but not too badly, we took it at its word and paid little heed to the absence of stars on the walk-in.

Three hours or so took us along the flatlands from Incheril across the bridge over the Abhainn an Fhasaigh, through the bogs afterwards, interminably up Coire Smiorasair in knee- and thigh-deep snow to finally reach the col by Meall Riabhach just as dawn was breaking. The rather grey and unconvincing dawn revealed what may be my favourite view: to the north-east, the massive bulk of the Atlantic Wall, whitened by snow and disappearing into the cloud; to the north-west, A' Mhaighdean dominating the empty land; and then south to Ben Eighe and Liathach. The sky was deep steel, the horizon black, the world reduced to monochrome and the wind biting from the west.

We turned to the problem in hand and set off through boulder fields to the foot of the wall, trying not to notice the first scuds of snow that suggested the weather might turn sooner rather than later. Reaching the bottom of the buttress we cast about for a weakness, and being great believers in following our noses, not descriptions, set upon what seemed the easiest line. A slight groove at the right-hand corner of the crag led up to a crack system. We convinced ourselves that this was probably the line of Parker's impressive solo in 1952 and would therefore be quite reasonable.

▲ At the base of Atlantic Wall, looking south to Torridon. Photo: *Guy Robertson*.

I led the first pitch – fine, thrutchy bridging, helped by convenient dods of turf leading to twin cracks. I laced them with gear and contemplated the world. The cracks were finger-sized and sloped left to right. About four moves away I could see turf overlapping a ledge. There were no apparent footholds, my glasses were steaming up, and my axes didn't want to stick in the cracks. On the belay Neil was beginning to shiver. I contemplated some more, told myself I'd wanted to climb this buttress for five years, took off my gloves, left my sack on a runner, and, front points scraping and axes dangling, laybacked the left-hand crack. When in range, I grabbed my right axe and swung for the turf and in one ungainly scrabble pulled and mantelled onto a ledge. The rest of the pitch was in the same idiom, until quite by chance after a series of physical moves I found myself sitting on a ledge, so I belayed. Neil came up grunting that Parker must have been a hard bastard! Pitch two was more of the same, but with turf and gear exactly when needed, making the hard seem easy.

We arrived on the first of the terraces, which was smaller than expected. A beautiful exercise in bridging then took us to a second terrace, more a very long ledge – a kind of pavement circling the buttress at two-thirds height. From here, climbing – that would have been pleasant but for the rapidly degenerating weather – led in three pitches to easy ground and the big square block that marks the top of the buttress. I'd arrived on its other side a month earlier with Charlie Hornsby after climbing a gully on the left flank. Above this a further 150 metres or so of grade II ground leads to the summit of the mountain, which must be traversed to get home.

Despite the now raging storm, I was confident we didn't have a problem. I remember turning to call to Neil when quite without warning I was blown off my feet and dumped violently back to earth. I lay stunned. As reason returned it dawned on me that we now had a very big problem indeed. I had never encountered such a wind in Scotland and never have since. I couldn't risk moving – when I tried I was flattened immediately. Communication was as impossible as movement, and to make it worse the snowfall intensified. For the first time I considered that in all likelihood the weather was going to kill me. Just then, a hand tugged my foot and Neil crawled up beside me. Clearly, 'impossible' was not a word in his vocabulary.

He screamed in my ear. I heard snatches of speech: 'stay!', 'die!', 'move!', 'out of the wind!'. I considered the options. He was right. Staying meant dying. Up was out of the question. Yet back down the way we had come would be into the full force of the storm. To our right was Easy Gully, if we could get into that we would be OK. We came to a shouted agreement, then, still lying down, retrieved the ropes and set up an abseil.

To our good fortune, every now and then there was a relative lull and in one of these Neil set off down the slope to our right. He was lost to my sight as soon as he departed, I was left alone in a maelstrom with a pair of taut ropes. After 40 minutes or so, they went slack. Shivering violently, I clipped on and, flattened by the wind and blinded by the snow, followed them down. (In the spring, when retrieving gear, Neil was able to walk down this abseil!) I found Neil on a sizeable ledge with an equally large belay. He pointed through the murk: in the light of the head torches I could make out an edge. We pulled the ropes, praying that they would come, and on the grounds that he could see more than me, Neil set off again. His light disappeared over the edge and again I was left alone with the wind. A long, long time went by. My shivering had become uncontrollable when the ropes went limp. I seized them as fast as shaking hands allowed, clipped on, and followed clumsily over the edge.

What a transformation. As soon as I was in the gully it was as if the wind had been turned off. I was in a snowflake world of silence. Below me I could see the gleam of a torch, surprisingly close, and when I touched down next to Neil I understood why. He was on a single foothold belayed to a single Friend 1½, whilst below him there appeared to be nothing but snowflakes and night. The gully walls were overhanging, the bottom out of sight. We considered the likelihood of the drop being greater than 50 metres and realised that in our state we didn't have much choice. This time as Neil had a foothold and I didn't, I went first. This was a spooky spinning descent; every now and again my torch beam would light up the gully walls, at other times I might as well have been in space. Eventually, white showed beneath me and I touched down in deep soft snow. I looked up, I could see Neil's light, something had changed – it was raining. Neil joined me, together we pointed out the obvious – 'it's raining and we are in a snow-filled gully'. And so, trailing ropes out behind us and fuelled by fear and adrenaline, we charged down to the open hillside.

Burns had become rivers and bogs become lochs. Twice we linked arms to wade through thigh deep water where there had been open ground in the morning. Our soaked sacks trebled in weight, and the distance had somehow quadrupled. 24 long hours after leaving the car, we stumbled back into the Ling Hut.

Guy Robertson on the first winter ascent of *Morgane* (VII,8).
Photo: *Roger Webb*.

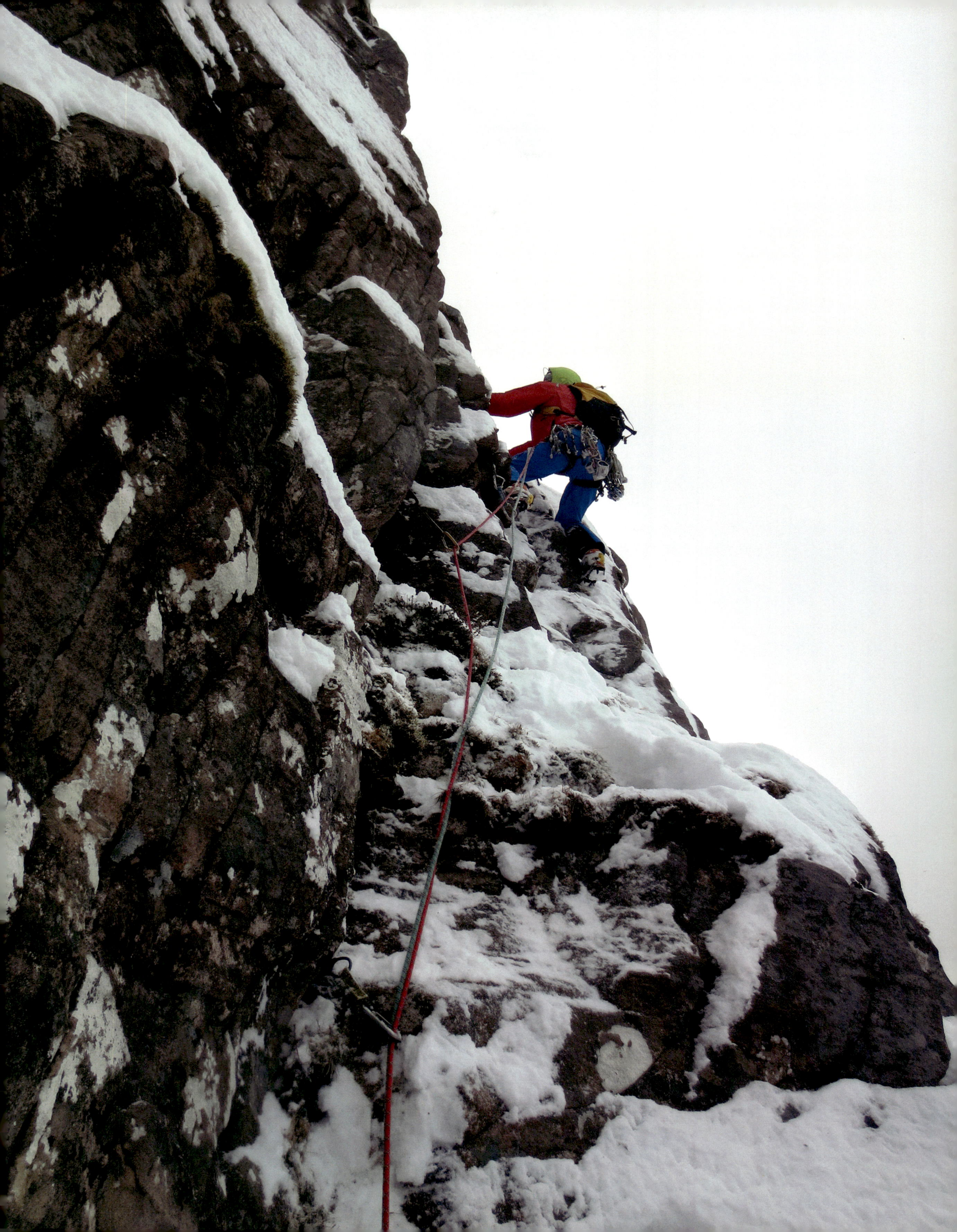

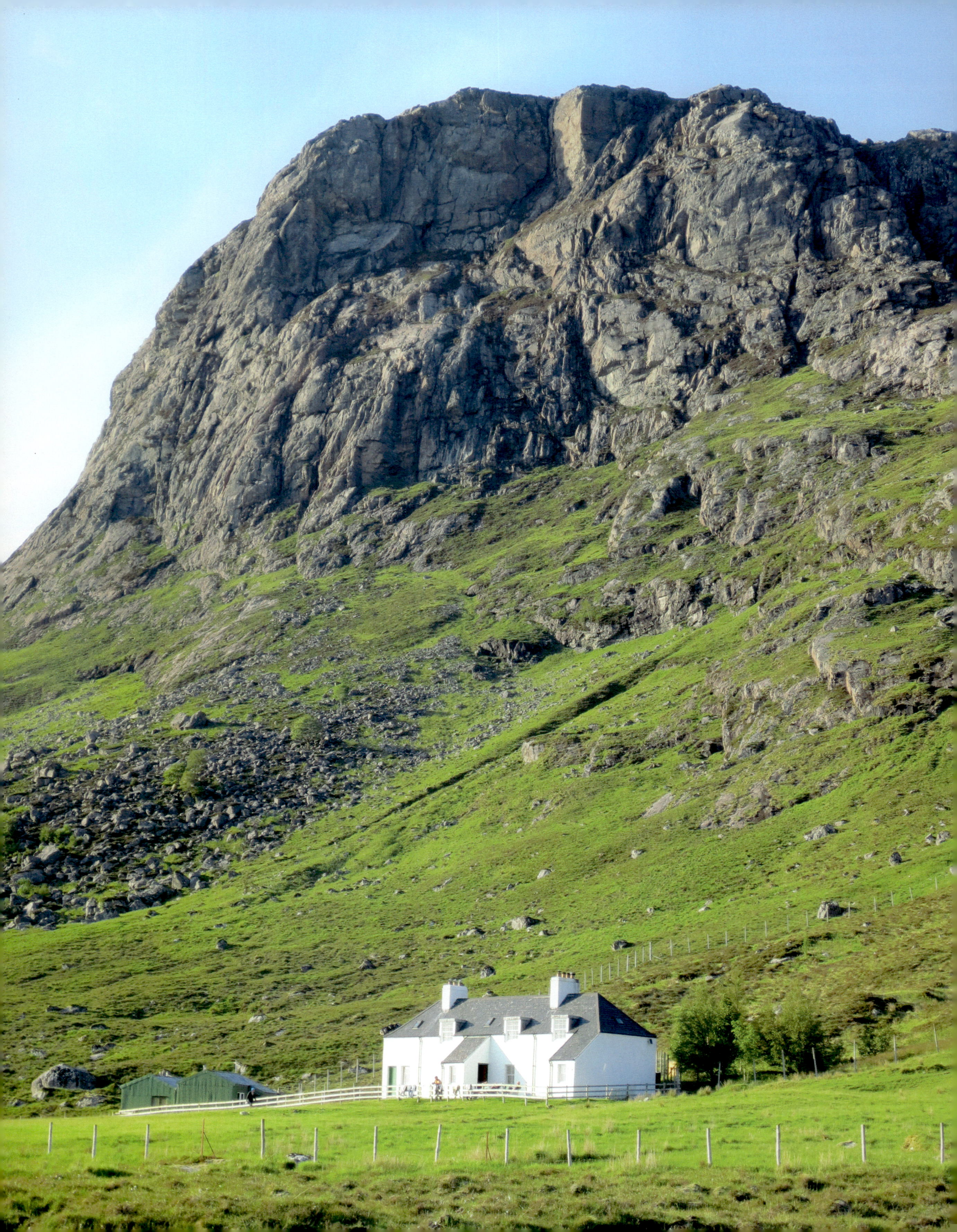

Cárn Mór – by Graham Tyldesley

THE PLACE

Cárn Mór is set close to the heart of one of Scotland's widest and wildest tracts of bog, heath, crag, mountain and loch. The contrasts inherent in this landscape reflect its impact on the soul. Look one way and a seemingly boundless desolation assaults the eye, but turn the other way and there is a grandeur that will lift your spirit. Here you can forget about yourself and your responsibilities, yet you are forced to contemplate your place in the world.

The dimensions of this expanse of roadless terrain both inspire and discourage. It is a land penetrated by few people, defended as it is on all four sides. In the south lies the mighty Loch Maree; at times benign, but in an instant whipped into a frenzy by a westerly squall. In the east the hills roll on and on before any road is reached. To the north An Teallach dominates, distracting most people from what lies beyond and fending off the rest. To the west this land spills out, funnelled through glens and spread into impenetrable bogs before civilisation is finally encountered, dotted about the coastal fringe.

This remoteness is integral to the Cárn Mór experience. People plot and scheme about opportunities to climb here. Should we nip in on the bikes for a quick hit, or lug in more gear for a weekend or longer? Can we borrow a canoe to cross Loch Maree or should we just shoulder the packs and get trudging? For climbers willing to make the effort, this is a place to immerse yourself in climbing, landscape and adventure.

THE CLIFF

The cliff itself looms above a tiny oasis of civilisation, the hunting lodge of Cárn Mór and its barn sitting rather incongruously at the head of Fionn Loch. When staring up from the banks of the loch what draws the eye depends as much on your agenda as it does on the immediate allure of the cliff. With the exception of a clear demarcation between upper and lower tiers, it takes a bit of effort to disentangle the various features from the hillside. However, once you focus on one part of the cliff, the routes begin to stand out.

The feature that perhaps does not need highlighting is the wide open book corner which sits proud at the top of the crag, just right of centre. The simplicity of its structure compels further exploration. Some may dismiss the corner and its binding walls as being short yet they hold much appeal to the modern climber. There are obvious lines that draw the eye across and upwards: a thin groove, a bold arête and a slice across both pages. The position of the buttress, and in particular of the right-most arete, rivals that of any piece of rock in the country.

Moving left beyond the great corner, an enormous roof sweeps across the crag terminating at the bulging barrel of rock through which two ferocious ramps cut. The walls and slabs leading up to the roof hold a mixture of delights: slabs, walls and corners. Before merging into the hillside again at the left-most end, slabs extend up the full height of the cliff providing continuous mountaineering routes to rival any in the country.

THE CLIMBING

As one might expect of a relatively low-lying and south-facing cliff, no winter routes have been recorded here. The character of the cliff is multi-faceted, therefore the climbing demands a comprehensive range of climbing techniques. Compact sheets of clean, thinly-featured rock standing vertically provide commanding lines that are surprisingly amenable – immaculate gneiss covered in positive crimps, sidepulls and undercuts provides superb, technical, occasionally run out but totally absorbing climbing. The most notable feature is the tremendous exposure, which is served up in equal measure by the vast, open outlook and a marked steepening of the rock on the upper tiers.

To warm up, there are rough pocketed slabs – for example, the first pitch of *Dragon*, leading up to steep climbing through capping roofs and flying ramp-lines. Randomly located across the crag are deep oblong pockets, which compel you to place cams, irrespective of how easy the climbing is, for the sheer delight of placing good solid gear. And you will never forget the flexing flakes, which provide good holds only to those light of touch and gear only to those light of head. The harder lines all contain bold sections, and this combined with the exposure ensures a cerebral experience as well as a good test of finger stamina.

Much of the initial development of the crag was carried out by teams from Cambridge University. I like to imagine these gents, with the aid of their butlers, ferrying in supplies for the weeks spent in the wilds: caviar, bottles of claret and Cuban cigars – all the necessities for some serious climbing. The number of routes they contributed is staggering and is sure testament to the protagonists' love affair with the place.

◀ Cárn Mór behind Carnmore Lodge.
Photo: *Guy Robertson*.

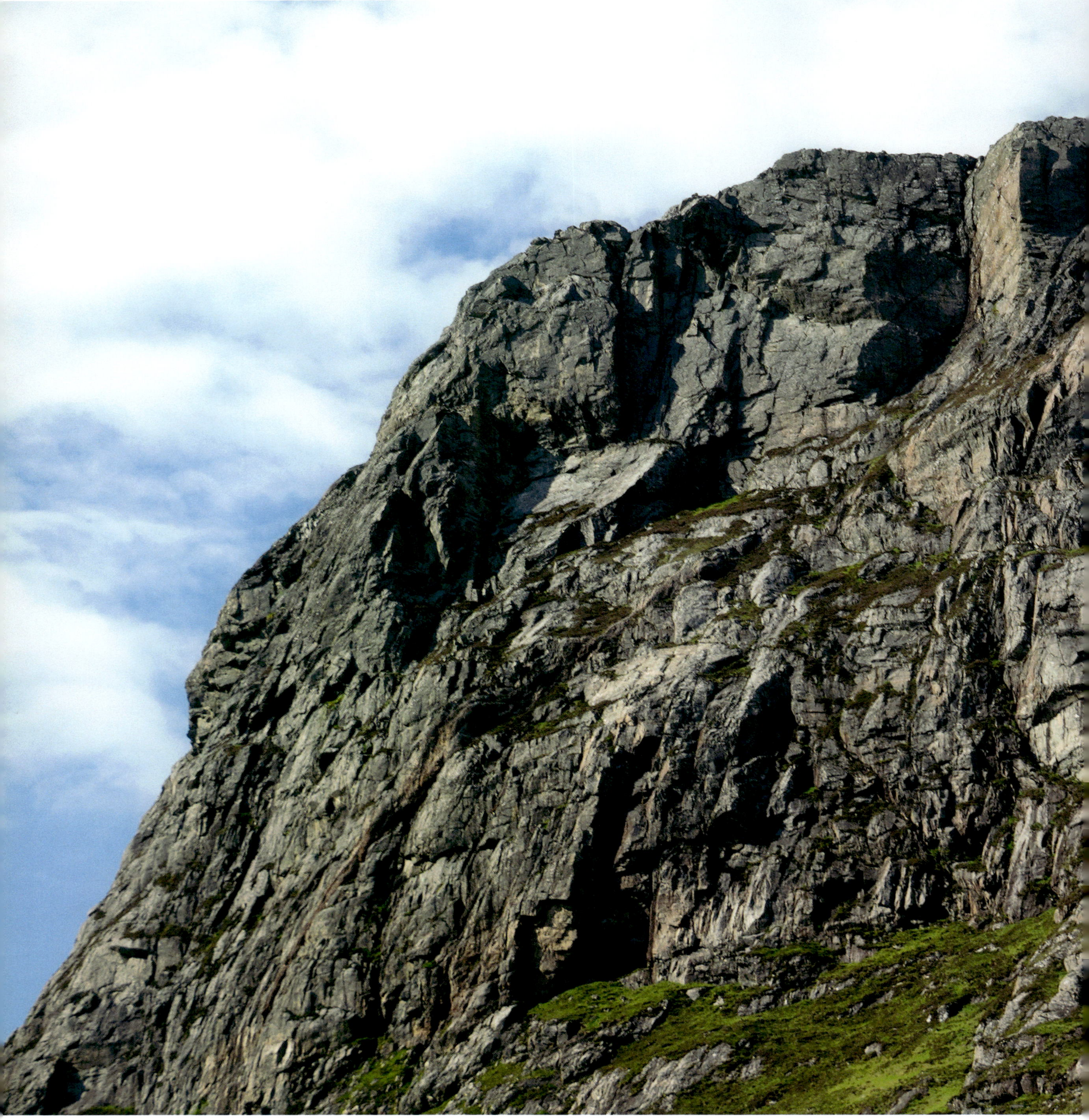

Dougie Mullin's *Wilderness* (E4) laid down a gauntlet at the start of the eighties. Previous new routes had been recorded even when the participants had resorted to the use of aid, yet here was a hard route put up ground-up, free and completely on sight. This route, leaving a crack line and forging up the seemingly blank wall above, was surely a daunting undertaking.

Since then the development of the crag has been largely the preserve of Aberdonians. Dinwoodie and partners ticked off many of the choice lines: *The Lion Rampant* (E5), picking its way across tiny flakes and edges, was emblazoned on the central wall in answer to the surrounding *St George* (E1), *Dragon* (E1) and *Sword* (E3); exquisitely poised, *The Orange Bow* (E5) was set aquiver on the right-most edge of the open book corner; and perhaps the most impressive route, *Deathwolf* (E6), clawed its way up the right-hand ramp line cutting through the steepness of the barrel-shaped buttress on the left. For this route Dinwoodie was partnered by Graeme Livingstone and they only gained access to its upper reaches after two days of sparring with the fierce first pitch. All went quiet for well over a decade until Guy Robertson and Tim Rankin added a couple of routes including the sure-to-be-classic *Fian Grooves* (E3). Great potential for exploration undoubtedly remains.

THE ROUTES

Fionn Buttress (VS)
A really big buxom climb for all comers; a good time guaranteed. It takes a long and complex line up the big buttress on the left edge of the crag

Dragon (E1)
Unforgettable. Full body wedge is de rigueur on the edge of the abyss. The line gains and follows the big left-slanting crack under the roof.

Wilderness (E4)
Clean, steep wall and crack climbing on perfect rock up the left arête of Cárn Mór Corner. One of the best climbs of its grade anywhere.

◂ Cárn Mór Crag.
Photo: *Colin Threlfall.*

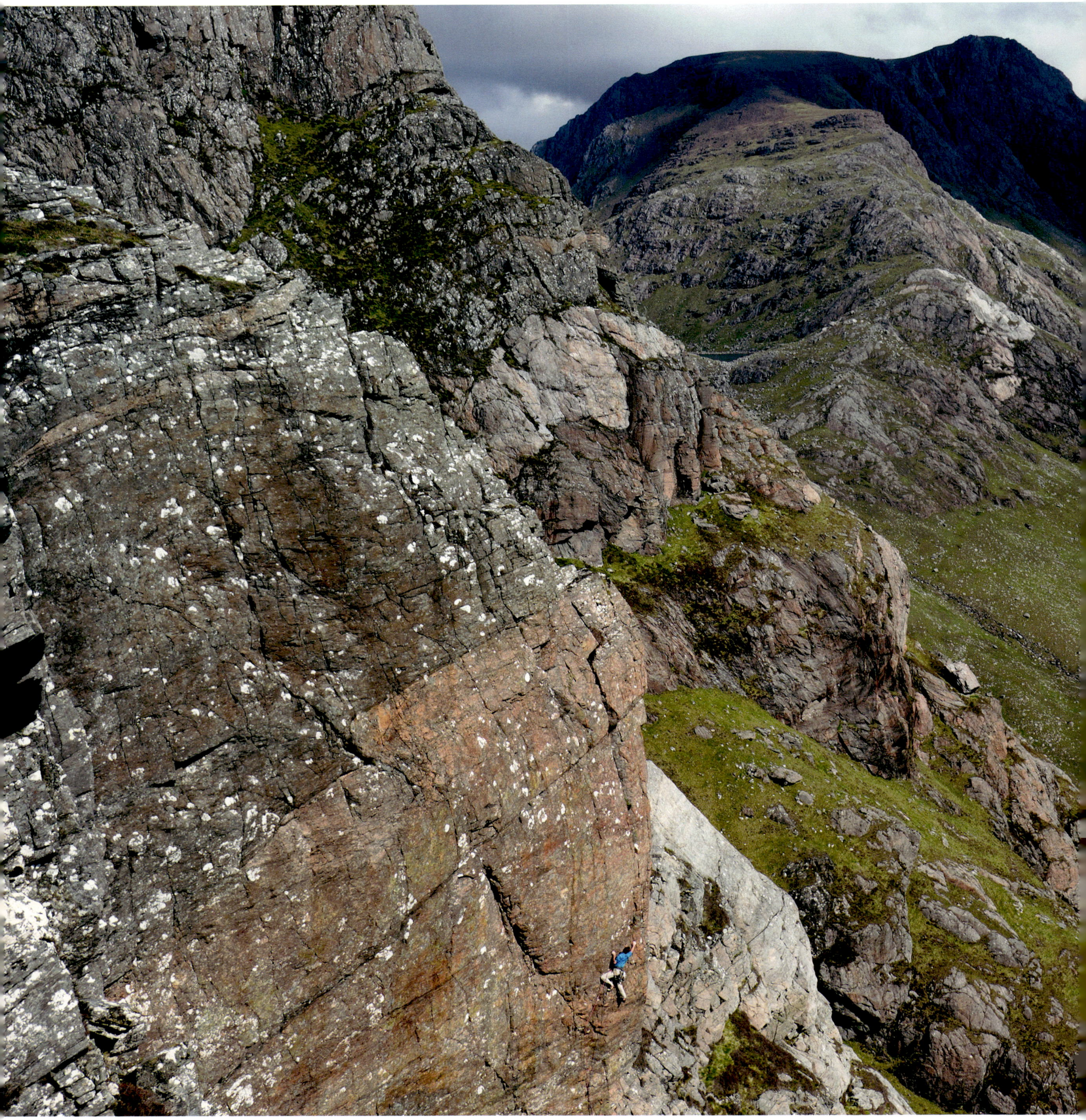

THE STORY

The capacity of a crag to captivate your thoughts, to set you dreaming, before, during and after a climbing trip, is surely the measure of it. For me, Cárn Mór has done this and continues to do it like few other crags can.

To start the process you need information, but a good dose of mystery helps too. The information does not have to amount to much, indeed for some people the plotting of adventures is most enthralling when that piece of information really is tiny, a mere kernel: just a photo in a book, a comment from a pal down the wall, or a glimpse of a crag as you walk past on your way into the hills. Most of us are inspired by the guidebooks we hoard. I love the challenges that guidebooks lay down. Some challenges are obvious — a three star route with immaculate rock in a stunning location, for instance. Others are slightly obscure: features that are described but that are not mentioned as routes; blank spaces on topos.

In the case of Cárn Mór I was drawn to the words 'seldom repeated' when I first read about it in the guidebook. These words and the route name *Wilderness* resonated in my head. And for me the grade was right for dreaming — it was just a bit too hard!

A few years passed before I made my way out to Cárn Mór. In that time I had improved a bit, the guidebook had been updated and *Wilderness* had been climbed a few more times. Suddenly it became a route highly recommended by the authors. Loose rock had turned into a pristine wall but the grade had gone up a notch. Still the words 'seldom repeated' were there, although how true they were, who knows. My motivation certainly had not changed. I had an enthusiastic partner, Russ, and a good forecast: brisk northerlies to keep the biting beasts at bay, some sunshine and no rain. Off we set.

◀ Guy Robertson on *The Orange Bow* (E5).
Photo: *Colin Threlfall.*

The crag appeared across the loch for the first time. It did not look like much when we were still an hour and a half's walk away. It seemed to almost blend into the hillside. We passed many crags and boulders on the way and wondered if anyone had laid hands on them before. On we marched, the spring in our step just about nulled by the weight on our backs. When we reached the barn, our accommodation for the night, we dumped most of our load and hurried up to the foot of *Balaton*, which was to be our route up to the terrace. A few creaky flakes, some steep, awkward climbing and finally a thrilling little traverse on the first pitch gave us access to the pocketed slabs above. Climbing them was a delight, the oblong pockets housing cams perfectly. A bulge to cross provided the crux but Russ barely hesitated as he pulled on through. The next pitch is not given a technical grade and I imagined I would be climbing some occasional loose rock amongst the heather. Instead I had the pleasure of motoring up a clean, rough, grippy gneiss slab for a full 60 metres. I grinned all the way until I heard Russ yelling from below that I was out of rope.

Then we hit the heather!

Soon we were positioned below the main pitch of *Wilderness*. Russ was gracious enough to allow me the honour: 'I suppose you'll want to lead this?' I climbed confidently: sure, precise, decisive movements. Gear spotted, placed and checked before examining the rock ahead and moving on. I quickly gained height. There was a sling hanging from a flake above. It pleased and irritated me in equal measure: it highlighted where to go, where I would get gear and sanctuary but any illusion that I was climbing in a wilderness was removed. Soon I was past the flake and pasted into the thinly featured groove above, the last gear just below my feet. I slowed. Doubt crept out through my muscles and tendons, tightening my once relaxed frame. Why had I climbed that section so fast? Why hadn't I placed more gear? Checked it more thoroughly? I wished that sling hadn't been there, urging me on in haste. I reassured myself and pushed higher into the groove, my feet pressed down hard. My limbs were contorted into a position to squeeze all that I could out of the thin edges of hard, clean rock. I twisted out onto the arête and was soon breathing deeply, and relaxing onto the monster jugs that only gneiss knows how to deliver. Phew, what a pitch! I raced to the ledges above.

But the route wasn't over. We had done most of the hard climbing, for sure, but the experience was far from complete. One of the best bits about climbing on Cárn Mór is the belaying, particularly when you've got a testing pitch under your belt. Sit back and relax. Watch the ravens barrelling down out of the sky above; listen to their throaty, rasping call. Look out to the south and east: a craggy, mountainous crown arcs around you, Gorm Loch Mor held high like a jewel. In contrast, to the west Fionn Loch lies low and flat reaching out, past the Bad Bog and towards the sea. Think about the miles of rough ground that lie between you and your car and appreciate every one of them! Take time to admire the striking arête of *The Orange Bow* or the menacing *Gob* roof curving along the cliff. Lay the fire that will ignite your imagination until the next time.

Despite having climbed the routes I most wanted to do at Cárn Mór I yearn to return more than ever. Unclimbed lines, unrepeated routes and other challenges that are too hard for me at the moment, all in that incredible setting where the ravens rule.

Top: Robert Durran on *Lion Rampant* (E5). Photo: *Dan Moore.*
Bottom: Stuart Walker above Cárn Mór. Photo: *Robert Mott.*

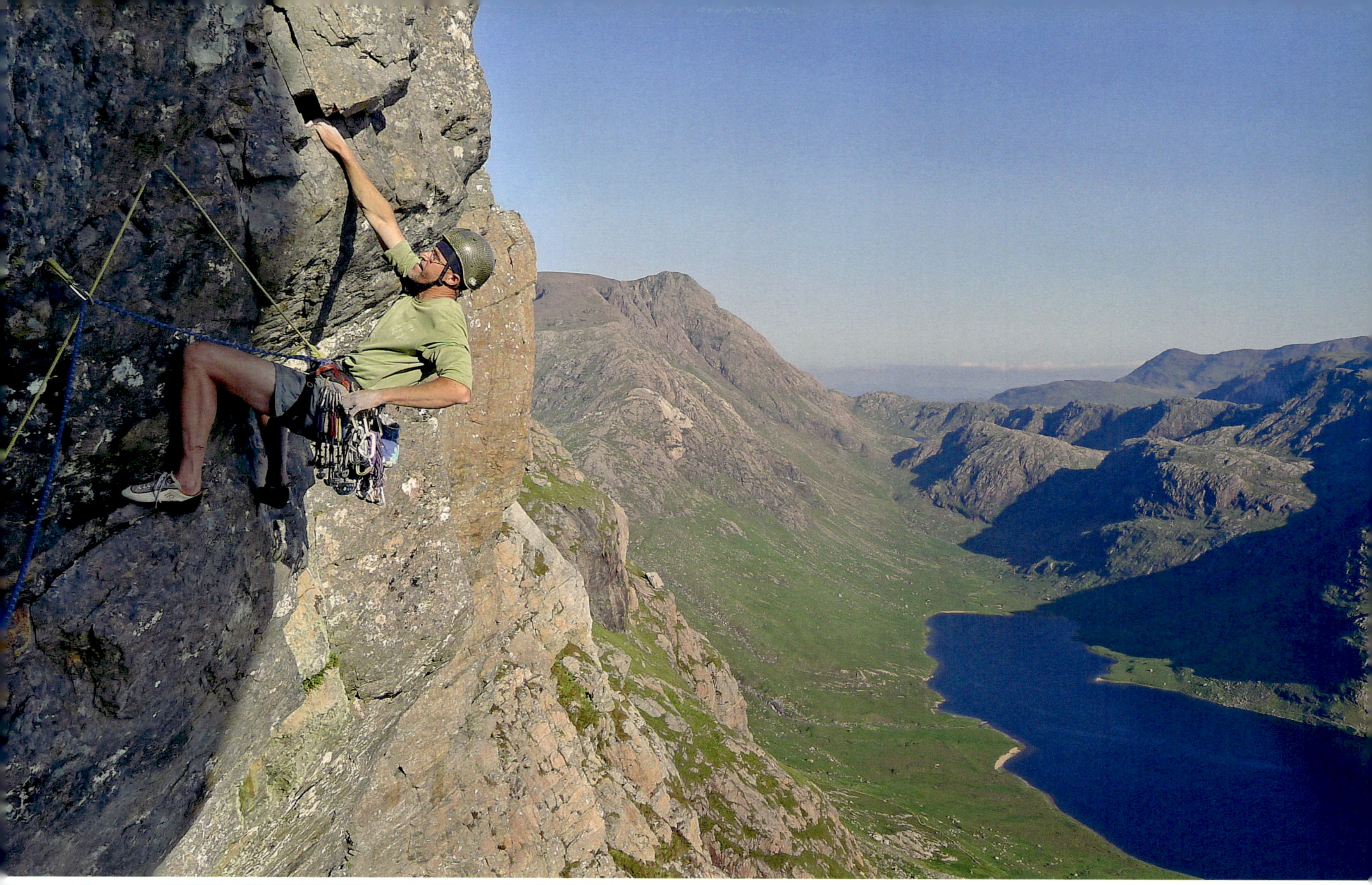

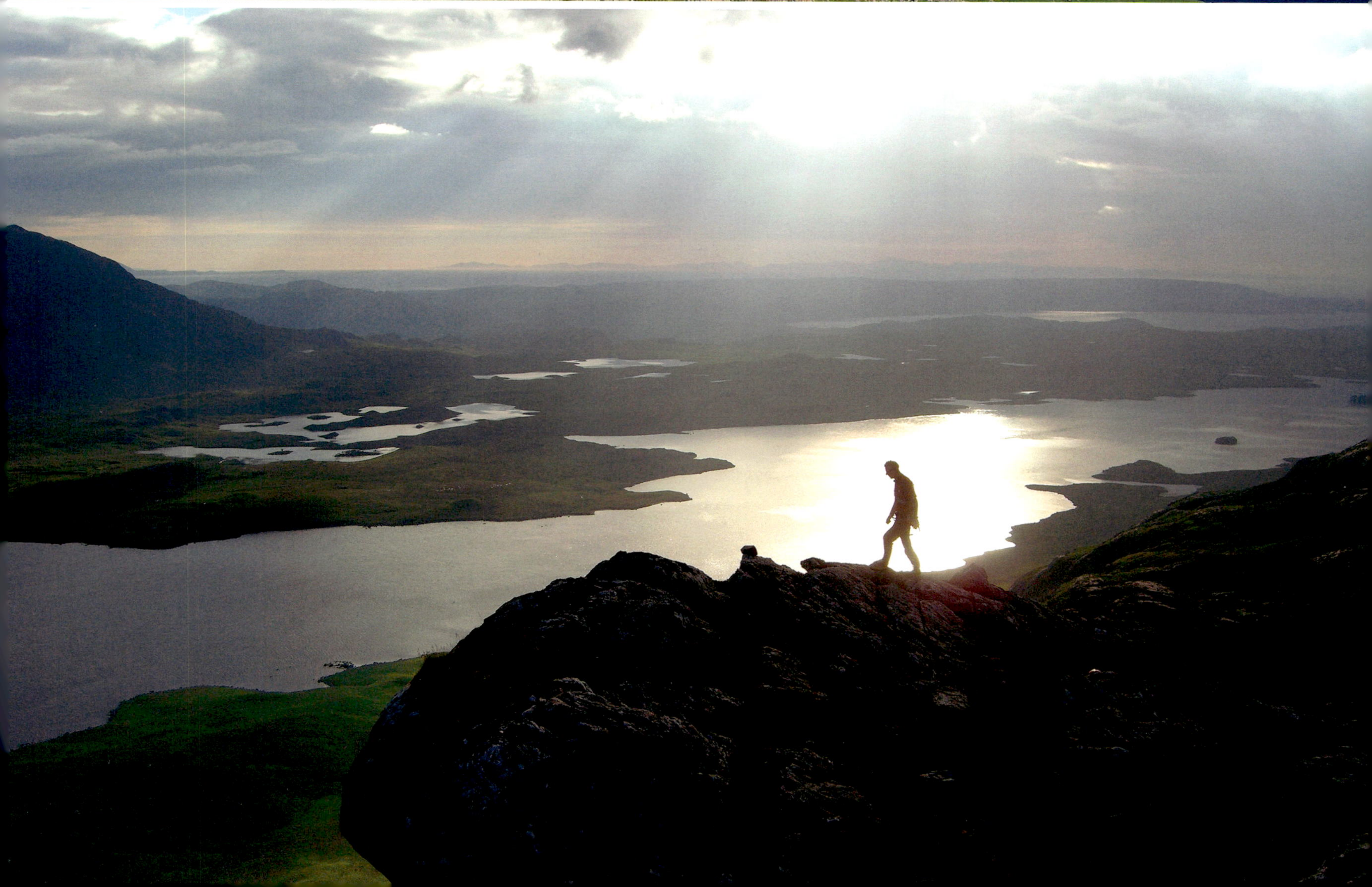

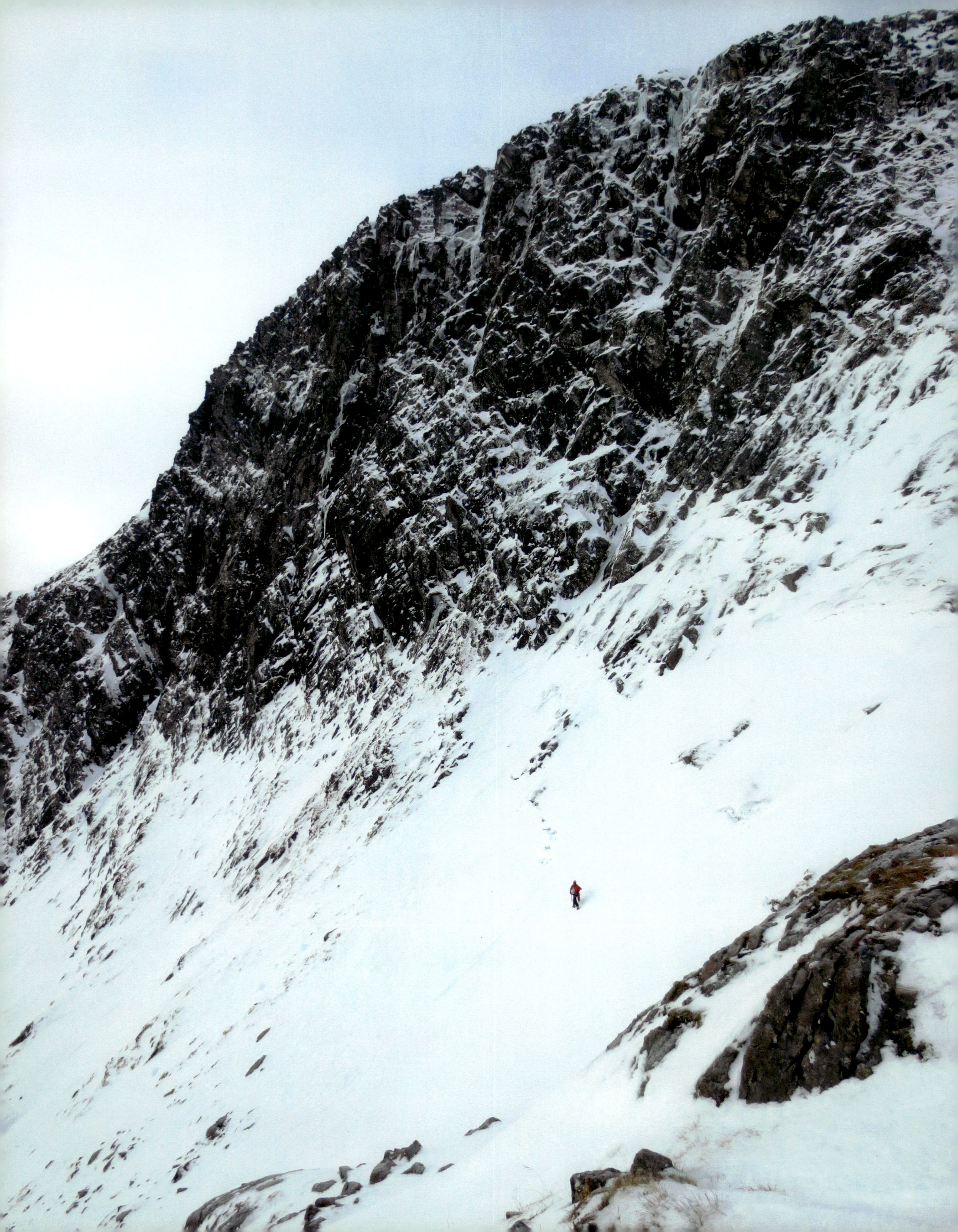

Coire Ghranda Upper Cliff, Beinn Dearg – *by Guy Robertson*

THE PLACE

Do I have any religious views? Yes – the view from the col at the northern limit of Gleann na Sguiab, looking down into Coire Ghranda of Beinn Dearg. From that vantage, the proportions of this most majestic of coires could most certainly be described as biblical.

The dank overhanging bulk of the Upper Cliff sweeps straight into a thousand dizzying feet and more of steep, crag-ridden hillside, treacherous with winter snow, and on down to a great sprawling loch, itself sided by steep crags, drawing the eye out southward to Loch Droma, the Fannaichs and beyond. The depth of exposure is breathtaking, the silence usually palpable. The approach is at least three hours in any direction, the two options being either direct over wild open land to the south from the head of Loch Droma, or, slightly longer but more travelled, on paths to the west from Inverlael.

THE CLIFF

The Upper Cliff of Coire Ghranda is not a place for the faint-hearted, and so far it has convincingly repulsed any attentions from rock climbers. It has all the attributes of the perfect winter crag – very steep, very vegetated and very wet. As is typical of the schistose crags in the North West Highlands, there are few defining features or lines, a fact complicated for the newcomer by a lack of vantage points from which to view the cliff.

Pride of place is given to the great central overhanging fault of *Ice Bomb*, though even this is defined largely by its moisture (or ice) content, rather than a particularly discrete topography. Much further right, almost defining the right edge, is the merely vertical fault of *Body Freeze*, whilst defining the left-hand side of the steep central wall is the similar but more defined fault of *Snort Trail*. In between are great leaning walls of unremitting steepness and complexity, sporting minor features here and there, but generally without continuous weakness. There is really only one way to find out where the weakness lies.

THE CLIMBING

The Upper Cliff will likely always remain the preserve of the winter climber. There are few if any continuous cracks and no easy routes; even those with relatively lowly grades have provided exceptional value on the rare repeat ascents. The rock does not hoar readily, so the focus is on turf and ice, which fortunately nature provides in copious quantities. Needless to say, therefore, less than typical conditions of heavy snow plastering the rock are required to justify venturing out onto the blanker walls between lines of drainage.

Due to the general dearth of cracks and protection, a 'rack for all occasions' is recommended. Friends are certainly useful for the occasional shallow horizontal breaks, while blade pegs, small and micro nuts and ice screws will all come in handy at different times on most routes. The routes are almost all mixed to some extent, typically starting on turf and rock and becoming icier higher up. Most lines have at least one pure ice pitch.

Development of the crag started late – not surprisingly, given the steepness – with the inimitable Mick Fowler commencing proceedings by plundering the great plum of *Ice Bomb* in 1986. Like so many of Fowler's great routes, this stunning line remained unrepeated for a great many years, and is believed to remain so at the time of writing – and like all his hardest winter routes, the grade is just a guess! Fowler went on to add other, easier but still fine lines up the faults of *Body Freeze* and *Snort Trail*. There followed a lengthy lull in activity until the late nineties when, with various partners, I slowly opened up the blank walls in between. First was *Cold War*, just right of centre, which while providing excellent climbing was essentially a failed attempt on the big ice plume. Then the intricate *Tickled Rib* further left, providing more mixed climbing than ice. The plum however was the sustained *Big Chill*, which succeeded in gaining and climbing the striking ice plume flowing from the groove not far right of *Ice Bomb*. My hardest addition however was *Final Destination*, venturing forth with gay abandon into the heart of the huge wall left of *Ice Bomb*.

◂ Andy Inglis approaching the Upper Cliff.
Photo: *Guy Robertson.*

▲ Andy Inglis on the first ascent of *Rebirth of the Cool* (VII,7). Photo: *Guy Robertson*.

▲ Heading into Ghranda from the north-west, with the Upper Cliff just coming into view on the right. Photo: *Guy Robertson*.

THE ROUTES

Ice Bomb (VI)

An outrageous Fowler enigma, up the great overhanging central fault. Unrepeated at the time of writing, this is clearly a first-rate route providing continuously steep and icy mixed climbing. It has been seen more or less fully iced.

The Big Chill (VII,7)

The first big icy line right of *Ice Bomb*. Steep turf and snowed-up rock lead to sustained, steep ice, which was thin to start on the first and only ascent to date.

Body Freeze (V,5)

The major fault at the right-hand end of the steep central section of the crag. This one has had at least one repeat, which found the climbing somewhat stiff at the grade!

▲ Andy Inglis on the first ascent of *Rebirth of the Cool* (VII,7).
Photo: *Guy Robertson*.

THE STORY

Side-stepping carefully out and left, one of the pair now scans the wall. A great icy canvas, as yet devoid of art. His eye traces keenly up, through familiar territories, to a previous impasse where it all ran out. The undisputed blankness that black schist often presents. Dwelling briefly on that point of return, of sure and sudden failure, he shrinks from memories of defeat. Tracing left now, across and away back down, he finds a subtle snow cone flirting with sheer rock; a weakness, a quick decision, and a flicker of his fire.

The ropes are unleashed at the base of the line, and the signs are good. A cooperative fault bristles with vegetation, slanting left to a bulge, from where a line of tenuous icy tears weeps back across right, and so on into a groove, it would seem, and the start of a battle unknown. A quick knuckle-numbing punch up the fault brings blood to chilled bones, then a sinker belay, and the second man soon flights up behind to kick out his place.

Into the fray now, teetering out on the tears, to where a searching grope right for the groove is rewarded with a pick in a crack. Both feet swing in tandem to settle on creases, and the unknown groove now bears gifts. Nuts tumble from the rack like coins from a slot machine. A thin seam yields a high torque on the left wall, for a high step up with the right foot, then the same again, rocking over, to both picks in good turf. A scrabble, a puff, a mantelling heave, and the turf sits solidly under his crampons.

Above is a corner – smooth, black and steep. There's no hint there of turfy goodness, and there's no faint slot for a pick to keep. So he swings back out left, blindly, popping up onto the crest, to where dragging ropes and a tempting eyrie force a second stance. Good cracks, good belay and some good progress for sure. Safe? Enough, at least, to ignore the threat of the bulging wall barring access above. Coils of rope are rushed in, and the shivering second is yanked from his bubble to hack and claw with stiffened limbs up the groove to the stance.

Their words of uncertainty are brief and in agreement; they are only mild in hope. Our second now leads through, from defence to attack, struggling with the sudden shock of the transformation. Soon he's ten feet or so up, axes dangling hopelessly from his wrists, spread-eagled, under-clung it seems on verglas, and looking quite the limpet. With nothing stopping him below, their stance becomes a target, a human bullseye. The belayer concentrates intensely, hounding every twitchy move, surely wishing he was leading and out of the firing line. But the limpet sticks, and slithers haltingly upward, nothing breaking the shared apprehension but the frightened, lurching gasps of his frozen breath. Until a pick is thrown suddenly, repeatedly and with conviction overhead. C'mon! C'mon! C'mon ya bastard! The pick finds a slot.

Several great gasping puffs, and an all-or-nothing heave confines their 'impassable wall' to the history books – for now at any rate. Watch me here! Not hard, but bugger all gear! No worries, it'll save some time, and it's running out for sure. A quick snack. Stomping feet and bouncing shoulders, as the rope feeds quickly out and the second's eyes gaze out into the murk, questioning the depth of the grey, and the lateness of the hour. Then the ropes go slack. Aye, slack, take some in then. What? But that's no ... **whaahooooaaaaayyaaaa**! The Banshee howl booms heavily round the bowels of the coire, both the ropes strike taut, and there's metal clashing metal.

Delayed impact ... **whhhhhhhuuump**!

Jeeezus man, you OK? Oh man, oh man, I don't know, I think so, give me a minute. Any blood?

When does falling become flying?

The clock's tick now echoes alarmingly, such is the hour, and the white murk is turning brown towards the sunset. At this, their third stance, the prospect is undoubtedly the grimmest yet. Any weakness above is reliably short-lived, and no line seems logical in any way. The grooves all fade to walls, all the walls are capped by bulges, and there's no glinting crack to catch the eye. But with battered pride set aside with such stalwart valour below, who would they be to shy away now? At least take a look man, take a look. So he looks, and he looks, and he looks again. Each time he probes tentatively higher, each time he is more committed, and each time the intensity of his awareness of that commitment grows, until he knows – there's no going back. A move up on more frozen moss than turf, with no bite for crampons, arms locked at the elbows and feet smearing an uncertain balance on the smooth, blank schist. Protection still eludes him, and his need becomes acute. The leader must not fall. Fate hangs like a guillotine, sharp and taut around him, as his moves become more frequent, more sure, but less cognitive. It's climbing by instinct. The belayer stares silent at the clean sweep of the rope, momentarily punctuated by a solitary peg, tied off and tokenistic.

The first bulge is beaten, trending left under the worst of it, the second succumbs to a more head-on approach, cranking hard towards the sanctuary of what appears to be a decent crack. Praying for mercy. Brief mercy there is, in the form of a nut, but the crack turns blind and forces wild swings out right, crampons all smearing again until a tiny spike accepts a sling. Then right again, and down. Down? He realises now that there is no line, only the desperate and chaotic clamberings of a man seeking escape, and there, at last, it appears, out of nowhere – a slim groove laced with ice. Once more the cracks all disappear but it doesn't seem to matter; there's a way out up ahead, and the trimmings of ice and turf have returned sure grip to both feet. Head down, into high gear, engage the exit ramps, and they're out of there.

Staring out into the giddying, amorphous expanse of a winter's dusk up high, he feels the clammy cool of relief on frosted cheeks. *The Final Destination*. It's over, and he knows it, but he's spent of any passion. Sleep whispers in his ears as he slowly heaves the ropes. Real life is a galaxy away – driving cars, tapping keyboards, drinking beer, sitting on sofas, watching telly. For a while up there it's just hot blood and wind, grey space and frozen ropes, until the faint jangle of the second becomes louder from below. And then the two are united, slapping backs and shaking hands, sorting the compass and the map and the who-goes-first, the slow grind down. •

Andy Inglis on the first ascent of *Rebirth of the Cool* (VII,7).
Photo: *Guy Robertson*.

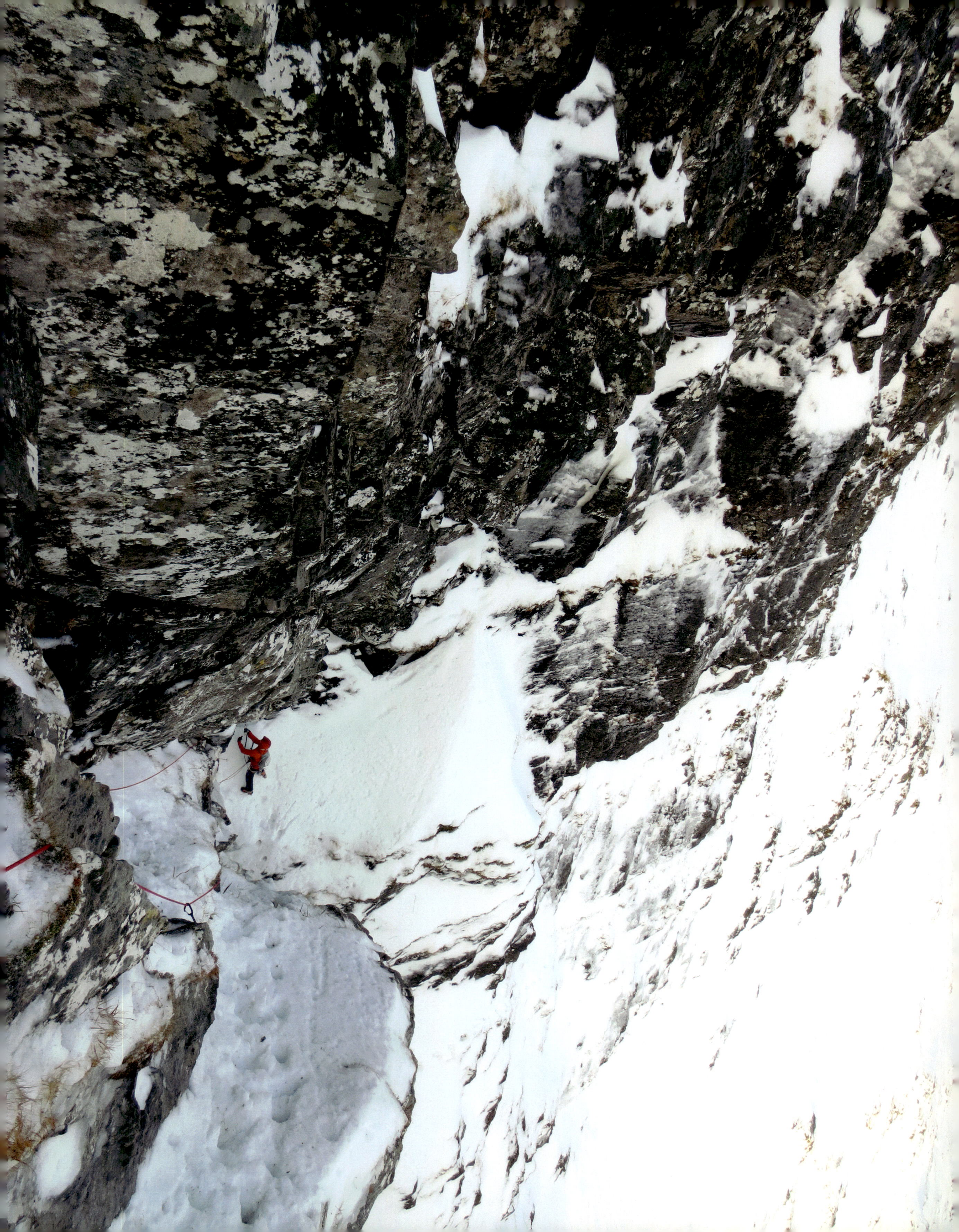

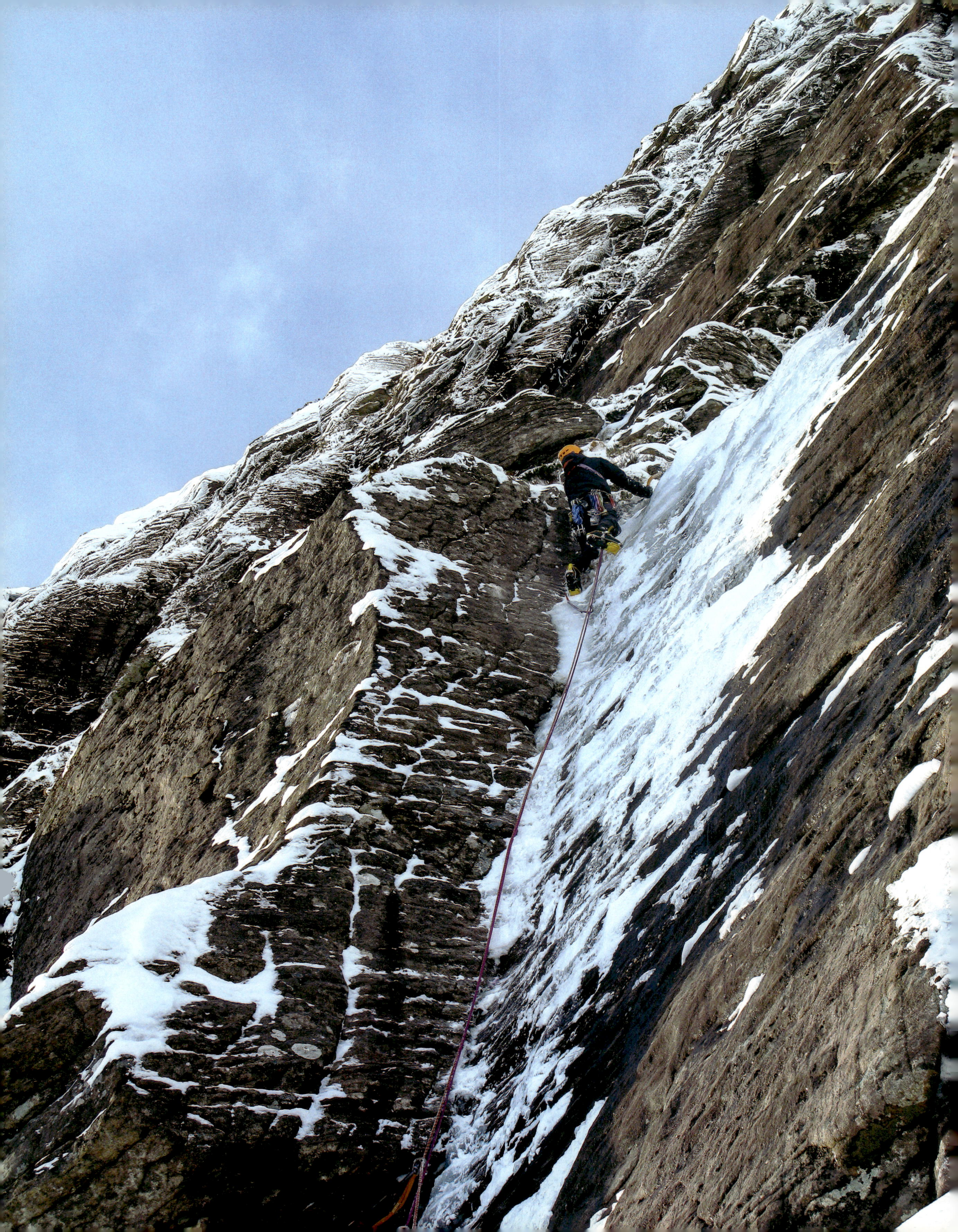

The Fhidhleir's Nose, Ben Mor Coigach – *by Simon Richardson*

THE PLACE

North of Ullapool is a magical land called Coigach. They say the gods practised making mountains here before they made Norway, and, looking at the distinctive peaks, you can see why. Isolated and proud, the steep-sided sandstone mountains rise straight out of a rocky undulating landscape of Lewisian gneiss.

Water is all around, and the surrounding moorland is peppered with countless lochans with the backdrop of the Atlantic Ocean behind. The mountain names – Quinag, Canisp, Suilven – have a mythical, almost Tolkienesque ring that perfectly matches the ancient rocks. None of the summits are high enough to reach Munro status, but the crags are big, steep and impressive and provide some of the best adventure climbing in the British Isles.

THE CLIFF

The northern side of Ben Mor Coigach is home to the main event, the remarkable 400-metre-high Fhidhleir's Nose. This superb Sgurr soars up in a graceful, narrowing arc, ever-steepening to a tapering crest below the summit of Sgurr an Fhidhleir (the Fiddler's peak). To its left, a huge sweep of high angle slabs stretch down to the screes below, and its right flank is guarded by a dark and foreboding vegetated face. The Fhidhleir's Nose is without question one of the finest pieces of mountain architecture in the Scottish Highlands. Nobody knows exactly who the eponymous fiddler was, but one can imagine no finer stage for a Celtic musician, perched on the edge of one of the greatest precipices in the country.

The Nose of Sgurr an Fhidhleir (pronounced *Scooraneeler*) rises up, broad and slabby at first, to the Pale Slabs at half-height. They are composed of lighter coloured sandstone than the surrounding rocks so that they stand out from afar, and are separated by three horizontal terraces. The term 'slab' is something of a misnomer because they are deceptively steep and formed a barrier to a direct ascent of the Nose for over 50 years. Above the Pale Slabs, the buttress rises more steeply for a further 90 metres to the Upper Shoulder where the angle eases and scrambling leads to the small sharp summit.

THE CLIMBING

The irresistible allure of the Fhidhleir meant the Nose was attempted as far back as 1907 by the redoubtable Ling and Sang. In a remarkable performance, they were forced right below the Pale Slabs onto the North West Face and battled up loose vegetation and crumbling rock to the top. Their efforts were not superseded for over half a century. A Cambridge University party led by Pat Baird followed a similar line in 1936 and their route had just two more ascents over the next 20 years.

By the 1950s, a direct ascent of the Nose had attained 'last great problem' status, but it was not until 1962 that it was finally climbed by the talented duo of Neville Drasdo and Mike Dixon. Their climb was a landmark in the development of climbing in the Northern Highlands, but like many great Scottish routes their ascent was more a result of serendipity than long and careful planning. The pair had admired the prominent outline of the Fhidhleir whilst driving south after climbing on Foinaven and then bumped into Tom Patey on his doctor's rounds near Ullapool. After several drams in a local hotel that night, Patey revealed the direct line on the Fhidhleir was still unclimbed and suggested they attempt it the next day.

Early next afternoon they set off up the climb and made rapid progress up to the Hansom Cab stance below the Pale Slabs. Here the angle increased considerably, the cracks became rounded and the strata dipped outward, resulting in a disconcerting lack of positive holds. They were being buffeted by a severe gusting wind, and as Drasdo moved up and right into a little sheltered corner he was soon confronted by a desperate-looking move. 'At first I felt that it was probably impossible and I pondered on the seriousness of a fall in such an isolated position but, as often happens, eventually I adapted to the situation and in one of the calm periods, after breathing out to get my centre of gravity as close as possible to the rock, I placed my foot on an improbably steep surface and found myself moving delicately upwards.'

◀ Chris Cartwright on the first winter ascent of *Magic Bow Wall* (VIII,8).
Photo: *Simon Richardson.*

▲ The Fhidhleir's Nose in winter. Photo: *Es Tressider*.

The 50-year riddle of the Pale Slabs had finally been solved. Patey went on to make the second ascent, and his success drew him back to the sweep of high angle slabs of the North East Face. The first line to fall was *Magic Bow*, climbed with Martin Boysen, which tackles the prominent right-facing groove in the centre of the face. This was followed by *The Phantom Fiddler* (a remarkable solo) and *G-String*. In 1979, the focus returned to the Nose itself, when John Mackenzie added the fine exposed *Tower Finish* to the *Direct Nose Route*.

In February 1979, the strong Aberdeen duo of Norman Keir and Bob Smith pulled off a remarkable coup with a winter ascent of the Nose, and then in 1987 another Aberdeen team consisting of Wilson Moir and Chris Forrest shattered the conditions myth by making the first winter ascent of the *Direct Nose Route*. They thought they were repeating the Keir-Smith line, and it was only several weeks later that Moir realised that they had climbed a completely separate winter route, following the true line up the very crest of the buttress. Thus was born one of Scotland's outstanding hard winter routes.

A winter ascent of the great curving corner of *Magic Bow* was attempted in the 1980s, but the complex route-finding required to negotiate the lower slabs proved too time-consuming. The scale and steepness of the Fhidhleir is both

▲ The Fhidhleir's Nose in summer. Photo: *Andy Moles*.

fascinating and bewildering. Angles are deceptive, and from below, it is often difficult to see a feasible looking line through the maze of hanging slabs and overhanging grooves. Chris Cartwright and myself took up the *Magic Bow* challenge in the late 1990s and made three attempts on the line over successive seasons before we were finally successful in January 2000. The 14-pitch *Magic Bow Wall* deviated from the summer line in the upper third and was characterised by complex route-finding, sustained technical climbing and punishing spindrift. We finally made it back to the car, hallucinating, after a gruelling 22-hour day. The route remains unrepeated, but I returned in 2009 with Iain Small to make a winter ascent of *Castro*. This provides the most natural winter route on the face with a similar standard to *The Direct Nose Route* and deserves more repeats.

In the deep freeze winter of 2010, Guy Robertson, Martin Moran and Pete Macpherson finally solved the riddle of a direct winter ascent of the *Magic Bow* corner with the superlative *Bow Direct*. These three winter lines have only scratched the surface, and such is the scale of the North East Face, that there are many stupendous challenges awaiting those willing to embrace the heady mix of steep technical climbing and complex route-finding up one of Scotland's big walls.

▲ Graeme Briffet on a winter ascent of *Direct Nose Route* (VII,8).
Photo: *James Higgins*.

THE ROUTES

Direct Nose Route Summer (HVS)

Without question this is the premiere mountaineering line in the north west of Scotland. Choose dry conditions and enjoy the exposure and north wall ambience. The original finish takes a crack to the left of the final prow at about 5a, but to savour the true Fhidhleir experience launch out on the *Tower Finish* (E1 5b) that traverses up and right above a huge void and reaches the Upper Shoulder on the very crest of the Nose.

Direct Nose Route Winter (VII,8)

The Fhidhleir's Nose is one of the most sought after high standard winter expeditions in Scotland. The length, sustained difficulty and feeling of commitment make it feel more like an alpine route than a Scottish winter climb. Despite its low altitude, it is normally in condition at least once every season, and has now seen approximately 20 winter ascents. Later repeats discovered a less technical variation to the crux groove, and this has now become the standard way.

▲ The Fhidhleir's Nose from below in summer. Photo: *Andy Moles*.

Castro (VII,7)

To the left of *Magic Bow*, an obvious line of vegetated grooves winds its way through the impregnable-looking North East Face. The steep corner on the third pitch is the technical crux, but it is the section through the band of overlaps above that will always be the key pitch. A tenuous line of turf threads its way between twin overlaps and is the key to gaining the easier upper pitches. The route is similar in standard to the *Direct Nose Route* and a good option for those who have done this great classic and are looking to return!

Bow Direct (VII,8)

The huge north-east side of the Fhidhleir is more sheltered than the Nose, and comes into condition even less frequently. The face catches the early morning sun, and the groove is a prominent drainage line, which means it takes an exceptional frost for the turf to freeze. The hardened winter aficionado seeking the ultimate Scottish alpine experience should look no further.

THE STORY

It's mid January 1991 and it's been below freezing for the last three weeks. Full of anticipation, Roger Everett and I are all set for a weekend climbing in the Northern Highlands, but while filling up with petrol at Inverness I scamper up the grass bank by the petrol station and kick the ground. The earth is as hard as rock. Could this be the moment? Could the mythical Fhidhleir's Nose be in winter condition?

We drop plans for Torridon and head north, Fhidhleir-bound. A quick kip in the car at Dundonnell Junction and we're up at 3 a.m. in a snowstorm. In Ullapool the plan falters as the car nearly fails to surmount a short steep snowy incline, but slowly we inch our way along ghostly white drifted roads, past Ardmair and along the tiny single track towards Achiltibuie. We leave the car at 5 a.m. and set off for the three-hour walk to the Fhidhleir through calf-deep snow.

Dawn breaks as we cross the frozen Lochan Tuath and the eerie purplish hue of a Scottish winter morning illuminates the cliff. It's huge! The massive Magic Bow Wall towers above as we round the prow to underneath the Nose. The way ahead is obvious – a long sinuous turfy groove leads up the lower section and is topped by a square-cut roof about a hundred metres above. By 9 a.m. we're on our way.

The lower pitches go smoothly and after three rope lengths we're below the Pale Slabs. The exposure is now beginning to bite. A solitary distant snowplough passes along the road a thousand feet below. It is a comforting sight and the only sign of people we see all day.

The first 'slab' is far steeper than it looks and I'm soon strung out high above protection facing an ankle-snapping fall. Front points desperately claw for purchase on small rounded holds, my calves are burning and my hands are slowly slipping out of the knotted tape wrist loops.

'C'mon Richardson ... get a grip ... fight the pump and concentrate ... '

I force myself to lock off with one arm and place a baby angle, then make a long reach to a good boss of turf and I breathe again. Little did I know that Patey's variation, now the normal winter way, avoids this difficult pitch by taking the heathery groove to the left of the crest.

Roger despatches another sustained pitch and I'm facing the Third Pale Slab. It's completely white, blanketed in a 15-centimetre layer of soft powder snow. Pitches like this are deceptive because it is natural to equate white with easy, but the snow is impossibly steep and provides no support for axes or crampons. Fortunately the odd single blade of grass pokes through the snow, and, heart in mouth, I set off linking these unseen havens of turfy blobs, picking my way protection-less up a sea of white blankness, to an exposed eyrie on the very crest of the buttress.

January days are short and it is already 4 p.m. Above is the crux pitch, a 30-metre vertical crack where Moir and Forrest had used their point of aid. Roger purpose-fully takes the rack and immediately sets to work. As the gloom of dusk rapidly envelops us, he makes the lead of a lifetime. He throws himself at the crack, and in a continuous dance he flows up it, past Drasdo's first ascent peg and onto the upper crest. Above, we scamper up the upper pitches through the night with the euphoria of a big route welling up in our breasts.

The long descent back to the car passes like a dream. We fall into a waist high bog and it starts to rain as we reach the car, but nothing can dampen our elation. We are supremely happy. We have just enjoyed one of the greatest climbing days of our lives on one of the finest mountain features in Scotland in the very depth of winter. Few experiences in this world can possibly compare.

Guy Robertson on the first ascent of *Bow Direct* (VII,8).
Photo: *Pete Macpherson*.

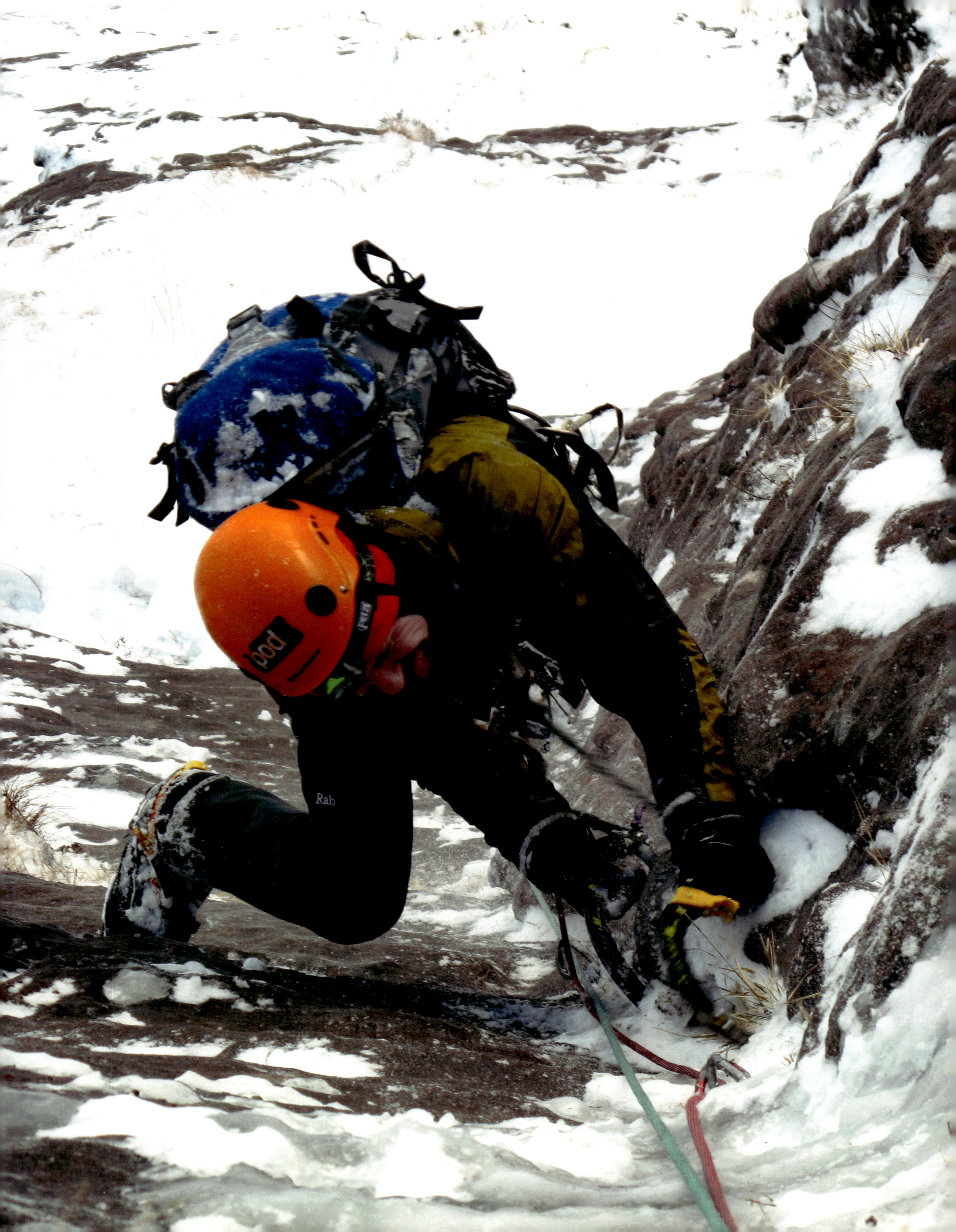
pod
Rab

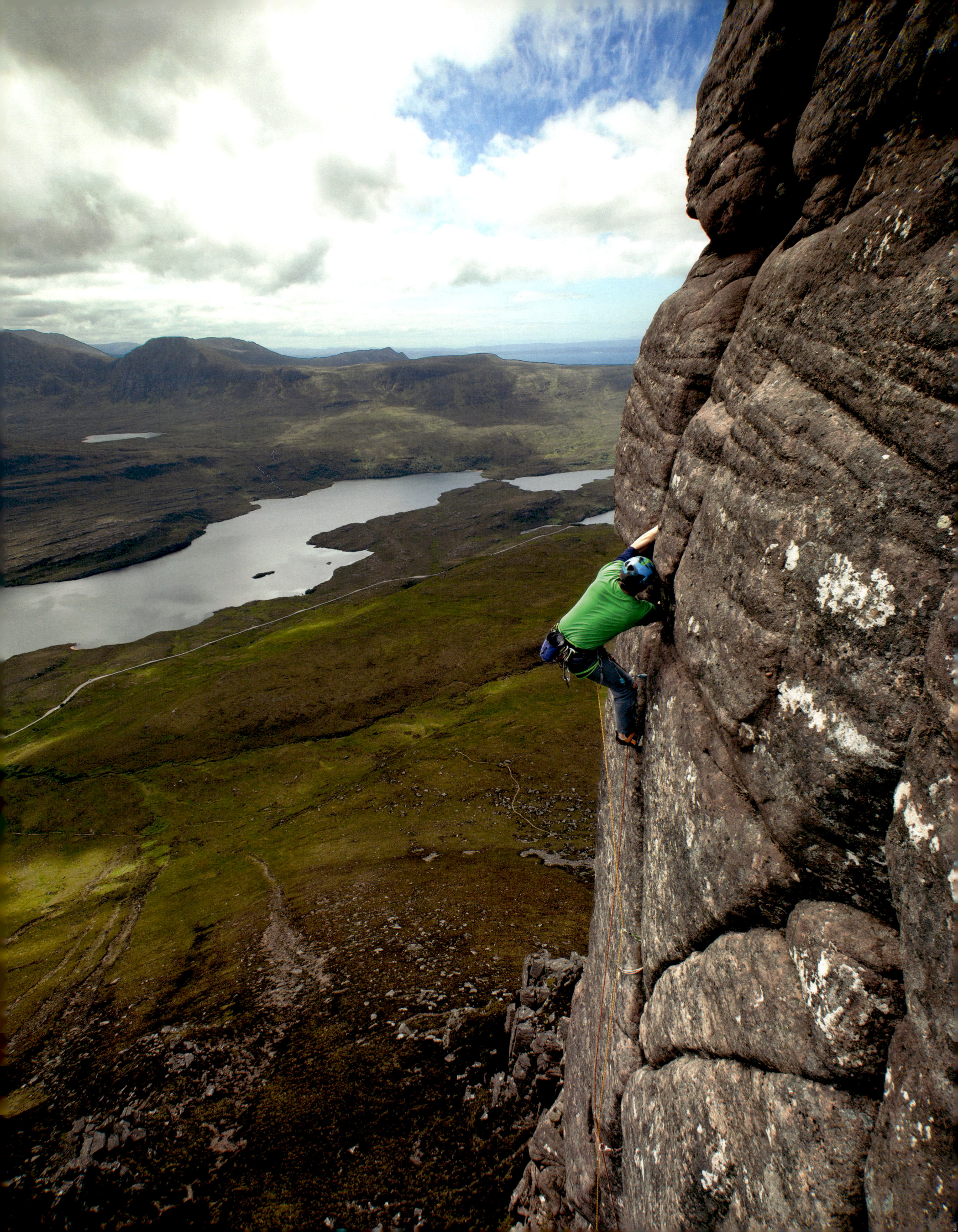

WEST BUTTRESS, STAC POLLAIDH – *by Ian Taylor*

THE PLACE

I first 'discovered' the amazing South Face of West Buttress one perfect June evening in 1988. A quick after-work scramble, up the original West Buttress, left me breathless on the summit. The view was simply stunning. Among the dramatic hills of Assynt, myriad lochans glistened in the setting sun and the burnished sea stretched westwards to the Long Isle and beyond.

In the gloaming I descended the gully back under the buttress to be confronted by an imposing crack-seamed wall. Brilliant, I thought, I shall climb all these amazing routes and become rich and famous. It was only on scrambling closer and peering up at the rapidly darkening wall that I could see a well-chalked line of holds ascending into the gloom. True to form, my 'discovery' was in fact someone else's.

THE CLIFF

There are few mountain crags in Scotland as accessible as Stac Pollaidh. The distinctive serrated ridge rises abruptly from the north shores of Loch Lurgainn on that mad road to Achiltibuie. Any number of Victorian romantics have likened the hill to a fossilised stegosaurus or an irascible hedgehog, but it always looks more like a pile of jagged rocks to me.

From the often-crowded car park the dauntingly steep approach is cunningly avoided via the left fork of a well-constructed path, which leads over to the western shoulder of the hill. When the path levels out, a traverse up and rightwards underneath the cliff base leads to the impressively smooth South Face, and all this in less than an hour.

The situation is dramatic, with the slope beneath the cliff falling sharply away, giving instant exposure from the moment one leaves the ground. The 60-metre sandstone wall is split in two by a large horizontal break. The lower half is raked with thin cracks and the upper wall is divided by a looming, jagged overhang, providing the crux of most of the routes. With the sunny aspect the routes dry quickly and there's often a welcome midge-defying breeze. Immediate impressions are of steep, smooth and unaccommodating rock, only partly relieved by occasional vertical weakness.

THE CLIMBING

Those used to the perfect wave-battered sandstone at Reiff might be in for a bit of a shock. Although it is finest Torridonian, the rock here tends more to the sand and less of the stone and has the occasional bit of lichen for interest. Aspirants are well advised to perfect the 'Stac Pollaidh wipe', this being the quick mid-move clean of your rock shoes on your trouser leg. The cracks, occasionally flared, but generally cam-friendly, can be rough and pebbly. Thin-skinned types might even consider taping up, though this is hardly in the true spirit. When you're climbing on Stac Pollaidh you're supposed to bleed.

The history started in 1906 when the roving Inglis Clark family, together with Charles Walker, ascended West Buttress. The 1950s gave the exceedingly traditional *November Grooves*, and then *Enigma Grooves* in a similar mould. In the 1980s, however, there was an explosion of new routes, and typical of these times there was competition for the plum lines. The result of these frenetic explorations is arguably the finest concentration of big sandstone mid-Extremes anywhere in the North West Highlands. All the routes here provide two long pitches, more or less on good rock and protection. The exposure is immediately apparent and considerable, and the climbing style often brutal. There are occasionally more delicate and technical crux sections, but most of the routes on this cliff will always involve their fare share of rounded grunt, jamming, smearing and brute force.

◀ Adrian Crofton on *Mid Flight Crisis* (E4).
Photo: *Colin Threlfall*.

▲ West Buttress from below. Photo: *Colin Threlfall.*

THE ROUTES

Expecting to Fly (E4)
The most amenable of the routes on the wall, taking the superb central line up a groove and exposed diagonal crack breaking through the prominent band of overhangs.

Walking on Air (E6)
An outstanding route taking on the full challenge of the wall blasting straight up the prominent crack-line and stepped corner slightly left of centre.

▲ Gordon Lennox on *Walking on Air* (E6). Photo: *Colin Threlfall.*

Mid Flight Crisis (E4)
A counter diagonal to *Walking on Air*, giving fantastic varied climbing ending up with a battle up the wild crack in the prow on the left side of the wall.

THE STORY

Apart from an uneventful ascent of the excellent *Jack the Ripper* sometime in the 1990s, it was a long time before I got back to that big flat wall. In fact it was almost exactly 15 years, and I had then become a climbing 'local' when Tess Fryer and I moved to Ullapool in the amazing hot summer of 2003.

In the intervening years I thought I'd learned a little about climbing, but I hadn't learned about the sneaky approach so we sweated buckets by taking the steep heathery slope straight on. A bad start. *Expecting to Fly* seemed like the best place to begin and I have to admit that nothing too exciting occurred – it was just a fantastic route. After an initial easy section, moves leftwards reached the main crack-line and the route gradually unfolded. Nothing hard, just nice continuous climbing, heading steadily for the overhangs above. Breaching the overhangs via a hanging groove was suddenly strenuous, fortunately with good protection, but the crux was still above. It all got a bit smeary and tenuous for a few moves before a welcome niche calmed the situation and a final flared crack led to the top.

Slightly more exciting was *Shadow on the Wall*, the leftmost route on the wall. I think we only decided to have a go at this because there appeared to be a large cam stuck a little way above an in-situ thread. Unfortunately the thread wasn't very good, so I pushed the boat out a little towards the cam and gratefully clipped it. It promptly fell out! Panic stations ensued for a few moments while I managed to get something else in, then I continued up to a large flake and traversed left to the belay ledge. Tess led up the supposedly easier second pitch, but this turned out to be especially hard work. An awkward chimney was followed by a dirty corner. Even seconding, the corner felt touch and go, with feet slipping around on gritty smears.

Gordon Lennox on Walking on Air (E6).
Photo: *Colin Threlfall*.

THE NORTH WEST HIGHLANDS | **WEST BUTTRESS, STAC POLLAIDH**

One day in the summer of 2006 we came back for *Mid Flight Crisis*. The first pitch gave very good climbing. Switching back and forth between two thin cracks, there were no desperate moves and the big break was soon reached. The belay was just to the left beside a big block. Glancing up at the second pitch didn't encourage me. It seemed dirty and there was a big moss-filled pocket that looked crucial. Anyway, I started up and, with decent protection in the crack, I was able to dig out the good holds and move leftwards into a corner. Reasonable moves up this led to an impasse. The description said move left, but all I could find were dirty sloping holds. After a period of up and downing my psyche was rapidly declining, so I bypassed the crux by down-climbing a few moves and traversing round the corner into a chimney that led back to a niche above the crux. An excellent piece of cheating I thought, but cheating all the same. Above the niche, an easy groove ended in a nasty-looking wide crack. Launching up this, I was tiring rapidly as the sandy jams slid out, and stopping to place gear just made things worse; but I struggled on until, pumped solid, I reached easier ground and collapsed on top. Buckled.

So that left *Walking on Air*. I asked around but no-one I knew had been on the route in more than ten years and no-one had even heard of an ascent post-peg. Dirty 6c was a grade I was very unlikely to on-sight, so I thought I'd just wait until I heard of it being done or maybe I'd just abseil down and give it a clean. Time went by and I detected a subtle shift in my climbing outlook. My new mantra became 'what's the worst thing that can happen? It is better to get on a long sought after route and fail, than never get on it at all'.

On a quiet midweek day in 2009, Tess led the first pitch with a certain amount of huffing and a great deal of cursing. Most of the difficulties were low down, but the gear was awkward to place and the crux was a long reach with dubious smears for the feet. The upper section was easier and she was soon relaxing at the belay. Seconding the pitch I was nearly off a couple of times, so my confidence wasn't sky high as I set off up the top pitch. But the initial moves were fine, as far as a triangular niche that had a good kneebar rest. Placing some solid wires, I had a good look up at the crux section, but it didn't really fit with how I'd imagined it. I'd envisioned a good crack, but this was just a slim groove with a seam which might take some small RPs. I gave it a half-hearted effort. By palming the edge of the groove, a long reach allowed a small pocket to be reached, but there were no good footholds and the pump was coming on quickly. I couldn't place any gear so it was 'fight or flight' and, looking at a nasty fall, I of course chose flight. Somehow I managed to scuttle back down to the niche. Decision time: I think we should just abseil off, but Tess suggests aiding past the crux. By placing a series of RPs I managed to ascend in a slightly scary fashion until I was able to get to a good hold and a solid nut. Well, now that I have myself a mini top rope I may as well try the moves.

I lowered down and gave it a bit of a brush. First go I got the pocket and continued trying to layback up the edge of the groove, but fell off trying a high step to get my foot in the pocket. Second go the foot goes in and with a bit of power-laybacking I'm at the good hold. The rest of the pitch goes OK except for one section over a bulge where I had to dig around in the moss for the hidden holds. Tess gets up the pitch quickly with one fall on the crux and soon we're both on top with the sun, the views and the tourists. Despite the appalling style I'm happy enough; at least my curiosity is satisfied.

And so I feel my affair with the wall is complete. But then Tess goes back with Murdo and they do a clean ascent of *Mid Flight Crisis*, including the crux section and there is still *Fear of Flying*, so maybe … •

Graeme Ettle (leading) and Joanna George on *Jack the Ripper* (E1)
Photo: *Dave Cuthbertson*.

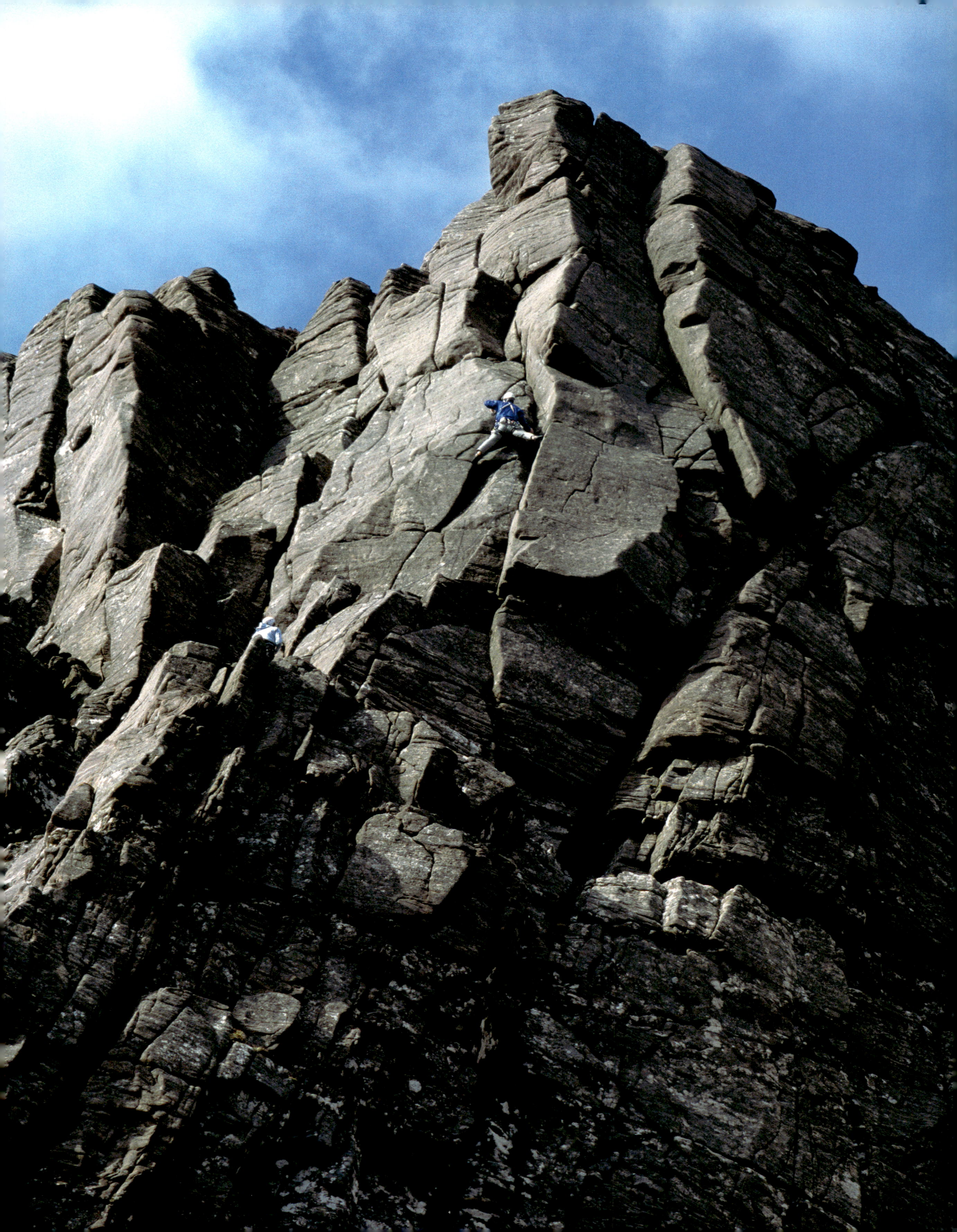

Stac Pollaidh. Photo: *Gerry Neely*.

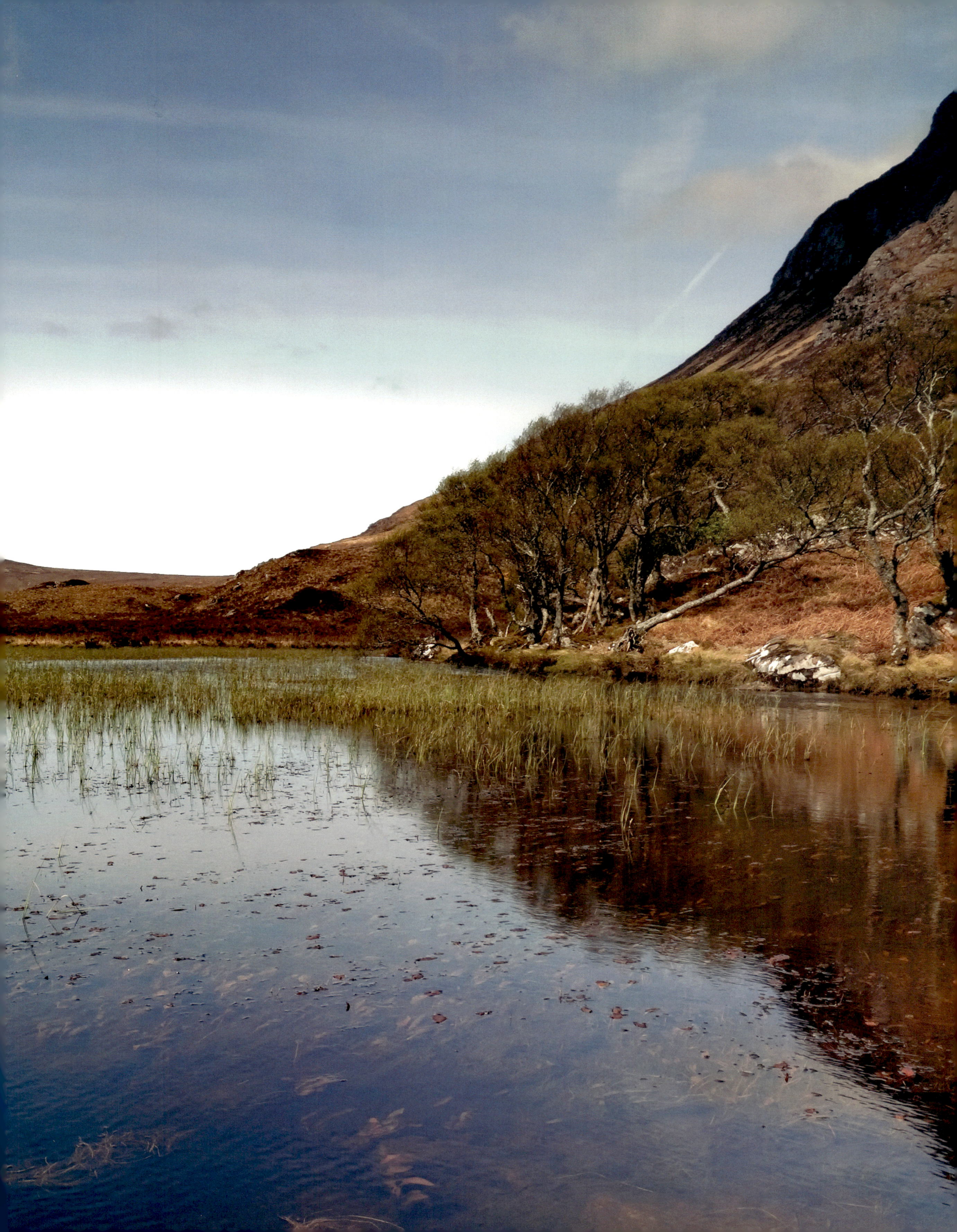

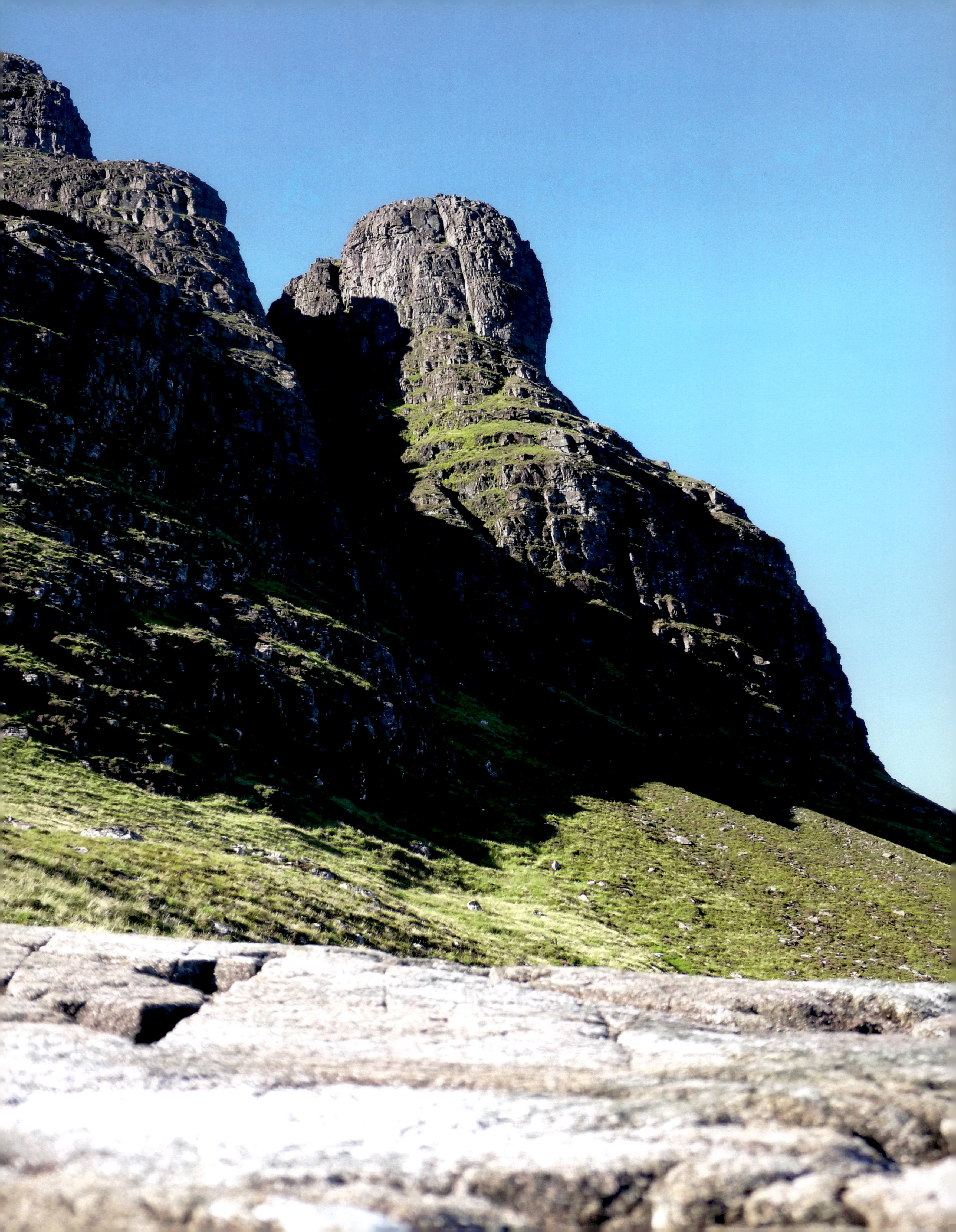

BARREL BUTTRESS, QUINAG – *by Roger Webb*

THE PLACE
Quinag is a big little mountain, its low altitude offset by its abrupt rise from the sea. Situated just north of Loch Assynt, with five peaks, its North East Face looms over Kylesku Bridge.

For the hill walker, it is magnificent, giving a walkway in the sky, views west to the Hebrides, north across empty Sutherland and south to the indecently glorious Assynt hills. At first glance it offers little for the climber. The crags, lost in the huge sweep of hillside, don't look worth the effort, but like the hill their stature is offset by their abrupt nature. These crags are concentrated.

THE CLIFF
Barrel Buttress, shaped as its name implies, sits upon a lower, much easier angled buttress, girdled at its base by a good ledge. Facing north, overlooking Kylesku Bridge, it is the single biggest lump of sandstone on Quinag's North Face. Access up the lower ground is straightforward at Moderate or grade II, depending on the season.

The barrel is split by a corner, the unimaginatively named *Direct Route*. On the left there is a slight easing of the angle. To the right the crag is uniformly steep. On each side are deep boundary gullies, Cave on the left and Cooper's on the right. It is possible to walk to Cooper's, but not to Cave.

The girdle ledge is an intimidating, shadowy place where resolution is tested by the knowledge that one can just go off rightwards for one of the best hill walks in Scotland, rather than endure several hours of physical and mental stress. In summer the added prospect of midge torment drives off all but the most committed. In winter, providing one can find that resolution, this crag comes into its own. The steep angle, the well-cracked rock and an abundance of turf make the cliff a mixed climbing gem. Excellent belays combined with the view add welcome relief for the suffering second who is likely to be in-situ for some time.

There are now about a dozen routes on the Barrel, roughly split between summer and winter. In summer, despite its northerly aspect, it is quick to dry and normally a couple of days will be enough. In winter it is a fickle venue. The combination of low altitude and prominence require the weather to be either very cold, settled and snowy, or, for the over-enthusiastic, very wild, to have a chance of decent winter conditions.

THE CLIMBING
The Barrel was first visited by Raeburn, Mackay and Ling, who climbed a line on the right wall of the central corner in 1907. It waited 55 years for more attention when Patey passed by, another 16 years for Nisbet and a further 15 for Webb and Steer. Development has not been swift.

Routes here do not fall quickly to well-practised balletic technique. Things are less obvious than they seem. What looks like IV tends to be VI, vertical steps have balance-destroying bulges, sometimes it's not turf in that crack but 'sandstone special' – evil frozen gravel which blunts your picks, and where they pop whenever you weight them (unless you hit it really, really hard); and of course, every now and then God forgot the footholds.

This is an arena for experts in the dark arts of thrutch, udge and grovel; where elbows, knees and heads are as valuable as picks and crampons. If you value your Gore-Tex don't come here.

Happily this isn't the land of the long run-out. Mostly, protection is superb. The main limiting factor is how much you can carry, so leave the ice screws behind but carry a full rock rack, turf gear and a few pegs. Occasionally there are bands where the gear isn't so good, but, if you push on, it will come.

◀ Barrel Buttress of Quinag.
Photo: *Adrian Crofton*.

THE ROUTES

Chang (V,7)
The last done of the four big winter routes on the front face of the Barrel, this route is the only one to finish up the open wall rather than the central chimney. Hence the last pitch gives magnificent exposure.

Badajoz (V,6)
This devious line was the first winter route on the central cliff. It outflanks the difficulties of the central corner by a rampline on the left. Interest and physicality increase with height.

Direct Route (VII,7)
The best route on the barrel climbs the central corner and chimney above. Looks are deceptive; the corner is far steeper than is apparent, and a positive attitude is essential. Possibly only VI if you have a very big cam.

Raeburn, Mackay and Ling Original Route (VDiff, VI,7)
Quinag's first route, climbed in the summer of 1907 by one of the best teams of the day, tackles the crack system on the right wall of the central corner. This is the cleanest rock on the cliff; in summer it gives a fine VDiff, in winter a technical climb that is less brutal than its neighbours.

Guy Robertson on the first ascent of *Beefheart* (E2).
Photo: *Adrian Crofton*.

THE NORTH WEST HIGHLANDS | **BARREL BUTTRESS, QUINAG**

THE STORY

It was Simon Steer's fault, he suggested it: Barrel Buttress on Quinag. Raeburn, Ling and Mackay did a route there in 1907, only VDiff, and sure to be a fun day out in winter – probably a grade IV and with more or less a downhill walk-in to boot. So one January day, happy in the knowledge that we were off for an easy but good time, we left the road far too late for the short walk to the foot of the buttress.

The weather was perfect: sunshine, blue sky, still and cold. Conditions were perfect: frozen ground and a white, well-rimed buttress. The view was perfect: west to the Hebrides over a sea as blue as the sky, and north to Foinaven, startlingly close in the clear air. Best of all, our intended line was stunning, if a bit short. The Barrel was split straight down the middle, from top to bottom, by a plum, left-facing corner. It looked like a four-star grade IV. Little did we know then how rare were the conditions, and how deceptive the angle of the rock.

As is often the case, the apron of easy ground leading to the main crag didn't seem quite easy enough to solo, so we roped it, and each thought the other was making a hash of his lead; faltering on the tricky, rather than the desperate, and faffing over belays. Too much time slipped by, and it was well after midday when we reached the base of the corner. It had all the hallmarks of a classic, the way to the top clear, taking a corner whose right wall was smooth and vertical, but the left apparently less steep. The first 20 or so metres appeared choked with turf, above which a bulge sported an offwidth crack.

I set off in confident mode, loving the initial turfy romp, bridging across little overhangs, at first not noticing that with each move the ground was steepening. By the time I reached the bulge the corner was most definitely vertical. The turf ran out into the flared crack, which was perhaps twice my height, and gently overhanging. Both retaining walls of the corner were impending. Our hopes centred on a chockstone a third of the way up. I couldn't see over the top of this, but expected more turf. Fixing some gear, I squeezed as much of my body in the crack as possible and started wriggling ... Without too much trouble I reached and threaded the chockstone.

▲ Roger Webb on the first winter ascent of *Direct Route* (VII,7).
Photo: *Simon Richardson*.

Above this the crack closed and overhung abruptly. I struggled upwards, attempting to bridge, but struggling as my front points skated repeatedly off the rock. My strength was rapidly giving out. Exhausted, I reached the top of the crack and, not quite beaten, I undercut the crack's end, swung high with my left axe, got a weak placement and peeked over. There was turf, but just beyond my reach! In between was a most unhelpful concrete mix of frozen mud and gravel. My last runner was just below my feet, the next perhaps six feet away. There was gear available, only I didn't have anything big enough. Slumping back down I conceded defeat, using the 'lack of time' ploy as cover. In reality it was more a lack of drive. Expecting a relaxed day I wasn't prepared to take risks.

Back in Inverness, disappointed by failure but even more inspired by the line, we planned a return encounter. It was a simple plan: get up early, psyche up, take a big wall rack, do the route. Over the remainder of that season we tried repeatedly and failed.

Sometimes the buttress was white but unfrozen, sometimes frozen but not white, while on other occasions the access road was blocked. So we had to settle for a lot of gullies on Beinn Dearg and some other interesting routes on Quinag, but we failed to climb the Barrel Buttress.

By necessity our plan was revised: get up, psyche up, take a big wall rack, drive up just before a blizzard hits and then do the route.

That March delivered a perfect, if rapidly deteriorating, forecast. A Homeric, rosy-fingered dawn saw us walking in over frozen ground, happy at the disappearing view, the rising wind and first signs of snow. The new plan was on track.

At the foot of the corner all seemed well, the right wall sheltering Simon from the worst of the wind and the route above in perfect condition. I'd visualised this for months, so bursting with motivation I set off. Again, however, it all came unstuck at exactly the same place. The problem with overhangs is that to overcome them you really do have to look up, and if you look up you get a face full of what's coming down, in this case large doses of freezing cold spindrift. If you are wearing glasses, as I was, this only adds to the problem. They steam up, ice over and generally become useless unless they can be wiped clear which is difficult to execute with leashed tools on overhanging ground. So I retreated to the foot of the crack. Below me I could see that Simon had a perfect cone of snow balanced on his helmet. We pondered the problem, screaming to each other over a rising gale. The solution – get out of the corner.

A few metres below a thin seam of turf snaked out left, so I dropped down to this to find out where it went. The turf was perhaps a few inches wide and the wall bulged above and below, so I ended up hooking my right foot on the ledge, left leg dangling, and hauling myself along strenuously by my axes. The snowfall intensified, and looking back I now appeared to be being belayed by a neat pile of snow. Spindrift continued to pour down and my glasses froze over again. Effectively blinded, I wormed slowly along until my right hand felt a welcome fin of rock in the middle of the ledge. I nudged forward, jammed my knee between fin and wall and so freed a hand to scrape my glasses. Looking around I found myself on a small pedestal, perched over nothing but empty space.

Simon was no longer in sight, nor could I hear him, but I could at least see a way forward. This was a shallow, overhanging groove directly overhead, mercifully out of the spindrift, and fortunately equipped with cracks on the walls. With great difficulty I contorted my body from prone to vertical and spent a happy time placing some badly needed protection. I contemplated belaying but reasoned that with the traverse ledge virtually unprotected and Simon carrying both sacks this was probably not wise, with potential for a big swing into empty space.

The groove was strenuous but well protected and this time I could bridge. Horizontal cracks and ripples in the sandstone gave my crampons purchase, while good turf in the back gave placements for picks. It was hard, obvious and sensational. Looking down between my legs I saw the ropes dangling free, disappearing into the swirling snow. My way was blocked by a small roof. Confident in my gear I swung out left and was rewarded by another groove. This was less steep than its predecessor and gave in more easily, but about halfway up, I realised three things.

Before me I could see that the angle eased, so we had probably broken the back of the route. Secondly, however, it was also now dark. Last but not least, I had no more rope. For once there was no gear and hence no choice. I shouted to Simon to climb and pulled the rope sharply three times. I put my head torch on, waited for the rope to go slack, and when it did I continued. This wasn't so reckless. There was now so much gear between me and Simon that the risk was minimal provided I reached a belay before he reached the traverse, and besides, I was out of options. Thankfully the major difficulties were over and after a few steep moves a large ledge appeared complete with satisfying thread.

I belayed and froze, and then froze some more. I was beginning to feel sorry for myself and resent Simon's slow pace, but when he appeared I understood. Despite having just climbed a hard 65-metre pitch in the dark, with two sacks, his clothing was still encased in a layer of ice. In fact icicles hung from his beard, helmet, eyelashes and eyebrows – he looked like a deep-frozen Viking.

'Long pitch,' he said. 'Bit steep for climbing together!'

A pitch later, we topped out. The siege was over – we could go somewhere else.

Three years later, armed with a new generation of gear and a contact lens, I returned and climbed the complete corner direct. In perfect weather, with bombproof protection, it was almost easy.

Guy Robertson on *Stout* (VS).
Photo: *Adrian Crofton.*

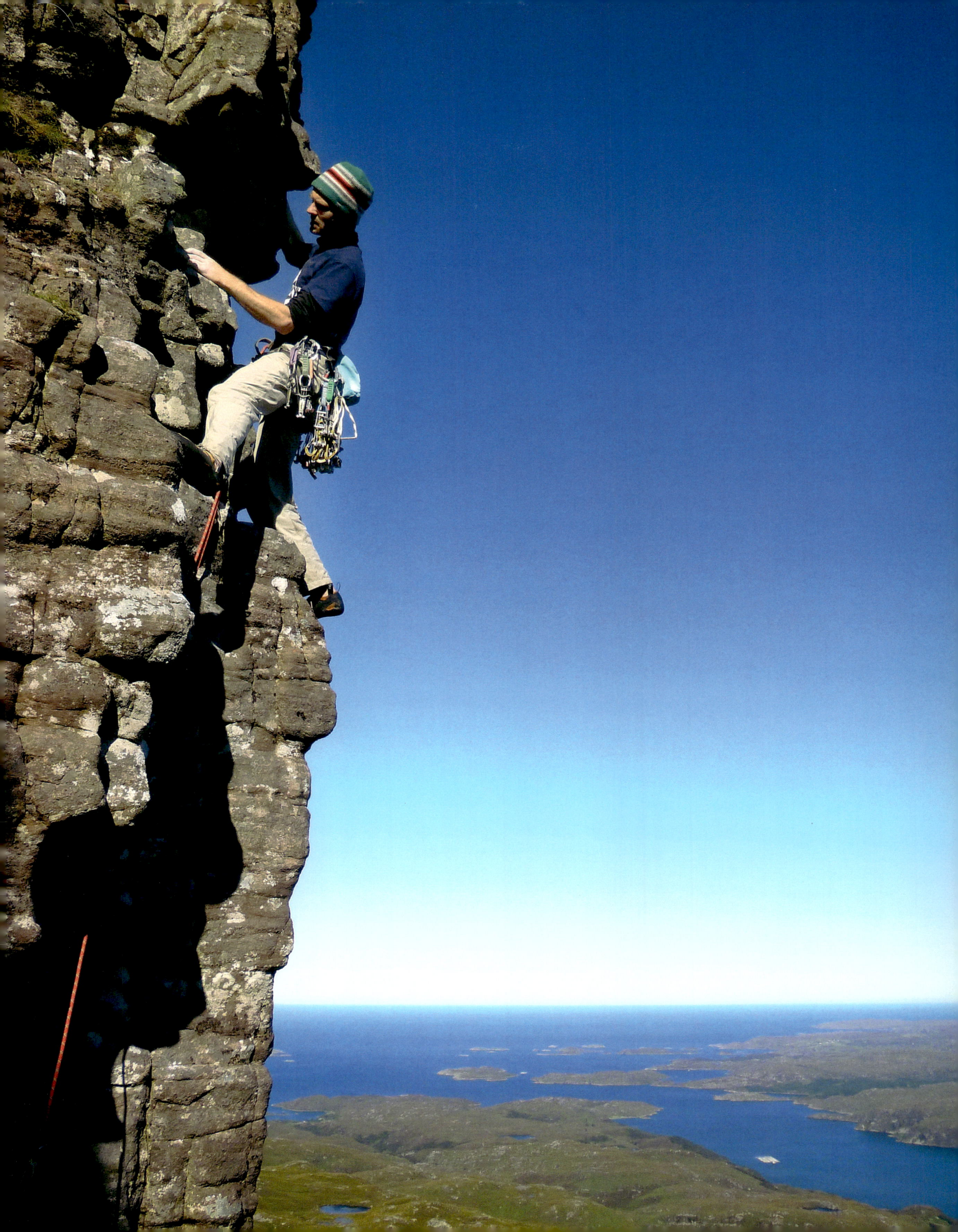

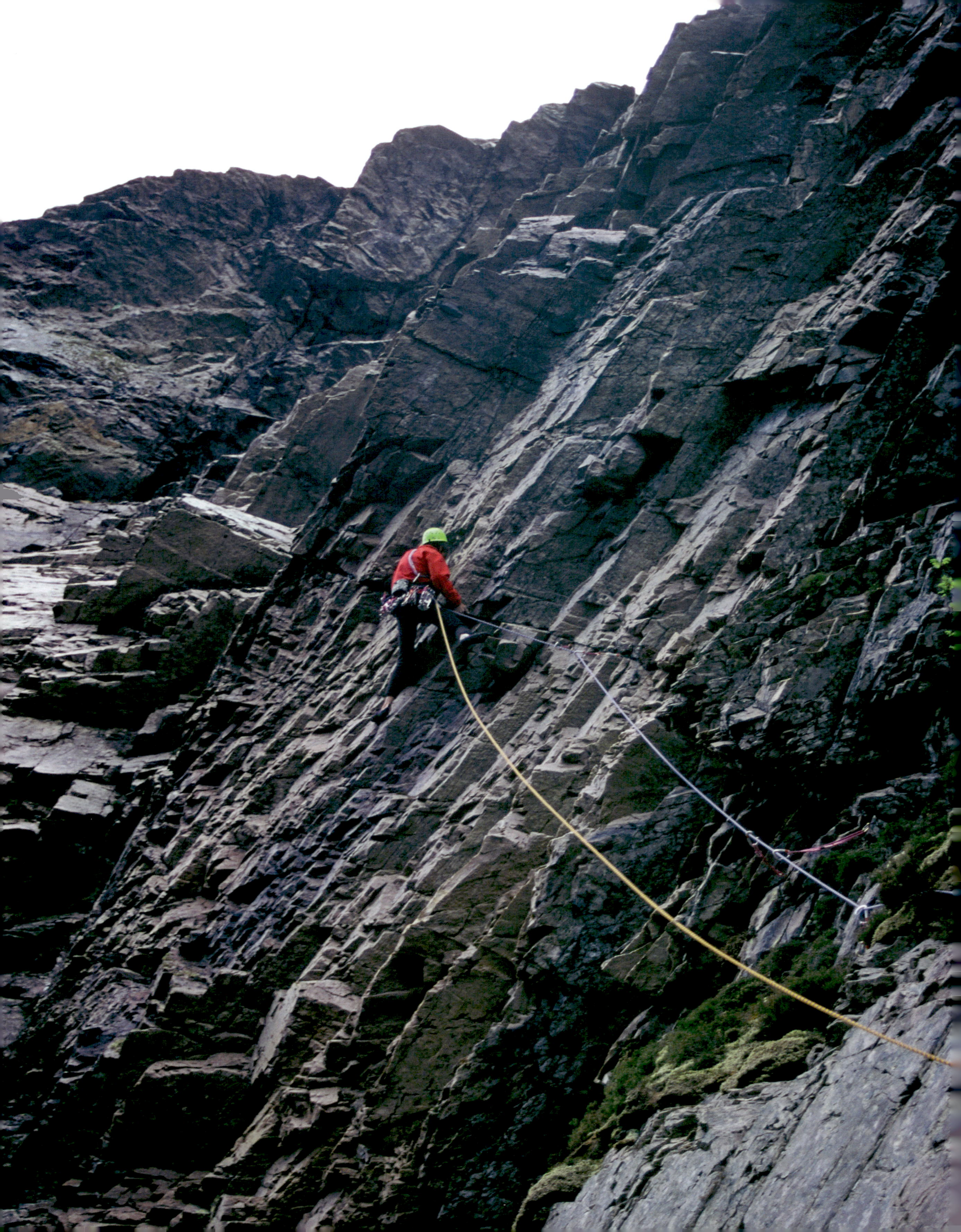

First Dionard Buttress, Foinaven
– by Rick Campbell

THE PLACE
The extreme north-west corner of Sutherland boasts the magnificent mountains of Foinaven and Arkle, set in some of the most rugged scenery in mainland Scotland. This is perhaps the wildest corner of mainland Britain, similar in many ways to South Harris with its lunar landscape of knotted gneiss outcrops and shapely lochans.

Foinaven, by managing to be a few centimetres short of a Munro, is blessed with a fraction of the traffic of the peaks on that list, and this is evident in the lack of eroded paths and the under-development of the local area. The long, scree-ridden flanks of Foinaven taper down at their south-eastern extent to the lonely trout-laden Loch Dionard at the head of the strath bearing the same name. First Dionard Buttress is the vast north-east-facing escarpment that overlooks this loch.

THE CLIFF
It is a sad fact that although Lewisian gneiss is many people's favourite rock, the stuff away from the coast that is steeper than vertical is often glacially polished, un-weathered and generally unpleasant to climb on. Aficionados of steep rock have therefore tended to look to quartzite for inspiration in this part of the world.

Impressive from afar, Creag Urbhard is not actually that steep, and rather too liberally furnished with incut holds to excite the modern climber. Directly above the loch, however, the First Dionard Buttress is an immensely impressive bastion with a huge roof at two-thirds height. There are further numbered buttresses up round the back, but none can hold a torch to this.

The lowest rocks consist of horizontal strata interspersed with heather ledges, above which is a long, small-ish roof with easier ground above. All the routes avoid this feature. There is a large left-facing corner to the right of the roof and fine vertical pale rock above this, leading to the main feature of the crag: the central roof. Stretching almost the whole width of the crag, this is a truly awesome feature. Two ramp-lines split the roof and these are taken by the two best lines here, *Millennium* and *Regeneration*. Above the roof the crag kicks back almost 90 degrees and offers little more than scrambling all the way up to a level shoulder where all the routes end.

Dionard One is not a crag that readily ticks all the boxes, unlike, for instance, Carn Dearg or the Shelterstone. The soul-destroying 12-kilometre approach up the rather dull Strath Dionard is a big minus for most, as are the many worrying areas of loose rock on some of the routes. The use of a mountain bike massively improves the access, and the *No Cycling* sign carries no weight in law. However, you had better hide your steed at the head of the loch because The Law and The Ghillie could be old drinking mates in this neck of the woods, or worse still, one and the same! Don't be put off by the loose rock, it's no worse than, say, *Freak Out* in Glen Coe, and where the quartzite is good, it's very, very good indeed.

THE CLIMBING
Other than Sròn Uladail on Harris there are not many cliffs in Britain as continuously steep on this sort of scale. This is impressive territory indeed. The high-lying quartzite of Beinn Eighe tends to have square-cut edges, all in a matt battleship grey making them hard to spot. Our crag of choice here at a mere 150 metres elevation has areas of similar rock, but also steep flaky cracks and juggy undercuts.

The early lines understandably sidestepped the main challenge of the crag and it wasn't until Paul Nunn and Clive Rowland arrived in 1969 to climb *Dialectic* (over two days) that hard climbing finally arrived. However, this early foray, though impressive in its conception, firstly avoids the steep lower wall by a mere shifty at the main roof, then turns on its heels and traverses wildly left across a bulging weakness featuring many aid points and a great deal of loose rock. Rather more satisfactory was the fruit of a return visit from Nunn in 1982 accompanied by Andy Livesey, when the pair climbed the highly rated *Millennium*. Still following an intricate line, the latter route is more direct and sticks to better rock.

◂ Rick Campbell on the first ascent of *Regeneration* (E6).
Photo: *Gary Latter*.

▲ Jason Currie on *Millennium* (E2). Photo: *Guy Robertson*.

THE ROUTES

Millennium (E2)
The line of the crag. Starts to the right of the large left-facing corner; a long traverse out right avoids the steep lower central walls. A couple of straight up pitches on vertical rock form the technical crux pitches, before a belay is taken in a bower under the right-hand and easier-looking of the two roof ramp/cracklines. This is ascended on good holds and gear in a wild position to easier rocks above.

Dialectic (E2 with aid)
Anyone fancy free-climbing the wild, loose traverse left under the main roof?

Regeneration (E6)
This should have been *Millennium* – it was climbed in 2000! A direct line immediately right of the left-facing corner. Worth persisting with nasty territory low down for the pump-fest higher up and the gob-smacking positions on pitch three. In places the rock is as good as the best in Torridon.

172 THE GREAT MOUNTAIN CRAGS OF SCOTLAND

▲ First Dionard Buttress. Photo: *Ian Taylor.*

▲ Guy Robertson on Millennium (E2). Photo: *Jason Currie.*

THE STORY

Gary Latter had somewhere got the notion that there must be a do-able line straight up the middle of Dionard One that had somehow been overlooked due to the remoteness of the crag. And so, one glorious Saturday in June 2000, Gary and I left the Achnahaird campsite at the crack of dawn to drive to Gaulin House, high on the moor on the Durness road, only to be greeted by a No Bikes sign. This was in the years before the Land Reform Bill, so it looked to us like it meant business.

The dilemma was resolved by the expedient that we didn't actually have any bikes with us that weekend. What we did have was a Latter-sized rack, incorporating three sets of Friends, three sets of nuts, 25 quickdraws, four cameras and several changes of under-garment. In addition, I had only the day before had confirmation from my GP that there was a jolly good medical explanation why one of my ankles was twice the size of the other and hurt quite a lot ...

After the interminable walk-in we found ourselves under the crag, scoping for lines. There was a curious lack of scree or boulders at its base. A good omen, we pondered? We gaped in awe at the size of the main roof, dominating the whole face in a most intimidating way. Clearly, though, there was a weakness straight through it. We were more concerned about the lower bulging wall. Stratified rock and heather led to a large bulge with easier rock above – all fairly uninviting though. To the right was the prominent square-cut central groove, the obvious feature on this part of the crag. Getting into this looked hard and the whole thing looked fairly devoid of protection. I was much more turned on by a crack in the red bulging wall just to its right which appeared to lead to more reasonable ground above the groove itself. By tilting my head slightly I managed to convince myself that this crack was merely vertical.

So, I set off up an unprotected though not unduly hard wall, which soon gave way to heather ledges where I needed to stop and work out just how many points of contact I would require to attain the platform lurking above. Eventually settling for the butterfly stroke through a brittle bulge, it was with some relief that the first solid runners bedded in to the base of the main crack.

'Holy cow this looks steep!' I launched up the crack and made a move left round a large hanging block that seemed solid enough to hold my weight. Soon, however, I found myself weighting the gear, prising off holds left, right and centre, before lowering back down to the platform. Another attempt saw ground gained up to a hard move though the capping bulge. More loose blocks hurtled down like grenades around Gary below. By now the remaining rock was solid enough, the crack well laced with gear, and the curious lack of debris at the cliff's base was now just a memory.

After a brief rest on the platform I girded my loin and went for the push to the top. Vertical crack, jam left over the block, layback wide crack to the crux, move through the capping bulge, long stretch left off a funny pistol-grip and finally a pumping fight with the flat holds above. By now I was well above the last runner. I realised that with strength failing there was little scope for anything but to flail onwards and upwards. Finally, I found myself in a position where I could take both hands off the rock and arrange a belay.

Gary followed the pitch, and as so often happens when seconding, the 'commitment gear' hadn't engaged, so when he started up the colossal groove on the next pitch he was moving rather tentatively. What was apparent was that the rock was the most perfect pale quartzite, a real joy to climb. After about 20 metres he quit the groove and moved out across the left wall to where delicate climbing led to a short overhanging wall. A stiff pull up this led to a small ledge and belay in an alcove at the base of the main roof. Up left now was an endless sea of overhangs. Imaginary lines for the 21st century were traced in abundance, but straight up was the groove-crack we were determined to climb.

The first move was a long stretch off an undercut jam onto a ledge where, to our surprise, we found a cluster of old stoppers on rope that someone had lowered off a very long time previously. Did the team who originally climbed *Millennium* try to go this way? The reason for their retreat was soon apparent. Directly above was an initially holdless groove, devoid of gear, while round the right arête was a pair of juggy but ridiculously steep cracks that disappeared out of sight. A solution was soon found by starting up the cracks for a few moves before swinging delicately back left into the groove above its blankest section. More awkward moves then led back right again onto a plinth. Above was a vertical crack leading to an amazing flying ramp going out right. The crux pitch of *The Scoop* in Harris came to mind, though fortunately this one appeared to have more for the feet. The position was, however, every bit as dramatic.

Tentatively I set off up the crack to the roof. The situation was mind-blowing. With my heart in my mouth, I committed to the flying ramp. I pulled moss out of a slot for a hold and Friend runner; a dice sized nubbin on the ramp was at first handhold, then foothold for a long rock-over to span a gap in the arpeggio of holds that led to the very top, where the ramp was no more. Literally vibrating with adrenaline now, I pulled over onto a ledge on the very lip of the roof.

Gary led up the next pitch climbing the continuing fault line directly on immaculate white rock. Apart from a move just above the belay the going was now substantially easier, and after a bit of scrambling we soon spied the shortcut down to our sacks, and with heads in the clouds picked our way back down. All that remained was the small matter of a 12-kilometre walk out, and the inevitable fist fight with the midges back at the car.

Guy Robertson on *Millennium* (E2).
Photo: *Jason Currie*.

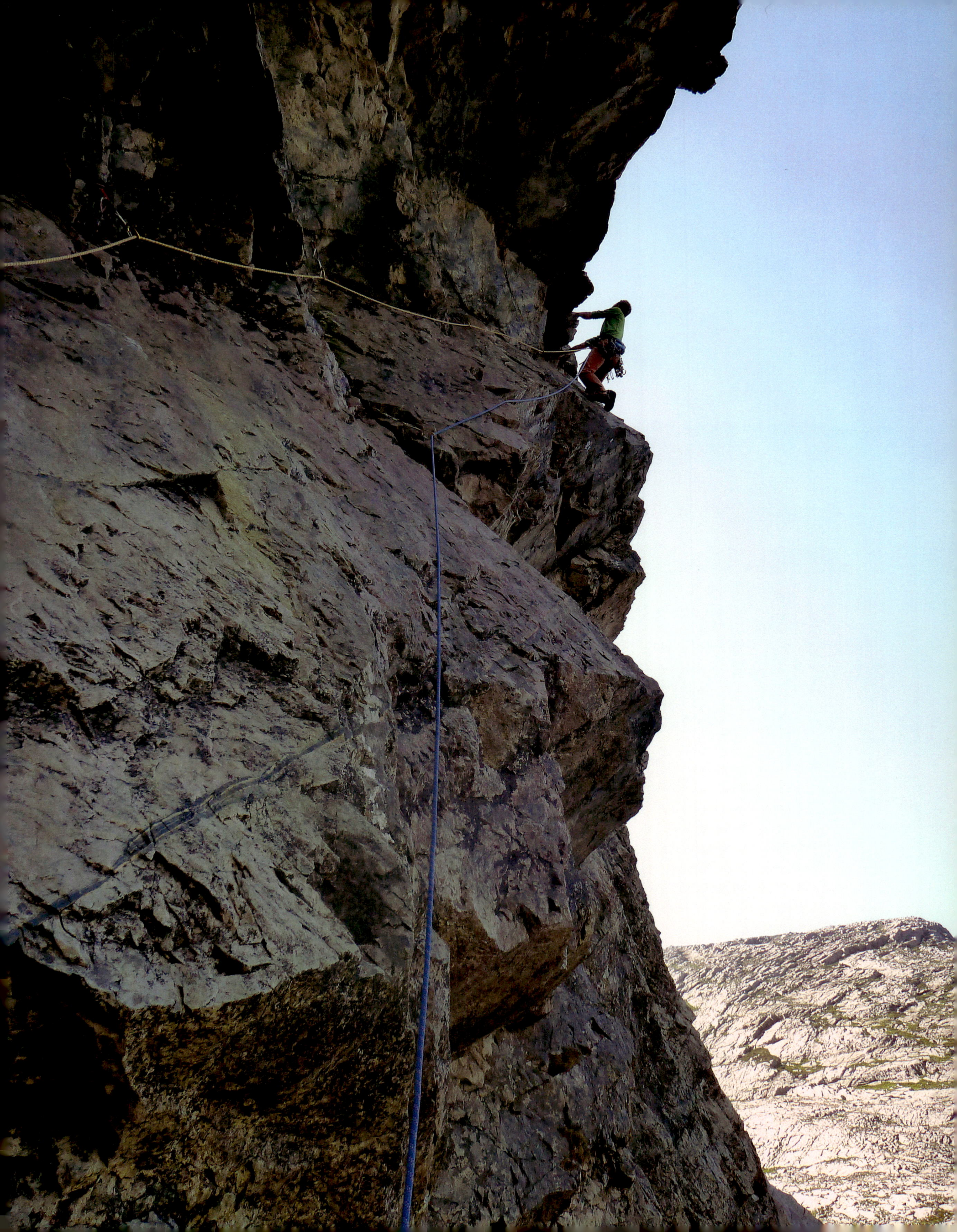

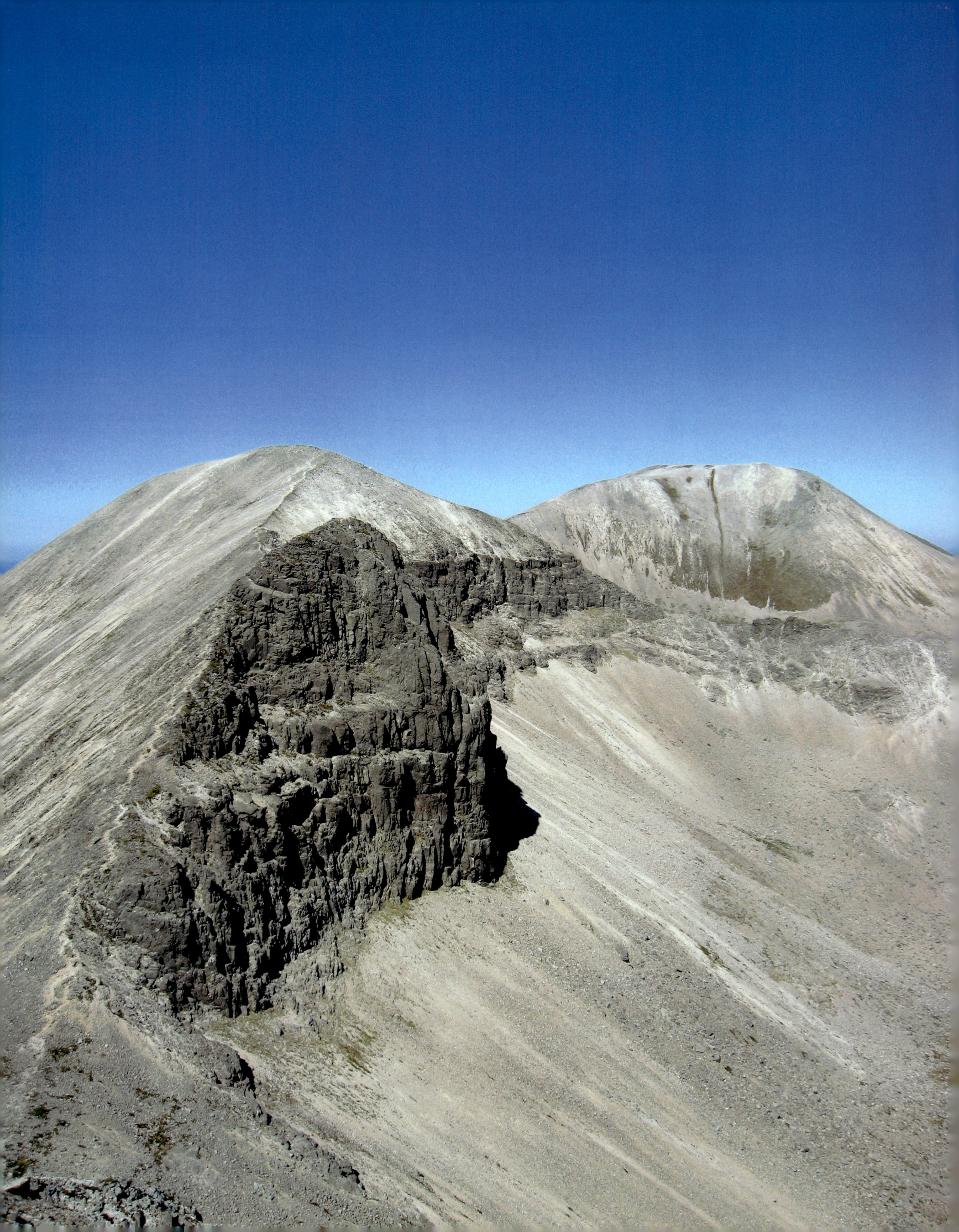

Lord Reay's Seat, Foinaven – by Malcolm Bass

THE PLACE

We live in a small, crowded country. But it doesn't feel like that when you're climbing on Foinaven. The impression of space is captivating: the mountain rises proud of its neighbours, which are few, so lines of sight are long across miles of moor and lochan to the sea. The hill seems to be perched on the edge of the habitable temperate world, facing out into the vastness of the Arctic north. In winter, with a northerly blowing, the Arctic feels very close indeed.

An air of mystery still clings to the climbing on Foinaven's seven major cliffs. Routes are climbed, recorded and never found again. The guidebook is full of guesses and uncertainties, daggers and points of aid. It seems a long way to come to waste a precious day blundering about through snow or sucking bogs, never to find your line. But take heart: the cliffs of Foinaven share little in common except their being on the same mountain. The confusion and aid pitches belong to the great sprawling buttresses that line Strath Dionard. For clarity and purity you need to go high, up to Foinaven's main ridge and Lord Reay's Seat.

THE CLIFF

The crag sits at the head of Coire na Lice, the most remote of Foinaven's three north-easterly coires. So the approach involves a 12-kilometre bike, walk and/or ski up Strath Dionard. If it's winter, and you've left early enough, dawn will come somewhere around arrival at the mouth of the coire, and, as you breast yet another heathery rise, you'll finally get a sight of the crag you've come so far to climb. It will probably be black.

The cliff faces due east and presents a very impressive, cathedral-like triangular appearance, holding court at the head of Coire na Lice. At its centre is a very steep nose, overhanging at its base, and as yet unclimbed. Right of this, the crag sports a prominent chimney – the line of *Fishmonger* – while to the left is another chimney line starting 25 metres up: *Pobble*. Beyond the two chimney lines the cliff diminishes in steepness, providing only a few easier climbs.

THE CLIMBING

In summer the crag dries quickly, there's little drainage or vegetation, and it gets a lot of sun, so a few days without rain should provide good conditions. Be warned, however, that this is no place for anything other than climbers with strong 'mountaineering spirit'. Anyone committing to the long and arduous approach expecting perfect rock is likely to be disappointed. On the other hand, those in search of commanding lines in the heart of beyond will be richly rewarded.

Winter conditions here are fickle in the extreme. Success on many of the first winter ascents required numerous purgatorial trips up Strath Dionard. It took two unsuccessful visits to find the chimney line of *Fishmonger* in acceptable winter condition in 1998. A similar experience was endured to produce the first winter ascent of *Pobble*. The only solution to the winter conditions problem on Foinaven seems to be to wait until it has snowed a lot, over several days, and without much wind. Ideal conditions are likely to be found when all the roads north of Ullapool are covered in a good even layer – at least two inches. But don't wait until it's stopped snowing and the sun has come out – the crag is east facing and sheds snow alarmingly rapidly.

The climbing style is largely as one would expect on a quartzite cliff: steep, angular, and positive. The existing lines follow strong continuous features, so chimneys, corners and grooves define the style of movement. Protection, on the whole, is very good.

The exploration of Lord Reay's Seat has followed an orderly progression, in keeping with the standard template. First a wandering line to get up the cliff any old how, then the obvious lines of weaknesses are climbed in summer, or some approximation to summer. The steeper chimneys had to wait until as late as the seventies, an indication of the crag's substantial resilience. The development of the steep ground away from the chimneys has been even slower, and quite sporadic.

◀ Lord Reay's Seat.
Photo: *Patrick Roman*.

▲ The eastern coires of Foinaven, with Lord Reay's Seat to the left. Photo: *Fionn McArthur.*

While the summer routes follow strong lines, they are, in places, quite shattered and will never win many accolades as high quality rock climbs. Winter, of course, is a different kettle of fish. It took until the nineties and beyond the turn of the millennium before quartzite mixed climbing techniques advanced enough elsewhere (notably on Beinn Eighe) for the routes here to become attractive winter targets. Roger Webb and Neil Wilson climbed *Fishmonger* on their third visit in January 1998, after two other parties had previously been to its base. Then in March 2006 Simon Yearsley and I (on our second visit) found the hooking in *Pobble's* overhanging chimneys to be as positive as we could have wished. In 2010, we returned to uncover *The Long March* (VIII,8) – the hardest winter offering on Foinaven to date.

THE ROUTES

Leftfield (E2)

An attempt to climb the frontal nose of the buttress directly, unfortunately thwarted by extremely steep and loose rock on the true crest slightly further right. The lower pitches are sustained, intricate and bold but never desperate and mostly on good rock, while the upper section takes in the great corner of *Pobble Direct* (E1), which is somewhat loose.

Fishmonger (Severe, VI,6)

An excellent winter route up the improbable-looking chimney system right of the central nose. The start looks desperate, but the crux is actually high on the route where the winter line continues directly and strenuously up the chimney, which is avoided by the summer route.

The Long March (VIII,8)

The overhanging corner crack of the second pitch is a fantastic winter feature. Steep and mostly positive it feels very committing once you've swung out from under the roof. The third pitch features a fine, sequency wall, then thin, bold climbing up an innocuous-looking groove. The last pitch, *Breakaway's* final corner, is a classic thrutch.

▲ Lord Reay's Seat in winter. Photo: *Simon Yearsley*.

THE STORY

The first weekend in March 2006 presented us with almost perfect conditions for a second attempt at a winter ascent of *Pobble*. The car began struggling on the snowy roads not far north of Inverness. Cheap snow chains won us a couple of dozen more slow miles before their final disintegration. They died in vain. The road north was definitively closed at Lairg and wouldn't be ploughed till the next morning. The bikes in the back of the car looked ridiculous, the snowshoes didn't. Over our pints that night we agreed that getting a day behind schedule was a small price to pay for the promising conditions. We finally began the human-powered part of our approach a mere day later. The bikes performed remarkably well. Only a few drifts forced us to get off and push. Snow showers kept blowing in and we cheered each one. At the outflow from Coire na Lice we swapped bikes for snowshoes and began the long plod. Dawn came in a gap between showers, and through gorgeous pink light we got our first view of the crag. It was white.

Simon led the first pitch smoothly, and as I took the rack I was full of apprehension. The chimney above was clearly very steep. We had come a long way and waited a long time to get here. Being in the right place at the right time is half the battle in winter climbing. But it is only half: you still have to climb the route. As soon as I got started I knew that the chimneys would go. Cracks in the sidewalls swallowed my picks whole and hungrily devoured wires. Chockstones begged to be swung from. It was hard work, but joyous hard work, the sort of positive mixed climbing we all like to imagine. Persistent snow showers sent occasional waves of spindrift down the chimney as we worked our way up. We took the final chockstone of the chimney system directly, avoiding the decadent sidewall dalliances of the summer. We wanted meaty, northern, winter thuggery and we got it in spades.

Above the chimneys the route changed character, abruptly turning all slabby. Chimneys are natural winter terrain, but slabs, unless iced or vegetated, are generally best avoided. *Pobble*'s 'grey crinkly slab' was neither iced nor vegetated, and I was glad it was Simon's job to balance delicately across it into the gathering gloom. Any slight features there might have been were buried deep beneath the powder. It was clearly imperative to take the shortest line we could find on the slab, so Simon made for an apparently loose corner that the summer description warns against. Careful footwork on thin edges saw him off the slab and into the vertical corner and the paradoxical world of loose ground: how do you trust enough to move whilst at the same time trusting nothing? A sudden awful clattering, a yelp, but he's still on. Having failed to eject Simon, the corner soon succumbed.

It was fully dark by the time we gathered at the final belay, and the snow was now continuous. Our position on the arête felt precarious, and above the ground looked improbably steep. To the right and left also the ground looked improbably steep. Going down was just unthinkable after all we'd just climbed. So out to the right I went, traversing unhelpful ground over unfathomable steepness with great reluctance. On all memorable climbs there comes a point when you stop climbing for pleasure and start climbing to get off the cliff, to go home. That point had just arrived. But the same things still had to be done, the same patient digging for gear, the same trawling for hooks, the same probing for cracks.

The rightwards traverse ended with a pull up left onto a final slab where I crouched, bunched up under an impending wall, trying to work out how to use a blind crack at the junction of the two. I wanted some certainty, not sloppy sideways torques that would require some weirdly precise tension if I wasn't to go scrattling down the wall. All those miles of driving, weekends and days off, phone calls and weather forecasts, all that cycling and walking, hoping and planning had funnelled down to this moment, to this troublesome little crack. I needed to make a couple of moves up and left along the slab. But the darkness, the insecurity of the moves, and the snow blowing in all directions sapped my courage and I stayed welded to the footholds.

Finally, I got so frustrated with my own inertia that I went for it. Leaning off the best torque, I reached out my left hand and got some sort of open-handed grip in the blind crack, then moved my left foot along the slab till it seemed to stick on something. I let go of the torque, matched hands, moved my right foot onto the slab, and scrabbled frantically along on awful handholds till I could spear a blessed patch of turf. A final little corner led to the ridge. I brought Simon up and we screamed our jubilation into the darkness.

We stayed roped up to descend the ridge and sent great slabs and sloughs of snow down its west side as we carved our way down to the col. Back at the sacks we ate, drank and slumped. Warmed by success, we now wanted to sit and talk through the climb. But we knew we had a long way to go.

It wasn't until we got back to the bikes and tried to ride them that it dawned on us. Snow had been falling off and on for most of the day. And it had been falling on the landrover track just as it had everywhere else. It was a long, slow push back down the Strath. •

Lord Reay's Seat in winter.
Photo: *James Higgins*.

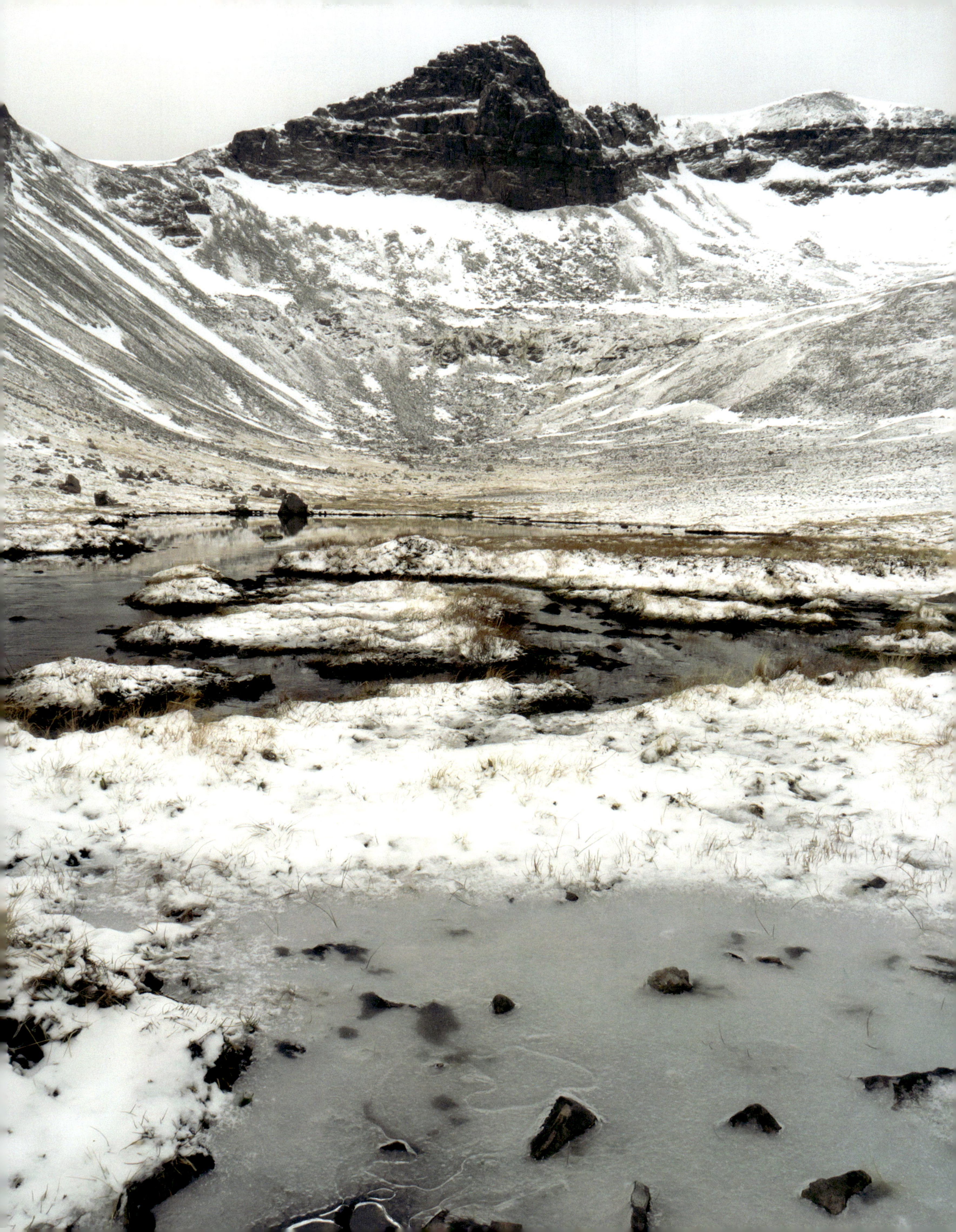

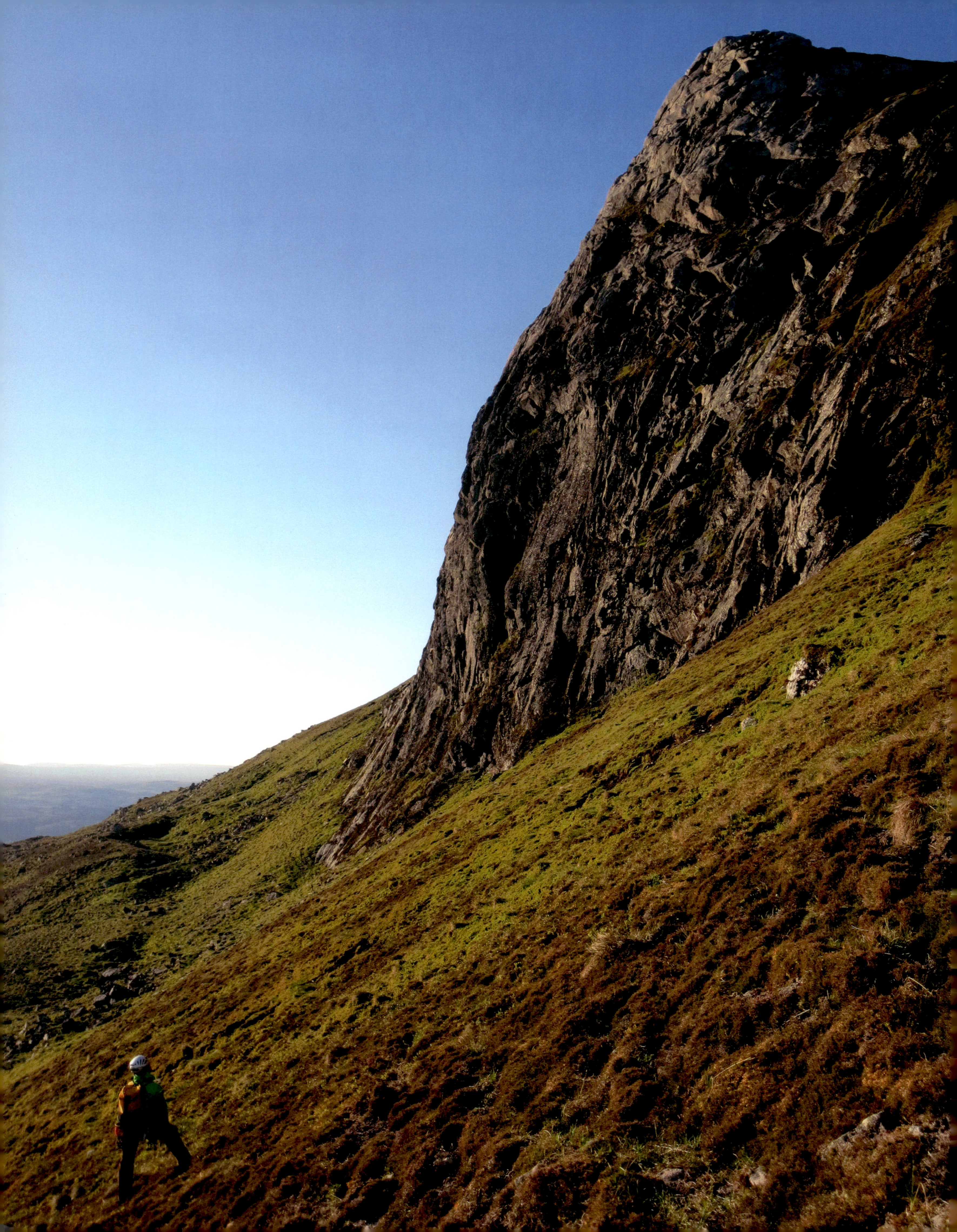

Sgor a' Chleirich, Ben Loyal – by Keith Milne

THE PLACE
Situated in the most northerly group of mountain crags in the UK, the wild and remote cliffs of Ben Loyal will not be encountered by chance.

It will take a deliberate plan to make a serious attempt at any of the long routes here. The mountain itself has an impressive profile when approaching from the north or south, its ancient granite tors rising majestically over the loch-strewn, desolate moorland below.

THE CLIFF
Sgor a' Chleirich (664m) is almost a peak in itself, a vast, steep west-facing slab of granite, its profile greatly enhanced by the beautiful lochan at its base. On closer acquaintance, the 250-metre-high crag reveals a variety of cracks and overlap features tempting the climber onwards and upwards. The rock is more properly called syenite, with occasional pockets and weathered gritstone-like features. Because of the conical nature of the buttress, it dries rapidly and wet patches tend to be localised. The west-facing aspect also has the added advantage of catching any available sun in the afternoon – quite unusual for a Scottish mountain crag.

The central route of the crag is the towering *Marathon Corner*, starting as a steep heathery gully and becoming more defined with height. To the left of this is a series of slabs that sweep upwards, apparently blank, towards a series of more featured overlaps. To the right of *Marathon Corner*, the impressive upper slabs are guarded by fierce overhangs and cracked walls. The routes finish almost on the rocky summit and the pleasant grassy descent is on the south side.

THE CLIMBING
The size of the cliff is very deceptive and because of its conical form it is easy to get lost amid the sweep of slabs. This is a major mountain cliff, one of the biggest in the country, and the leader's route-finding and gear placement skills will be tested to the limit. A big rack and lots of long slings are particularly useful here, to take advantage of the cunning and often rather lateral runner placements. Having said that, protection is mostly good on the existing routes, with only a few run-out sections, though there is certainly scope for some bolder routes in the E4 to E5 range. The potential in winter is less clear, though clearly with one existing line there must be something still on offer.

The grassy diagonal line of *Priest's Rake* was the first line to fall, back in 1958, and 11 years later the more direct *Marathon Corner* was climbed. In the exceptional cold winter of 2010 it saw its first winter ascent. In the seventies a much harder route was climbed on the right-hand side, mysteriously named *Gog*, but it was not until after the millennium that Aberdeen-based climbers added two new routes to the large areas of clean slabs, ignoring reports of excess vegetation.

◄ Sgor a' Chleirich. Climber: Richard Biggar.
Photo: *Guy Robertson*.

THE ROUTES

Milky Way (E2)
This route climbs the series of inspiring slabs on the left side of the crag. Mostly climbing in balance with the exception of a hand-jam crack near the start and a strenuous overhang near the finish. A lot steeper than the Etive slabs, this is a great route if you like slabs with holds and like to rest before the difficult sections.

Gog (E3)
The full details of this groundbreaking climb are lost in the mists of time, but we know from the first ascensionists that the meat of the lower section takes a narrow, discontinuous gangway slanting from left to right. A small overhang blocking the way is taken with an acrobatic move. Eventually reaching the central grassy bay of *Marathon Corner*, the route now makes a hard traverse right under some overlapping roofs to gain some clean slabs to finish.

Marathon Corner (E1, VIII,7)
Tackles the monolithic corner cleaving the centre of the crag. Be prepared for some route-finding difficulties and commitment. Once the grassy ledge system has been reached, a direct finish up *Gog* would make this arguably one of the best mountain routes in Scotland.

Richard Biggar on *Mars* (E4).
Photo: *Guy Robertson*.

THE NORTH WEST HIGHLANDS | SGOR A' CHLEIRICH, BEN LOYAL

▲ Pete Macpherson on *Marathon Corner* (VIII,7). Photo: *Iain Small*.

THE STORY

For many adventurous climbers, new routes offer the most rewarding experiences, although taking more effort and having a more uncertain result than going to the same old places. I first read about Ben Loyal in Ralph Storer's *50 More Routes on Scottish Mountains*, which contains a wonderful photo of the cliff. However, the area guidebook was not so encouraging. It told of experienced climbers repulsed by steep vegetation and treacherously loose rock, and the route descriptions were vintage.

With visions of Lost World greenery in mind I made a reconnaissance in 2002, but was pleasantly surprised by the large areas of clean rock with very few recorded routes. Was this a place others were keeping secret?

So, in the perfect weather of spring 2003, I joined Steve Helmore for a serious attempt. Starting on the left side of the crag, we moved tentatively up towards an obvious crack. The heather in this succumbed to hacking with my old north wall hammer, brought along specifically for the purpose. Gritty jams led to more pleasant ground and soon put us onto a ledge system. The heather was remarkably short and peeled off the slabs unnervingly. Craning our necks upwards, the way wasn't obvious and there was clearly a risk of becoming

186 THE GREAT MOUNTAIN CRAGS OF SCOTLAND

▲ Tess Fryer on *Milky Way* (E2). Photo: *Ian Taylor*.

overcommitted without protection in a sea of steep slabs with limited belays. However, by sneaking left a little we found a hole for a welcome cam. Above this, a promising overlap coming in from the left was disappointing: it was totally blind. The final run-out section to an enticing edge was made more exciting by some seepage and a doubtful hold. The next pitch was memorable – as good as you will find anywhere – using a crack, a shallow corner and more teetering up the slabs. We were making good progress.

Unfortunately we were now stumped by a band of large overhangs. Initial attempts at a direct 'boulder problem' mantelshelf proved futile. The afternoon sun was beating down incongruously and I almost said it was too hot (this was northern Scotland in April!). To the left, that Lost World greenery had now become reality. Yet after some cleaning further left again to place a large cam and open up a hand-jam, we cracked the overhang and reached another system of slabs. This turned out to be sprinkled with fine incut holds and surprisingly good runner placements. A great pitch, and a sense that the end was now close. Finally, more clean, pleasant climbing delivered us on the summit. It's not often in the north of Scotland you can relax in the hot sunshine at 650 metres, having completed a substantial new route on a remote cliff.

In September the following year I had the good fortune to return to Ben Loyal, this time with Mark Atkins. We arrived in the afternoon and set up camp next to the lochan. Looking up we could see that the lichenous rock to the right of *Marathon Corner* featured a band of overhangs near its base, and the easiest line above was not obvious. We approached up the heathery hillside until we were tip-toeing on worryingly steep grass (I should have brought the north wall hammer again). After a depressingly long time we managed to set up a poor belay, more akin to alpine exploits than Scottish mountain rock. The first mossy ten metres of climbing above were precarious, but the rock soon improved, leading to pleasant, well-protected climbing up a rib to the first major difficulties. The continuation line was direct, but the groove was sprouting ferns and rattling with blocks, so I placed some good runners and made a committing step right into an exposed recess. After a moment of excitement pulling off a loose hold, I fixed good runners in a parallel crack which I had spied from below. I was almost in balance, but it was obvious that the route would have to go back left after a few metres. With the setting sun reflecting orange on the lochs to the west, I lowered off, pleased that we had at least got past the overhangs and that the rock was better than anticipated.

We slept early, our minds busy thinking of how to tackle the challenge ahead. The following day the weather wasn't as good as advertised, and we plodded around in the drizzle hoping for an improvement. It wasn't until early afternoon that we were back in-situ. In wetter conditions, we repeated the precarious approach and a cool wind sapped our enthusiasm and tugged at our thick jackets. After some thrashing around at my previous highpoint, I was fully fired up. Using a long layaway move, I managed to get back left to a sharp spike and continued steeply, rope dragging, to reach a large ledge. Recovering my breath, I brought Mark up to join me. I was glad I hadn't tried this route too early in the season. There was a good block belay, but we had been acutely aware of the black and blank looking nature of the corner above. It didn't look any better on closer acquaintance, and Mark set off tentatively up the left wall, brushing off lichen as he went. There was a long way to go and I was worried, but I relaxed somewhat when he unexpectedly found a thread runner just below a bulge. He tackled this with conviction, his right foot waving in vain, trying to bridge onto the smooth wall. I gripped the rope tightly in readiness of a fall. With tiny footholds crumbling in his wake he managed to belly flop unceremoniously onto a sloping ledge.

The tide was turning on the mountain. The obvious line led left and up pleasant cracks and slabs. The rock was now very clean. Straight above was a beautiful slab, but as expected it lacked protection. The alternative was to climb a continuously interesting grooved arête on the left. Once this faded, we decided to traverse back right towards an obvious belay and more into the line of the route. It seemed prudent to leave a runner for the second to avoid the potential pendulum. As Mark led on again I glimpsed him weaving to and fro across the expanse of slabs and overlaps. I followed the balancy moves and was delighted to see that we were now on *Priest's Rake* after four long pitches, the major difficulties now behind us. With time pressing, we scurried rightwards on up giant sculpted slabs, until once again an abrupt step finished just metres from the summit.

There's been talk in the past of leaving the climbs of the North West unrecorded, but I don't concur with this view. Providing descriptions of routes enables and inspires other climbers to add their own ascents to cliffs they might otherwise not visit. Amid the wild and lonely grandeur of Ben Loyal, far from the nearest bouldering mat, it's surely time for today's hungry young tigers to leave their mark on the Lost World.

Guy Robertson on Mars (E4).
Photo: *Richard Biggar.*

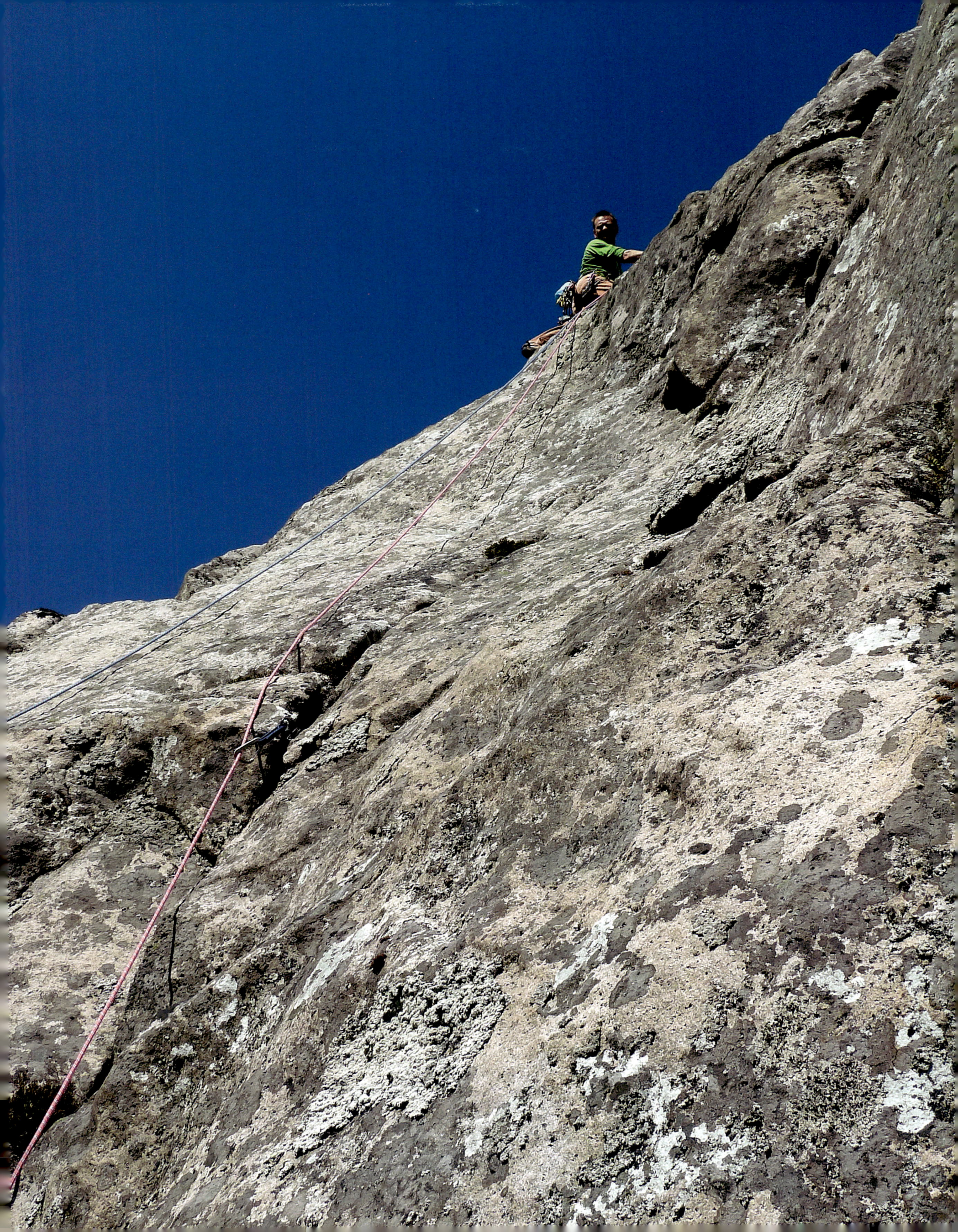

Ben Loyal from the north.
Photo: *Colin Threlfall*.

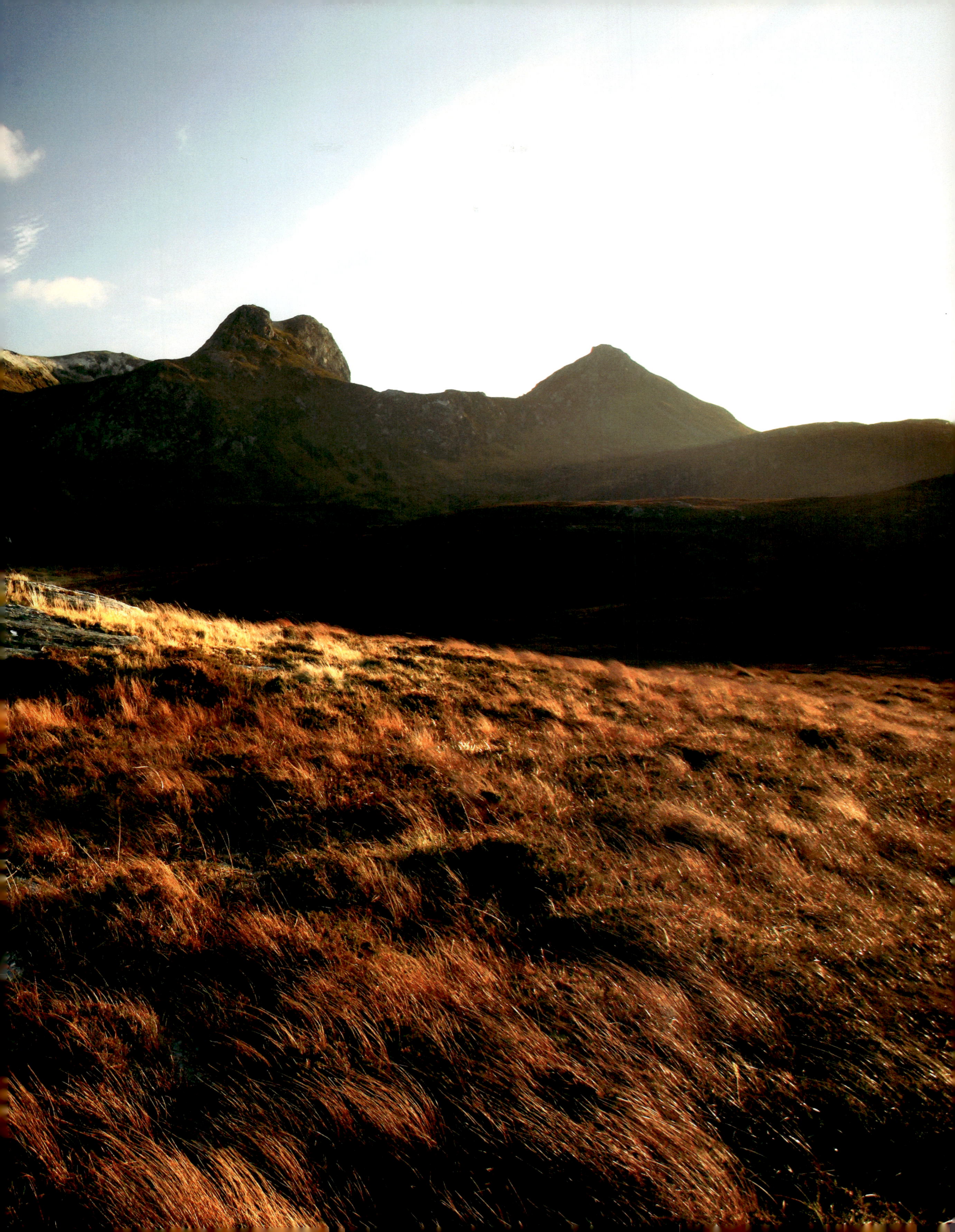

THE ISLANDS

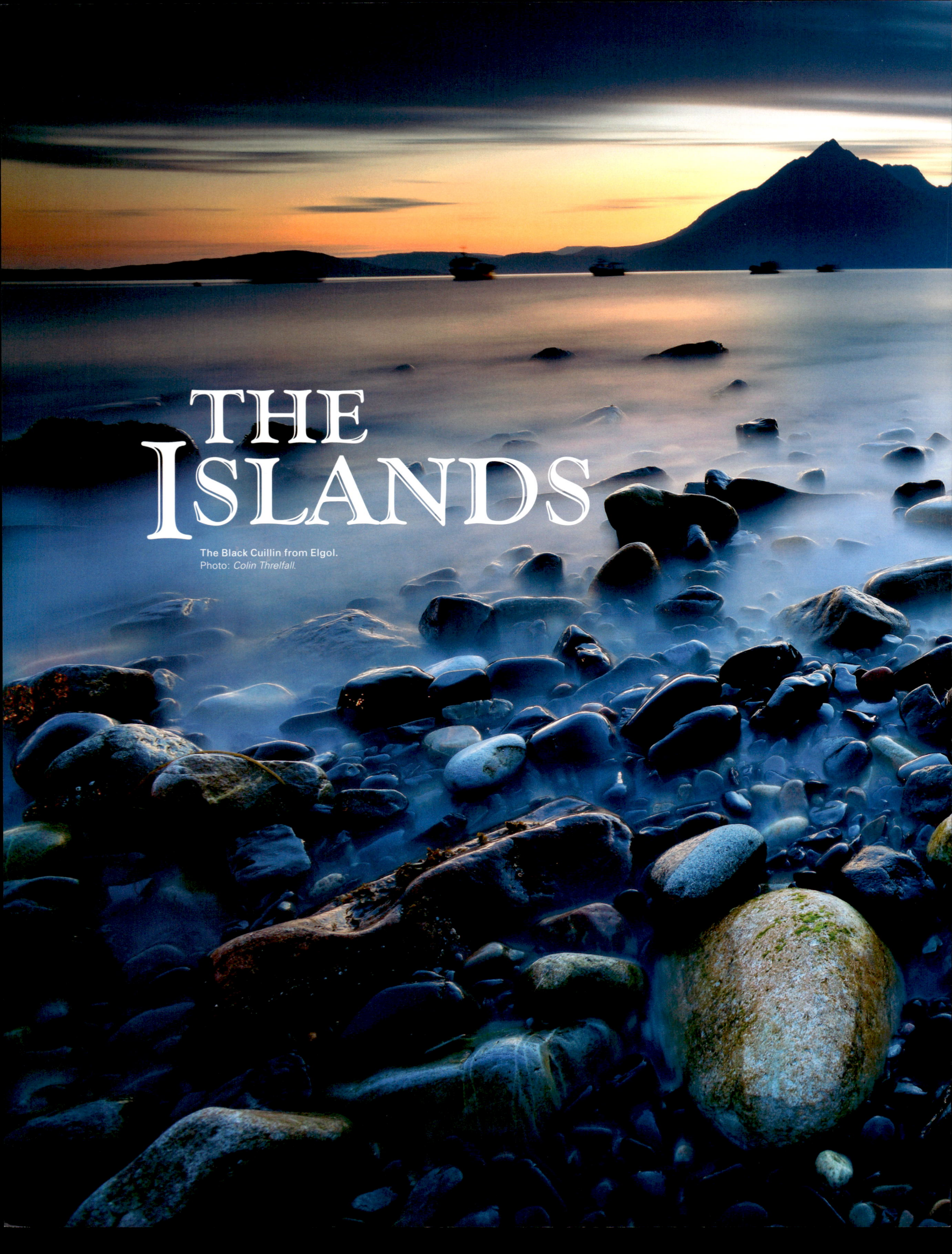

The Black Cuillin from Elgol.
Photo: *Colin Threlfall.*

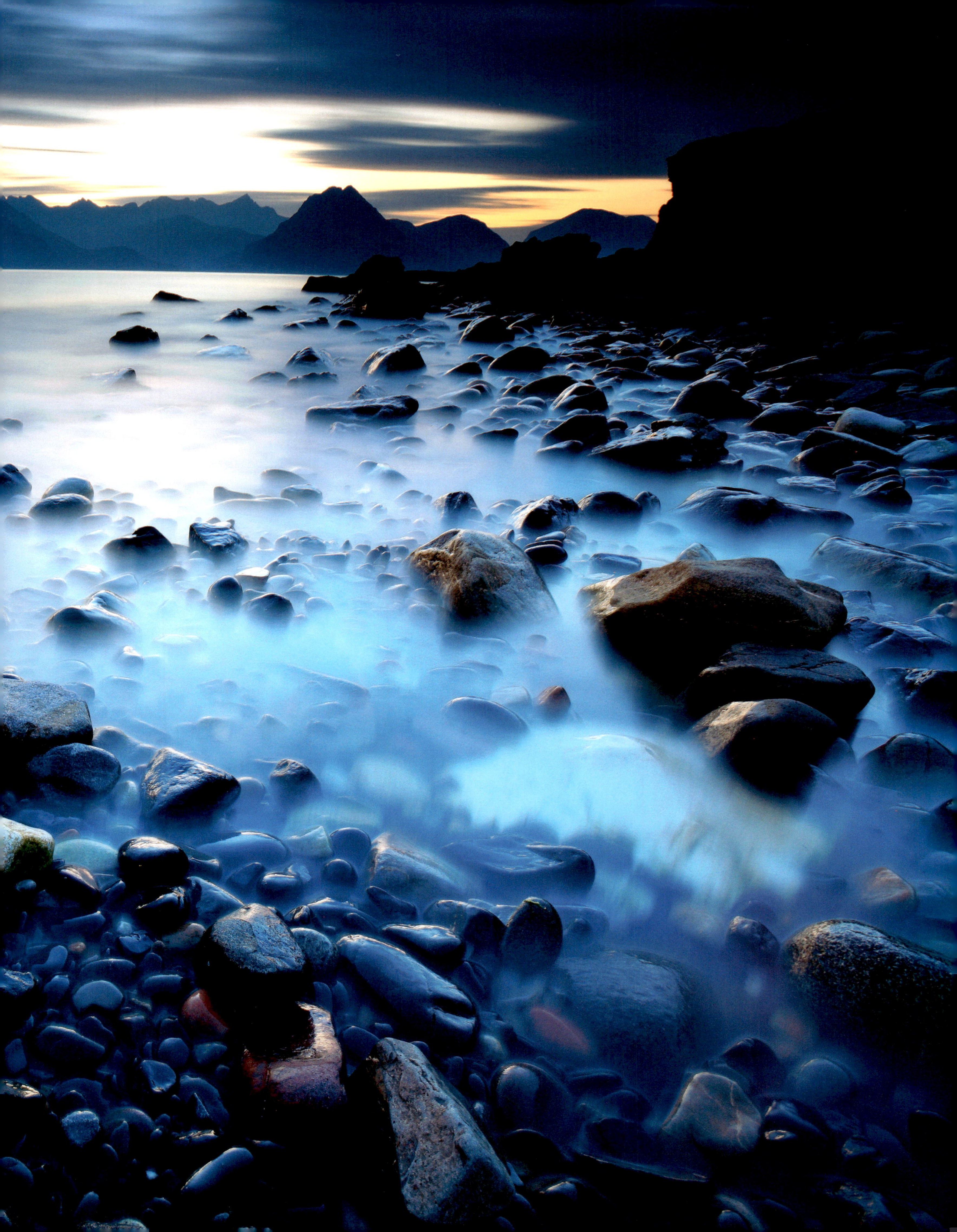

Martin Moran exploring the north side of
Am Bhastier, Skye, in winter.
Photo: *Guy Robertson*

Islands
by Stuart B. Campbell

*Here you can look over the edge
into the half-life of the earth,
see: the spoor of dinosaurs on the Jurassic shore.
We camped on the footprint of a croft
a man once kept at Coruisk;
little remains, everything so far removed.*

*We climbed the peak of the young men,
because we were young men and
older, yet still eager, sought the inaccessible:
pinnacles, geos, ridges. Crimps, smears,
jams, jugs; dream-rock: moves flowing from moves.
You give everything; to risk it,
not the falling, but that exaltation:*

> *feeling the great skua's effortless levitation,
> kinship with the sure-footed stag;
> in that abstracted moment,
> a foregone sense of self; even the contours
> of your fingerprints are eroded.*

*For what? An eagle feather for your cap,
like Hector Mór na Beinn;
to name a new route: Star of the Sea,
Sunset Slab and Yellow Groove, or
Reul na Mara, Leac na Gréine agus
A' Chlais Bhuidhe,
as he once might have known them?*

Introduction to the Islands – *By Blair Fyffe*

Imagine a wild and windswept archipelago surrounded by an ever-changing ocean – sometimes calm and quiet, sometimes furiously battering the shore. A hint of peat smoke to the air, old crofts, and grassed-over lazy beds hint at a bygone age. Now throw in white sand beaches and some of the finest mountain and sea cliff climbing in the country, and you may be getting an idea of what the Hebridean Islands have to offer the adventurous climber.

The Hebrides consist of two groups of islands off the north-west coast of Scotland. The Outer Hebrides form a chain of islands over 100 miles long, beyond which there is little more than the dark, angry north Atlantic Ocean for over 2,000 miles. The most northerly of this chain, and the largest of all the Hebridean islands, is Harris/Lewis. This is one island which consists of two different sections, Lewis in the north and Harris in the south. Together they are sometimes known as the Long Island. Here are found two of Scotland's greatest yet least known mountain crags: the huge overhanging bastion of Sròn Uladail on Harris, and the compact wall of Creag Dhubh Diobadail on Lewis.

The Inner Hebrides consist of a number of islands which lie much closer to the Scottish mainland. The largest of these is Skye. During the last Ice Age, when sea levels were lower, this island was joined to the mainland. Since 1995 it has again been attached to the mainland, but this time by the slender concrete thread of the Skye Bridge. Skye is famous for the Cuillin Ridge, the finest mountaineering expedition in the British Isles. Scattered along the flanks of the main ridge are many quality crags with great long routes, at all grades, on typically perfect rock.

Being tucked away at the furthest corners of the country, Hebridean crags tend to get discussed more than visited. Skye is probably the busiest of the islands in terms of climbing activity, but even here most head to a handful of popular locations, while other less well known, but high quality crags remain deserted. Indeed, on most mountain crags in the Hebrides you are likely to have the place to yourself. Many of these crags face away from the road, out into a wilderness of peat bogs, streams and lochans, and often remain hidden on the approach until you are almost underneath them. This all adds to the sense of remoteness and adventure associated with climbing here.

With so little human disturbance, these crags offer a great opportunity to see wildlife – especially creatures which, like the mountaineer, enjoy wide open spaces. The Cuillin, for example, has the highest density of nesting golden eagles anywhere in the UK. The barren moorlands and lochs thrive with a variety of bird life, including divers and greenshank. The sea – which is never too far away – bustles with marine life. Seabirds, often from huge colonies, cruise these seas where seals, otters, dolphins, minke whales and even basking sharks are not an uncommon sight.

The weather in the Hebrides can often be better than on the mainland, especially in the Outer Isles, where incoming Atlantic weather tends to pass over rapidly, as the rain-inducing upland areas are much smaller than on the mainland. As with the rest of the north-west, midges are a hazard. They tend to be worse between June and September. However, as these islands are some of the windiest places in Britain, there is often enough of a breeze to keep them at bay, especially in the hills.

Despite the close proximity of Skye and Harris/Lewis, their geology is very different. All of the Outer Hebrides, apart from a small area around Stornoway, is made up of Lewisian gneiss. These are the oldest rocks in Britain and have a history that spans roughly 3,000 million years – over half the age of the earth. Despite a century of research, these rocks have not yet given up all their secrets. What is known is that they began life as a variety of other rock types, such as granite. Plate tectonics resulted in them being buried under great mountain ranges, heated to near melting point and folded by unimaginable pressures. Deep within the earth's crust they cooled slowly, allowing the formation of large crystals, which provide great frictional properties thousands of millions of years later.

Over aeons of time, the overlying rock has been eroded away to leave relatively rounded hills that can be ascended quite easily on foot. However, in a few locations the glaciers of the last Ice Age have carved out some magnificent crags: large and compact with few features. Just a lot of steep, solid, rough rock.

Lewisian gneiss is a tough rock. Contorted patterns hint at its violent past. It can appear granite-like – with long positive flakes and corner cracks, or gritstone-esque – rough, rounded and solid. To the climber it is generally very user friendly with good holds and protection. Intrusions, such as veins of quartz, are often compact and give bold climbing.

In contrast to the ancient Lewisian gneiss of the Outer Isles, the rocks of Skye are mere youngsters. About 58 million years ago a dome of molten rock welled up under the earth's crust. This broke through the crust under what is now Skye, in a huge volcanic eruption. The lava flows that were extruded now make up the majority of the rocks on the island. Other smaller plumes of magma pushed up towards the surface, some of them breaking through the crust to form the igneous rocks that make up the island of Rhum and parts of the coastline of Antrim in Northern Ireland. Other plumes failed to break the surface and cooled slowly to produce the much redder coloured granite of the Red Cuillin. Eventually, the great Skye volcano became blocked, and the magma cooled very gradually to produce a large-grained, dark-coloured rock called gabbro. This dark, clean rock forms what we now call the Black Cuillin. The gabbro found here is one of the roughest rock types in the country, great when standing on sloping ledges, or in the damp – but a few hours pulling on small holds and your fingertips will know all about it.

Weathering has not yet had time to grind these mountains down; they are still young sharp peaks reaching for the sky. The advantage of this is that there is a huge amount of climbable rock packed into a relatively small area. The main Cuillin ridge is about eight miles long, but there are many subsidiary ridges harbouring plenty of fine crags.

The history of climbing on the Outer and Inner Hebrides is also quite different, but this time it is Skye that has the long history. Skye's widely visible, jagged peaks have always attracted the more adventurous visitor, and the first rock routes here were climbed over a decade earlier than those in more accessible areas such as Ben Nevis. Initially climbing in the Cuillin was an activity for the rich and privileged, and locals were often hired as guides, as in the famous pairing of Collie and Mackenzie. The first guidebook was published around 1908, and led to an increase in popularity. With economic depression and the loss of almost an entire generation in the First World War, activity slowed in the twenties and thirties. During the Second World War, many allied troops were sent to the Cuillin to train. This resurrected interest in climbing in the area. Classic routes like *Integrity*, *Arrow Route* and *Commando Crack* were pioneered during this time.

As with other areas in the west, it was the arrival of the working class hard men of the Creag Dhu that heralded the rise in standards that produced the first Extreme standard climbs. The first of these were *Trophy Crack* and *Bastindo*, put up on the same day in 1956. Through the 1960s many classic easier Extremes were added. After a quiet period during the early seventies, harder technical advances came later that decade, with the development of better protection. With ascents of *Dilemma* and *Enigma* (E3) and the freeing of *Creag Dhu Grooves* (E3), East Buttress in Coire Lagan became – and remains – a popular destination for fine technical, high standard mountain routes. However, the highlight of the era was Fowler and Thomas's ascent of *Stairway to Heaven* (E5) on the Great Prow of Bla Bheinn in 1977, an impressive, serious route on a vast smooth wall. Although the great cliffs of the Cuillin now contain many fine routes at all grades they are far from climbed out. Perhaps Dave Birkett's 2007 route in the heart of the Coruisk wilderness – *Skye Wall* (E8) – gives an idea of what awaits modern climbers willing to make a bit of effort. This is one of only a handful of routes harder than E5 in the Cuillin, an area that has more good quality rock than anywhere else in Scotland.

Going climbing on the mountain crags of Harris and Lewis requires more than a little extra effort. This, and the fact that the classic lines on the big crags tend to be in the mid E-grades at least, perhaps explains why development began much later than on Skye. Although a few forays had been made onto the main face of Creag Dhubh Diobadail during the seventies, it was not until 1980 that Mick Fowler climbed straight up the centre to create *Panting Dog Climb*. He returned a year later to climb *The Big Lick*. Although a couple of new routes have been added since then, this crag boasts a remarkable amount of perfect unclimbed rock.

Due to its steepness, Sròn Uladail has always been an intimidating proposition. In the sixties a trio of fine routes around HVS were climbed on its right-hand side. The main face was first tackled in 1969 when both *Stone* and *The Scoop* were climbed using aid. The former was an attempt at a free route that required some aid to complete, while the latter was a pure aid route right from the start. During the seventies and early eighties the crag became one of the last bastions of British aid climbing. A pointer of things to come came in 1980, when *Stone* was freed by Mick Fowler – yet again, the main pitch being one of the finest anywhere on British rock. The big event, though, came in 1987 when young anti-heroes Johnny Dawes and Paul Pritchard free climbed *The Scoop* over seven eventful days. This mind-blowing route remains one of the longest, most sustained and sought-after mountain rock climbing experiences anywhere in Britain. Strangely, since the ascent of *The Scoop*, the Sròn's history has been dominated by talented English and Welsh raiding parties. It now contains at least a dozen high quality multi-pitch routes of E5 and above. However there are plenty of lines left to climb, and two aid routes are still awaiting free ascents.

So next time you are planning an adventurous climbing trip, consider heading to the Hebrides. The climbing out here is all about adventure and escapism, far from the hustle of the modern day climbing scene. The combination of wild moor, rugged scenery and open spaces which give the islands their unique and captivating atmosphere, is a great antidote to the rat race of modern existence. Whatever your experience of the area, one thing is for sure, a trip to the islands will repay your efforts and leave you wanting more.

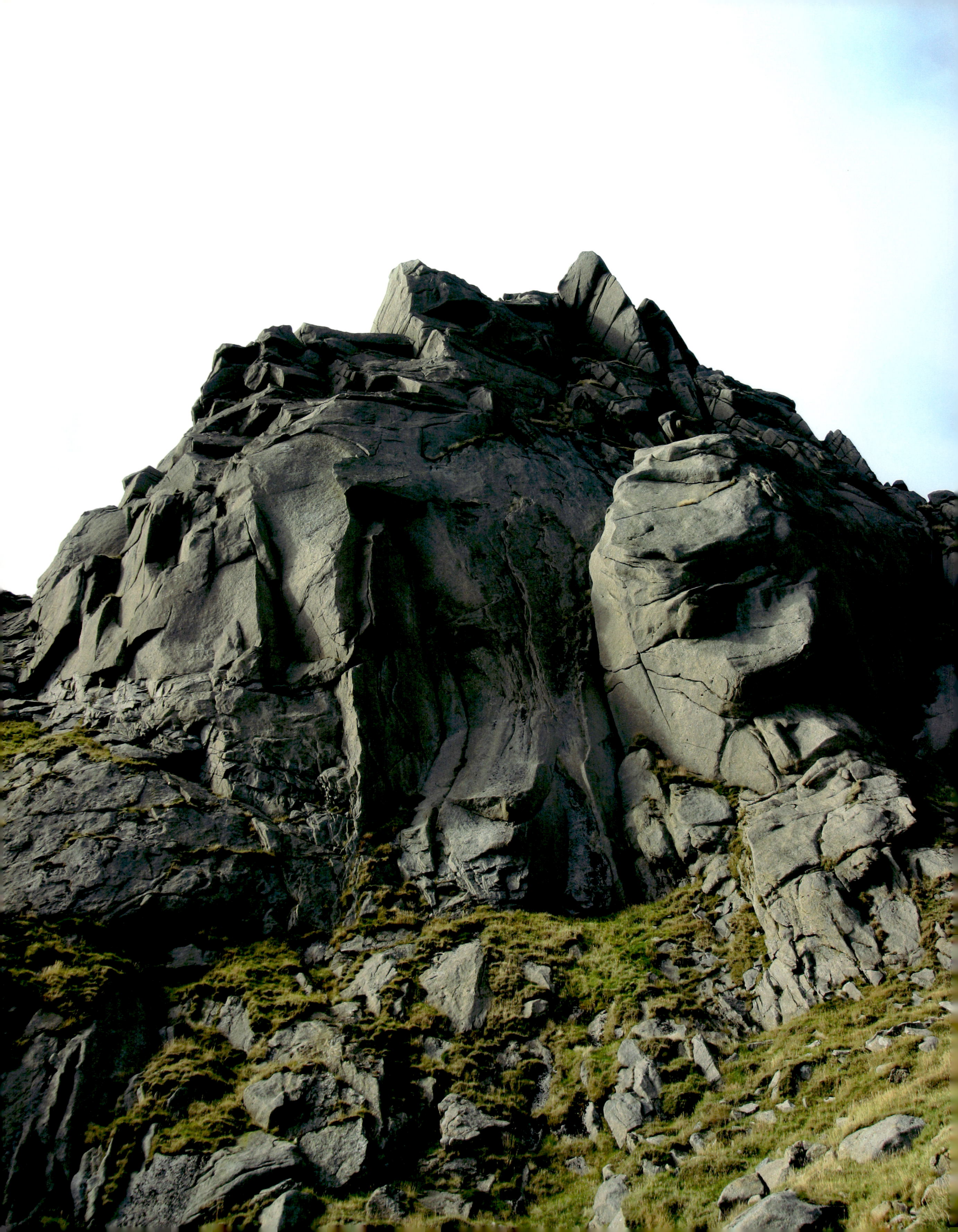

Cir Mhor, Arran – *by John Watson*

THE PLACE
Arran is the island that gets many Scots climbers hooked on that 'big mountain feel'. For me, it was the cover shot of Ken Crocket's 1989 *SMC Arron, Arrochar and the Southern Highlands* guide that inspired renewed visits to the island. It showed helmeted Lego-man climbers hunkered to a belay on the great sweeping flank of Cir Mhor, overlooking the long watery U-bend that is Glen Rosa.

They looked intent and busy, as though trying to shut out the alpine intimidation of what lay above them. It was an inspiring shot and had a new generation of climbers reaching for the phone. The next two decades were to see a watershed in what was possible on granite. Arran underwent something of a gold rush. Strong climbers arrived to tiptoe gracefully, if tentatively, away from the old classics, and a long legacy of big-booted grunting gave way to focused precision and exposed athleticism.

My first experience of Cir Mhor came late one April morning when I went to climb the famous South Ridge. It was almost silent as we ascended blindly through the mist into Fionn Coire, a distant breeze swooshing through the invisible crags above. With one puff of wind the view cleared before us, and there it was, the pristine colossus of Cir Mhor.

THE CLIFF
The natural geology of Arran granite is predominantly eroded blocks layered upon each other like the leaves of a giant book, with cracked slabs often vanishing into nerve-shredding blankness. The rock of Cir Mhor is perhaps the best example of this perplexing geology: an impeccable array of white-grey granite reflecting the light like burnished metal.

It is often compared to the armoured chest of a gladiator – the sternum being the South Ridge, flanked on the east side by steeply shouldered walls and on the west by the overlapping 'armour' of slabs. The top is a classic apical peak converging at the 'Rosa Pinnacle', giving the impression of a gladiator helmeted and tensed for the ring, the shadows of great roofs resembling his embattled brows. The subsidiary ridges of Prospero's buttress and Caliban's buttress supply suitable biceped arms to the image.

THE CLIMBING
In 1958 the first climbing guide to Arran was published as a slim 84-page, neatly-illustrated booklet by J. M. Johnstone. This signalled the end of the classic period; all things vegetated and crumbly would soon be forgotten. From here on in, the blankness and cleanness of the better granite would be explored with longer ropes, rubber-soled PAs and improved protection.

Most of the modern routes are based either on ridiculously strenuous overhanging cracks or, more commonly, delicate and bold slabs. The slabs are a little steeper than their famous Etive counterparts, but provoke a similar confusion and terror as to what can be stood on and what will result in skint knees, hands and chest! Gear is plentiful in the long deep cracks of the jointed granite, but often these are left behind where infamously 'disappearing cracks' lead to rounded scoops, sills and basaltic intrusions with lips and shallow pockets often forming the holds. Some of the harder and steeper lines lead unremittingly straight into the maws of obvious features, where the body is twisted into such demanding improvisations that placing gear becomes difficult and sequences strenuous and inescapable. Things are hard on the granite, but more often than not a sudden nervous sequence will lead to generous holds in a tremendous situation, and all is forgiven. The higher you climb on Cir Mhor, the easier things become as the rock lies back, allowing time to absorb the exposed vistas.

◄ The upper buttress on the east side of Cir Mhor's south ridge.
Photo: *Guy Robertson.*

THE ROUTES

South Ridge Direct (VS)
First climbed in 1936, the South Ridge provides one of Scotland's most attractive and distinctive long VS climbs. The route meanders up between impenetrable roofs via the famous 'S' and 'Y' cracks, before cleverly negotiating the final roofs via immaculate pitches such as the Layback Crack, one of the best pitches on Arran, irrespective of grade.

Skydiver (E3)
An utterly tremendous route, notoriously desperate for E3, taking the great bottomless hanging groove on the East Face, then the blank walls above. A delightful exercise in bridging and technique, sustained but nowhere desperate, followed by an altogether fundamental second pitch and a bold final headwall.

The Sleeping Crack (E7)
In 2001, an embryonic Dave MacLeod climbed the quietly named but desperate *The Sleeping Crack*. The crag had slept for over a century before this. It takes the vanishing crack striking out right on the bulging bastion to a hanging thread belay, before regaining the crack to an exposed finish onto a slab and the elation of more straightforward padding.

Iain Small on *Whispering Crack* (E6).
Photo: *Guy Robertson*.

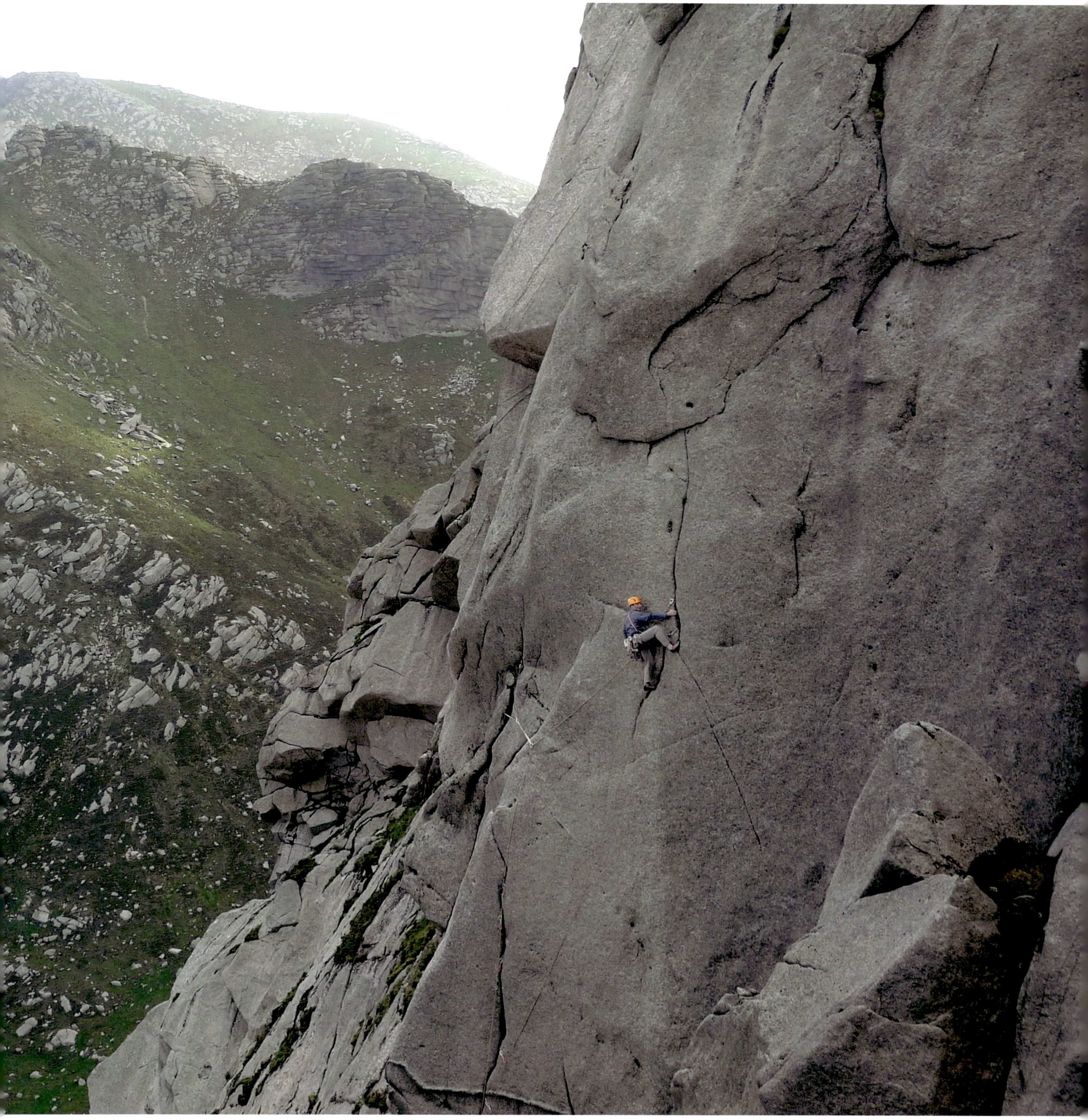

▲ The west side of the South Ridge of Cir Mhor. Photo: *John Watson*.

THE STORY

Dave gets it bad: functional fear. We have been in the city too long, working too much, we need a purpose and we've suddenly found a window of 24 hours. If you're a Glasgow-based climber and ache for the mountains, Arran is the cure.

We jump the afternoon ferry. Galley staff dish out chips and beans in jobsworth portions. Dave and I look at each other like unpopular prisoners. We take a window seat and amuse ourselves trying to translate the purser's announcements on the loudspeakers, before being disgorged onto the island, wobbling on bikes with 50-litre sacks as though on one wheel rather than two. The rattling ride up to the Garbh Allt bridge and a further hour's hike finds us at the bivi boulder by the moraine humps of the Fionn Coire ford. Cir Mhor and the Rosa pinnacle sweep grandly above us like full sails.

By now it's 8 p.m. Dave still has the city twitch – he suggests a romp up into Coire Daingean and an evening solo ascent of Boundary Ridge and A'Chir. Tent set, but still dangerously early to hit the hip flasks, I agree. The hike up into the coire goes easily with the usual minor sacrifice of sodden feet. Stags eye us

▲ Tony Stone on *Hardlands* (E4). Photo: *Guy Robertson.*

suspiciously as we scamper up the ridge towards howling winds gathering pace in the darkening sky. The slabs of Goatfell cling to a final flush as we breast the ridge and find a Japanese-flag sunset over Loch Lorsa, the clouds purple with inner rage and the water battened down like the hatch of a submarine. My Pertex jacket balloons out and I am spurred to dance along the ridge in Ninja slippers, my calves cramping. 'Look like an elf, you do – Legolas' the elf …

Our Tolkien world dissolves into the west as we skitter down the ridge like spilt mercury, back into the coire and down past the adder-ridden boulders to the tent. It is now 10.20 p.m. and the dram has found its hour.

Stories … nothing but stories fill our lives. Hot stove water ekes out the whisky, and precedes a restless June sleep.

We've overslept, and it's colder than we thought, so our plan is mutually set in limbo and we stomp up to the bottom of Anvil Recess by 9.30 a.m. It's as good as the guidebook suggests but we're still weary and the wind is throwing us wobblers on the slabs. Things get interesting at the junction of South Ridge, where Dave eyes a more direct chimney line.

'Looks bloody brutal!' he spits. 'Painful – offwidth territory. Hate offwidths.'

Dave loves this kind of challenge. Half an hour of gurning and he's up. 'More like E5!'

'Never been repeated till now, I bet. Bit chilly for *Skydiver*, don't you think, my fingers are numb. Anyway, I don't fancy it in this wind.' Dave says nothing, which means it's worth a look.

We slither down Old East to the bottom of the best route on Arran: *Skydiver*. I give Dave the nod on the first pitch as a spur for me to lead the crux second pitch. I have the 4.40 ferry in mind and I'm ashamed of my out-of-form attitude, my lack of fitness and ashamed of my shame! Dave nurses my apprehension with slick climbing and ecstatic chatter, he beams down at me from the first belay. True to form, the pitch is a beauty, gritstone-esque, positional, generous and technical all at once.

I look at my Scarpa slippers, a little baggy now at the toes, and I've been struggling to hold the granite for 24 hours. I take a step left onto polished patina-edges of micro-granite and immediately slip off. I am caught by Dave's hooked foot as though he doesn't quite trust the belay. The fear monster does a little dance in my belly. 'Christ! Sorry, Dave, can't keep my feet on today.'

I gather my wits and scoff at my glaikit-ness. A short traverse under the blind roof and an awkward cam placement leads me to a nervy peek into the blank groove round on the left. Beneath me, by my Elvis knees, it drops into nothingness. I'm freaked out: by the unexpected fall, by my worn boots, by my failure of nerve and by the drop below.

'It's blank, Dave!' It takes just one glance to see the corner is as featureless as a cabinet corner. Dave shrugs from the comfort of his nest of cams.

'Your lead, mate.'

What follows is a flurry of stress, knuckle-ripping climbing, slips, recoveries and general calamity. At one point, above the sickening drop, I am wedged in against the big lug of rock on my right, left toe smearing wildly on steep blank granite, right shoulder jammed against my cheek, screaming at my inability to get at the gear loops on my wedged hip. Then it comes, like it has come before: a great calm takes over. I take one deep breath, and focus. Time and the fear monster both vanish like so much smoke, leaving only this big empty space with no backwards or forwards, no Dave, no me, just the unstoppable urge to climb. Stretching up to a previously-unseen and positive ripple on the left, I get my shoulder out and turned and wedge a foot against the stubborn lug of stone. I grab its flat ear thankfully and haul myself up to better holds and a ledge with a detached flake belay, which has no right to still be attached to the cliff, but that's all there is. I clip in.

Ten minutes later, Dave smears up efficiently but with gritted teeth above the drop. He sets off with some relief onto the final pitch, which proves sticky, technical and bold, but he cruises it in Dave-fashion and seconding it is not a patch on the struggles just gone. Everything resolves itself back into shapes; identities are reassumed and time begins to pressure again. We find ourselves on the terrace below the Rosa Pinnacle, elated and clapped out. It's 3.10 p.m. I suggest the early ferry is still an option.

An hour-and-a-half later, panting onto the ferry, we replay the fear in laughter and cosy reminiscence. Dave's broad smile and thousand-yard stare tell me what we did was far from functional. I leave it at that as we demolish our plates of chips and beans.

Tony Stone on *Hardlands* (E4).
Photo: *Guy Robertson*.

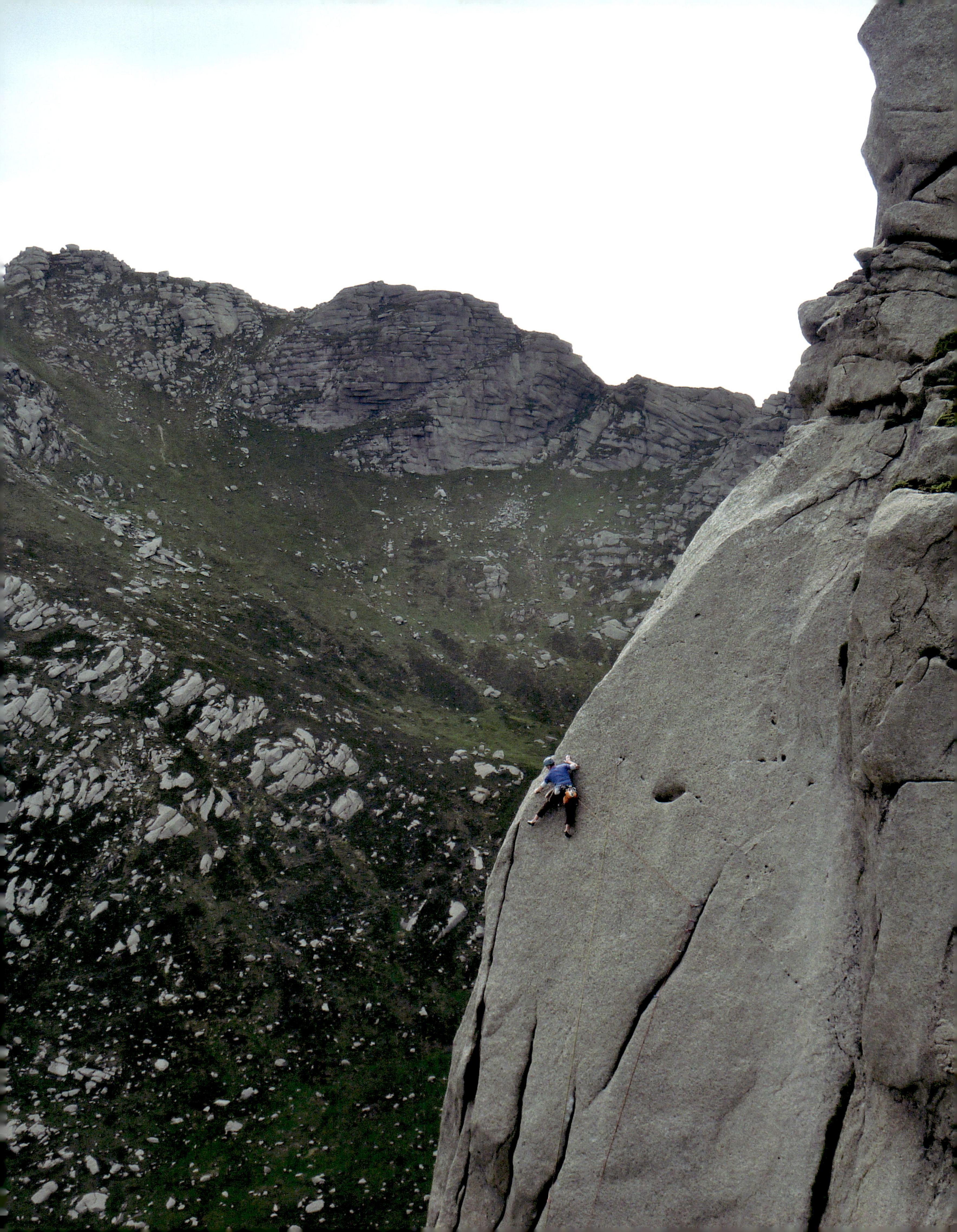

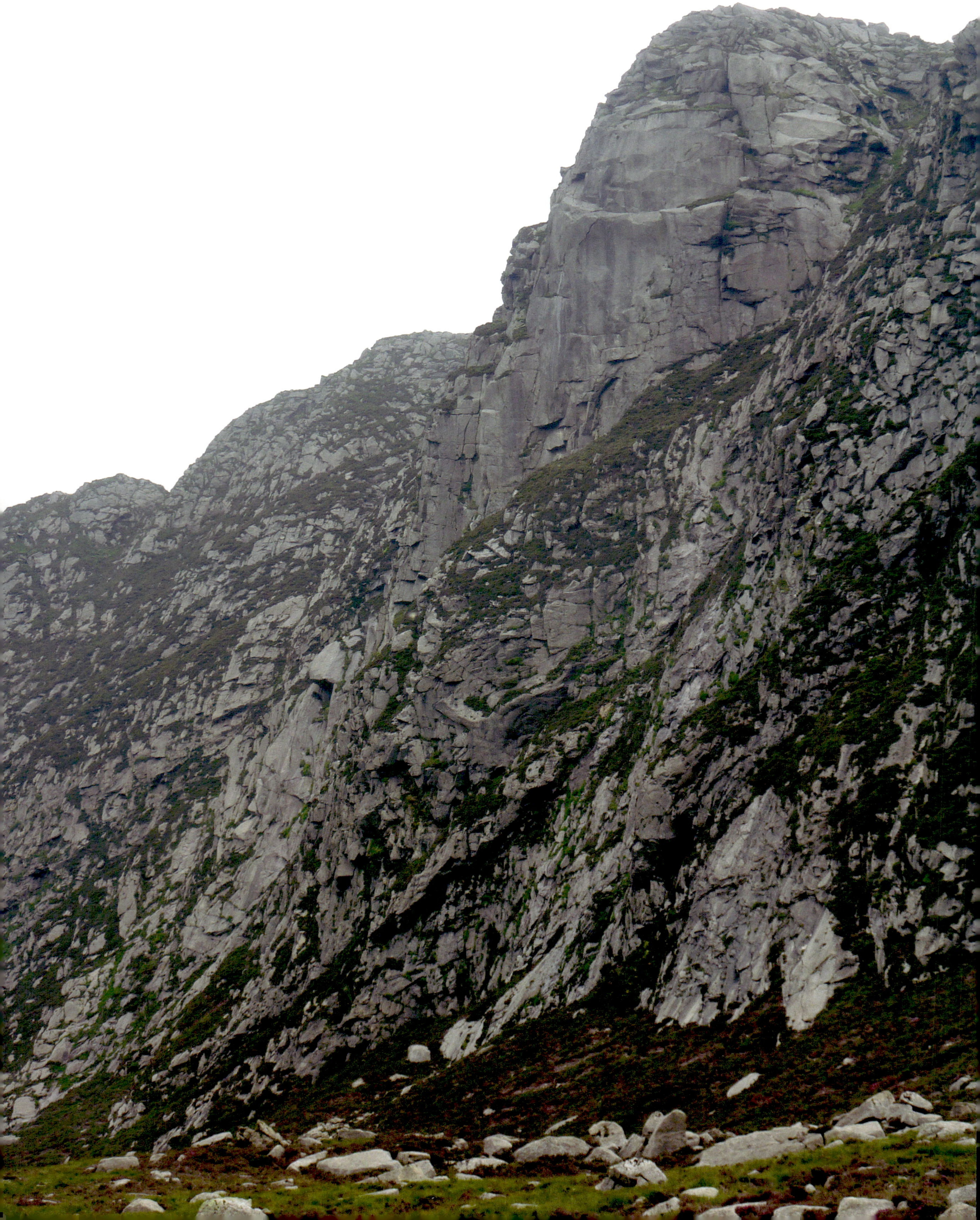

The Bastion, Cioch na h-Oighe, Arran
— by Kevin Howett

THE PLACE

Arran and its climbing have always been a bit of an enigma. This little island has for years been blessed with the accolade of being 'Scotland in miniature' – all the best of the mainland, but without the worst. It should, therefore, attract a wide audience, and yet I know of many climbers who have never even visited.

There are some huge cliffs on Arran, bigger than most climbers realise, but without doubt the jewel of them all is The Bastion of Cioch na h-Oighe. Located high in one of the most impressive coires on the island, tantalising glimpses can be snatched as you walk down the hawthorn-shrouded lane out of Mid Sannox. Suddenly, breaking free of the trees, the open expanse of Glen Sannox lies before you, and high on the left are the smooth bare flanks of the Cioch.

The route up to the crag follows a stream that flows from the springs dotting the base of the coire floor. Entering the Devil's Punchbowl, as it is affectionately known, is an almost spiritual experience; the cathedral-like rock architecture arches over you in full Gothic mode. If this was in Catholic Spain a pilgrim route would take tourists to its healing springs, and a giant crucifix would be suspended high between the coire walls.

THE CLIFF

A thousand-foot wall dominates the coire. Five huge diagonal ledges dissect a disjointed series of lesser walls, slabs and goat grazings. Composed of heather, unstable grass and unsound rock, ascents of these ledges have not helped the cliff's reputation. However, look closer and between two of the higher ledges, rising to near the summit, glistens a 100-metre sheet of perfect steep granite – a modern rock climber's Nirvana, home to some of the most stunning lines on the island. This is The Bastion.

Unusually for any cliff, the most striking line is the hardest – a scintillating line of vague flakes dissect the steepest and longest central section, providing the dubious possibility of gaining the left-most of two giant 'pincer' flakes high up. Left of this is a complex area of smooth rock broken only by slight grooves, intermittent cracks, ledges and overlaps. Left again and the cliff diminishes in height, but the features here are stronger with a number of powerful grooves and arêtes.

THE CLIMBING

In climbing terms, Arran development has been sporadic – the result of small bands of aficionados taking up the challenge every now and then. As a result, the history of climbing has not followed mainland trends, but is instead intertwined with the personalities of the climbers and the state of the virgin rock. Looseness, scale and a strict on-sight ethic have combined to dictate the style of most first ascents on The Bastion to date.

The diagonal ledges were first breached in 1894, but The Bastion itself waited until the forties for *Midnight Ridge Direct* (VS 5a) to be climbed. The Devil slumbered for another 20 years until Andrew Maxfield found his stunning route *Tidemark* (Severe) in 1960, providing a giddying girdle traverse of the cliff. Maxfield's further addition of *Klepht* in 1967 was still regarded as one of the hardest routes on Arran by the time of the 1979 SMC guidebook.

The seventies however belonged to Bill Skidmore. With Graham Little he formed a formidable partnership exploiting a passion for engineering and judicious use of bolt belays. The pair's ethics were undoubtedly out of step with the rest of the country, but nonetheless their vision produced such quality routes as *Abraxas* (E4) penetrating the imposing central section of the crag. Little described this seminal route as *'my dream, my fixation, my creation, but was it a bold concept marred by my cowardice, or a masterpiece flawed in its making?'* The bolts certainly won't provide much comfort on the crux sections – go and climb it and decide for yourself!

The last great unclimbed line on The Bastion had been cleaned as early as the seventies by Little, but proved too hard for an attempt. After a tip-off, Yorkshireman John Dunne broke the ethical mould with his only north-of-the-border raid to claim the line as *The Great Escape* (E8), head-pointing the great central flake line with a pre-placed sling for protection. An on-sight ascent of this magnificent challenge remains one of the most exciting prospects Scottish mountain rock has to offer.

◀ The Bastion of Cioch na h-Oighe.
Photo: *Guy Robertson.*

▲ Kev Howett and Graeme Little on the first ascent of *The Brigand* (E6). Photo: *Kevin Howett Collection*.

▲ The approach into the Bastion, with the crag clearly visible just left below the summit. Photo: *Guy Robertson*.

THE ROUTES

Tidemark (Severe)
A remarkably exposed route at a modest grade that takes you into spectacular territory.

Abraxas (E4)
One of the best multi-pitch Extremes in Scotland, with continually fascinating climbing and astonishing positions. It takes the only true weakness of cracks in the centre of The Bastion, the line unfolding beautifully and logically.

The Brigand (E6)
Arêtes are always exciting; like in-your-face arguments, they thrust towards you from the shoulders of the cliff inviting conflict. This route tackles the most prominent arête on the cliff. A dancing first pitch to a stance is followed by a punch-up through a band of disintegrating rock and a length of intricate ducking and diving leaving the knockout blows to the end.

The Great Escape (E8)
A major Scottish mountain rock climbing challenge, taking an obvious natural line into the heart of the cliff. The climbing is reputedly as bold as it is hard.

▲ Tony Stone on *Abraxas* (E4). Photo: *Guy Robertson*.

THE STORY

Glen Nevis in the late eighties, a basic life of subsistence climbing paid for by a government grant for those without normal livelihoods. During long days of rain, arguing about ethics and scouring guidebooks, Gary noted the plethora of aid points remaining on Arran and even worse, the presence of bolts. On a mountain crag! We were apoplectic. A plan was hatched. The team was Gary Latter, Dave 'Cubby' Cuthbertson, Callum 'Hugo' Henderson and myself. Our quest was the free ascent of *Abraxas*, ground-up without the bolts, a line untouched since its first ascent in 1980.

There was a problem though, as we all wanted the coveted free ascent. One look at the line and a team of four was dismissed as too cumbersome so we settled with Cubby and Gary having first go. Callum and I would follow after having dispensed with the aid on *Armadillo*.

Whilst I was trying not to part company with the crux of *Armadillo*, as the grit that had glued a huge turf to the crag failed, Gary and Cubby were taking longer than anticipated on *Abraxas*. Clearly it was not a foregone conclusion. Back at the tents there was banter about pegs, bolts, and a disintegrating belay. Most of the in-situ gear was easily dispensable, but high in the centre of the wall was a unique feature – a bucket seat allowing you to comfortably sit with legs dangling over the abyss, however, it possessed no natural runners, and so two bolts had been placed.

A bolt-free ascent would have to bypass this, stringing two pitches together across a contorted horizontal foot traverse; initially hard and protected, then unprotected and easy.

Cubby had dispensed with the use of the bolts but Gary had back-roped from one of them. Callum and I still had a bite at a completely bolt-free ascent.

Callum was perfectly capable of seconding E4. But an attempt at the traverse with the difficulties of retrieving my gear and an arching sweep of featureless granite drawing his eye 100 metres to the coire floor saw him back-roping from one of the bolts as well. Who could blame him? He was a bit unnerved by my belay: stoically refusing to clip any bolts including the one right next to me, I only had one cam embedded within a crack of Weetabix rock, and Callum weighed 15 stone.

Although tainted, we were happy with our ascent. A day later, Cubby and I went back up to try a new line. On the way we were surprised to bump into folk heading back down! It was Craig Macadam, Derek Austen and Andy Tibbs. We chatted leisurely in the warm heather and discovered to our misery we had been beaten to the free ascents of *Armadillo* and *Abraxas* by just a few days. They had, however, all used all the bolts.

In addition, the new line Cubby had spied had been attempted by Craig that day. Coincidences like this have plagued me on numerous occasions but this time Craig graciously said it was an open project.

It was incredibly humid as Cubby sweated with the steep initial pitch, yet I was cold at the belay. By the time I was up and leading the second pitch I too was drenched in sweat and now Cubby was shivering. It was the strangest weather.

My memory of my on-sight and the moves of this pitch remain vivid as it was similar to my first E6 in Glen Nevis, *Flight of the Snow Goose*. A necky but easier third pitch completed the fine *Token Gesture* (E5) – the first of its grade on the island and suitable compensation for missing out on *Abraxas*.

More coincidence followed. On arriving back in Lochaber we met Graham Little himself in the Kings House Hotel and there proceeded a lively discussion on the use of bolts, which was beginning to get rather heated as the beer flowed. This first meeting with Graham could have been the last. But not long after, he appointed me to the post of National Officer for the Mountaineering Council of Scotland. I was directly responsible to Graham as Prèsident and we soon struck up a climbing partnership.

Graham's obsession over Arran rubbed off. We went on to climb ten new routes here through the nineties, righting previous wrongs and snatching some plumbs. On The Bastion our new route followed a blatantly obvious arête that had been ignored. An initial attempt was thwarted by a snowstorm forcing a fraught abseil down ropes that were blown upwards into the white void, but it succumbed soon after on a hot weekend with Lawrence Hughes. As we topped out we could see the ferry arriving. Decamping tents from the Punchbowl and racing for the connecting bus all prolonged the excitement of the climb. *The Brigand* (E6) for me provided everything that is Arran climbing: superb rough granite, hidden pockets in blank rock, disintegrating Weetabix, tremendous exposure and pure pleasure all the way. All the raw uncertainty and adventure that drew us to this beautiful island in the first place. ●

Tony Stone on *Abraxas* (E4).
Photo: *Guy Robertson*.

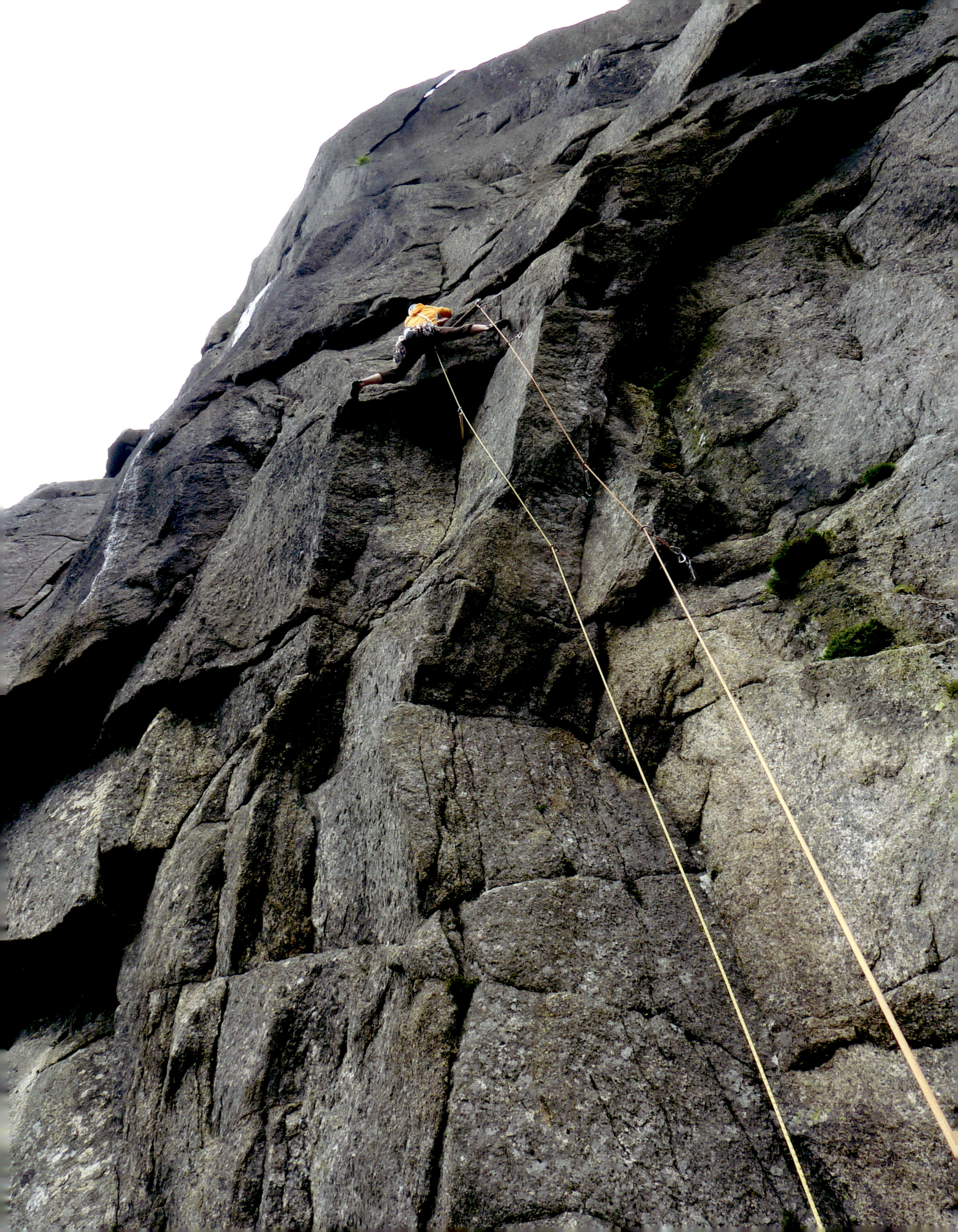

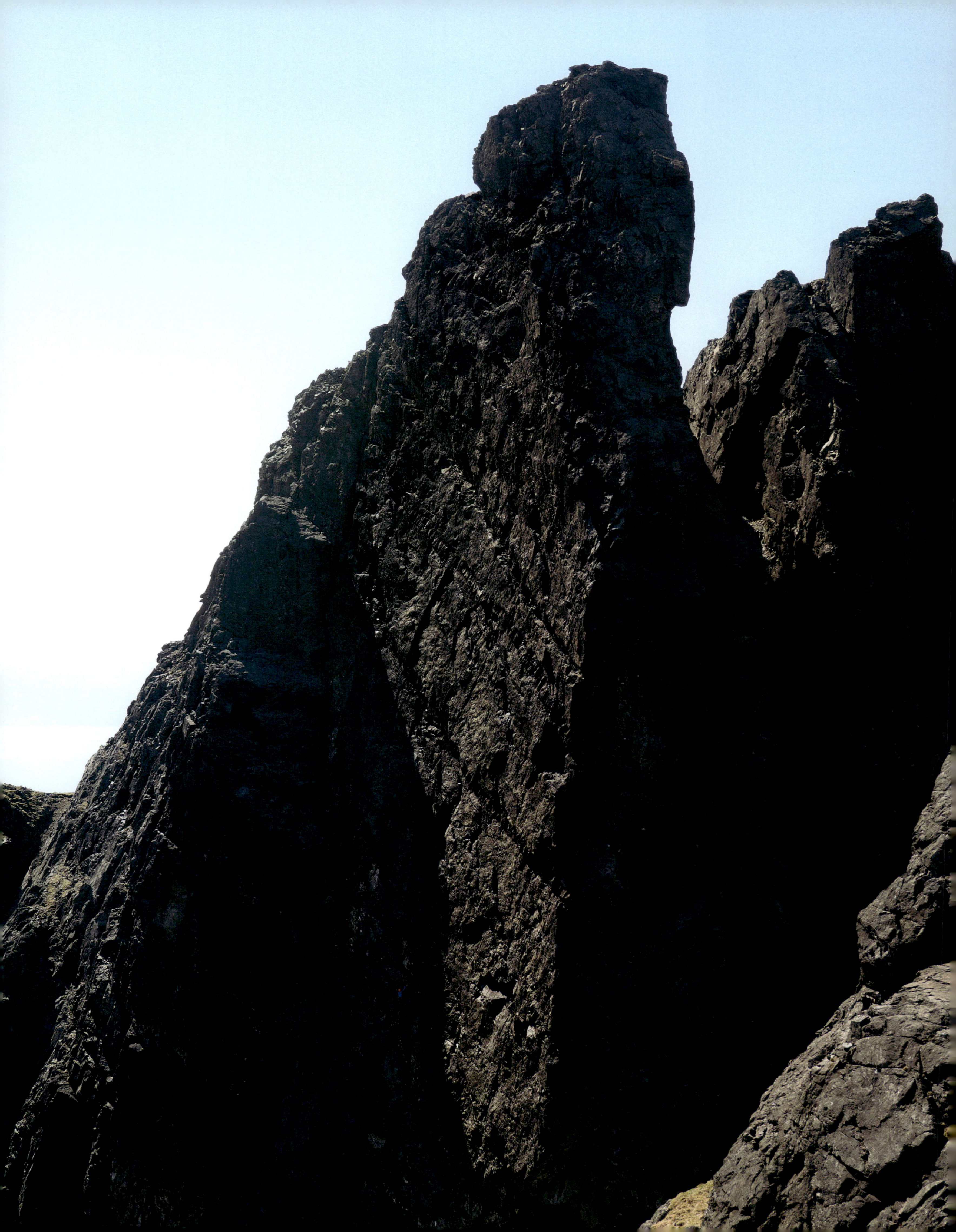

The Great Prow, Bla Bheinn, Skye
– by Grant Farquhar

THE PLACE

I first went to Skye with my parents. I was five years old. I literally thought we were going to the sky and I wasn't sure how we were going to get there. The Ford Cortina didn't look up to the job. I trusted my parents, but brought my Corgi Messerschmitt 109 just in case. I might have been five years old but I wasn't entirely mistaken. A trip to Skye does indeed involve a journey upwards – physically and spiritually. It has the potential to catalyse significant personal transformations through the initiations, heroics and sacrifices engendered by peaty waters, mountain zephyrs and sea gales. These rare ingredients combine here to create, amongst other intoxicating things, Talisker – a very fine and spicy single malt whisky.

The Gaelic name for Skye is An t-Eilean Sgitheanach which means 'the winged isle'. It is a magical place, especially so in early summer. Slightly less magical are the winged biting insects that appear in number around this time. These can be ferocious. Admittedly, they seem less of an objective hazard than that faced by Neil Howie, the protagonist of The Wicker Man. Pagan human sacrifice by immolation is apparently no longer a regional hazard. Nevertheless, on the winged isle, genuine bloodsuckers in the shape of midges and clegs[1] still await.

In Celtic mythology, The Cuillin of Skye take their name from the Gaelic hero, Cuchulainn – 'The hound of Cullan'. Cuchulainn learned the art of war from the warrior queen Sgiathach, who dwelt in The Land of Shadows on Skye. A fertile imagination might conjure up a mental image of a Celtic Xena the Warrior Princess replete with leather mini-kilt ensemble practising ancient Scottish martial arts above vertiginous cliffs.

THE CLIFF

The Great Prow lies at an altitude of approximately 2,200 feet on the eastern face of Bla Bheinn. An outlier of the main Cuillin ridge, Bla Bheinn itself is a forbidding fastness of rock with spectacular views of the surrounding Skye peaks, islands and the sea. The steep, scree-ridden walk in from the road near Loch Slapin takes around two hours to the base of the routes.

There are many great crags on Skye, but this one has a character all of its own. The height and sustained steepness of such a monolithic blade striking out from the mountainside make for particularly exposed and giddying climbing. As with all the great Skye mountain cliffs, the setting is magnificent. This massive, jutting sheet of rock is undoubtedly one of the most imposing and impressive walls in Scotland. 400 continuous feet of blank, unbroken and vertiginous rock. It's not called The Great Prow for nothing.

The left side of the wall is defined by the big corner of *Jib*. *Stairway to Heaven* finds a line up the vast expanse of wall book-ended by this and the striking right arête, which is taken by *Finger in the Dyke*. The eponymous route itself can be found around the arête on the very nose of the prow. Scupper Gully lies to the right and provides a useful descent route.

There are practically no defining features on this wall – indeed, apparent unrelenting blankness is its very essence. Occasional and horizontally inclined basalt dykes offer some respite, but other than the extremities of left and right, there are no significant features to carry the eye from bottom to top. This is a place for the route-finding connoisseur.

THE CLIMBING

The Skye mountains are rightly famed for their gabbro and the quality of the rock on The Great Prow is no exception. However, unlike the crags in the nearby Black Cuillin, the stark contrast between climbing at one moment on the super-rough igneous gabbro and the next on smooth extrusive basalt dykes provides extra variety to the climbing. Protection when you get it tends to be good, but it is sometimes sparse, making for bold, committing climbing.

Such a jaw-dropping feature as this 'mini Cerro Torre' will always be a siren's call to adventurous climbers. *The Great Prow* – the name given to the square-cut edge defining the right side of the wall – was first climbed in June 1968 by a St Andrews University Mountaineering Club team comprising William Band, Phil Gribbon, Neil Ross and Wilf Tauber. Unaware of the St Andrews team ascent, the second ascent was made by Hamish MacInnes and Ian Clough the same year, who then returned the following year teaming up with Martin Boysen and Dave Alcock to make the first ascent of *Jib* up the striking corner defining the wall's left side.

◀ The Great Prow.
Photo: *Colin Threlfall*.

[1] A 'cleg' is what the Scots call horse flies.

▲ Another view of The Great Prow. Photo: *Colin Threlfall*.

THE ISLANDS | **THE GREAT PROW, BLA BHEINN, SKYE**

▲ Tim Rankin on *Finger in the Dyke* (E5). Photo: *Guy Robertson*.

Not surprisingly, the main challenge of the smooth frontal wall waited until the seventies before succumbing to English raiders. Mick Fowler and Phil Thomas ascended the *Stairway to Heaven* in June 1977 – a typically audacious and bold on-sight first ascent. It was the hardest route on Skye at the time and originally graded E4. The consensus grade these days appears to have settled at bold E5 and it is therefore a strong contender for the first E5 in Scotland. Fowler was only 21 years old in 1977, although he was already by that time a renowned on-sight and loose rock specialist. He had put up one of the UK's first E6 climbs only the year before. Developments then stalled for over two decades, although Fowler's creation had emerged as one of the country's most testing and inspirational high standard routes on rock. *Finger in the Dyke* was climbed by Paul Thorburn, myself and Gary Latter in June 1997 and its quality confirmed by a repeat ascent in 2010.

Although unlikely to become a quality winter crag, *The Great Prow* itself was always an interesting and exotic prospect if anyone ever managed to find it in acceptable condition. True to form, Simon Richardson and Iain Small stepped up to the mark on a rare 'white blanket' day in 2010.

THE ROUTES

The Great Prow (HVS)

This striking feature is climbed in four pitches and was originally graded VS. Scottish VS was for many years a notorious grade. Nowadays it is still an improbable line for HVS.

Stairway to Heaven (E5)

A four pitch E5 with a spooky reputation, it swaggers up the massive left wall. Although the climbing is never desperate for the grade, it is sustained and complex and there are some taxing run-outs.

Finger in the Dyke (E5)

A spectacularly positioned outing clinging to the very edge left of *The Great Prow*. The three big main pitches ascend in descending order of difficulty.

▲ Blair Fyffe on *Stairway to Heaven* (E5). Photo: *Tony Stone*.

THE STORY

Far away from Skye, I sit sweating in Bermuda on a hot and humid August night. More than 15 years have elapsed since our first ascent on *The Great Prow*. Due to the inevitable tricks and lapses of memory, I am perhaps an unreliable narrator. I feel alien to the person I was back then. Do I even like him? Would he recognise me? Heraclitus tells us you cannot step twice into the same stream. Maybe so, but I will dip a toe into the upstream waters of the burn of my life in order to recount this tale. Please bear with me as I dredge my memory banks. Maybe a medicinal dram of Talisker will help, and Runrig on the stereo to drown out the whistling song of the tree frogs outside.

> *Memories are old ghosts*
> *Mountains of black and gold*
> *Sunsets falling over the moor*
> *Oh take me there*[2]

In 1997, it had been a long drive to Skye with plenty of time for contemplation. Driving across the bridge from the mainland, I'm dozing off, and my thoughts, memories and dreams are drifting below with the blue men. I'm transported back 12 years to 1985. Local heroes Runrig are performing at the Isle of Skye Music Festival. A guest female vocalist and what looks like the band's entire extended families are on stage. I'm with my Dundonian climbing school friends. We have been eating Haggis and drinking McEwan's Export. The sun is setting and tomorrow we will climb. Happy days. The Black Cuillin hills provide a stunning backdrop as she sings the bridge:

> *Chi mi'n t-eilean uaine (I see the green island)*
> *Tir nam beanntann arda (land of the high mountains)*
> *Ceo a'tuiteam tron a'ghleann (mist falling through the glen)*
> *Na shineadh air do raointeann (stretching out over your land)*[2]

Unlike the bridge of the song, the road bridge did not exist in 1985. In those days, the ferry from Kyle of Lochalsh on the mainland deposited you at Kyleakin on Skye to be instantly covered as if by magic by a black blanket of midges. Welcome to the islands. This was to be my first experience of climbing on the rough black and gold gabbro of The Cuillin. It left an indelible impression and a yearning to return.

[2] *Skye* – Runrig

And now here we are, 12 years later. I awake with a start as the car stops. A passenger no more, it's time to get out. Sluggishly, I stir into action. The sky is blue and the sun is shining. There are no midges. We are parked up near the head of Loch Slapin. 'That loch is like your heid Gary' I joke; 'It's slappin'. Gary laughs good-naturedly and retorts, 'Och I've got wavy hair – it's waving goodbye to my heid'. We take our rucksacks out of the car and shoulder them.

After a long, thirsty slog in the sun up the Allt na Dunaiche we reach Coire Uaigneich and then the base of the wall. Up close, the Great Prow is, dare I say it, a gigantic phallic Rorschach test of gabbro veined with basalt. I can imagine it looming out of the mist on occasion but not on this bluebird day. The sky above may be blue but we are now deep in the tenebrous shadowland of the coire. Fleeces and woolly hats are duly donned.

I can't remember which one of us suggested the plan to climb the arête of the Great Prow. In the crag photo in *Hard Rock* it was a blatantly obvious unclimbed challenge. Pay attention to the images contained in this book in your hands at this very moment: many unclimbed treasures and future testpieces may be depicted within.

We had in mind a ground-up ascent. This means on-sight climbing with no abseiling for cleaning, pre-inspection or practising moves. Such ascents feel harder than the later consensus grade of the route. This style is therefore only possible when the first ascencionists are either particularly inspired or the grade of the climb is well within their personal limit. We had no idea whether the latter would prove to be the case but we were psyched!

On closer inspection the route looked improbable, to say the least. The base of the arête was severely overhanging and revealed little in the way of climbable weaknesses. Directly beneath the prow is an overhung closet. We fossicked around for a bit looking for a way onto the arête. Eventually we came out of the closet with Paul in the lead following a perverse path initially away from the arête leftwards then straight up for a while before bending back horizontally rightwards along the very lip of the roof and moving rightwards and up to belay. This pitch was a superb achievement and a route-finding masterclass from an expert climber at the top of his game. An on-sight flash through sustained and sometimes bold 6a territory, taking the easiest line up a superb and vast natural feature, accomplished with apparent ease and continuous casual conversation with the belayers below. A telltale photo in an old book may have marked the X on the map, but Paul had found the key to the treasure chest. We were in!

Gary and I prepared to second, each on a single strand of the double nine millimetre ropes. I set off, removing some of the pieces of protection on my rope and clipping some crucial others into Gary's rope to minimise any potential swing on the long traverse back right. I joined Paul at the hanging belay in a crack, swiftly followed by Gary. The next pitch was my lead. Looking up from the stance, it looked steep but the rock was impeccable and I felt pretty confident. Steady moves flowed directly above the hanging belay on perfect gabbro and basalt blobs. Mindful of the possibility of falling and landing on my seconds, I paused to place gear. Bridging and steep dyke-grappling led out right to the arête where easy gangways continued right, and turned a blank-looking bulge to gain a logical stopping place. I belayed Gary and Paul simultaneously through my belay plate, carefully draping the coils of rope over my legs. Eventually, all three of us were clustered at the anchors, spectacularly positioned on a hanging belay with several hundred feet of fresh air beneath our feet. We drank some water while Gary surveyed the vertical terrain above. He re-racked the gear for his lead, being careful not to drop it. At least there was no guidebook to carry. We were pirates in uncharted seas in the sky. It looked like we were going to steal the prize of the first ascent.

In patience we wait for the light
I am a climber
I am a thief
Oh kingdom of Gabbro[3]

Paul and Gary were ready to go. Gary took over the sharp end and led a long entertaining pitch, gradually easing to follow a wide crack and easier angled terrain towards the summit. The blue sky was long gone and the mist was clagging in atmospherically as Paul and I seconded the last few metres. We exchanged a few celebratory profanities and then coiled the ropes, each of us trying to ensure that the others were carrying more hardware than themselves before scrambling back down the gully. Reunited with our sacks at the base of the prow, we craned our necks looking back up at the route we had just climbed.

It was a privilege to climb such a dramatic feature ground up and on sight in such an amazing place and with such splendid and talented company. Unlike Cuchulainn, no dogging or heroics were required. Cue bagpipes.

Blair Fyffe and Tony Stone on *Stairway to Heaven* (E5).
Photo: *Colin Threlfall.*

[3] *Nightfall on Marsco* – Runrig

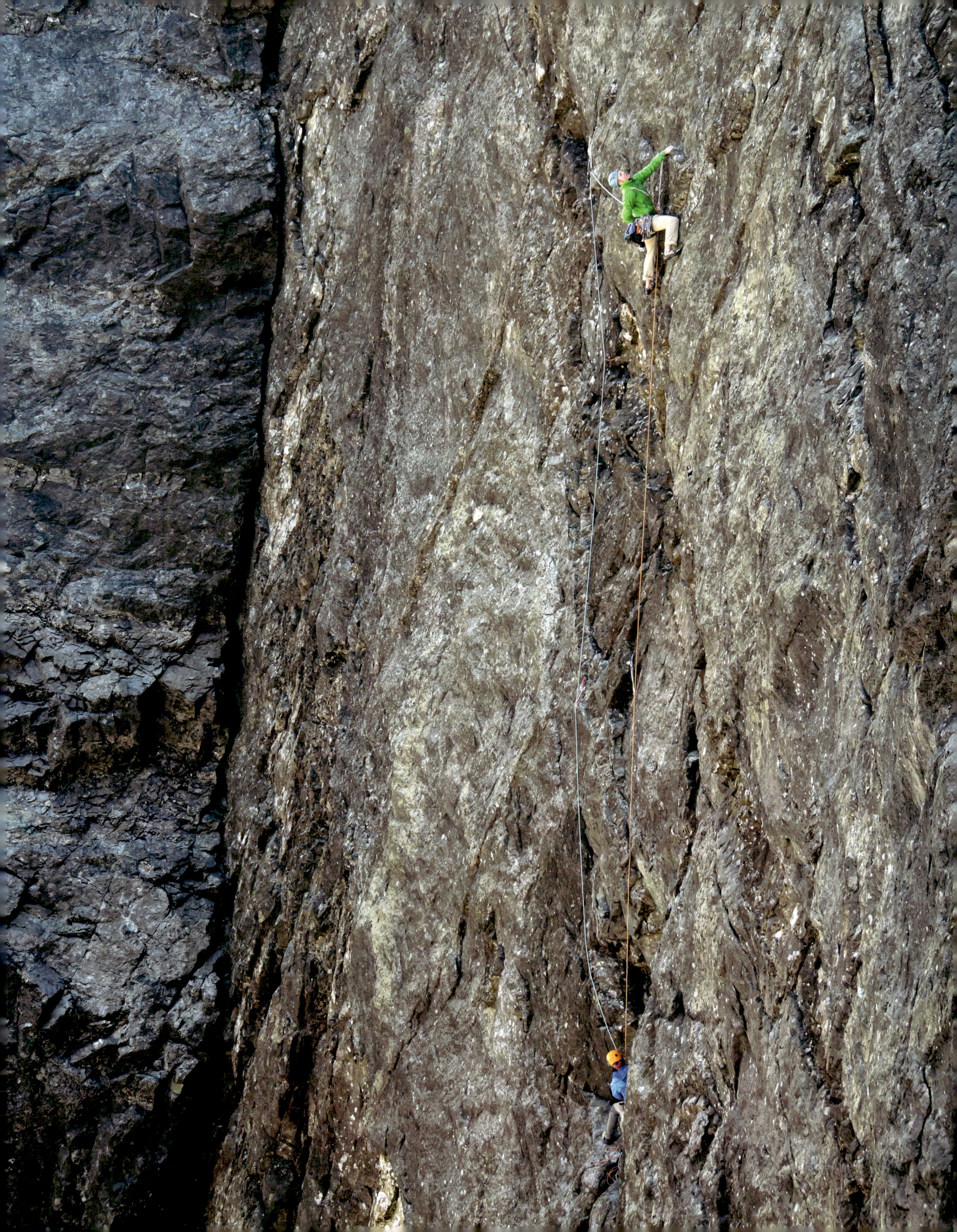

Tony Stone and Blair Fyffe on *Stairway to Heaven* (E5).
Photo: *Colin Threlfall.*

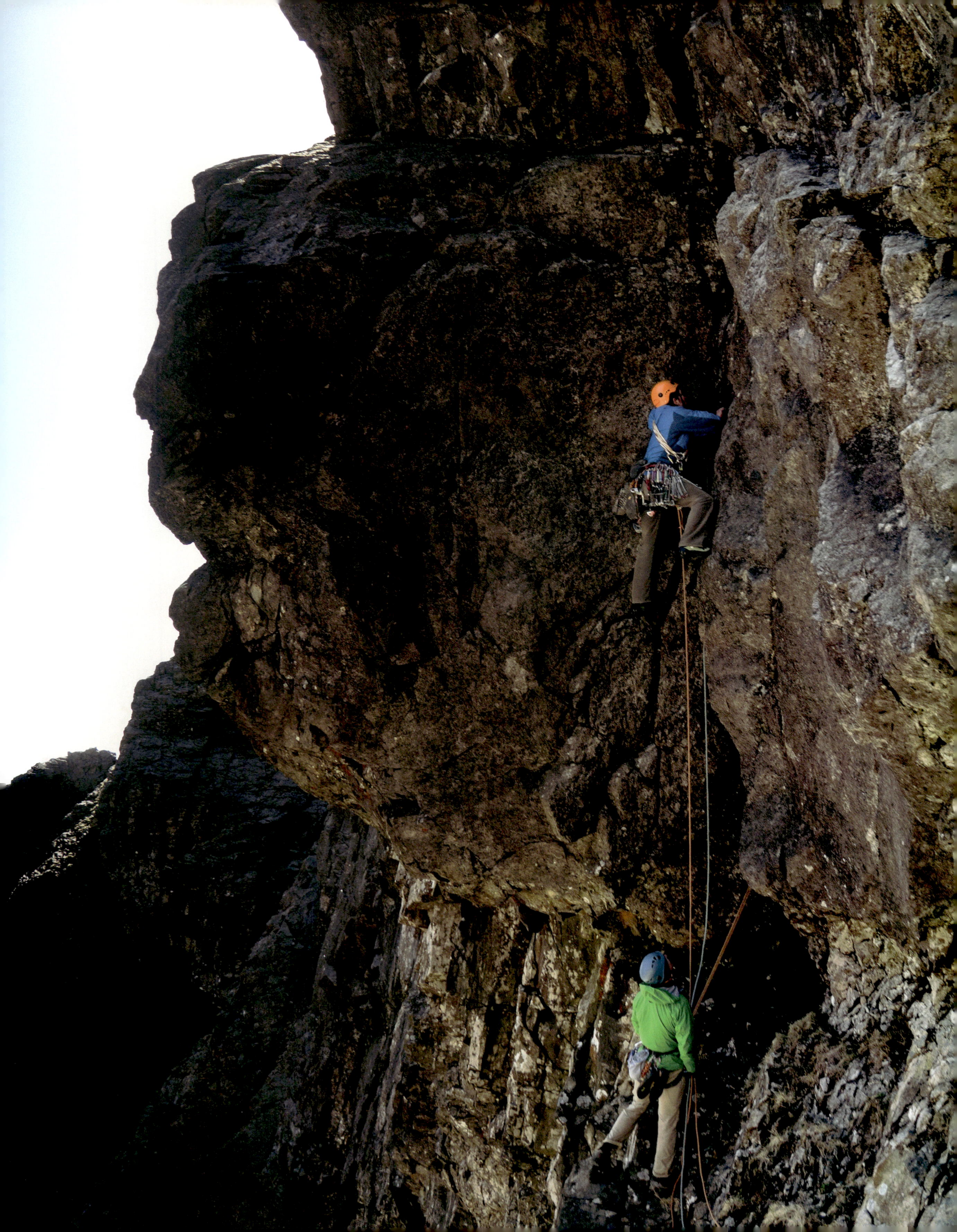

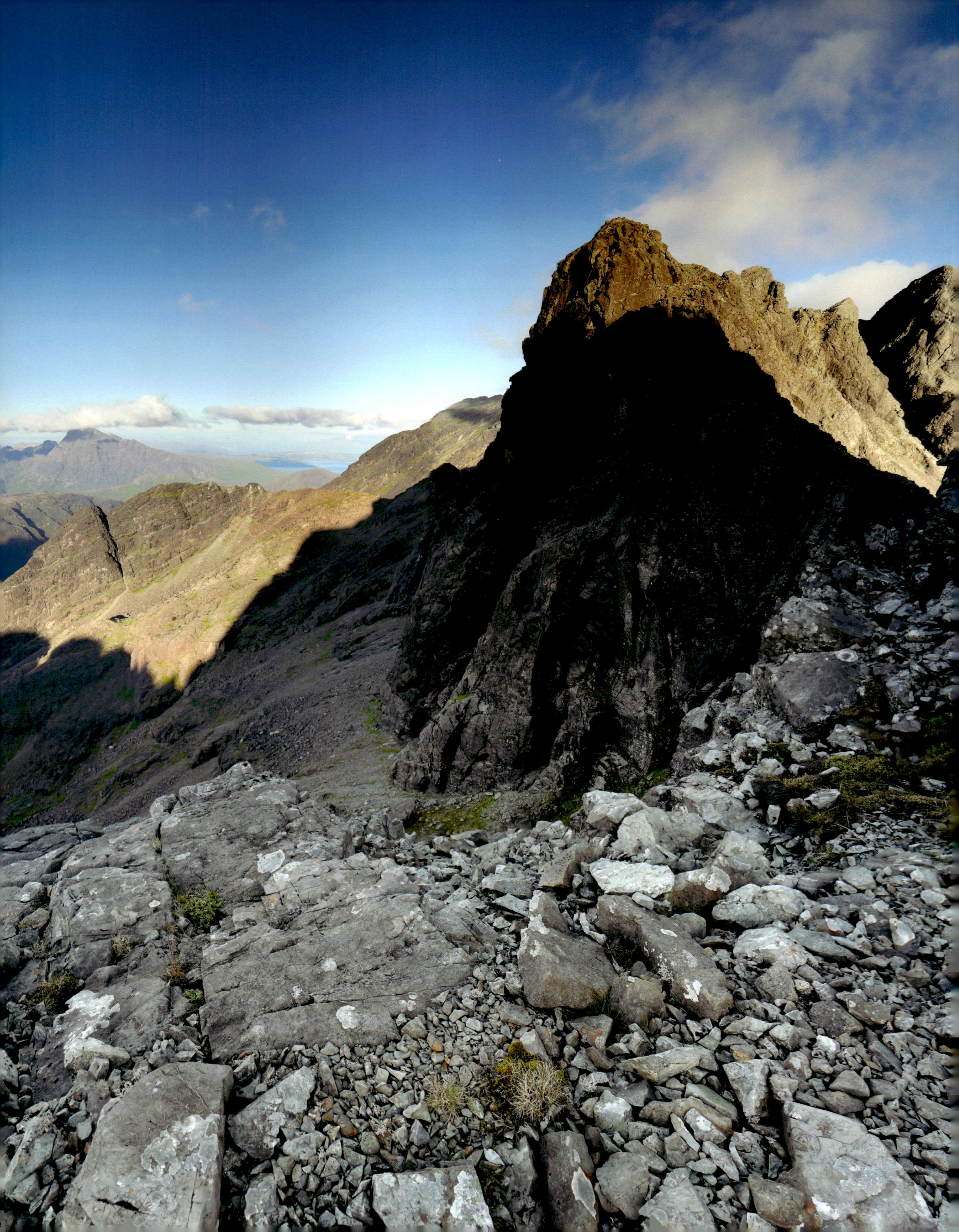

Sgùrr Mhic Choinnich North Face, Skye – *by Mike Lates*

THE PLACE

At the heart of Skye's mountains is the Coir'-uisg basin, a huge rocky arena overlooking the dark waters of Loch Coruisk. The coire is the inner sanctum of a castle whose huge walls are the Black Cuillin, further defended by the sea and long rough approaches. Mike Dixon called this 'The Forgotten Coire', a name used by many even today.

By whatever means you approach The Forgotten Coire, the feeling of isolation and commitment is intense. The best approaches are probably by boat from Elgol, or if pushed for time, over the ridge from Coire Lagan and down Rotten Gully. Pulling the ropes after rapping the gully, you will find yourself double checking all essentials are packed and that there's no sign of rain. An expedition here by either of these approaches requires an early start, complex logistics, good navigation and a high level of self-sufficiency.

THE CLIFF

The 1969 SMC guidebook described the Upper Cliff as *'the most impressive cliff in the Cuillin, containing steep continuous rock some 700ft high'*. However, only a tantalising hint of the climbing is visible from the main ridge. From Bealach Coire Lagan, at the top of Bealach Buttress, the plumb vertical profile of the Upper Cliff can be seen dropping from high on the snaking crest of Sgùrr Mhic Choinnich.

Peering over the edge it continues to screes a long, long way below. From this vantage point the lower cliff will always remain a blur of 3D features from a 2D perspective. The adjacent Bealach Buttress is intrinsically linked to the climbing here, having been developed in the same era, and routes there can be studied relatively easily from the crest of the main ridge.

Once the central bay at the foot of the Upper Cliff is reached, the start of most routes is obvious, while continuation pitches blur as they attempt to break through the steeper upper section. *Dawn Grooves* and *Crack of Dawn* tackle the initial steepness by powerful groove and crack lines, starting up the same clean crack in the east-facing wall of the bay. *Mongoose* links the obvious central line of discontinuous corners, starting with a fierce layback. Further to the left *King Cobra* starts up the prominent open-book corner then weaves a more complex line through the steepness above. There are no lines carrying the eye the full height of the crag: good route-finding is essential.

THE CLIMBING

Gabbro is the bedrock of the Cuillin, providing legendary adhesion for hands and feet – far fiercer than any gritstone. A climber's confidence in their medium always increases with familiarity but this phenomenon seems exaggerated in the Cuillin. A warm-up route will often feel desperate as the brain struggles to cope with the alpine atmosphere – exposure, steepness, occasional loose holds and a shortage of obvious protection.

Conversely, an acclimatised and gabbro-confident team can feel some of the harder classics reassuringly soft-touch for the grade. Although the routes have seen relatively little traffic they are remarkably free of loose rock on this face. There are precious few signs of passage. Although most of the climbing follows corners and cracks, these are in multiple-choice format and the routes will always retain their adventurous nature.

This is an old cliff with a long history, starting way back in 1903 when Raeburn led his SMC party up the North Face in full winter conditions. Since then a host of British mountaineering luminaries have left their mark, testifying to the quality of the climbing and the ambience here. Of his sixties classic, *King Cobra*, Chris Bonington is rumoured to have reported that it was 'certainly the best route I've ever done' – high praise indeed.

Not surprisingly, the cliff is still in its winter infancy. Mick Fowler and Andy Cave climbed the esoteric *Exiguous Gully* (VI,6) in 1995, but Guy Robertson and Mark Garthwaite really brought the cliff up to speed with a winter ascent of *Dawn Grooves* (VIII,8) in 2008.

◀ The North Face of Sgùrr Mhic Choinnich.
Photo: *Colin Threlfall*.

▲ Guy Robertson on *Rainman* (E5) on the neighbouring Beallach Buttress. Photo: *Pete Benson*.

THE ROUTES

King Cobra (E1)
The best route of its grade on Skye. 'King Cobra was the best new route we did that summer and certainly the best route I've ever done.'[4]

Dawn Grooves (HVS, VIII)
A long, sustained and varied route, with delicate climbing low down and more strenuous fare higher up. It takes a powerful line through the heart of the cliff and provides a tremendous adventure in summer or winter.

Rainman (E5)
You'll have to look very hard to find a better E5 on Skye, if not the whole of the western Highlands. This route blasts a direct line up the centre of the 'impossibly blank' wall just right of the central arching corner on Bealach Buttress.

THE STORY

It was a rare situation for me: bone dry rock and no work commitments. Coming down off Gillean I had played out the fantasy in my mind. *King Cobra*, *King Cobra* ... 'one of Skye's great routes, low in the grade with good protection and situations'. *King Cobra* ...

Down in the cool of the Sligachan bar the first pint hardly touched the sides, but I soon discovered my usually reliable climbing partner had been coaxed off the island to the Etive Slabs. Just as the bubble seemed set to burst I got chatting to a young lad called Jonno who'd come over from Australia with his dad. Hearing my tale of woe he granted my wish like a fairy godmother: you shall go to *King Cobra*, sport!

On the walk-in I shared with Jonno what I knew of the cliff's daunting reputation and admitted that just seeing it close up might be enough. Even this degree of respect didn't prepare me for the impact of the place. A vertical wall over 200 metres wide and four times the height of the mighty Cromlech (which had had a similar effect on me many years before). No obvious lines to conquer here though,

224   THE GREAT MOUNTAIN CRAGS OF SCOTLAND   [4] Chris Bonington reflects on a summer's climbing with Tom Patey.

Mark Garthwaite below *Dawn Grooves* (VIII,8).
Photo: *Guy Robertson.*

just a myriad of grooves and discontinuous cracks and the whole lot distinctly overhanging in the upper reaches. It was time for some mental blanking and well-practised routines. Jonno spied the Cobra's head whilst I buried mine, racking up and uncoiling ropes.

Scrambling up to the first stance I hardly even glanced at *Exiguous Gully* rising to my left, a winter masterpiece that Andy Cave had described to me as part of a 'mystery trip in the mist with Mick [Fowler]'. Reaching solid rock and confidently on route, it was time to relax and enjoy the ride ahead. Stretch out the limbs as the jugs and footholds appear on either side of the corner crack. A spacious ledge, a bomber belay and obvious holds leading out right to the crux corner and we were rocking. In fact the unclimbed direct continuation looked possible, but I thought 'let's just stick to the classic; don't want to ruin this fantasy route by scaring myself ... '

In 2005 Julian Lines visited the Cuillin and soloed a number of routes. *King Cobra* was by no means the hardest but does appear to have given him the biggest fright. His description of the crux provides a perfect account of how I – mere mortal with rope and belay – felt for the few minutes I was engaged on this section of the climb:

I swung right to the base of a bottomless groove and stood on a ledge that Patey described as 'large enough for a roosting seagull' with more than 60m of space beneath my feet.

I carefully studied the groove and worked out all the options. Two rusty stains in the back of the crack were no doubt from the first ascent. All I had was a shallow fingerlock for the right hand and a good hold on the right wall that was too low for the hand and too high for the foot. The left hand was a poor layaway and all other holds were red herrings. The footholds were just on smears on either side of the groove.

Right foot up to a toe smear: 'Wow I'm still sticking,' I thought to myself, now I will just step down for a wee breather and then commit next go. But then it all went horribly wrong. I tried to put my foot back down but could not bring myself to re-weight the right foot in case I slipped. In a split second my unconscious and conscious minds went into a state of combustion. For once there was no indecision between them; preserve life no matter what. The adrenalin surged and my soul had changed from being frightened and frozen to a 'Give it everything you've got and climb for your life' scenario. I slapped for a reverse layaway then a good lock and then out to a bridge. The holds were better now and I started really enjoying the pitch and the exposure in this smooth groove.

Fortunately, I survived the shock, hauled up the sack and let off steam to Jonno before tackling an easier pitch up a broken rock rib. This was only a brief interlude in the tension which rose alarmingly as the belay ledge yielded not a single decent runner or break. My partner's jovial company only mildly eased the stress as I wandered back and forth trying to unravel the puzzle. The E3 direct pitch went up off the left end but looked full value at the grade. A central possibility was unprotected, and a similarly unattractive option lay five metres further right, just before the wall dropped into a huge void with the line of *Mongoose* well and truly beyond reach. Down-climb, abseil off and run away was looking an increasingly attractive option. By the third lap, frustration and desperation dictated an extra step towards the void, *et voila*!

A juicy nut crack was within easy reach. I feasted with three runners before even looking up to study the climbing ahead. The moves looked steep but positive. Where they led was less clear. The headwall above contained a big, dark, damp-looking corner system. I hoped the route would not take me up there, but I opted not to worry myself with anything but the immediate moves. One absorbing problem followed another, positive and well protected, to the base of the corner where a peg finally gave me hope that I was still on route. I seemed to have missed half of the features described but 'climb out on the left wall of the groove and swing across to jammed spikes' could be made to fit, and even looked quite feasible. A ten-metre rising diagonal line gave a sling on a small chickenhead low down before some real spacewalking out to the spikes. Not wanting to test these fully I pondered the last move and accidentally glanced between my feet. The screes were in the shade now, but definitely still straight beneath me after five pitches of climbing. Blanking this and finding just the right foothold to complete the sequence, I treated myself to another look down before pulling into the tiny crow's nest belay.

Fatigue and hunger began to gnaw. A zigzag pitch broke the wonderful rhythm, it felt like the fantasy was coming to an end. Awkward route-finding brought me back to the present. Finally features began to fit the description once more – the end was in sight. Reaching the top was everything it should be; spectacular views, space to sit, but mostly the indescribable endorphin rush of a climbing dream come true. It didn't disappoint in any way. I had confirmed what I'd suspected: this cliff really is the best in the Cuillin. •

Susan Jensen on *King Cobra* (E1).
Photo: *Guy Robertson.*

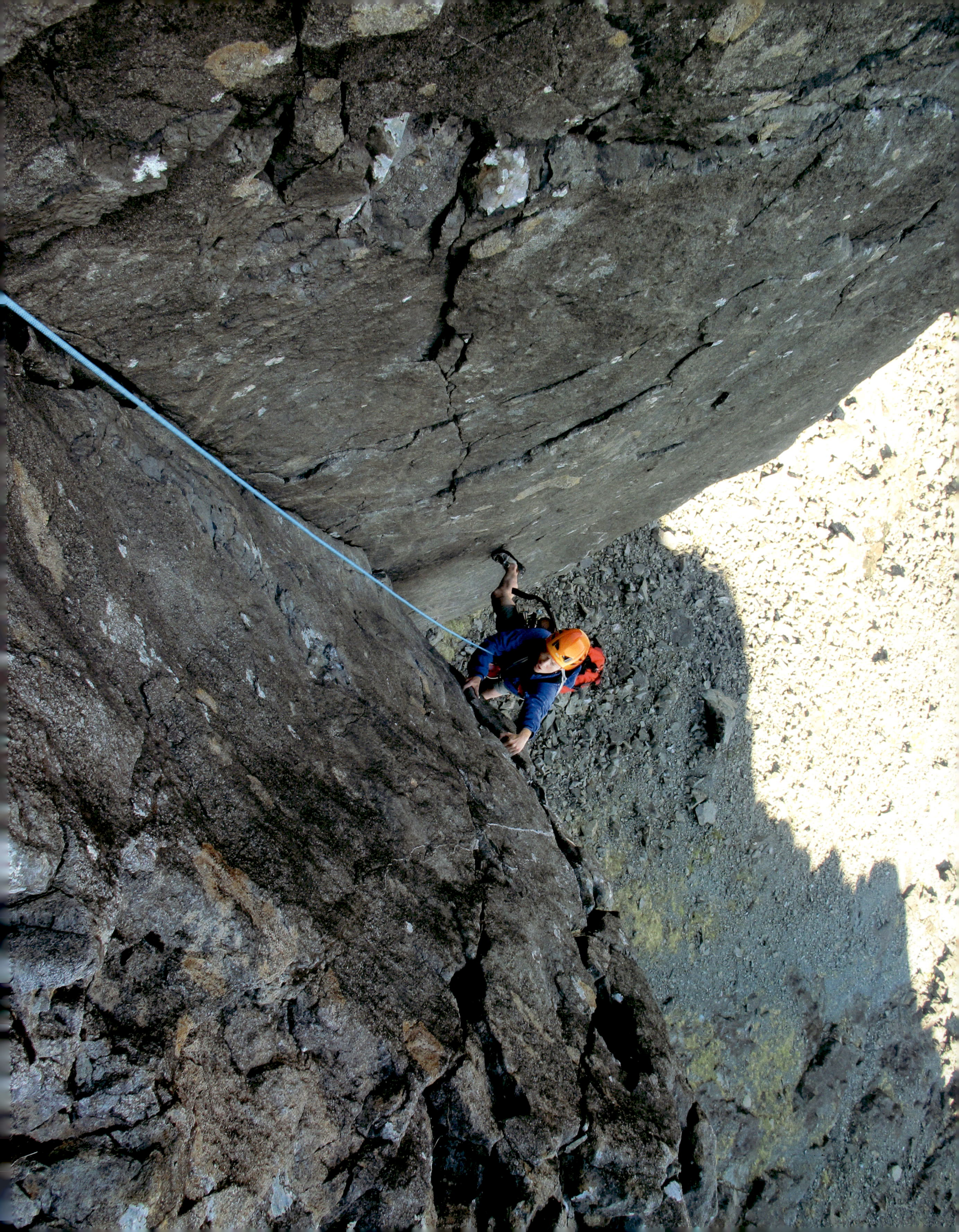

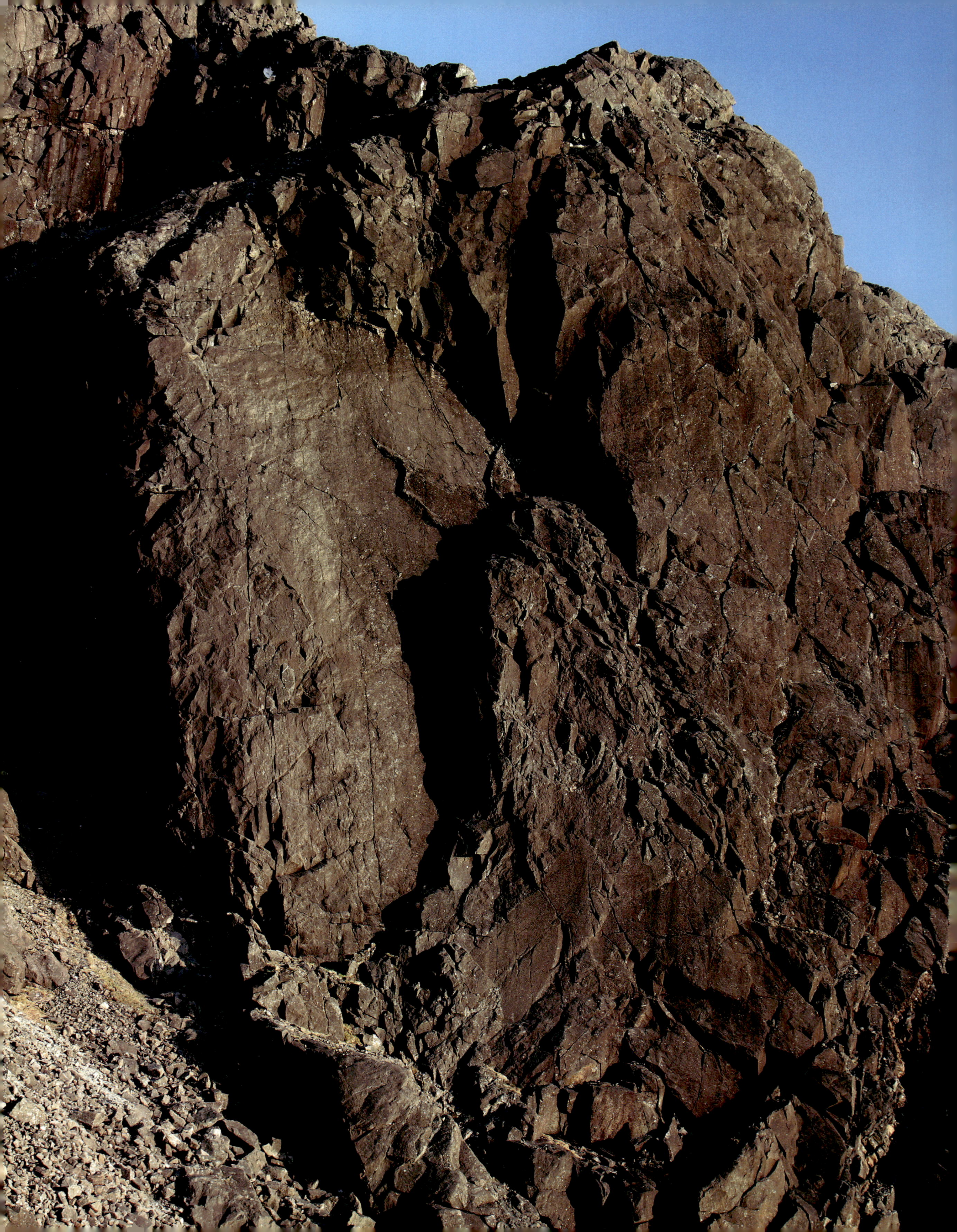

East Buttress, Sròn na Ciche, Skye
— by Kevin Howett

THE PLACE
'The Soul of the Gael is on the Summit of the Mountain.' There is, in Gaelic culture, an affinity for high places that goes beyond the simple naming of geographical features. The Black Cuillin is Scotland's Alps, and as such has a special resonance for the Gael.

The Victorian pioneers sought out local guides, and, not surprisingly, the highest peak of the ridge, Sgurr Alasdair, is named after its first ascenscionist, a Skye native. The most impressive of the Cuillin's five main west-facing coires is Coire Lagan. Ensconced in the heart of this vast amphitheatre, however, there are great peaks in all directions, save for the endless sea to the west. Here, tucked up high on the right wall beneath the great sheet of pocketed gabbro that is the East Buttress, one is at once enveloped by dark volcanic rocks, kissed by cool maritime breezes and arrested by the blazing Atlantic sunset.

THE CLIFF
Coire Lagan is undoubtedly the hub of Cuillin rock climbing. With the extensive thousand foot cliffs flanking the north side of Sròn na Ciche, the quality and quantity of rock surpasses any other Skye coire. Sròn na Ciche's Western Buttress is a monolithic thousand-foot 'old school' wall where exploration is the name of the game. Left of this is the famous Cioch Buttress. East Buttress begins where these cliffs start to recede towards the ridge.

Although diminished in comparison to its western neighbour, East Buttress is still over 130 metres high, and what it lacks in stature it more than makes up for in raw quality. This is some of the best rock that Skye has to offer. The crag is actually two sheets of rock separated by a striking chimney, and the routes are what Tony Hancock would have laconically described as 'modern shaped'. This is epitomised by routes in the Vulcan Wall area — an unbroken sheet of perfect rough gabbro. The lines here are best distinguished on very close inspection — from a distance this facet presents an alarmingly blank impression. Left of this great sweep of rock the crag terminates at a striking blunt arête — the line of *Spock* (E3). To the right lie the magnificent soaring inset corners of *Creag Dubh Grooves* (E3), while right again a more broken and complex lower wall leads to another superb, near-vertical face higher up.

THE CLIMBING
Due to the high altitude and the impeccably clean, dry rock, East Buttress will likely always be a summer venue. The style is best described in one word — poise. The generally easier-angled nature of the rock, and its unparalleled frictional qualities, means the emphasis is on balance and faith rather than brute strength. Grunters need not apply. However, the angle is about as acute as it could be for these comments to apply, so anticipate plenty of tiny edges, pockets and nubbins to support your pumping calf muscles.

It is also fair to say that unlike most other Skye crags, there is a disproportionate reliance on mental rather than physical fortitude; here you must commit 100 per cent to self preservation, as falling would grate — quite literally. Clean rock and almost no vegetation mean that many of the climbs dry quickly after rain, although grease can linger in some of the deeper cracks. The late afternoon and evening sun provides an enchanting climbing experience, and in the height of summer can be sufficient to dry out weeps that may have persisted through the day.

By Skye standards, the history of climbing on East Buttress is recent, and the work of a genuine cross-section of Scottish climbers: Glaswegian hard men, new wave East Coasters, relocated Englishmen, and displaced Londoners. Ian Clough and Hamish MacInnes kicked off with ascents of *Vulcan Wall* (HVS) and *Creag Dhu Grooves* (E3) both with some aid, in the fifties. Little was added until the late seventies when Mick Fowler and Phil Thomas added *Dilemma* (E3) on a raid from London. A strong Scottish team, Murray Hamilton and Dougie Mullin, climbed *Enigma* (E3) in 1979, and Pete Hunter and Cameron Lees followed up with an ascent of the blatantly obvious crack of *Strappado Direct* (E2) and the stunning *Spock* (E3) in 1980. *Pocks* (E3) was added by George Suzca and Colin Moody, and two final lines on the buttress were added by myself, with Tom Prentice on *Uhuru* (E3) in 1990, and with Scott Muir on *Clinging On* (E4) in 2001.

◀ Vulcan Wall in the evening light.
Photo: *Colin Threlfall.*

▲ The Coire Lagan face of Sròn na Ciche – East Buttress lies immediately right of the white, scree-filled gully just right of centre. Photo: *Colin Threlfall.*

THE ROUTES

Spock (E3)
Cracks and grooves up the blunt left edge of the buttress, overlooking the Sgurr Sgumain stone shoot, give a tenuous yet surprisingly strenuous excursion. Its hanging position accentuates the steepness and the passage through a small roof to gain easier ground is memorably bold.

Vulcan Wall (HVS)
Although not hard by modern standards, the obvious crack-line up the left side of the smooth wall epitomises East Buttress climbing. Superb, technically sustained climbing up a perfect wall with great atmosphere and two equally good pitches for a team to share.

Clinging On (E4)
A long and lonely lead up the heart of the smooth wall, with ever-increasing difficulty and a real sting in the tail. Protection exists but becomes less and less apparent as the strain of the lead reaches its crescendo after the 50-metre point.

THE STORY

This is a story spanning 20 years. It all started as the bad taste seventies and punk were fading. I was at Exeter University. I had just started climbing before moving down from Northumberland, school friend John Griffiths enticing me with his Joe Brown style washing-line adventures in Northumberland. Although the catch-all 'Extreme' grade existed, very few routes had E's to their name. There were also mysterious 'Mild XS' and 'Hard XS' routes. I had repeated some of these, but they varied wildly. We were yet to climb in Scotland.

Fate played a hand, and ultimately changed my life's direction. We were in the student's Ewe Bar at Exeter. 'Portsmouth Paul' was passing through on a road trip with 'a guy from Scotland' – Dave 'Cubby' Cuthbertson. This unassuming Scotsman had been quietly repeating most of the hardest routes across the UK. Over a pint, Cubby painted a very different picture of Scottish rock than we were being fed by the climbing press. Being fiercely patriotic, with a conviction that Scottish rock climbing should be better known, he invited us north with the promise of accurate advice.

A year later the eighties heralded a fresh era. Punk was dead, Dire Straits were about to hit the big time and climbers were soon to wear Lycra. Taking Cubby up on his offer we set off on a road trip up to the west of Scotland and found ourselves camping in Glen Nevis in the rain. We tracked down Cubby working in Fort William and he recommended a trip to Creag Dubh where he had recently established new routes. *Acapulco* (E4), he said, was a good climb to get started! Sensing some, albeit unwitting, sandbagging we decided to head for Skye despite the forecast.

The following days were thwarted by terrible weather and although I was desperate to get on the harder lines we were well and truly spanked by *Vulcan Wall* (HVS). We retreated to Northumberland and considered Scottish grades.

A few years' residence back in England followed and I started climbing with Alan Moist. Alan was loosely a member of the Sunderland Club, on the fringe you might say, as I was, hooking up with 'Macum Men' Jimmy Whin, Mick Gardiner and others for trips away in three-wheelers. Alan and I made more winter trips and by 1983 decided to move north and lodged ourselves at Laggan Locks. A Skye trip was but a short hop away.

We blagged our way into the Glen Brittle Hut where we shared convivial surroundings with a group of walkers. Our first day dawned to a dreich, wetting mist with visibility just across the road. The pull to stay by a warm fire was hard to resist, but we took a stroll up into Coire Lagan, just in case. Below the base of the cliffs, we stepped out into bright hot sunshine: one of the best inversions I have ever seen in the mountains. When quizzed later by the walkers about 'the weather up on the ridge' we thought we'd play a little and said it had been just as bad as they could imagine. As this inversion persisted and we returned day after day ever more sunburnt, our joke became increasingly difficult to sustain.

I vanquished the ghost that was *Vulcan Wall* and finished it with the recently added *Chambre Finish* (E2). Strangely, the harder finish seemed easier than parts of the original, but I put that down to the psychology of revisiting the scene of previous failure. I liked the climbing here – a mixture of balance and brawn.

Years passed. I wanted to return to make my own mark on East Buttress. On an early season visit Tom Prentice and I repeated Mick Fowler's outrageous *Stairway to Heaven* (E5) on Bla Bheinn and feeling brave we then found a line beside *Vulcan Wall*. *Uhuru* (E3) was born.

Uhuru made me realise there was a gap up the centre of the wall and these things tend to linger in the subconscious waiting for a chance to surface. This notion returned to me over a coffee in the Glenmore Lodge bar with Dave Simmonite. Dave was looking for subjects for a series of photo-shoots on rock in Scotland for a new book project. Fame was guaranteed! I persuaded Scott Muir to come along and at the first opportunity a phone call from Dave saw us heading through driving rain to meet the photo team.

Midges and mist slowly evaporated as we headed into the coire with the weather curtain opening before us once again. Whilst Scott got to grips with a nearby route for the cameras, I eyed up that central line. I even had a name in waiting: *Clinging On*.

With Dave installed on his abseil rope I headed off. Within a matter of metres the difficulties were considerable. Legs were burning, toes screaming. The shoes were too tight. I should have worn the older, bigger pair. I was getting pumped in all the wrong places. Just over halfway, a respite offered itself as I found myself just a stride away from *Uhuru*. It seemed like a chicken-run but my calf muscles were now cramping up. It also seemed churlish to ignore the natural line of the route, so I stepped left and relaxed. Unfortunately at that point there was little protection (unless I traversed a little further) so complete karma was far from achieved.

However, with at least partial physical recovery I headed back into the line of the thin crack, even thinner now, and curving up rightwards into black boiler plate blankness. With each new move I left security further behind. My toes started to scream once again, but now my arms were pumping too, and my fingers began to cramp. The pain everywhere became almost unbearable. I knew this was mainly down to a lack of recent climbing, but I had convinced myself I could do the route no matter what.

Dave was some way up and right taking pictures. When the holds ran out I shouted across 'anything up there?' but I heard only a muffled reply. I don't really think I was listening for a reply anyway – it was a form of psychological preparation, like placing a poor runner that you know won't hold a fall, but you do it anyway to give you confidence. I reached blindly over a slight bulge and found a flat edge. The next few moves were performed in fluid subconscious motion, brain engaged but not actually available for anything else. I don't remember anything at all. I noticed the world around me again as I grasped good holds under the capping wall and started to shake a little as it dawned on me how far above gear I had travelled.

And so I had, finally, painted my own portrait upon this stretched and blackened canvas. Sitting on the belay bringing Scott up behind me, the whole experience brought back distant memories of the raw excitement of going to Skye for the first time all those years before. That feeling of entering a different place, with a different language. 'You'll no be understanding the Gaelic then,' proclaimed the woman in the caravan shop all those long years ago. Perhaps now I did understand, just a little. •

Top left: A busy day on the Vulcan Wall area of East Buttress – unknown climbers on *Pocks* (E3) and *Vulcan Wall* (HVS). Photo: *Alistair Robertson*. **Top right**: Unknown climber on *Spock* (E3). Photo: *Ian Hey*. **Bottom**: Julian Lines on a solo ascent of *Uhuru* (E3). Photo: *Dave Cuthbertson*.

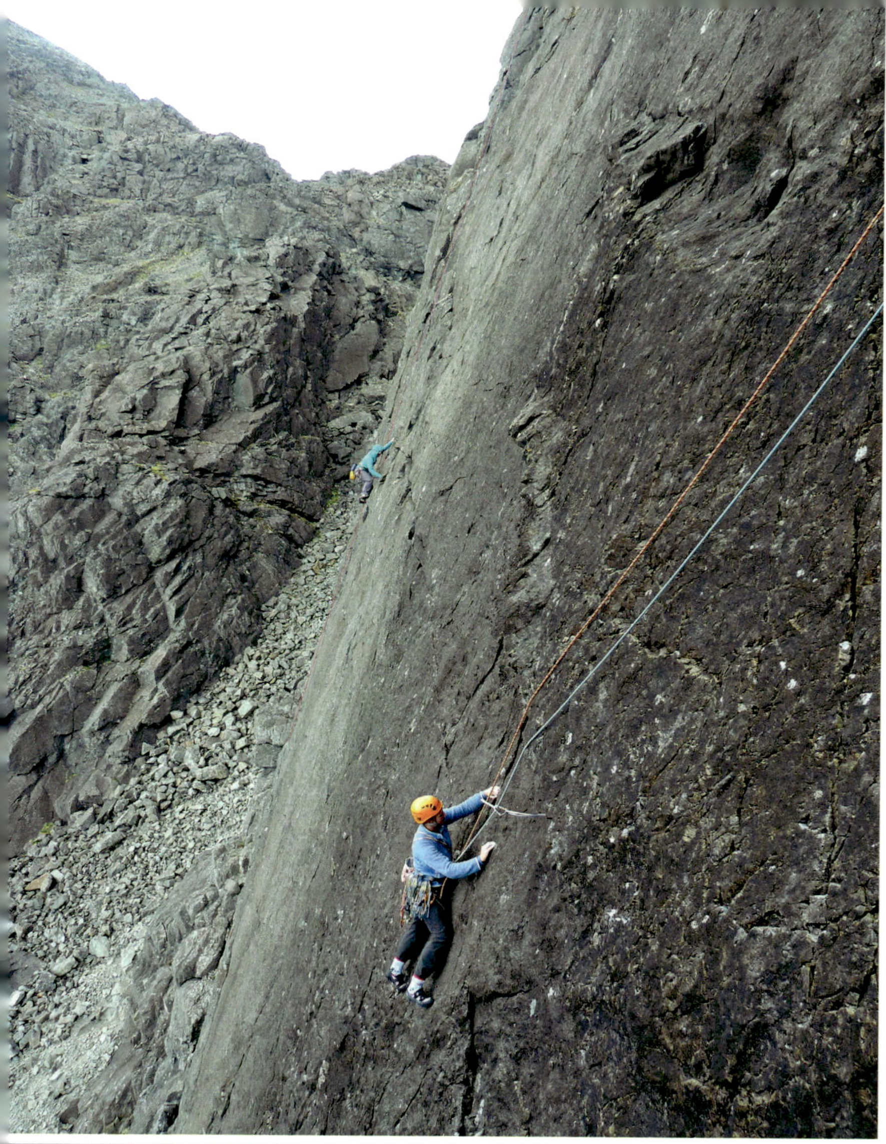
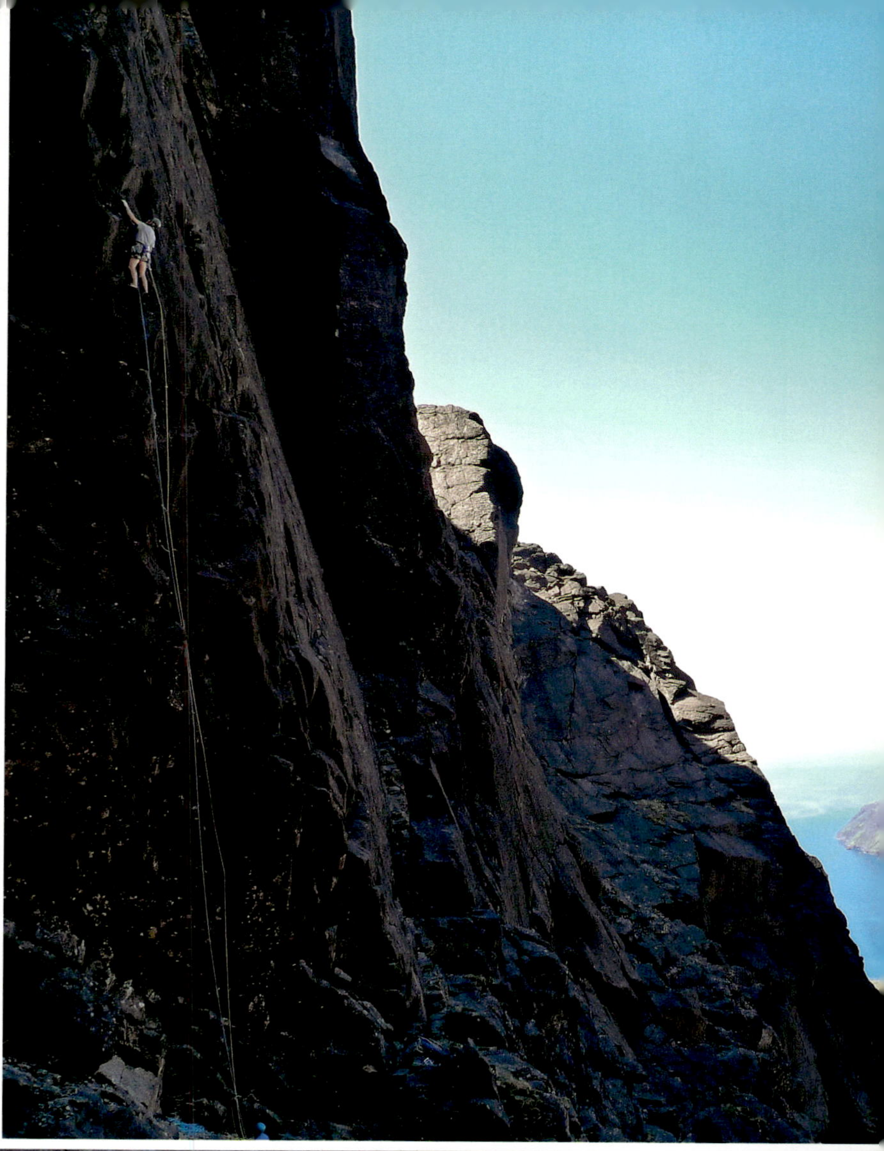
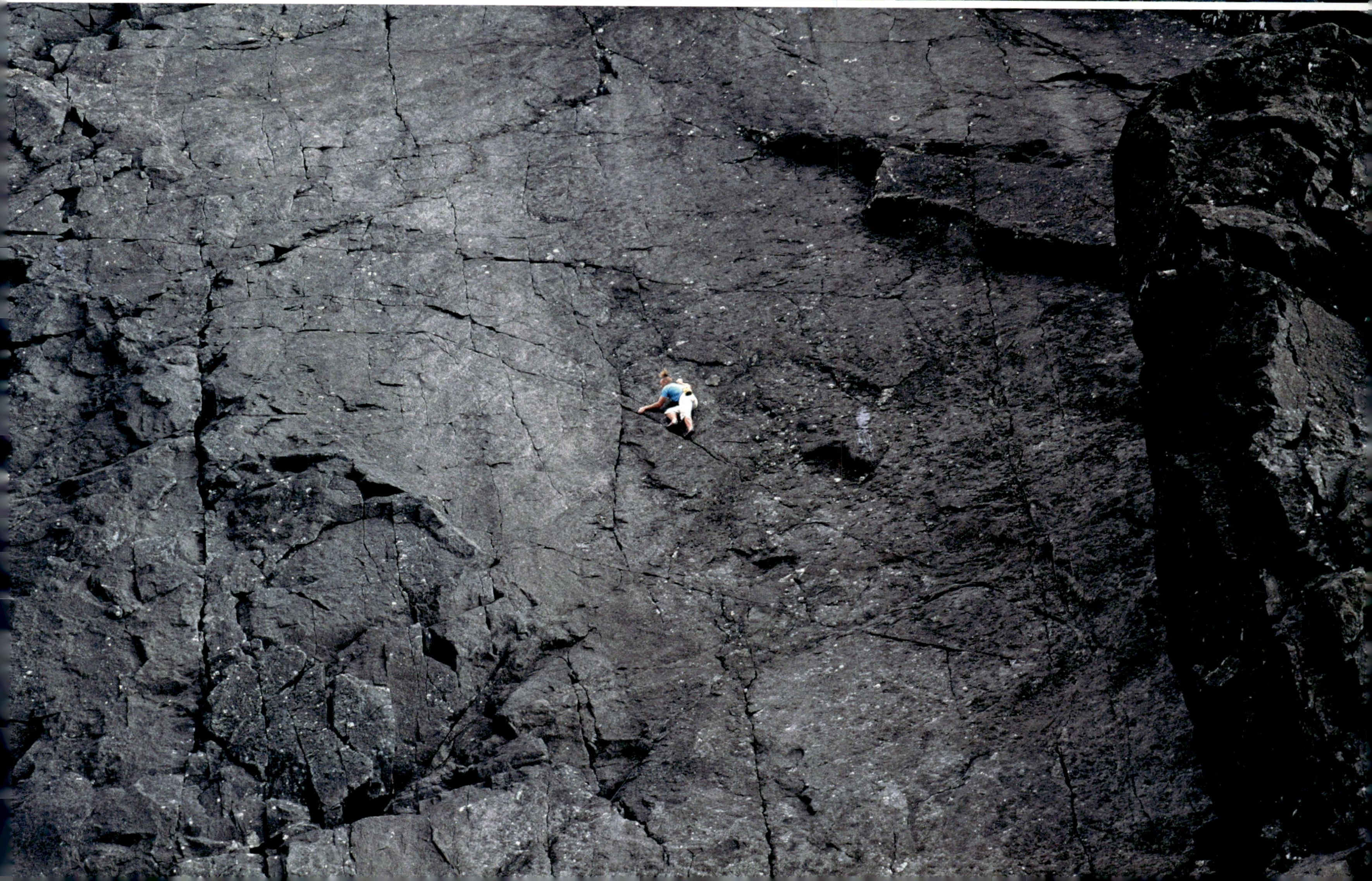

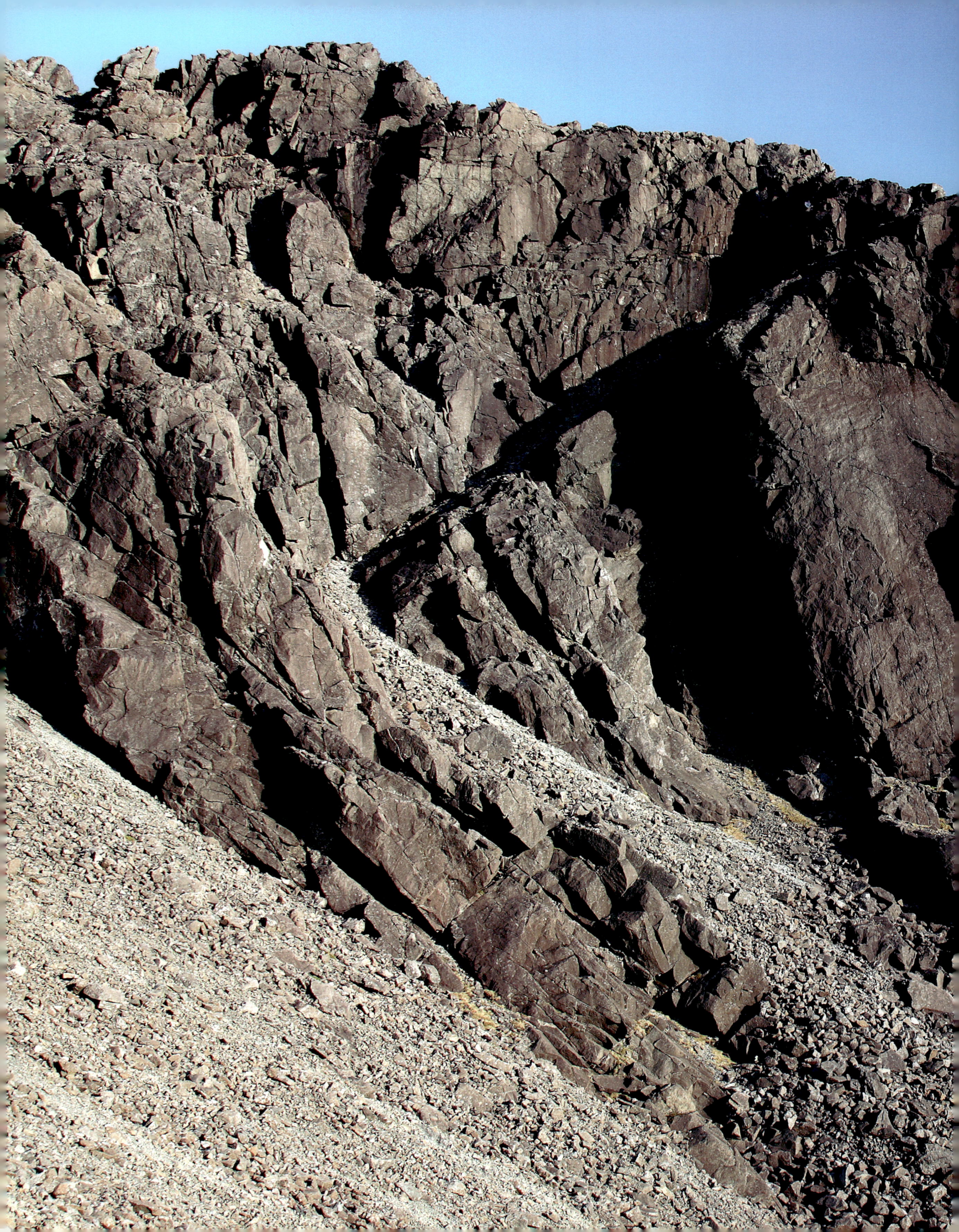

The East Buttress of Sròn na Ciche in evening light.
Photo: *Colin Threlfall.*

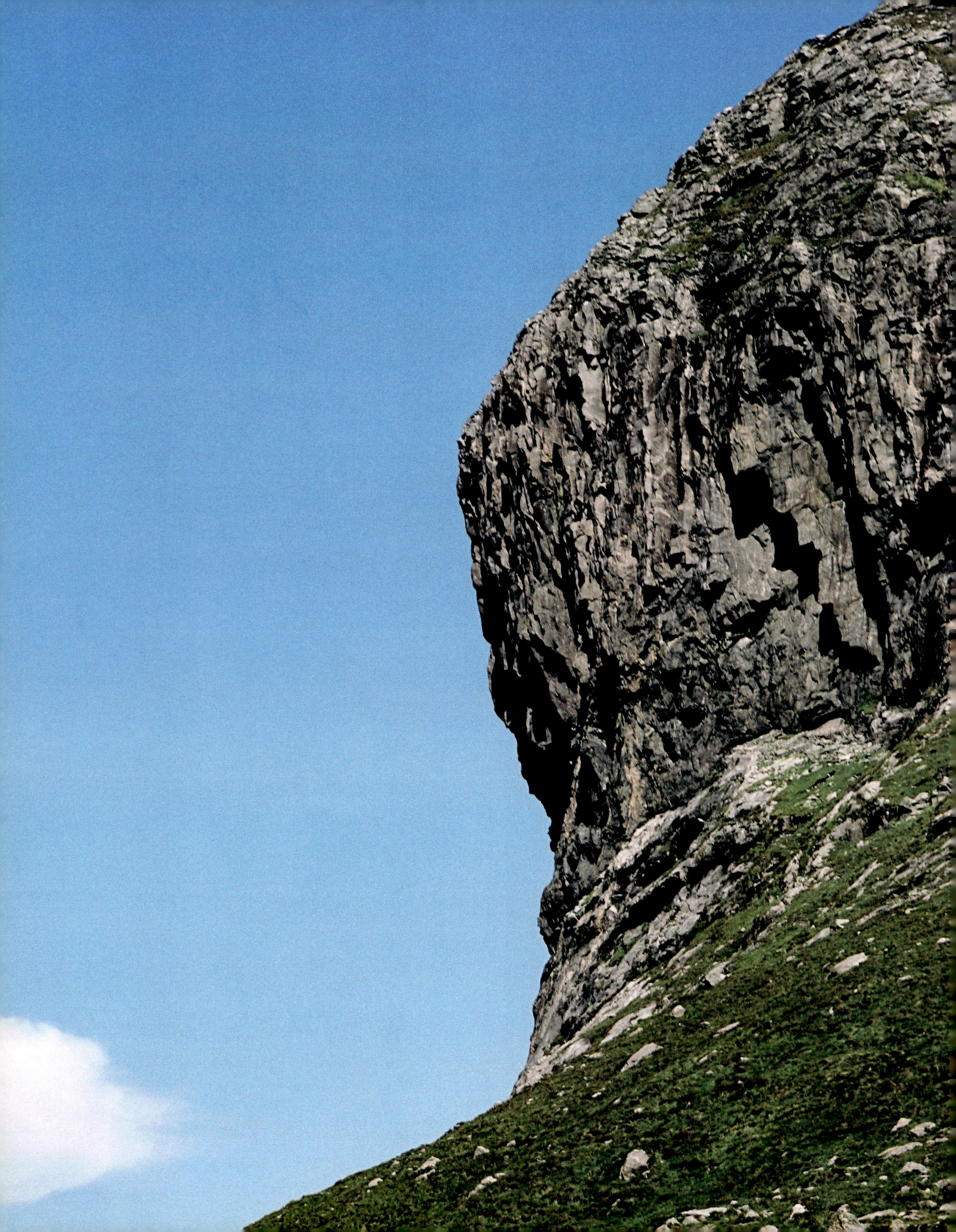

Sròn Uladail, Harris – *by Tony Stone*

THE PLACE

Sròn Uladail is unmistakeable. The mighty scale of the towering rock face is incomparable to anything else in the UK. The largest overhang in the UK protrudes out some 50 metres at the steepest part of the 200-metre tall cliff. The Sròn broods over a bleak kingdom, an empire of seemingly unbounded emptiness. Undulating moorland of several shades of green is pierced in places by the underlying bedrock. Dark lochs and lochans with ragged edges are sketched into the heath and the grey dots of boulders are liberally scattered throughout. It is a magnificently beautiful place, fit for the monarch of British mountain crags.

From the Huisinish road just east of the grounds of Amhuinnsuidhe Castle, a private road strikes off from the coast and up into the hills. The road ends at a hydro dam from where a well-defined path leads past two lochs to reach the col at the head of Gleann Uladail. The crag is revealed as the path sweeps gently down through the glen.

THE CLIFF

The Sròn remains a seldom-visited crag despite having been included in both *Hard Rock* and *Extreme Rock* and also the venue for a recent BBC outside broadcast. For the majority of UK climbers the journey here would involve driving past many excellent cliffs in the Scottish Highlands just to get to the ferry port. Add to this the yearly bird ban between April and July, and it is clear a trip to the Sròn requires some effort. However, the Sròn is unique, and a pilgrimage to pay one's respects to this worthy cliff will be well rewarded.

The Sròn is the result of a glacier having sliced through and removed a large part of the hillside. Since the recession of that carving glacier, the exposed cliff has been further eroded over the millennia by the ravages of the weather. The great boulders lying below the cliff are testament to this. The same boulders now provide climbers with shelter from the weather, though not against the midges.

Fortuitously for a west coast venue, the North West Face of the Sròn is an overhanging amphitheatre. It is so steep that much of it stays dry even in the rain. Further right the cliff overhangs much less and seepage can be a problem after prolonged rainfall.

◀ Sròn Uladail.
Photo: *Rob Reglinski*.

THE CLIMBING

This is, to remind you once more, Britain's steepest mountain cliff. It is so steep that retreat from any distance up the crag could be a complicated, if not futile affair. However, don't be fooled into believing you'll be jug-hauling above good protection, for despite the unrelenting steepness the routes are surprisingly technical and delicate. They follow intricate lines, linking corners and grooves, to sneak through the myriad blank roofs. Very quickly you find yourself far above the ground as the hillside falls further away from below your heels. The Sròn really is Britain's very own big wall.

Early climbers sought to scale the cliff by any means possible. At that time this meant aid climbing, still an impressive feat since the cliff overhangs so much that aiding is a slow process and retreat and re-ascent an arduous business. The leading lights of the seventies, eighties and nineties all made their pilgrimage here. Some came armed with pegs and hammers, others with just vision and athleticism. Initially, efforts were focussed on freeing the original aid lines, but this soon progressed to forging completely new, all-free lines of their own. The legacy is an unparalleled selection of hard, high quality mountain routes.

THE ROUTES

Stone (E5)

The easiest line up the main section of the cliff is no pushover. Four pleasant pitches weave a way up to the base of an overhanging corner crack. After trucking up this for a while, a swing rightwards gains yet another steep crack – all very tiring. This leads to a 'hanging basket of Babylon', before gaining the massive ledge. One final pitch leads to the top.

The Chisel (E7)

This stunning adventure forges up the right edge of the overhanging amphitheatre in the cliff. With sustained high quality climbing throughout its length, the route takes the climber into some spectacular positions unrivalled in the UK. The outrageous crux pitch, between airy hanging belays, follows a soaring technical groove then cuts left along a savagely strenuous jagged flake. Above three finishes exist. Respectively, *The Original*, *The Gloaming*, and *The Roaming*. None of these provide an easy escape, ensuring success is well earned.

The Scoop (E7)

The cliff's most famous line and one of the wildest mountain routes in the UK. The free version takes a mind-boggling line up the steepest section of the crag. The very technical first pitch, aptly named the 'Rude Awakening', sets the tone and the crux 'Flying Groove' is just that, 150 metres of air nipping at your heels. The route well deserves its reputation: featuring much old fixed gear, some large booming flakes, and a final scary tenuous traverse at the very top, this is not for the faint hearted. Finally, totting up the individual pitch grades, award yourself 31 E-points for the on-sight.

Tony Stone on *The Scoop* (E7). Photo: *Iain Small*.

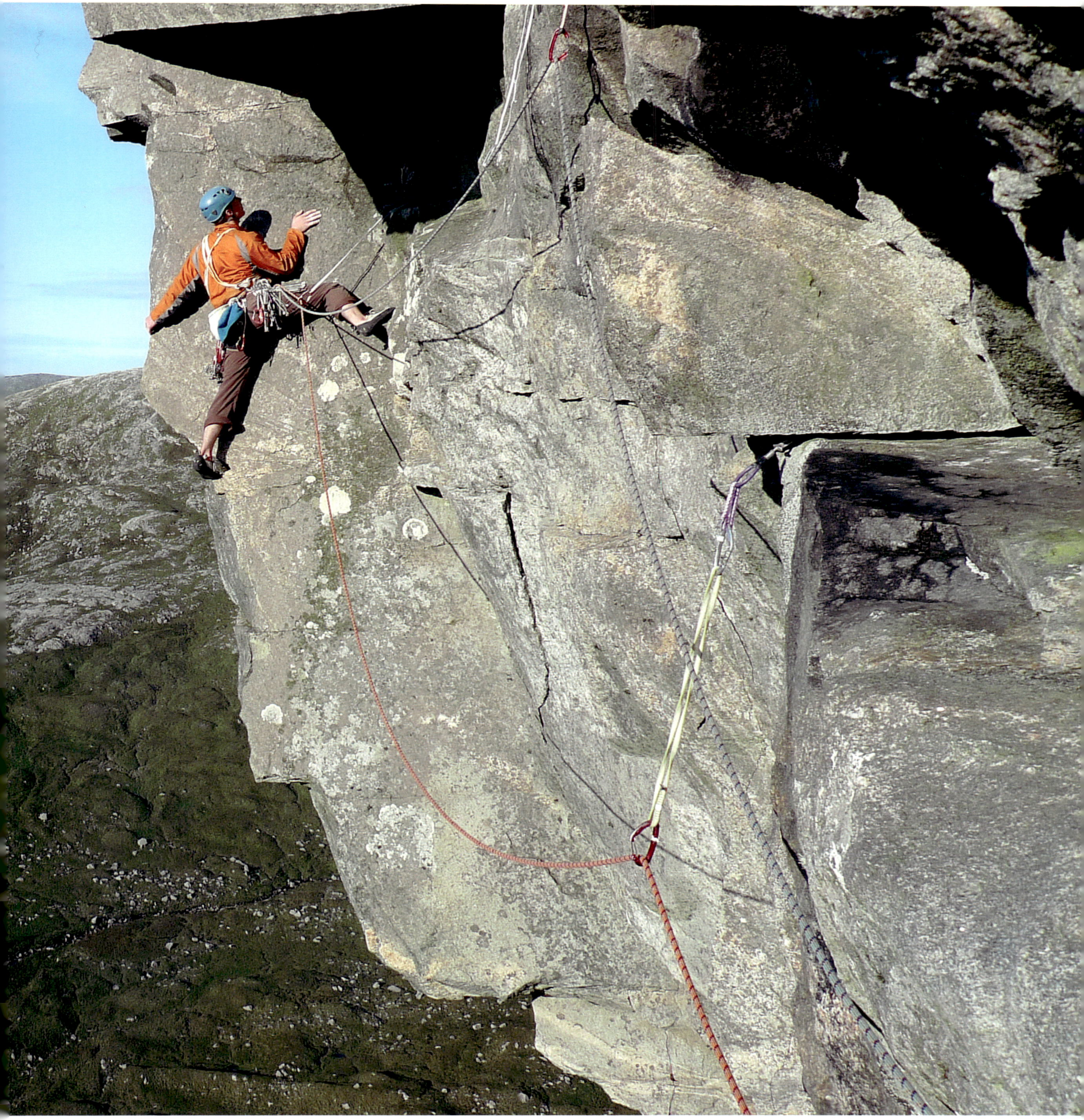

240 THE GREAT MOUNTAIN CRAGS OF SCOTLAND

THE STORY

We had done it. Or had we? The crux pitch of *The Chisel* lay beneath us, along with four other tiring pitches below that. A mere 70 metres above, but still well out of sight, lay the top of the crag. We hung from the belay on a measly footledge, a tiny pedestal perched right on the very lip of an enormous overhang. Loch Uladail shimmered seductively below us and I thirsted for it. We had been on this rock for nine hours. Surely the worst was over?

As we wearily shuffled the gear off Iain's harness and on to mine I felt strangely confident. Despite my tired body and mind, I was reassured that the guidebook description gave no cause for alarm. I set off upward. And so it began.

The innocuous-looking initial groove was far from it. I squirmed my way awkwardly upward to an impasse. Above loomed a brown and lichenous bulge, the first dirty rock we had encountered on the route. How bad could it be? I timidly tested the ground. Up, down, up, down. The trad climber's modus operandi. My probing was unproductive — I wasn't going that way in a hurry. Damn that guidebook of lies! Giver of false hope! And stuff the first ascensionist's line!

A good hold winked at me from way out right on a steep rib of rock. At full span I curled the tips of the fingers of my right hand around its lip. My face was pinned tightly against the brown lichen, both arms trying to tear the other from my torso — crucified. There was nothing for it but to commit to the hold. I hung with both hands now tightly wrapped around the hold as the rock below teasingly rebuffed the advances of my feet. As stomach muscles strained to keep my toes in contact, I attempted to stuff a cam into a slot beside my hands. Damn that broken Camalot! The trigger was held together with some elastic cord and as I strained to pull the cams narrower they strained, mocking me. That cam nearly flew over my shoulder before I remembered it belonged to Iain and would be expensive to replace. Eventually, irritated, I somehow wiggled it in.

◄

Iain Small on *The Scoop* (E7). Photo: *Tony Stone*.

THE ISLANDS | **SRÒN ULADAIL, HARRIS** 241

I had lost my excuse for staying in the same place – this place with the big hold – so now I would have to move again. Damn. I shook one arm down by my side, then the other, and repeated this process for a few minutes. All the while I pretended to look around for where to go. Eventually I thought I had better really look around. There wasn't much to aim for, but I glimpsed a tiny ledge a few metres further right. As a self-confessed ledge-lover I thought I should better investigate.

So I shimmied on right. Almost immediately I was disappointed with the paucity of protection and decent holds. On the plus side, I had a lot of air to play with beneath my feet should gravity take over. On arrival at my little ledge I was dismayed to find that I could not take a belay and was therefore forced to continue. A groove ran upward from the ledge, and with the rationale that grooves are usually easier than faces I decided to follow it. I pasted my feet onto small edges and crimped my way onward. Only a few metres beyond the ledge the groove terminated, abruptly. The joys of rock climbing on gneiss – it can be so clean and so compact that sometimes there are literally no features. To my right was yet another groove, and although it looked no more promising than the previous one, it was the only option available.

A rising sense of apprehension enveloped me as I traversed ever further right toward an uncertain outcome along my untrodden path. I thought briefly about retreat, but I was now some ten metres horizontal of Iain's belay and not much above it. Below me was the void. Lowering off simply wasn't an option. So with all the fragile self-assurance of 'what will be, will be' I ventured yet further forth, now quite pale and dipping frequently into my chalk bag.

The second groove was in fact friendlier, even accommodating a small micro-wire, but it too terminated prematurely. This time though, the thin rib forming the right side of the groove continued a little way beyond. It offered little in the way of protection but it formed a path through bulges above, permitting access to the bottom right corner of a near-vertical wall of bright white quartz. The wall of quartz was wonderfully compact; not large, probably just four by four metres and beautifully patterned with the intricate geometry of countless crystals. A rising diagonal foot-rail of gneiss ran from right to left across its base. A feeling of tempered optimism rose up inside me. It mingled with the terror. Tiptoeing left along the rail I scratched my fingernails on tiny crystal edges as the wall thrust out against my torso. Looking down at my feet I couldn't help but peer beyond, down to my last protection, then staring further down until the green and grey of grass and boulders blurred together. Oh Damn! Damn! Damn! What on earth am I doing here? Why didn't I retreat when I could? Idiot!

My eyes are bulging, my breathing shallow as I try desperately now to stay in balance. I can maybe just reach the left edge of the quartz wall, but please – please – let it get easier beyond. After tiptoeing left and up a little further I see the cliff now grants me mercy.

The gross crime of climbing on-sight into unchartered territory on this beguiling, omnipotent crag, even if just for one pitch, has exacted a heavy toll. The cliff generously pardons my offence on this occasion; perhaps I'd been punished enough. I take my chances and run for glory.

A comfortable ledge and protection await beyond the beautiful wall; above, an uncomplicated road to the top. I pull round onto the horizontal, thankful for this gift, my feet aching from two hours spent desperately seeking the path of least resistance. Only then did I know, for sure, that it was over. Finally.

Tony Stone on *The Scoop* (E7). Photo: Iain Small.

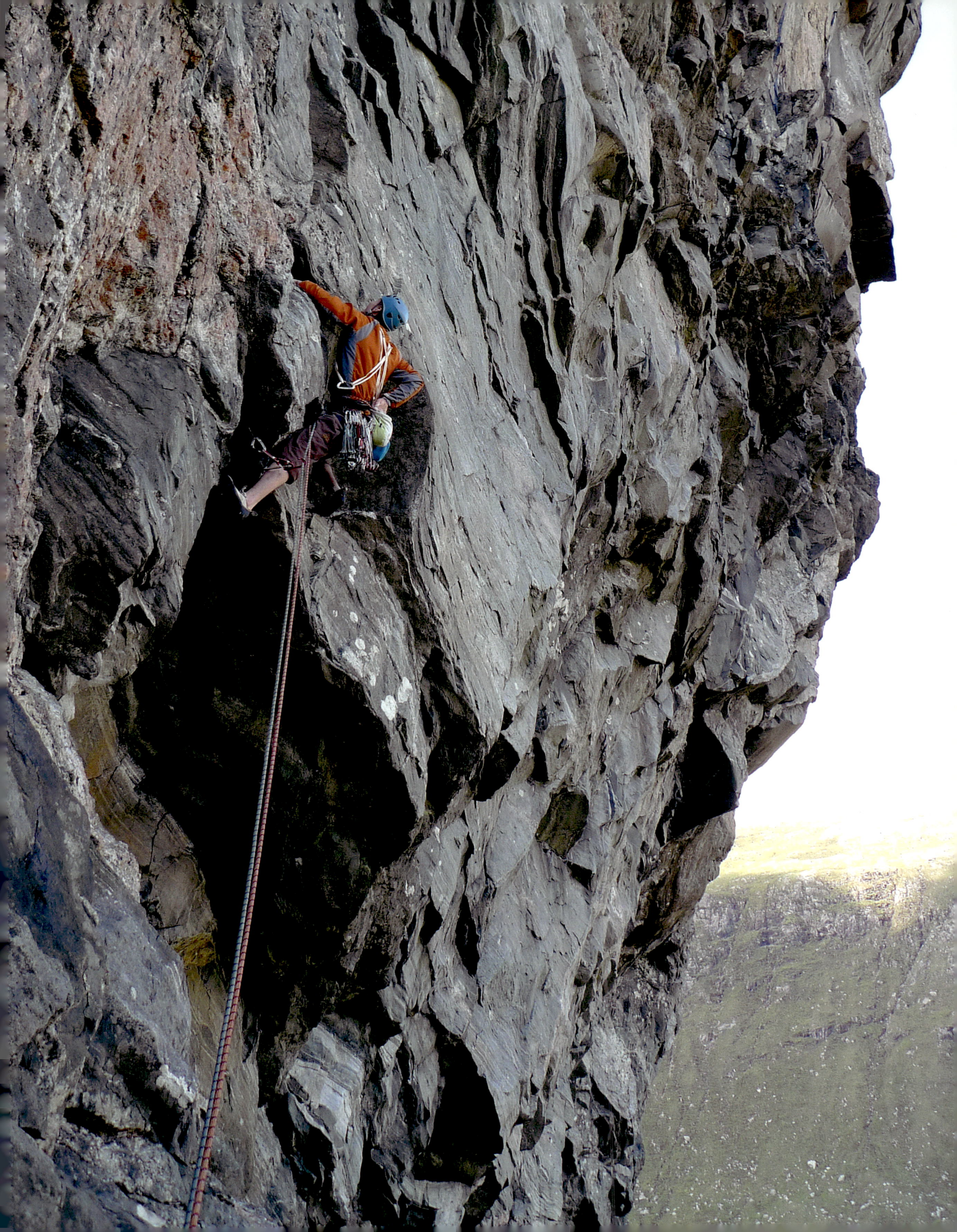

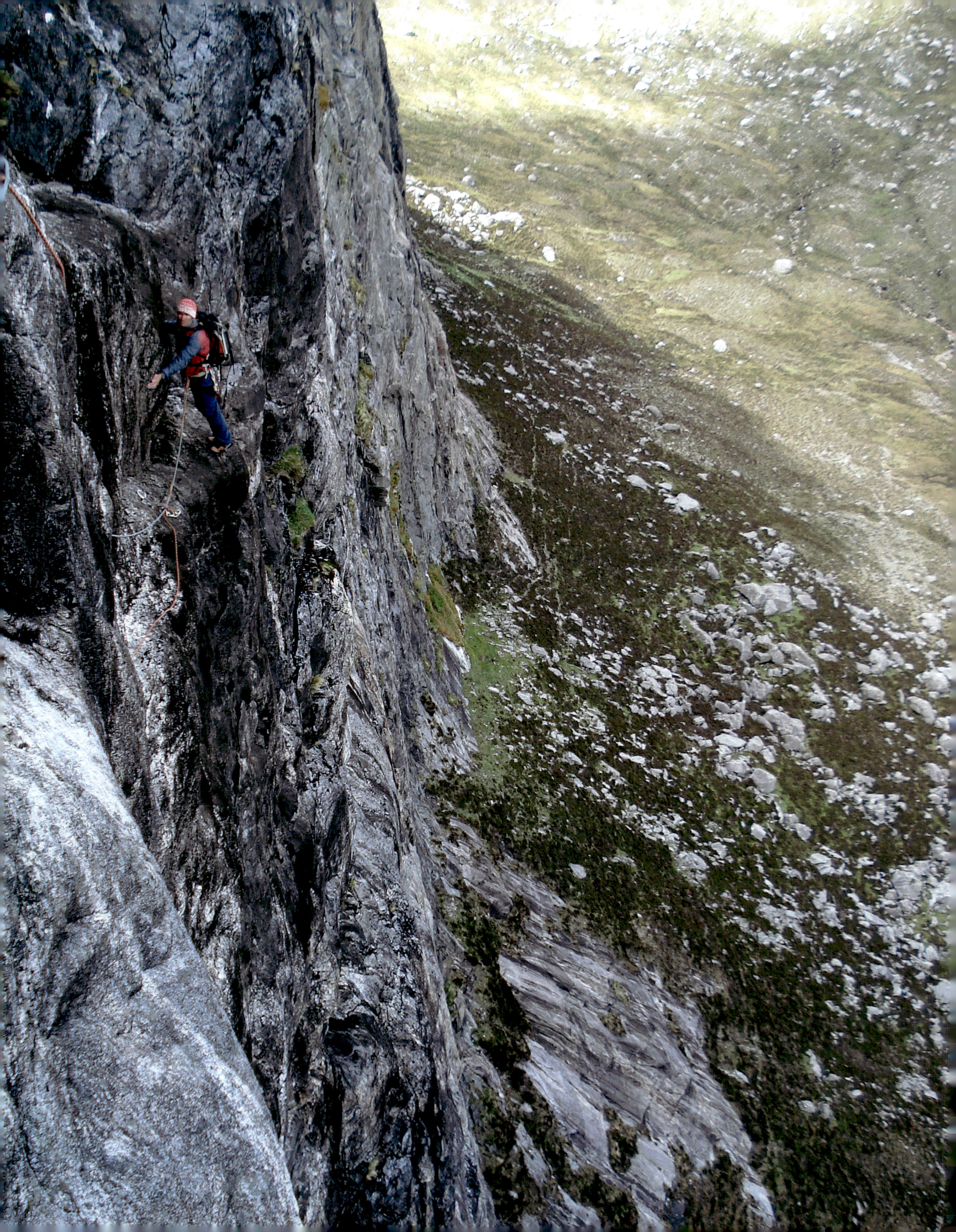

CREAG DHUBH DIOBADAIL, LEWIS – *by Tony Stone*

THE PLACE

If Sròn Uladail is the climbing jewel of the Outer Hebrides then Creag Dhubh Diobadail is the forgotten gem. In times past generations of Breanais people regularly walked past this giant of a cliff on their way to summer grazing pastures. Nowadays in the course of a year only a handful of intrepid hill-goers will pass by this remote and hidden place.

Whether by choice or coerced by the weather, most climbers visiting Lewis climb only on the island's many excellent sea cliffs. It is certainly an easier choice to forego the long march into the mountains. But if conditions in the mountains are right, to miss out on Creag Dhubh Diobadail is to miss out on the adventure of a lifetime.

A gravel track leads off southward from near the southern tip of Traigh Uige. There is a locked gate after less than a mile. Four more miles on foot, or more sensibly on a mountain bike, through a strangely beautiful landscape of scattered boulders and undulating moor, gains the track's high point overlooking Loch Tamnabhaigh. From here a steep pull leads to the marshy col at the head of Coire Diobadail and an easy downward stroll is all that remains.

THE CLIFF

Creag Dhubh Diobadail forms one side of the great trough of Coire Diobadail, which overlooks the vast treeless expanse of Morsgail Forest in North Harris. It makes up much of one flank of the modest hill, Tamnasbhal. Although very much a mountain crag, it is low lying – its base just 200 metres above sea level – so it is sheltered somewhat from the notorious Hebridean winds. The crag faces north-east, so receives only the early morning sun, although at these latitudes during the height of summer this is not insignificant. Nonetheless, a few days of warm, sunny weather are required to dry out the seepage.

For the climber, Creag Dhubh Diobadail is something of a coquette. The vast sweep of grey gneiss seems at first glance pleasantly attractive, but on closer inspection does little to further the climber's progress. Between two steep faults, several hundred metres apart, the cliff towers up nearly 200 metres with no chimneys, corners, cracks or ledges. Instead, the way is barred by pristine, near vertical rock with the odd overhang thrown in for good measure. All this goes some way to explaining why there are still less than ten routes recorded here.

THE CLIMBING

The extremely compact nature of the rock is both good and bad for the climber. There is very little vegetation and the rock is unusually clean, with virtually none of the slippery lichens and mosses that are normally associated with mountain crags. Moreover, Lewisian gneiss, having weathered over three billion years of existence, is very solid and provides excellent friction.

The price of all this, at least to the climber, is that the cliff offers relatively few cracks which accept wires or cams. It is certainly worth carrying micro-wires to increase the odds of finding a useable crack. A bold approach however is essential on all the routes. In general, away from the cracks, the climbing is on positive finger edges. So while run-out, the climbing does not usually feel too precarious, although on occasion it may be necessary to pull on the occasional gneiss sloper!

It's not surprising then that the first routes put up in 1968 avoided the blank central section. Six years later, Geoff Cohen and Rob Archbold became the first to tackle the central wall. They pioneered *Joplin's Wall*, taking a somewhat wandering line for three pitches before scurrying off rightwards up a ramp. It took until 1980 for the wall to be breached head-on. It was that man again, Mick Fowler, with Arnis Strapcans, who made a much more direct ascent. They started up and cut through *Joplin's Wall* to give *Panting Dog Climb*. The route was named after a meeting on the ferry with a dog that had 'a particularly pink lolling tongue', apparently reminiscent of the pink quartz feature from which the route commences.

With the exception of *The Big Lick* there have been few other additions to the crag since *Panting Dog Climb*, and Creag Dhubh Diobadail remains relatively untouched. So for those with sufficient finger strength, and the mettle to match, the potential pickings are rich.

◀ Blair Fyffe on *The Big Lick* (E4).
Photo: *Tony Stone*.

▲ Blair Fyffe on *The Big Lick* (E4). Photo: *Tony Stone*.

▲ Creag Dhubh Diobadail. Photo: *Adrian Crofton*.

THE ROUTES

Via Valtos (E1)

Initially climbed at HVS with a little aid, this climb was a tentative effort on the left-hand fringes of the steep central wall. Uniquely for the crag, the route is reasonably well protected. It follows the attractive, steep crack with only fleeting deviations onto the flanking walls. It is the easiest way up the main section of the cliff.

The Big Lick (E4)

The cliff clearly made a great impression on the irrepressible Fowler, returning to pluck the classic of the crag just a year after putting up *Panting Dog Climb*. Starting from the left side of the pink quartz tongue, the climb struts its way through some very bold ground, only slinking off slightly when close to the top. Constantly engaging, whether mentally or physically, it is sustained throughout, saving the crux move until the last.

Dominis Vobiscus (E4)

The most recent addition to the crag is a demanding line: future ascensionists may very well hope God is with them! The hardest of the bold heart-stoppers, it is the only route on the central section not to start on the pink quartz tongue. Instead, it carves a way through the steep ground bravely linking what few features there are, even resorting to gneiss slopers for progress.

▲ Tess Fryer on *The Big Lick* (E4). Photo: Ian Taylor.

THE STORY

The Scottish walk-in is a breed apart. In the Lake District, certain mountain crags can be reached in 15 easy minutes. In Wales, a mere five minutes up scree gains some so-called mountain crags. But in Scotland most valley crags demand at least half an hour, and it doesn't count as a mountain crag unless the walk-in is mainly uphill and at least two hours long. Or so it seems.

Lewis's high point may only be 574 metres above sea level but Creag Dhubh Diobadail still required a two-and-three-quarter-hour walk-in. At least the going was fairly gentle. It might even have felt relaxing had it not been for my anticipation. Blair strolled along unperturbed some way behind, seemingly lost in thought while we wandered through the desolate lunar landscape that surrounds the track. It seemed to me to go on forever, but eventually we cut off the track and struck steeply up the hillside to a col.

From the col we viewed an even more secluded valley. As we tramped downward, the ever-steepening hillside on our right turned from minor bluffs to cliff, which grew in height and curved round the hillside out of sight. We consulted the guidebook and attempted to match various route descriptions to visible features. Nothing matched. So we continued with something of the feeling of a couple of children in a sweet shop: this giant cliff was virtually untouched. Finally, we spied the tongue of *The Big Lick*; a pink quartz slab flowing down the hillside from the towering cliff above.

THE ISLANDS | **CREAG DHUBH DIOBADAIL, LEWIS** 247

This was the route we had come here for, the classic of the crag and the *Extreme Rock* 'tick', though there seems little danger of this one becoming polished. So we ignored the impressive virgin walls of steep, compact blankness to our right and instead focused on the imposing wall of steep, compact blankness in front of us. We made our way to the base of the cliff proper and decided who was to climb first by the fairest means of all: scissors, paper, stone.

It was a terse scissors-cut-paper win that ultimately led to me chalking my hands with some trepidation. It was certainly a remote cliff. Stunningly situated above Loch Diobadail, the cliff maintains a height of at least 150 metres for its near half-mile length. In a valley with no tracks and few remaining signs of human settlement, it was a foreboding piece of rock to climb.

The first few moves were straightforward as the quartz tongue gave easy access to the steep solid gneiss above. From then on, however, ground was hard won and protection even more so. The gneiss was so compact that there were few cracks to yield reasonable placements, but at least it was solid. Big spans between small flat edges, with bigger spans between protection, forced me to move with care. The rock was excellent and the climbing technical. Eventually I made it to the belay and could relax only a little, acutely aware that there was still a long way to go.

The next pitch was Blair's. From what I could make out, he had either lost his ability to climb or the pitch was somewhat under-graded. I was hoping for the former, unfortunately I found the latter. When I made it to Blair's belay we were both ready for a break — it was only pitch two! I wondered how many more pitches would be like this. After a quick snack we ploughed on upward. The next two pitches were easier and better protected, and I was starting to relax as I pulled up onto Blair's palatial sit down ledge, of which he was taking full advantage. We were lost in a sea of rock enjoying the most spectacular views over Loch Diobadail and the empty moorland beyond, all the way to the distant hills of Harris.

While Blair enjoyed his belay, I tiptoed tentatively leftward along a narrow sloping ledge. My hands groped for non-existent edges on the steep wall in front of my face while my feet smeared on rounded gneiss. After what seemed an age, but was in reality probably only a few moves, the tenuous balancing on next to nothing gave way to easier ground. From my belay I had a perfect view of Blair as he fought the will of our rucksack and clung limpet-like to the rock on the traverse. He joined me, without incident, below the final pitch. Glory was barred only by a slightly overhanging bulge at the base of the final groove just above.

It was a somewhat weary Blair that strained his foot high round the bulge, and with not a little effort pulled himself up into the groove. He scurried upwards to easy ground while I hung back on my belay safe in the knowledge that we had made it to the top. With the ropes tight above me I soon joined him. We sat on top enjoying the long Hebridean evening sunset, not only pleased to have climbed a route of such quality and character, but more than satisfied by the adventure of it all. That is really what climbing in the Hebrides is all about. •

Tess Fryer on *The Big Lick* (E4)
Photo: *Ian Taylor.*

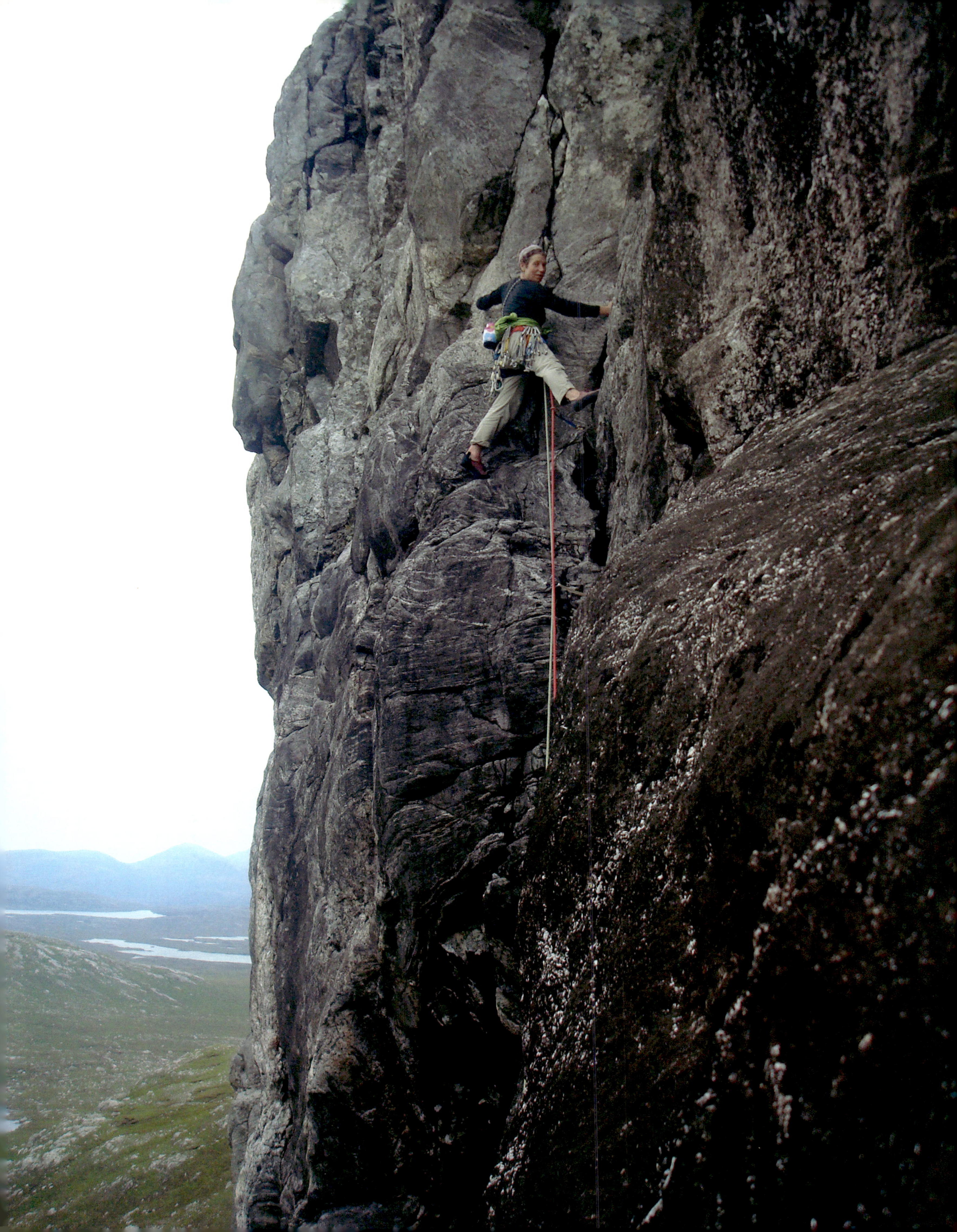

The Bla Bheinn group across to Beinn na Cro (right) from Camas Malag. Photo: *Colin Threlfall*

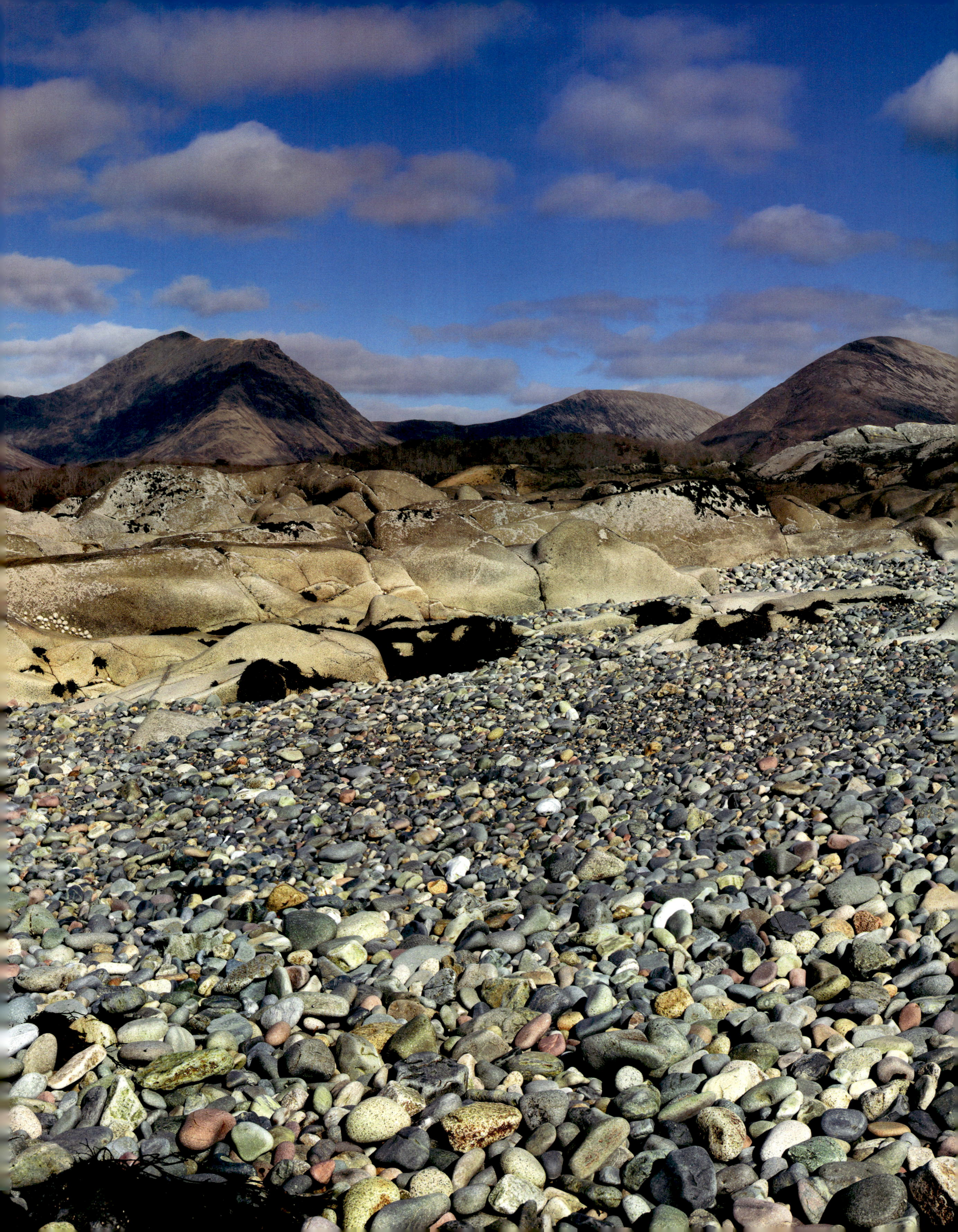

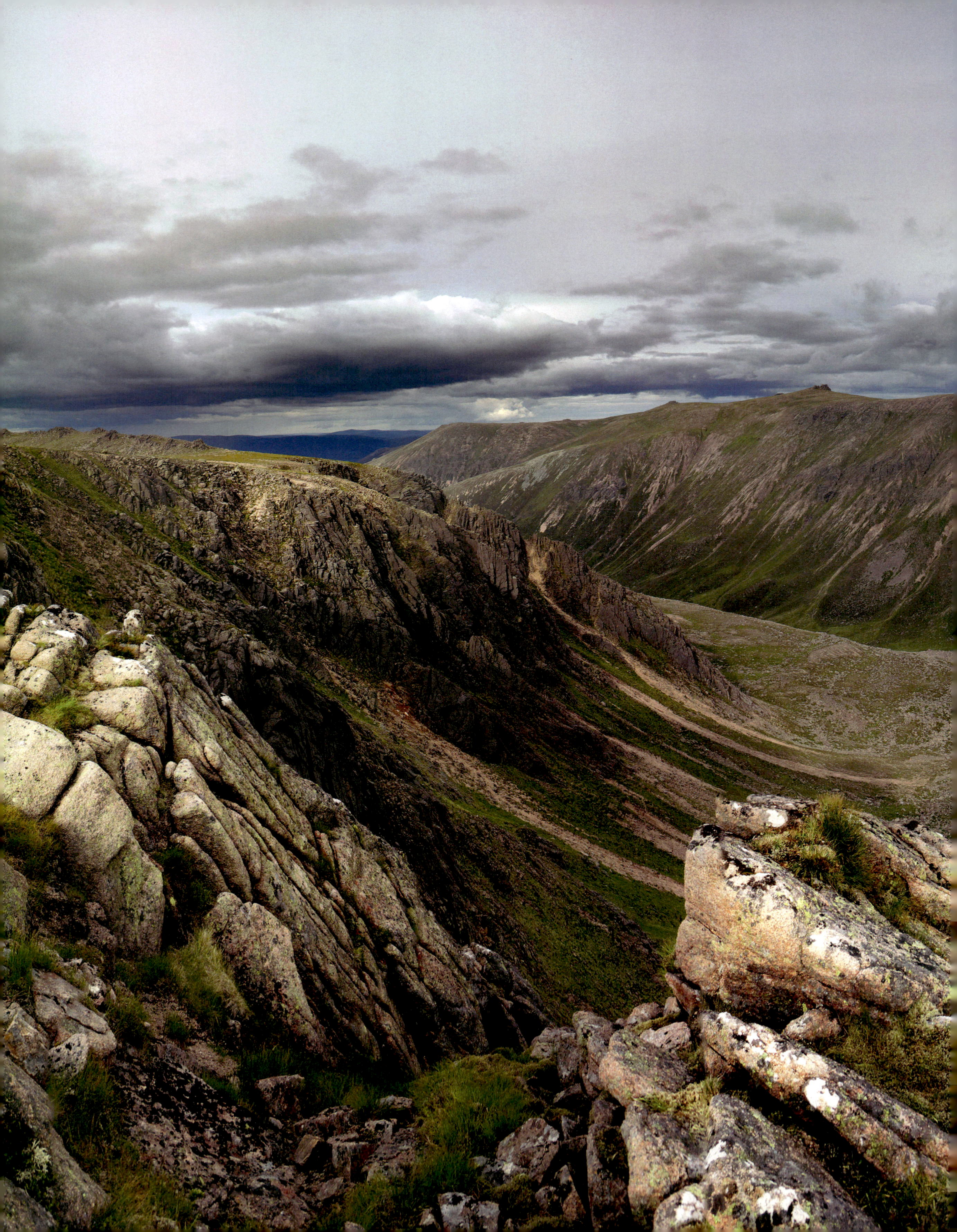

The Cairngorms & Central Highlands

Garbh Choire of Beinn a' Bhuird with the West Face of Mitre Ridge catching the sun on the right.
Photo: *Colin Threlfall*.

Guy Robertson and Pete Macpherson on the first winter ascent of *The Gathering* (VIII,9), Coire an Lochain.
Photo: *Simon Frost.*

Cairngorms
by Stuart B. Campbell

Stick your sticky, slick rubber sole here,
on a crystal of quartz; jam
your cam into that gummsie maw
of a crack ... maybe this is Djibangi; you imagine
on Vertigo Wall, Eagle Ridge, Sticil Face:
not the skyte-mark of a skidding crampon, but
from a tricouni — and feel that
same rough, red granite; feel that,
like Bell, Brooker, Patey — men
in Harris-tweed and Woolies' gutties — you
want the same: The Icon of Lust, The Hurting ...

Oh aye, loon, it's this you're after:
Bad Karma, on The Needle; a first step on To Hell
and Back (and a night suffocating
in the Shelter Stone); to make your mark, but
that last move was just a striation,
a scratch, on the surface of a slab
that's seen the slow passing of ice-sheets.
There's nothing short and fast here, nothing
that can be gained, except in the dignity of solitude,
in the long walk-in to Whispers and the primeval plateau.

Introduction to The Cairngorms & Central Highlands – *By Adrian Crofton*

THE CAIRNGORMS

Our heads sticking out of our bivi bags, we looked up at a bright starry sky over a very cold, white Cairngorm plateau. 'If,' ventured the glaciologist, 'you were to take the Cuillins and stick them on top of the Cairngorms … ' he inhaled with great authority, 'you would have the greatest climbing range in the world.'

Thankfully we were never granted planning permission, so the ranges have retained their distinct character and feel. Not the least loss would have been the obliteration of the Cairngorm plateau, and it is good to know that with the creation of the National Park in September 2003, this wonderful landscape may yet be left for posterity.

Bill Brooker used a beautiful phrase for the opportunity to be had in the Cairngorms – 'the dignity of solitude'. This seems particularly resonant in that place – a world above a world – as if to walk over its edge would be to plunge back to the tawdry separate existence below. Falling off the edge is, of course, a real risk in bad weather, and knowing this sharpens the sense that this is a special place, to be gained with difficulty and escaped just the same. Difficult on one occasion, perhaps, because you are loath to leave a magical, sun-kissed dream world under its vast, luminous blue firmament, or on another because you need to muster all your skill and energy to escape the murderous maelstrom of a winter whiteout after dark.

The Cairngorms are very different to the other mountain environments of the British Isles. Their scale and curves are greater, and often deceptively so. The massively featured landscape with its monolithic rounded shoulders of gravel and rock seems austere and barren in contrast to the intimate nooks and crannies of, for instance, Glen Coe or the Lake District.

The making of the region is more dramatic than first appearances suggest. The story began about 500 million years ago when a vast schistose range was uplifted, into its roots flowing the hot pepper stew which cooled to form a unique combination of feldspar, quartz and mica crystals – the basic ingredients of the granite pluton from which was fashioned the hills we have now. All this occurred just as fish began to appear in the oceans and leafy plants on land. Then over the following 350 million years or so this lump of granite was first worn down by wind and rain to a sub-sea level nubbin, then raised back up over a kilometre high to be bared to successive ice sheets that carved out such great troughs as Loch Avon and Loch Muick. And, of course, our current crop of cliffs. Fresh pink rock scars on the retaining wall of *Parallel Gully B* on Lochnagar and the top pitches of *The Giant* and *Cougar* on Creag an Dubh Loch make clear that this process is far from over.

Today the range forms a great granite nipple whose jointed and varied rocks have been cut through in many places to provide some fantastic outcropping – a halo of accessible schists to be enjoyed when the central massif is out of play. Glen Clova and Dunkeld to the south; in the north, Huntly's Cave; and Creag Dubh to the west. The Cairngorms are, in effect, as Robert Macfarlane points out, a land-locked island.

The three great rivers of the area – the Spey, the Don and the Dee – have their origins in these mountains, most notably on the Braeriach plateau where luminous sphagnum beds mark the spring source of the Dee which cascades spectacularly down the back wall of Garbh Choire Dhaidh. Fittingly, the ascent of the Dee waterfall was the first recorded climb in the area. The mighty glacial trough of Loch Avon is also fed by the burns flowing over vast slabs from the Ben Macdui plateau. This natal amphitheatre, birthing pool of the River Avon, can be appreciated from any of the great northern crags of the main massif.

Considering the size of the range and its height, the number of individual crags is perhaps fewer than in, say, Wales or the Lakes. But it is the quality of the rock and the size of the Cairngorm cliffs that sets them apart. The east-facing cliffs of Lochnagar and Creag an Dubh Loch lie to the south of the Dee. In the northern half of the range, the Shelter Stone Crag shares this same aspect, whereas the climbing in Garbh Choire of Beinn a' Bhuird is west and north facing. Between them, these crags offer the best climbing in the range, boasting routes of up to 330 metres in length with a great variety of style and character – the common theme: beautiful, high quality, adventurous climbing in grand surroundings. The suspended boiler plates of the Central Gully Wall; the castellations of the Citadel and Mitre Ridge; the monolithic overhanging menace of the Broad Terrace and Black Spout Walls; and the peerless sweep of the Central Slabs.

There are many wild spots here where a night out can be spent before or after a day's climbing, so as best to absorb the place. The climbing culture of the Cairngorms has been forged around the howff and bothy – which appear in many forms and locations scattered through the hills. They provide an opportunity to immerse yourself in the mountains and to enjoy the company. The unearthing, construction and in many cases destruction of these 'hotels of the hills' would warrant a book in itself.

Some have bemoaned the long walk-ins of the Cairngorms. But for those with eyes to see there is a wealth of life here, from tiny voles and crested tits to capercaillies and pine martens. Coming down the hill after a long winter day there is shelter and the welcome smell of life among the native Scots pines. The long walk-in should be regarded as seasoning for your main course of finest quality granite climbing – it is at the very heart of the Cairngorm climbing experience.

Technical interest and subtlety can be found on any rock type, but they are the essence of Cairngorm granite. Fluency, intuition and quiet momentum will bring rewards here that no amount of power endurance and static strength can. It can be puzzling, infuriating and terrifying – perched on a slight fold at the edge of an overlapping boilerplate, out of sight of the last runner, unable to see anything obvious to move onto or back to. Yet the confidence to move on is mandatory: you give it all up to the rock and suddenly you have arrived. Likewise, in winter, no amount of dry tooling or overhanging 'M' action will equip you for the balancing on rounded nubbins, the serrations of your axe caressing those vital few crystals that will allow you to gingerly reach and excavate that beguiling furrow of frozen turf – or will it be tungsten-hard gravel?

Although in sheer numbers of routes climbed, the Aberdonians can be seen to dominate the development of these cliffs, such is the quality of the rock that talented outsiders have been repeatedly drawn to the area. So where should you go if you are chasing the hardest and the best? Back in the forties when he forged his masterpiece, *Eagle Ridge*, on Lochnagar, J. H. B. Bell noted that the three great cliffs of the Cairngorms were Lochnagar, Creag an Dubh Loch and ... Sgoran Dubh. 'Sgoran Where?,' you may ask. The Shelter Stone is not even mentioned in his commentary in *Bell's Scottish Climbs*, but Sgoran Dubh has a lengthy section all to itself – such is the power of tradition. Perhaps it was just that its impregnable appearance meant that the Shelter Stone did not even feature in a climber's imagination at that time. Warnings of utter impossibility seem to feature in Cairngorm guidebooks, yet each new generation has thrown such caution aside – Brooker on *Route 1*, Patey on *Vertigo Wall*, Lines on the Central Slabs. I recall looking over from The Pin to the pristine sweep of impossibility that is the Central Slabs. I was awestruck. How could anyone climb such steep featureless granite? Just then those portentous guidebook pronouncements seemed sane, not silly, and it is the style of their eventual refutation that has been incredible. Indeed, it was here that the limitations of traditional chalk-free, on-sight style were reached when even the talented and driven Dinwoodie was forced to hammer in a few aid pegs to complete his ascent of the long elegant cedilla of *Cupid's Bow* in 1980, each hammer blow sounding the end of an era. The new era can be said to have dawned in 1982 when, over the following two summers, it seemed almost every remaining great line was climbed. Climbers from the Lakes and Edinburgh took the lead: static lines were used shamelessly, the ancient lichens and mosses brushed away to leave some of the most tremendous and difficult multi-pitch rock climbs anywhere in the British Isles.

The pattern and pace of development of winter climbing has been different to that on the summer rock. This is because the great rise in standards occurred in the early and mid fifties, and the hard routes of these times still feel hard, in the same way that the rock routes of the late seventies and early eighties do. These routes are still memorable landmarks in the progress of the modern aspirant. The Aberdonians, in winter as in summer, were traditionalists to the core: the style of the ascents of *The Sticil Face* or *Djibangi* by step-cutting may have seemed by that time atavistic, but the standard certainly was not. Even so, the winter first ascents list in modern times seems positively cosmopolitan. Compared to the great venues of the west coast, the relatively continental climate of the Cairngorms means that reliable conditions – the most precious of qualities in a warming world – are more often found in this range than anywhere else in the country. It can be surprising to come to these mountains in October to find great fields of consolidated frozen snow and ice already, only weeks after you were there on a hot August day kicking up clouds of heather pollen. These are Scotland's premier winter mountains, and this transformation at the end of summer is often disconcertingly rapid. In summer the appeal of these cliffs may extend to other parts of the British Isles, but in winter their reputation is becoming international. That's not to say they are crawling with French climbers as the Alps teem with Britons, but rather that a discerning group of the very best have often come and left their mark, in no small part thanks to the international meets held at Glenmore Lodge in recent years.

For many the Cairngorms now means reliable 'roadside' mixed climbing in the form of the ever-crowded Northern Coires, where excellent short climbs can be had any time from October through to April, often with only the briefest of preceding snowfall. The combination of road access, elevation, aspect and modest size have transformed this once lonely and neglected area into an 'easy' hit for huge numbers of winter enthusiasts. At the same time these very qualities have delivered a bonanza of technically hard mixed routes — a spawning ground for climbers going on to do greater things on the wilder and bigger crags which require more forethought and effort. More committing adventures are not too far away — just over the plateau on the Shelter Stone's main bastion, on the remote cliffs of Garbh Choire of Beinn a' Bhuird, and of course on the enormous hulking slabs of the Dubh Loch. *The Cardinal*, *Slochd Wall*, *The Steeple*, *Vertigo Wall* — these are all serious and involved winter expeditions, rewarding richly only those with sufficient guile and determination.

There are still plumb lines remaining, and in some cases it doesn't take much looking to see where they are. So, rise up from your bouldering mat, take up your wire brush and static rope and head to the hills!

THE CENTRAL HIGHLANDS

From Loch Linnhe across to Speyside there is a girdling belt of Dalradian schists worn jauntily aslant the country's girth, studded with igneous gems such as Glen Coe, Ben Nevis and Binnein Shuas. But where these rhyolites and granites beloved of climbers are lacking, this unpromising base material has occasionally been artfully glaciated, most notably at Creag Meagaidh, where it forms a spectacular vertical arena which comes into its prime when winter brings snow and ice. The delightful micro granite or pegmatite of the south facing cliffs of Binnein Shuas stand in contrast as a magnet for the summer climber. From the road at Loch Laggan one can access the best long steep ice lines in the country (going north) or at other times of year some fantastic rock-climbing (walking south). Access is incomparably easier now for us — consider Raeburn first cycling from Dalwhinnie to climb on Meagaidh. Whilst we can still enjoy adventures on these cliffs, the utter isolation and strangeness of the mountains must have been positively exotic then.

The character of these archetypal Central Highland venues is an amalgam of east and west, a transition between the dramatic sharp-ridged peaks of the west and the drier hills of the east with their extensive high plateaux. The decimation of the Highland forests which has progressed steadily over the last two millennia has left a worn sparse mat of vegetation at their base, but magical nooks of birch and oak forest can still be appreciated, and the more sympathetic reforestation of recent times promises more of the same for the future.

The adjective 'dolomitic' is often applied to the cliffs of Coire Ardair with some justice — the horizontal banding, the downward slant with each vertical layer slightly undercut, giving at times nauseating exposure, in particular on the Pinnacle Face. Jimmy Marshall's ascent of *Smith's Gully* in 1959 in the company of Graham Tiso was the first of the great lines to breach the defences, and later the pencil line of *The Fly Direct* in 1983 by Mick Fowler and Vic Saunders showed that the exposed blank face itself could be climbed.

This, then, is a place in between, traversed by raiders, armies, and poor herders across the centuries. We, then, are a historical anomaly: left in peace to pursue our sport in this beautiful place. •

Ross Hewitt on *Vertigo Wall* (VII,7), Central Gully Wall, Creag an Dubh Loch.
Photo: *Guy Robertson.*

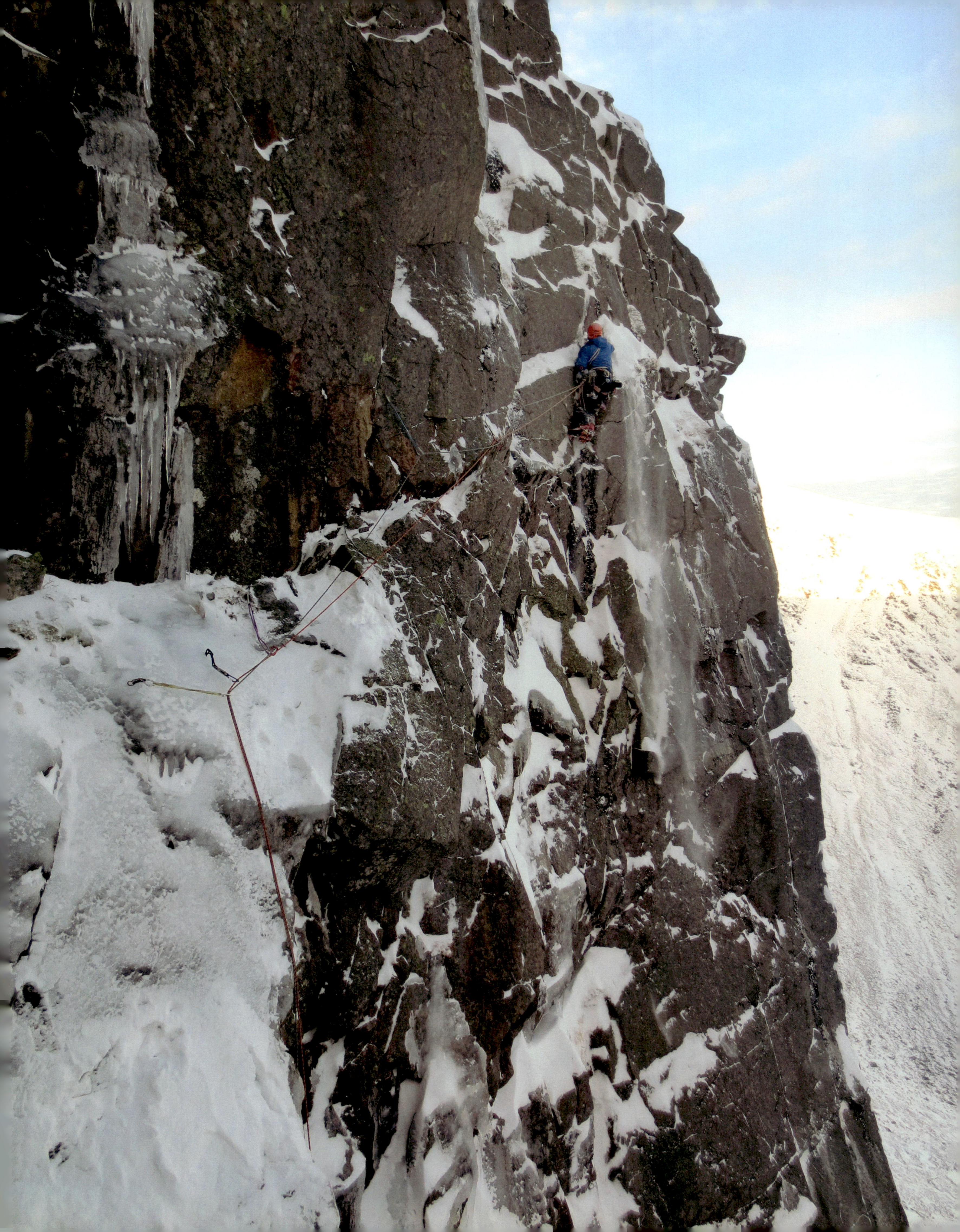

Julian Lines pioneering an as yet unfinished route on Creag an Dubh Loch.
Photo: Dave Cuthbertson

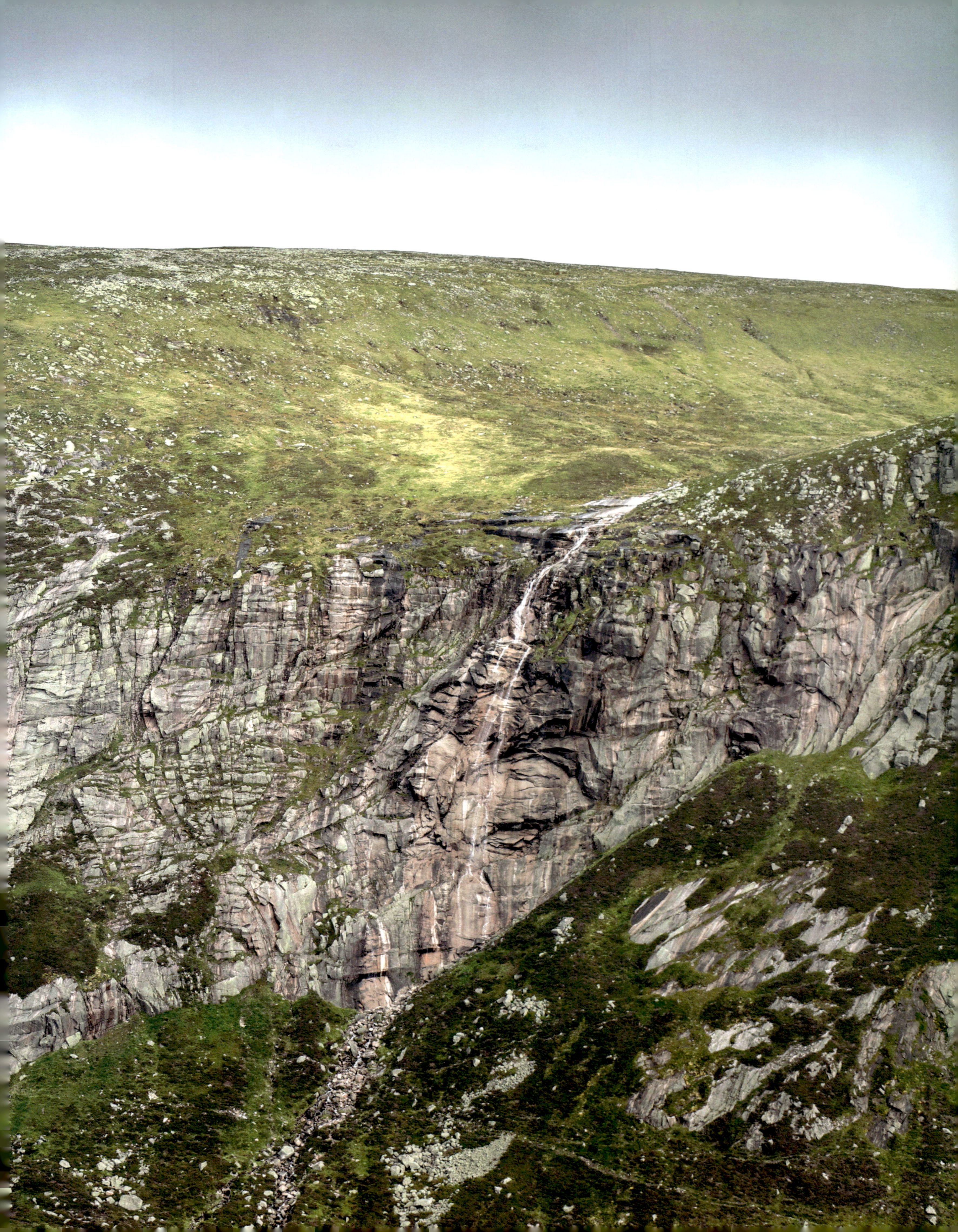

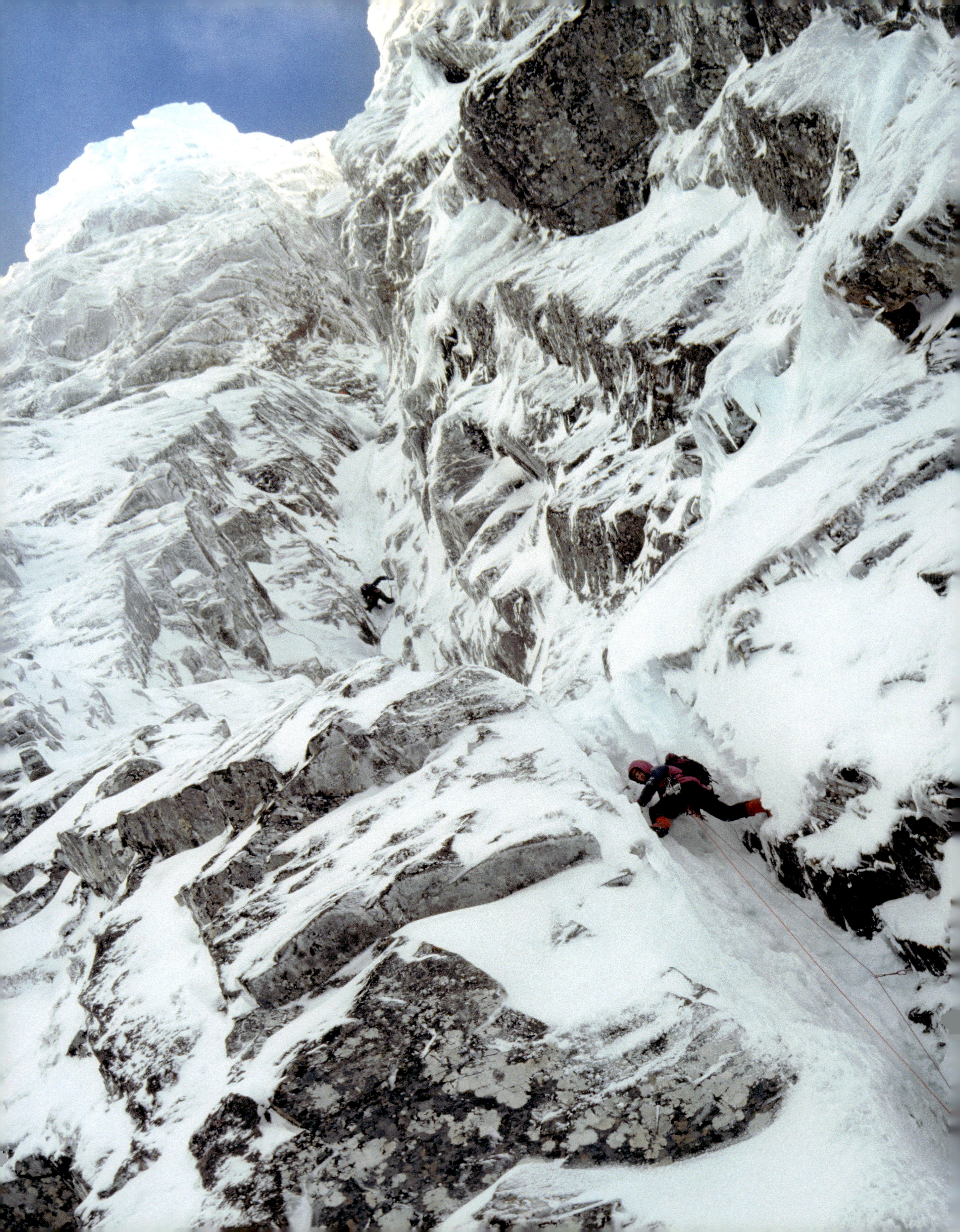

Pinnacle Buttress, Creag Meagaidh – *by Es Tressider*

THE PLACE
Creag Meagaidh always strikes me as a slightly secretive crag, hidden as it is up a long glen, its steep cliffs nestled among much gentler, rounded hills that offer little hint as to the sort of adventures to be found here. The nature of the climbing seems to add to the mystique.

It is not somewhere that people climb in summer, so there is never the luxury of having a feel for the topography and atmosphere of the place outside of the harsh temperatures and weather of winter. Compared to other big venues, there is not always 'something to do' here, so it's not somewhere you would go just for a look. It can also be very dangerous in poor conditions. As a result of all this, people tend to plump for either The East or The West and often fail to consider The Middle. In many winters the crag stays largely off the radar. For me this air of mystery only makes the routes more alluring, and the taste of success that little bit sweeter.

THE CLIFF
On the long, gentle approach from Aberarder farm to Creag Meagaidh, it is the Pinnacle Face that first grabs and holds the attention. Standing forward from the rest of the coire, it presents a vast face of uncompromising steepness, only occasionally interrupted by the horizontal striations common to Creag Meagaidh.

In good conditions it is the gully lines that immediately grab your attention; from the top left, *Ritchie's Gully* and then *Smith's Gully*, then from a generation later *The Fly Direct* and *The Midge*. All these routes were standout ascents in their time, and they are no pushover today, even with modern technology.

In between the striking gullies are great bulging terraced walls, providing some of the most exacting winter-only mixed climbs found anywhere in Scotland. There are very few prominent features on the buttresses, the routes requiring instead an intimate practical inspection to link horizontal ledges, tenuous grooves and improbable slabs and walls hopefully sporting just enough turf and ice.

THE CLIMBING
Creag Meagaidh offers superb icy mixed climbing combining rock, ice, snow and plentiful vegetation. There is a good reason there is no summer climbing here! The older routes tend to follow deep gullies, predominantly steep ice and snow, hence they often feature long run-outs and dubious protection.

On the steeper routes the protection can sometimes be a bit better but is rarely 'bomber'. However, away from the gullies on Meagaidh the fear factor is usually maintained by an urgent feeling of pump and an increased likelihood of falling off! The routes are all huge, so plan to be fast or start and/or finish in the dark. It is unusual to be able to climb here early in the season since quite a long period of cold weather is required for good conditions to form.

Because of the paucity of protection, on the harder routes it is worth carrying a rack large enough to offer a good broad selection on the occasions when gear opportunities arise. Expect to do a lot of digging for your belays and bring a decent selection of pegs and turf gear, in addition to a few ice screws.

◂ Unknown climbers on *Smith's Gully* (VI,5).
Photo: *Dave Cuthbertson*.

THE ROUTES

Eye Candy (VII,7)
Superb climbing following icy ramps up the arête right of *Smith's Gully*. Expect varied and always interesting climbing, fantastic situations overlooking *Smith's Gully*, some baffling weirdness getting through a roof on the third pitch and, if you're lucky, it sports a hanging icicle on the final pitch.

Extasy (VIII,8)
A stupendous route taking on the challenge of the big wall between *The Fly Direct* and *Smith's Gully*. Very sustained with lots of pitches warranting technical grade 8. Long viewed as a 'last great problem' by those in the know, and justifiably lauded at the time as a standout route in an exceptional season.

The Moth (VII,8)
Excellent icy mixed climbing, finding a way up the complex wall between *The Fly Direct* and *The Midge*. The first ascencionists spent much time finding a way through the complex lower section, and consequently finished the route in a murky dark storm.

Guy Robertson and Es Tressider on the first winter ascent of *The Moth* (VII,8)
Photo: *Dave Cuthbertson*.

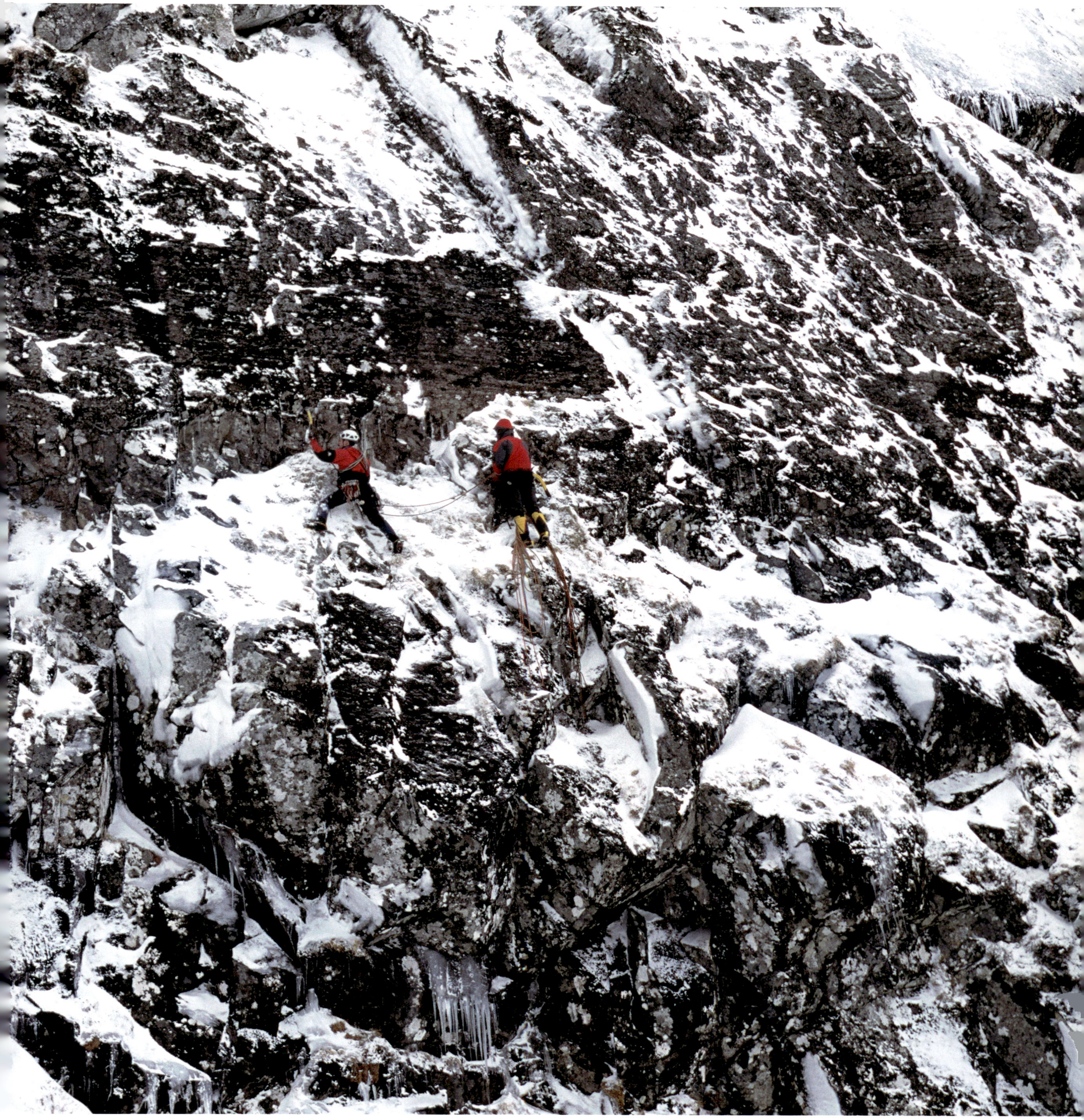

▲ Approaching Coire Ardair with Pinnacle Buttress directly above the walker. Photo: *Andy Nisbet*.

THE STORY

Like many people, my first impressions of Creag Meagaidh were informed by the iconic black and white images in *Cold Climbs*. Perhaps more than any other cliff featured in that book, Creag Meagaidh's grandeur and geology seemed to lend themselves to monochrome photography. One photo stood out from all others, a superb full-page spread of the Pinnacle Face. Here was a face of truly alpine proportions. Steep buttresses split by fantastic soaring gullies; incipient corners defined by lines of white in black rock; snowy ledges throwing the eye sideways, shadows cast by a weak winter sun. My young eyes, still in the first flush of obsession, saw new lines everywhere, but it was more than five years before I finally turned interest into action.

Superb conditions coincided with the BMC International Meet in 2005. Every day, motivated and strong teams were out doing the most impressive routes. I'd had a good week myself, and was feeling exhausted after back-to-back big days with Slovenian guest Primož Hostnik. Though I felt I'd more than fulfilled my duties as a host, showing Primož a variety of styles from Beinn Eighe to Ben Nevis, there was one vital aspect of the Scottish Winter Experience that I had neglected – climbing new routes ground up.

This missing link nagged at me constantly, so it was with exploration in mind that I recruited Guy Robertson for the last day. We decided on 'Meggy' and the Pinnacle Face. One of the best new routes of the meet had been the stunning Extasy earlier in the week, so conditions were clearly exceptional, and Guy and I knew there was more for the taking. As we walked in, however, I fought motivational demons, seizing on everything that wasn't quite right about the day as reason to turn back. This is the problem with Scottish winter climbing

▲ Guy Robertson on Extasy (VIII,8). Photo: Pete Benson.

— there's always something not quite right, so assessing whether or not to continue is a constant battle between prudence on the one hand and pessimism on the other. As we reached the gearing-up spot I voiced my intention to turn back. Guy was incredulous. But almost as soon as I'd spoken I changed my mind. It was as if voicing my weakness had exorcised it, and suddenly motivation returned; I now wanted more than ever to see what the long-dreamt-of Pinnacle Face had to offer.

We scoped our options, finally plumping for a sinuous icy ramp-line in the right arête of *Smith's Gully*. Guy started with the first pitch of *Smith's Gully* before handing the rack to Primož where we left the gully for new ground. Though Primož impressed me, as host I still felt protective, and worried about his protection and the difficulty of the climbing. I needn't have worried: by chance I had given Primož the finest pitch on the route — a superb 'out there' position, ice on one side of the corner, and a perfect crack on the other. I seconded the pitch with a huge grin on my face, content to have carried out my duties as host and local expert to the full.

Another bulging ice pitch followed, and higher up Guy found a way through an unlikely overhanging wall on weird, off-balance ramps — never strenuous, but very insecure and quintessentially Scottish. We were silently pleased when our Slovenian ropegun fell off seconding. The route ended with a pitch more suited to his style though — a fine, free-hanging icicle bringing us right to the plateau.

At the final night party, excitement was fuelled by alcohol, and a constant loop of motivating images from all the adventures lit the wall of the bar. Three photos stood out for me, all from the new mega-route *Extasy*. It was clear that while we had had fun on our new route, *Extasy* was in a different league of quality and difficulty. Guy and I made plans to return.

The following weekend we returned to find conditions still good but an imminent thaw on the horizon. As ever, things had evolved considerably, and in addition to ice there was now hard snow in the most unusual places, smeared and sculpted onto walls and arêtes where normally there would be either bare rock or powder. We chose to go for the vast unclimbed wall between *The Fly* and *The Midge*. It looked improbable, but after our experience the previous week, we figured it was worth a go.

Guy led a pumpy, bold traverse pitch to gain a line we'd scoped from below. Axes in turf on an overhung and undercut ledge, with Warthogs for protection. Above, the way was far from clear. A short crack led to a long curving overhang from which sporadic thin ice drooled over the blank wall below. Could I link those streaks? If so, where would I get past the overhang? What would happen if I went a step too far and couldn't find any gear?

From the top of the crack I voiced my dilemma to Guy. A series of non-decisions were made before Dave 'Cubby' Cuthbertson – taking photos from the gully below – shouted 'if you carry on traversing you'll find yourself in big trouble!' When someone like Cubby voices concerns about your route, it is worth taking notice. I had to find a way through the overhang as early as possible. Fortunately with adequate protection, the solution was hard, strenuous and balancy – just enough snow ice stuck to overhanging walls to enable a classic gut-wrenching Scottish mantelshelf.

Higher up, as a storm gathered, we began to understand where Creag Meagaidh had got its reputation for serious climbing. While the crux was well protected, the easier grade VI climbing in the upper pitches was exceptionally bold, and belays took time and motivation to find. Near the plateau, with darkness taking its psychological toll, the thaw arrived early, turning our route to unclimbable mush. So with heads down we escaped out right on a ledge that skirted the final tower. The void below beckoned in the darkness, and it was with great relief, some 13 hours after starting out, that we emerged on level ground and the top.

That thaw marked the end of one of the most productive winter seasons I've ever had. I went from never having climbed at Creag Meagaidh to climbing two major new routes on a face that I had long dreamt of. The week of the International Meet still retains a magical air in my mind. One day I'll go back to Pinnacle Face. I hope it doesn't break that spell.

Another view of Guy Robertson and Es Tressider on the first winter ascent of *The Moth* (VII,8).
Photo: *Dave Cuthbertson*.

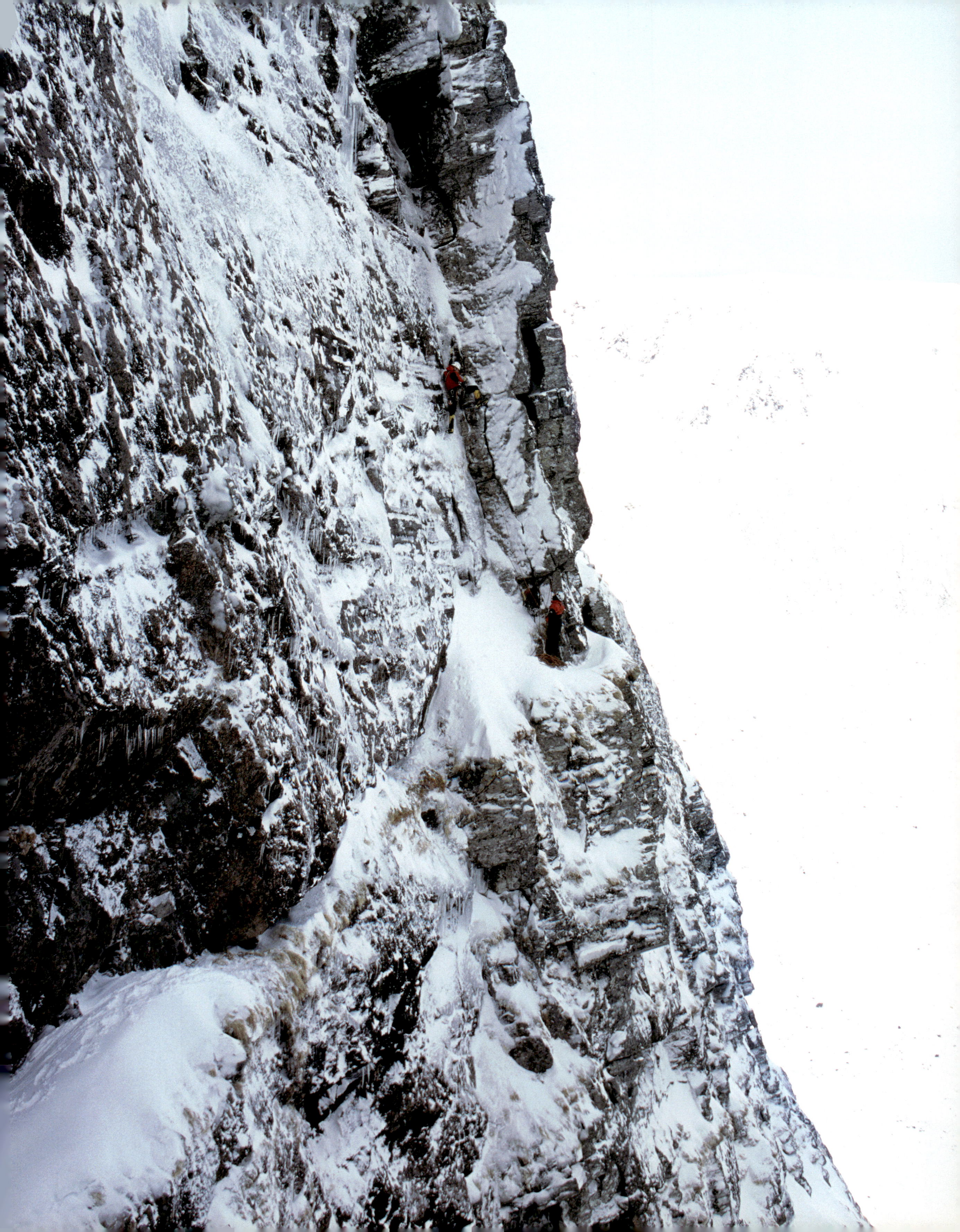

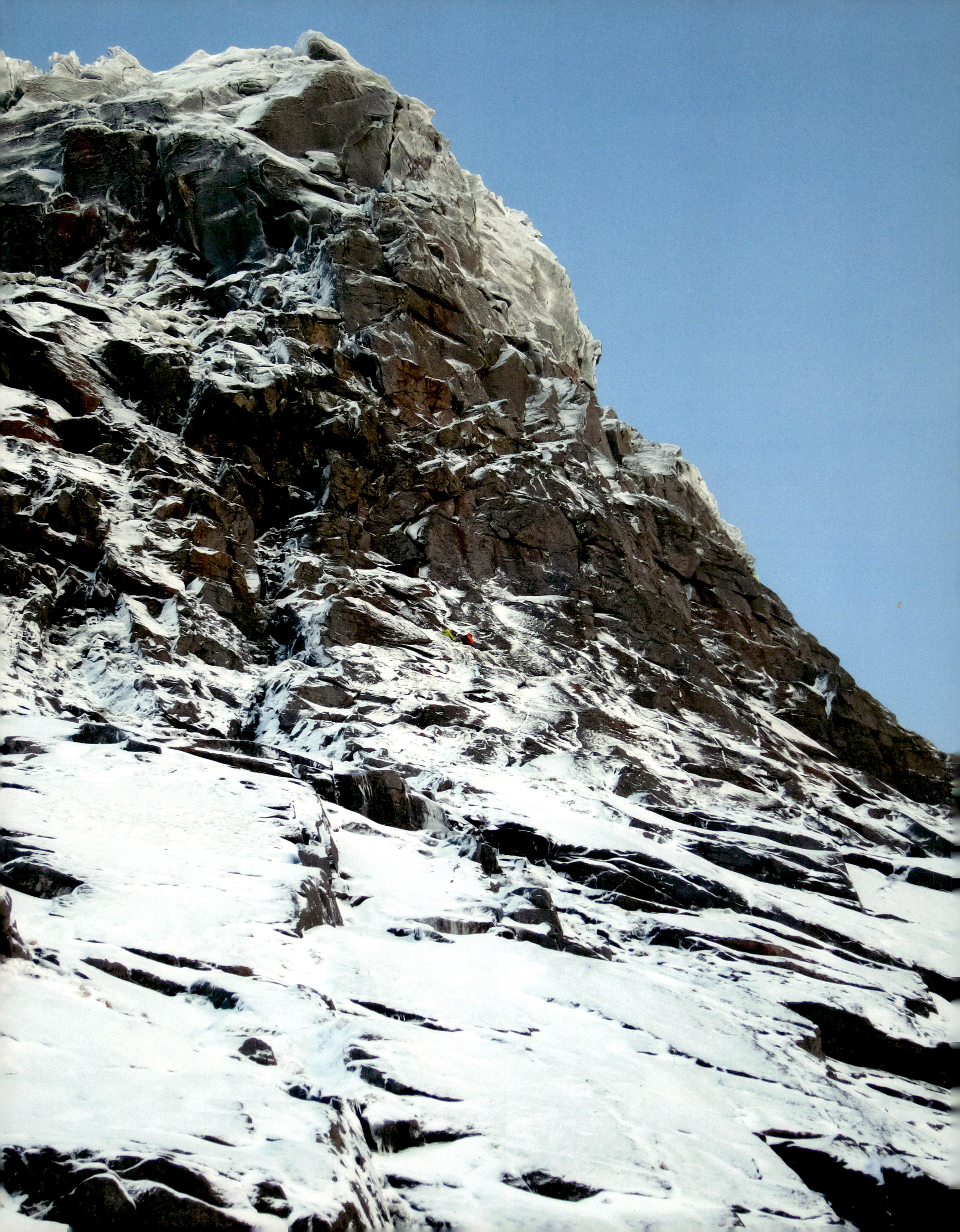

Shelter Stone Crag –
by Guy Robertson, story by Rick Campbell

THE PLACE
Cut deep into the heart of the northern Cairngorms, a great glacial trough extends eastwards, mellowing as the landscape flattens towards the Moray coast. At the western limit of this long elegant glen broods a dark loch, ensnared by a gang of towering granite cliffs. Shelter Stone, Hell's Lum, Stag Rocks, Carn Etchachan – there is more steep rock and good climbing found at the head of the Loch Avon basin than anywhere else in central Scotland. Despite the passage of time and development of a ski resort nearby, it is still far enough from the road to demand that extra dose of commitment. It's a place of lengthy approaches in all seasons, and home to some of the best and longest climbs in the country.

THE CLIFF
Shelter Stone Crag describes the huge mass of rock extending from Castlegates Gully on the left through to Pinnacle Gully on the right, both easy-angled water courses, or grade I snow climbs in winter. The two facets of most interest to the modern climber are undoubtedly the smooth, high-angled sweep of the Central Slabs and the great flat-topped monolith of the Main Bastion. The two could hardly be more contrasting. The former is a perfect palette of pristine granite set at an angle of around 70 degrees, and around a hundred metres high. The latter is a steadily steepening and tapering fortress, starting as slabs but rearing up to a vertical finale; almost a thousand feet high and broken substantially only by a halfway terrace.

The Slabs are undisturbed by any horizontal relief. They are characterised by a number of powerful, yet mostly discontinuous upward-curving grooves and corners, offering strong lines and perhaps some sanctuary, but leading invariably out into blankness. Even the natural weaknesses provide rock climbs in the mid to high Extreme bracket. The blank spaces in between are only penetrated by climbs of the highest order of difficulty. The Bastion, on the other hand, offers more continuous, vertical lines of weakness, punctuated by occasional ledges, providing relatively complex route-finding and potentially interchangeable pitches. A series of parallel lower and upper corner systems are connected by steep walls above a broken lower terrace. In most cases these central walls provide the crux of the routes, with relatively fewer continuous cracks. In winter, however, after five or six exhausting lower pitches, it will likely be the upper pitches that prove the most taxing.

◀ Guy Robertson and Pete Macpherson on the first winter ascent of *Stone Temple Pilots* (X,9).
Photo: *Brian Duthie.*

THE CLIMBING
Shelter Stone Crag is arguably the most dramatic climbing venue in Scotland. For seekers of extreme slab climbing in summer, or long and arduous routes in winter, few other venues can compare.

The rock is generally impeccable mountain granite, though less rough or reliant on friction than other cliffs in the Cairngorms. It is also considerably less rounded, and instead more square-cut, so the routes are generally characterised by more positive holds and features. In winter this means that even long sustained pitches can often be climbed quickly and positively, even through very steep ground. The slabs are out of bounds in winter, and the more obvious features require sustained finger and foot work, with usually at least adequate protection. Routes tackling the blanker sections, however, are invariably intensely bold and technically demanding 'head games', requiring a full repertoire of slab techniques. Long ropes, extenders, a large selection of RPs, micro-wires, and small cams are all de rigueur, as is the ability to set one's faith in the integrity of in-situ pitons! On the Bastion, however, protection is never an issue, with all the routes following big features with plentiful runners of all descriptions. Individual pitches are often based around long, soaring corners or grooves, gradually steepening as they go, to a giddying (and tiring) vertical crescendo up the final impending headwall. Layback skills will generally help, as will the ability to avoid placing your entire rack before climbing even halfway up a pitch!

It's not surprising that the crag attracted a lot of interest among Cairngorm pioneers. Such a fortress of rock so clearly devoid of weakness was bound to fire the passions of any self-respecting Cairngorm Tiger. Indeed, it is fair to say that while the crag takes pride of place in the Cairngorms massif, it also has a lofty status in the wider context of Scottish climbing history. With the possible exception of Ben Nevis, there are few venues where generation after generation have pushed the boundaries of what is possible. From Patey, Grassick and Nicol et al. forging the first hard winter routes in the fifties, to Campbell and Lines venturing boldly out onto the blank sections of the Central Slabs through the eighties and nineties, the Shelter Stone has consistently provided 'touchstone' testpieces across the seasons, and is home to many of Scotland's hardest multi-pitch routes to this day.

▲ Julian Lines on *Realm of the Senses* (E7). Photo: Dave Cuthbertson.

THE ROUTES

The Needle (E1, VIII,9)

A Robin Smith classic. This was the first of the big routes tackling the Main Bastion directly, taking a scintillating line aiming for the big open corners high up. In summer the climbing is never desperate for the grade, but the route is very long and sustained. The winter route is rapidly gaining modern classic status.

Aphrodite (E7)

The first E7 in the Cairngorms and a stupendous line. It takes the unrelenting crack-line striking diagonally up right from just above the big Snipers overlap at the bottom left of the Slabs. It could be said that other routes — notably *Run of the Arrow* — 'dip into' this line, but it has to be followed all the way for the ultimate Shelter Stone slab climbing head game!

▲ Ian Taylor on *The Missing Link* (E4). Photo: *Rob Durran*.

Sticil Face (V,6)

The original and best winter route on the crag, taking the big dirty (that is to say 'icy') depression left of the Central Slabs. The route has a crux that might just bite the unsuspecting grade V leader, and there is some awe-inspiring exposure on the terraces high up.

274　THE GREAT MOUNTAIN CRAGS OF SCOTLAND

THE STORY — *by Rick Campbell*

Teetering across *Missing Link*, with its three meagre runners but reasonable holds, it is hard to imagine how the blank, leaning *Thor* overlap only a few metres above could ever be free-climbed. With the adequate protection available in the great dihedral it is just possible to keep your toes moving onwards and upwards.

Having seen Grant Farquhar and Kim Greenald yo-yo their way up the first pitch in 1988, and having myself already placed a couple of new pegs on the second, Neil Craig and I walked in to try our luck one fine July morning in 1989. Incredibly we found ourselves in a bit of a race with Gary Latter and Graham Lawrie, who, by sheer coincidence, had similar plans – on exactly the same day some 20-plus years after the original aided ascent!

Risking broken ankles haring across the plateau, we managed to get on the line first and zoomed up the easy first pitch to a belay at the base of the main overlap. The pitch started steadily enough (in common with several other lines) until a point was reached where an unhelpful flake above the overlap was used to place a crucial RP. The granite beyond here appeared very blank and, with the vultures gathering on the belay below, I committed to a sequence of full-on friction moves up into an alcove under a slight roof. This was the original belay – on a single drilled peg – but since it was clearly not a 'hands-off rest' I was forced to continue. By this time I was struggling somewhat, and maintaining marginal contact with the rock I launched into a thin traverse blindly out right, eventually reaching the sanctuary of a hanging flake and good peg belay.

I had already been down on a rope to place a couple of peg runners in the next pitch. So having clipped a knifeblade just above the belay it was straight into a really awkward long move right to a decent hold. From here I elected to crank straight up into a crescent-shaped crack where, after a quick mantel, a good rest was taken. Panting for breath and with that slightly dizzy feeling brought about by an overdose of adrenaline, I paused to weigh up what lay ahead.

◀ Shelter Stone Crag catches the morning sun with Carn Etchachan behind.
Photo: *Guy Robertson*.

Top left: Julian Lines (leading) and Jonny Baird on *Realm of the Senses* (E7). Photo: *Dave Cuthbertson*.
Top right: Unknown climber on *Steeple* (E2). Photo: *Ewan Lyons*. **Bottom left**: Guy Robertson on the first winter ascent of *Stone Temple Pilots* (X,9). Photo: *Pete Macpherson*. **Bottom right**: Jason Currie on *The Needle* (Winter Variations) (VII,8). Photo: *Guy Robertson*.

The overlap was now only about 15 centimetres high, blank and horizontal. A solid ring peg provided the moral support to throw my right foot way out right onto a smear, crimp a tiny crystal, drop low, flag with the other leg and rock up into a standing position. Above was a worrying line of ancient RURPs, tied off with rotting cords, but fortunately the climbing here settled back to about Severe in standard, so it wasn't long before I was lashed to a belay at the top of The Pin. Neil followed and we sat back to watch Gary working his way across our recently completed pitch. Electing to stay below the overlap the whole way, he found a sequence across it that was less technical, nearer the gear but somewhat more sustained.

The obvious line up the face above the base of the *Thor* overlap – *Run of the Arrow* (E6) – was climbed to the satisfaction of most by Lakes cragsman Pete Whillance in the days before sticky boots. Since then, the crux move – a long bridge onto a smear and hands-free weight transfer left – has seen its fair share of leader falls onto the marginal gear placements. Some time after my own ascent of this now classic scare-fest in 1988 I decided the line should really continue directly from below the crux to finish up the blank slab above. I also wanted to free-climb the *Snipers* roof below this, and link it into the start of the original Whillance line. Furthermore I strongly felt it could and should be ascended from the ground up. 1990 was to be the year; the only minor problem being my lack of fitness following a long lay-off after a large chunk of Pembroke had smashed my shoulder blade. Still, I reckoned I'd be OK for a bit of slab climbing.

The stoical Alistair Moses was just the sort of chap to have on board for this adventure, considering the inevitable belay marathon on the main pitch. While expressing a preference for the pocketed limestone of Buoux, he was game for the project as a whole. With a sigh he settled in at the first belay for what he expected to be a protracted battle with the *Snipers* roof, only to find (somewhat to his surprise) that Chicken Man, as he liked to call me, had cracked it first go! Left hand next to upper peg, poor low undercut for the right, Gay Gordons-style volte-face, moving butt cheeks through 180 degrees followed by a desperate slap for the top with the left hand. The ensuing mantel was straightforward enough.

After regaining some composure, a runner was fixed a short way up *Snipers* before teetering rightwards into a seam that led easily up to where *Run of the Arrow* comes in from the right. Those insecure moves above with poor RP protection will never feel easy, but soon the gentle romp up to Whillance's crux was at hand. Back then – but no longer – there were two very poor and rusty hammered nuts to protect the move up to place gear for the crux. Micro-cam out right in a flake, micro-stopper in a tiny short crack and a large nut dovetailed into a shallow placement. This was to be the last gear for some 25 metres to the top.

Straight up there wasn't much, but some tufts of grass protruded from a crack out right. At full stretch I managed to scrub it clean with a wire brush, only for it to spit out any pro that I tried to seat in it. Eventually I committed to move up, gaining a distant edge and trying frantically to mantel onto it. I could feel the tissue in my over-used shoulder starting to tear, and quite convinced I was in mortal danger I just kept pulling until I found myself standing upright on a foothold.

A featureless sea of blank granite stretched on above me. To go on looked impossible. Should I down-climb and jump off? I was far from sure, however, that the distant protection would hold. My belayer was incommunicado below. Malcolm Smith was nearby on *Thor* (the world's strongest climber – on a slab?). Was he near enough to execute a rescue?

Never before had I felt so keenly that I had taken my climbing to a genuine point of no return, and if I said that there was pleasure in the sensation I would surely be lying. On a mad impulse I launched rightwards on mere friction for some eight long metres, thankfully reaching a juicy cam placement in *Cupid's Bow*. Now with head full of steam, charging up this my ropes came to an end, so I pulled up half of one rope, extended the other, and continued to the top.

That night I lay sleeplessly in the howff below the crag. I started to doubt I had really given my all, and that my indirect route was incomplete. Surely with abseil inspection the 'true' direct line would go?

So the next day Al and I whizzed back up *Snipers*, and he lowered to a belay in *Thor* while I checked out the headwall from the safety of a rope. It was less steep and more textured than other parts of the slabs, so clearly it was climbable. After lowering down and pulling the rope I re-climbed the crux and set off. Reasonable smears but incredibly committing climbing led up to the infamous *Cupid's* mantel, which felt simple by comparison.

The resulting route, *Aphrodite* (E7), left me with confused emotions. Pleasure to be sure, and a high that would last for several weeks, but at the same time a curious emptiness and the sense that I would never take it that close to the limit ever again.

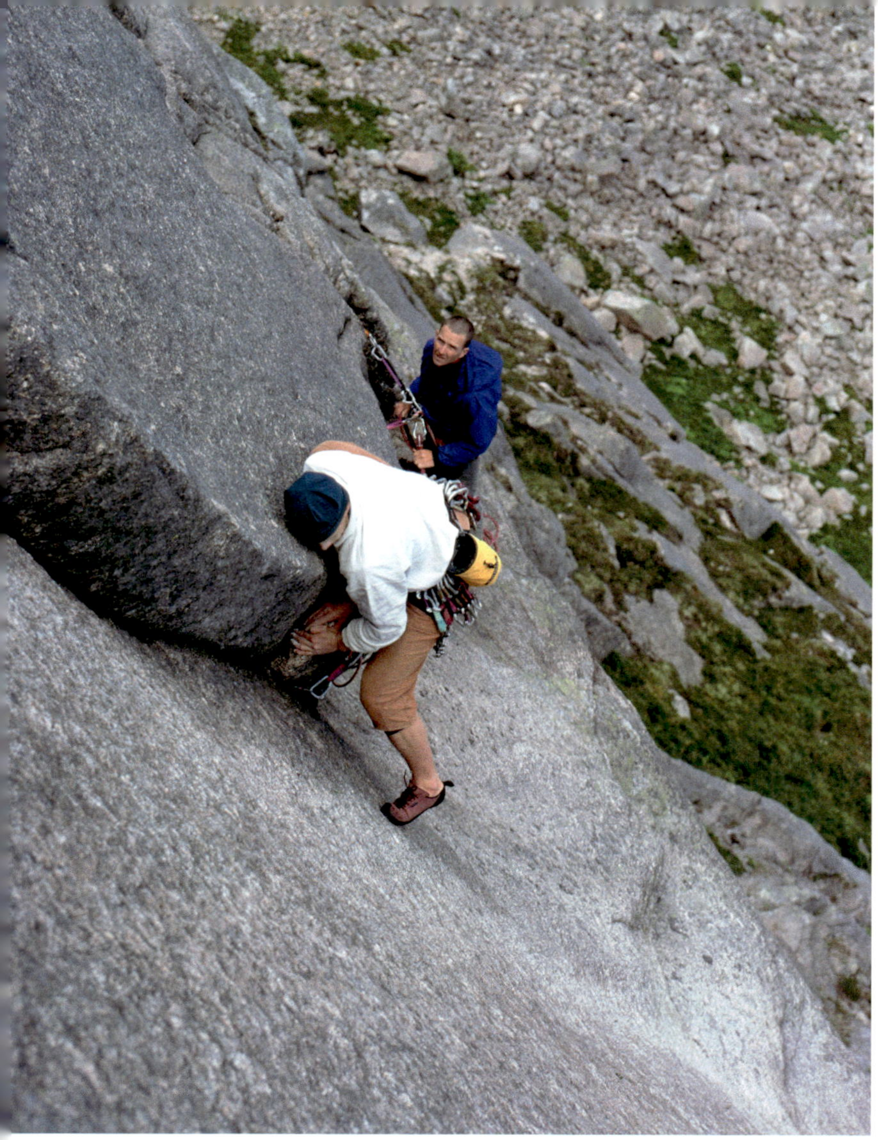
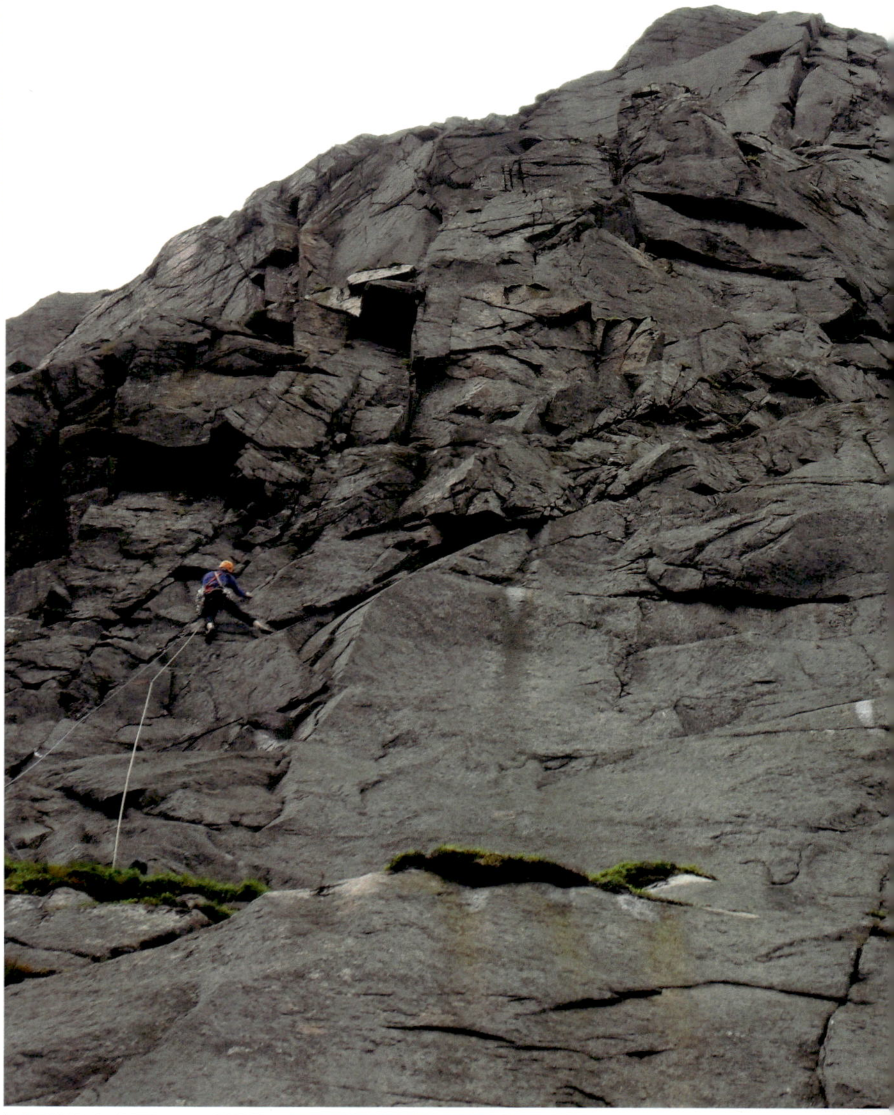
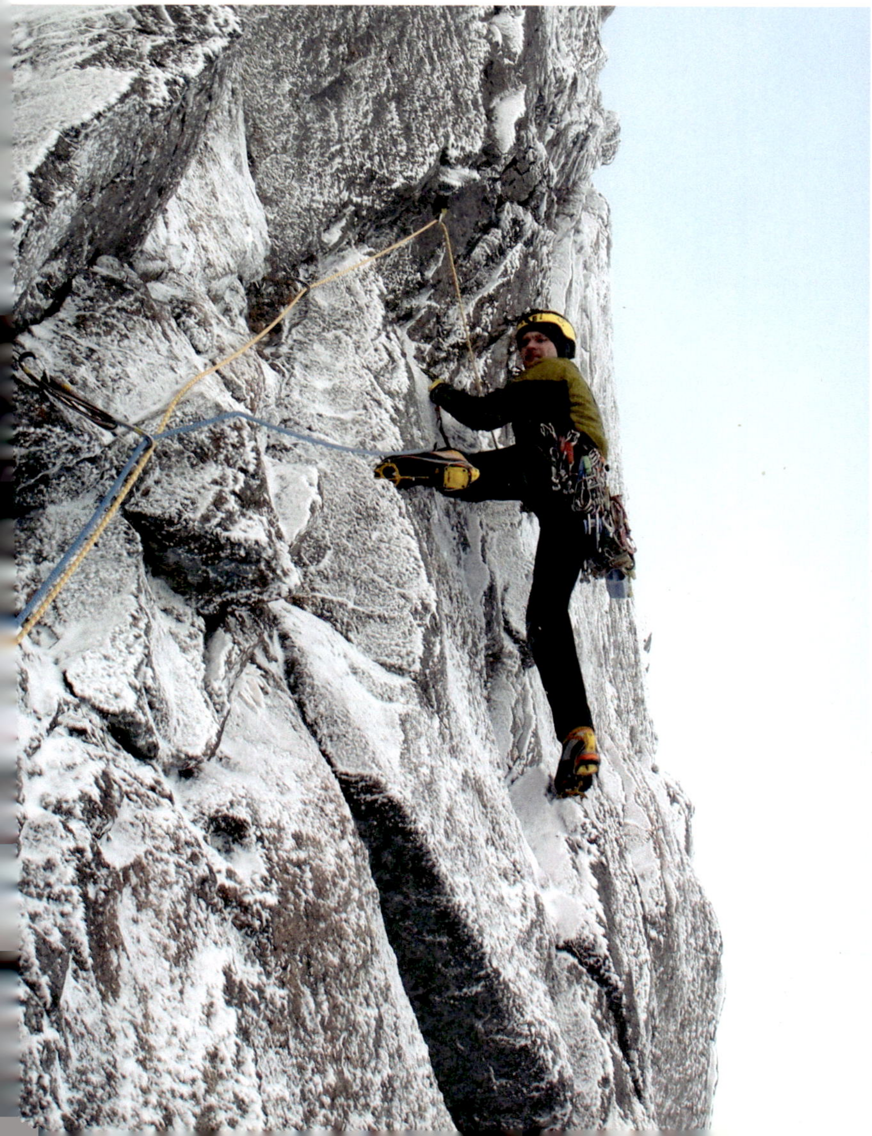
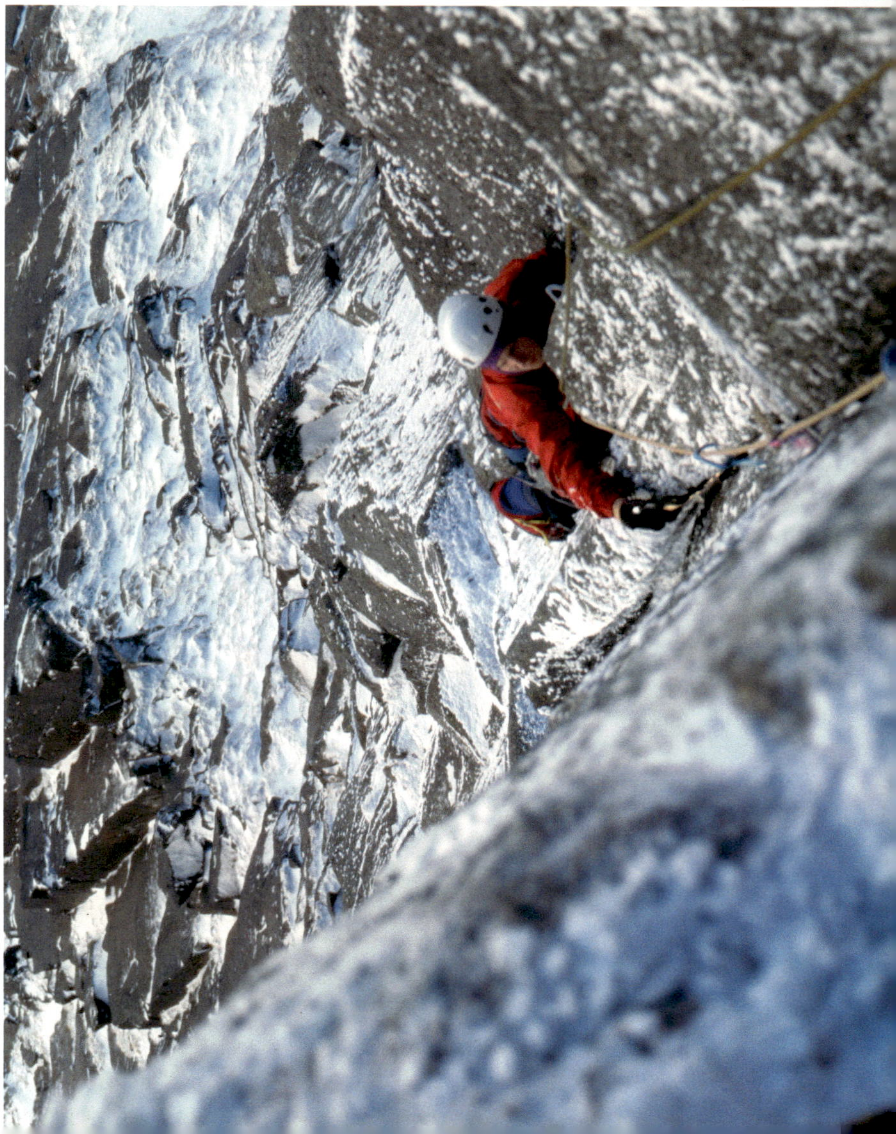

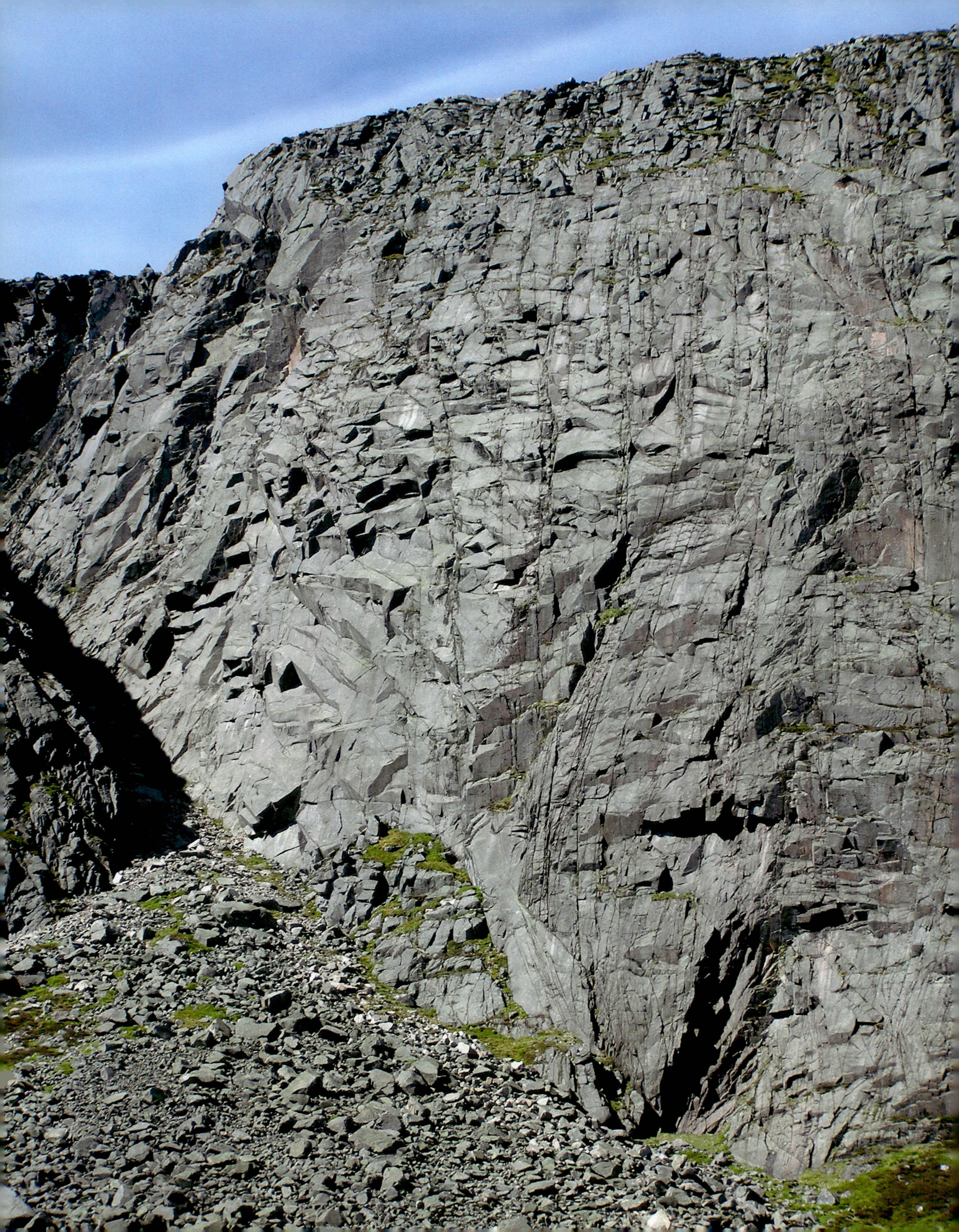

Central Gully Wall, Creag an Dubh Loch — *by Julian Lines*

THE PLACE

Aside from the 'Royal Mountain' of Lochnagar, the remaining heather-carpeted hills of Deeside roll on passively to the horizons – deer stalking country. That is the view travelling west from the southern end of Loch Muick, when suddenly, up ahead, and quite out of character, appears a massive granite cliff, over a kilometre in length, ploughing destruction into the glen below. Towering a thousand feet above the eponymous loch, Creag an Dubh Loch is Scotland's mountain-climbing Mecca, coyly concealed and shrouded behind the spray of a distant waterfall.

If one travelled to the Dubh Loch to climb at will, undoubtedly the Central Gully Wall (CGW) would be your chosen objective. The eyes linger there longer, discerning possibilities, trying to decipher a means of passage amongst its devious features – a series of impenetrable overlaps and alluring slabs, like ancient, colossal roof tiles. They're neatly cleaved and clean too, laced with lime-coloured lichens welded to smouldering, grey granite. As one approaches the cliff, its vastness oppresses like an awakening stone giant. The smell of cordite reinforces the awareness that the physical force of gravity and geological carnage are not that far away.

THE CLIFF

Every time, without exception, I just stare in awe at this face. For those who have climbed or aspire to climb its walls, it is the most precious 'extreme' real estate that Scotland possesses. Under winter's garb too, this most improbable of walls harbours a few secrets that rank among the very finest in the country.

The open, sweeping frontal face is characterised by a series of long crack-lines that are convex in nature – steepest at the bottom before merging into easy ground higher up. However, as the wall curves round into the gully, it begins to show its true mettle; a complex armour of monstrous slabs, walls and overlaps, seemingly offering little chance of progress. But take a closer look, stretch your imagination, and you'll begin to pick out the occasional tiny, connecting groove, ledge or feature, not much for sure, but possibly just enough. The few continuous lines there stand clear and proud – the great, soaring, vertical corner of *The Giant* quite central, and the huge, overhung scoop of *Vertigo Wall* further up. Central Gully Wall is a place that is simultaneously perfect in its simple, geometric grandeur, and full of intricate, and almost infinite, possibilities.

THE CLIMBING

There's a real art to climbing on the Dubh Loch – indeed the climbing is unique, and subtleties of improvisation in body tension and balance are required to tackle these formidable overlaps, blank grooves and smooth arêtes. Holds are sparse, but uncannily there are always just enough to get by. Honed, strong men with rubber tendons and pliers for fingers aren't going to find these climbs easy – there is frankly no substitute for experience here.

In winter the cliff feels more subdued when the gully hardens with neve and the walls are glossed with snow and ice. In most winters, *Vertigo Wall* (VII,7) silently transforms from an ugly duckling into a golden goose, while its more direct offspring, *Vapouriser* (VIII,8), and the nearby icicle-factory of *Goliath* (VII,7) are two of the most ephemeral, atmospheric, and sought after icy mixed climbs anywhere in Scotland. Undoubtedly these compelling winter routes will be complemented by even sterner offerings in years to come.

The early pioneers, who arrived here later than on most premier cliffs, were typically drawn to the vilest looking routes; they clearly knew their limitations. It wasn't until 1977 that the central section of cliff was first breached by *Cougar* (E3), tracing a weakness across the cleanly cut cubes above the entrance to the gully. This opened the floodgates for a torrent of hard and bold extremes pioneered through the eighties and nineties: *Ascent of Man* (E5), *Naked Ape* (E5), *Perilous Journey* (E6) and *Web of Weird* (E6) – the route names tell all. Despite periods of relative obscurity since those halcyon times, new challenges have continued to be scoped out by the next generation of devotees. Perhaps the most legendary of these was the bald, bold arête of *The Origin of Species* (E6) by Paul Thorburn and Gary Latter. Snapping off a flake when leading the main pitch, Thorburn took flight, but the flake knocked the belaying Latter unconscious. With the rope hanging limp, Thorburn fell 70 feet into the gully bed below, before dusting himself down and soloing back up to rescue his belayer! The pair returned to claim their prize within the week.

◀ Morning light on Central Gully Wall.
Photo: *Guy Robertson*.

THE ROUTES

Vertigo Wall (VII,7)
Possibly the most sought-after mixed winter route in the country, taking a devious line to crack the huge, overhung scoop high up on the left side of the crag.

Voyage of the Beagle (E4)
A real voyage that sniffs out another devious passage, weaving right to left through inset hanging slabs above the gully mouth to finish high above the central reaches of the gully – a challenging mix of bold, technical and mentally absorbing pitches.

The Origin of Species (E6)
This direct line through the *Naked Ape* is truly outstanding. The blunt arête cuts chillingly through the air that in turn tests both skill and bravery harmoniously. The atmosphere here matches the massive proportion of this section of cliff. The climbing is as good as mountain granite gets.

THE STORY

Spring 1990: it was 80 degrees Fahrenheit. The surface of Loch Muick held no secrets because there was no wind, no ripples, just the sound of four wheels turning. Wilson Moir was ahead – just a rucksack with a pair of legs, his tyres kicking up soft plumes of dust. The track soon ended and we stowed the bikes and set off on foot.

Waterfalls echoed, granite baked, the air shimmered, and behind it reared the Dubh Loch – startling, almost fantastical – with, as always, a band of snow lingering above Broad Terrace Wall, like an albino's eyebrow.

Wow. It fires the desire and makes your legs work harder every time.

We pitched the tent on the shore of the loch. The sun encouraged and I kept staring upwards, mesmerised by this huge, overwhelming cliff. Central Gully Wall immediately caught my eye: pristine, offset slabs, alluring – like huge, inclined mirrors waiting to reflect our destiny.

'Which route do you want to climb?' Wilson asked.

'All of them!' I replied.

I was young and naïve, but full of energy and aspiration. Wilson looked at me incredulously and said nothing – he was wise, experienced, and rather quiet too. Somehow I felt kind of invincible having a partner who had made the third ascent of the *Naked Ape* the previous year – anything seemed possible. We chose *Voyage of the Beagle*, which I conjectured we could climb as a precursor to *Perilous Journey*.

We clattered up the gully, humbled by the mute power of the tilting walls, the boulders and the heat; it was idyllic – we had the cliff to ourselves. Wilson tied in and made haste, ropes snaking out quickly. A well-formed granite groove was my first touch of the Dubh Loch's texture – a strange medium – weird movement, but somehow simple too. We swapped leads, the groove continued, hot to touch. It soon blanked and diverted me left to a thin seam – devious. I was nervous, lost and totally out of my depth. I placed an RP2 blind – a first; they're tiny, but look good on a rack, professional-like. I dared not retreat; instead I tore at the seam, keen, brave – all fingers and toes – out of balance and way short on technique. Whoosh ... 30 feet ... I bounced on the elasticity, staring Wilson in the face, the RP dangling uselessly from the rope.

▸
Neil McGeachy on *Cannibal* (E6).
Photo: *Neal McGeachy Collection.*

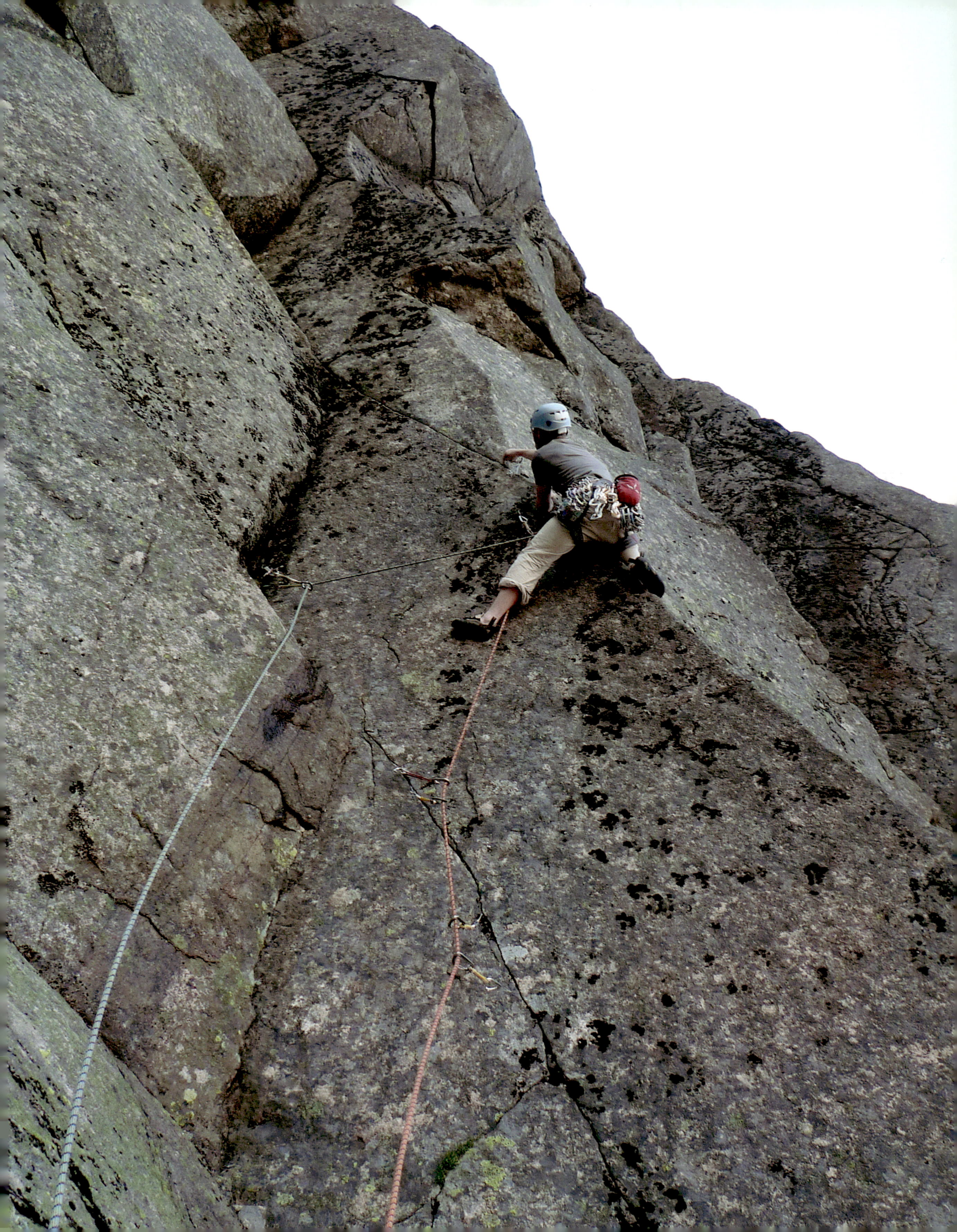

Wilson took over the sharp end and I watched, hoping to learn something of the technique required. I followed, battling to keep in harmony with the rock's tune, thinking to myself that these mountain routes aren't easy at all.

Above the seam a huge inclined slab teased leftwards, hemmed in by giant overlaps. It was a haven: easy, lovely architecture and colourful, a chance to reflect on the past and the future here, as *Cannibal* fires up from beneath and bisects ...

Fast-forward two years. It was a moody morning beneath the *Cannibal*. The cold wind had found us, as it often does here, chilling us to the bone. The sharp end was mine, the first pitch was steep and honest – unusual hereabouts, but it bullied my forearms into a flash pump. Not wanting to fall, I flopped panting onto the belay, all wrists and knees. The pitch above looked gorgeous – a thin runnel to an overlap, then a dearth of anything – vanishing, Dubh Loch style. A huge span rightwards and power is required to reach the next belay. Above, an acute, left-leaning corner cleaves its way to beneath the *Cougar* slab. I surrendered the lead to Wilson; he accepted with that familiar fire in his eye. He climbed smoothly to a wee overlap, and then fell. Thoughts of failure swirled in my head, but I just held the ropes obediently and attentively. Finally he mastered the sequence of moves required – a case of 'doing the unobvious'. Then, above him was The Mantelshelf – scary, but he committed and disappeared in an instant onto the *Cougar* slab.

The easy-angled *Cougar* slab is a gently inclined patio with a beautiful view – a place to de-stress from the rigours of hard climbing, affording brief but essential respite before attempting the so-called 'hospital moves' above.

Wilson spread-eagled into the corner and spun a strange web, the Dubh Loch granite, as always, controlling the game. Then it was my turn. The corner seduces: rough textures, palms and pads, then turns blank, the right rib winks with chalk, mantel out, recuperate, and then fall back into symmetric bridging. Absorbing, minimalistic and brilliant.

Wilson was in high spirits but drained, and glad of someone to talk to after his bold lead. I lamely offered to lead the final pitch, but he continued his heroic effort.

Voyage of the Beagle, unlike *Cannibal*, didn't go up; instead it sidled leftwards onto a lower slab, dripping with exposure as it tilted above the gully. It felt cute at first, but as the slab narrowed it became quite harrowing. The following pitch continued in the same exposed vein; partway along this section is where *Origin of the Species* joins from beneath. I secured the second ascent with Tim Rankin over a decade later with a lot more experience and technique in my armoury. A hanging nose was then reached with indescribable atmosphere and exposure. I tussled with it and then onto a delicate wall, eyes popping, thoroughly grateful for Wilson's rope above my head. A final overhanging crack was the last verse. Fitting.

We abseiled on our 50-metre ropes into the void, the trail of the *Naked Ape* beneath my feet, its Gothic slab hanging there like a stone picture framed by precipices. While descending the gully, the boulders chuckled underfoot. Wilson stopped to point out the line of *Perilous Journey*: 'Your lead now!' he muttered jokingly. I replied with a hearty laugh. •

Doug and Uisdean Hawthorn (leading) on the first winter ascent of *The Giant* (VII,7).
Photo: *Robin Clothier.*

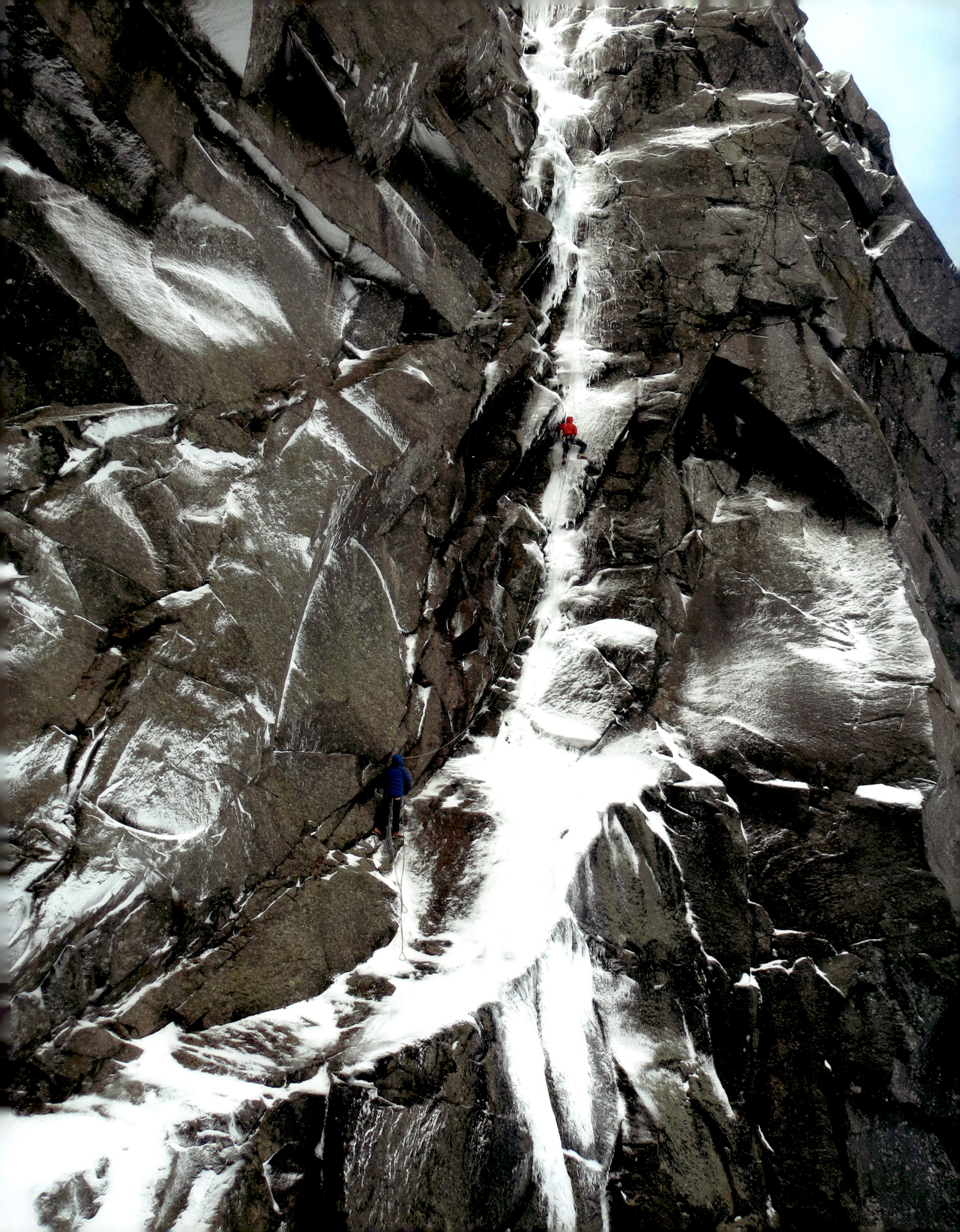

Julian Lines on *The Origin of Species* (E6), Central Gully Wall.
Photo: *Dave Cuthbertson*.

Unknown climber on *Goliath* (HVS), Central Gully Wall.
Photo: *Guy Robertson.*

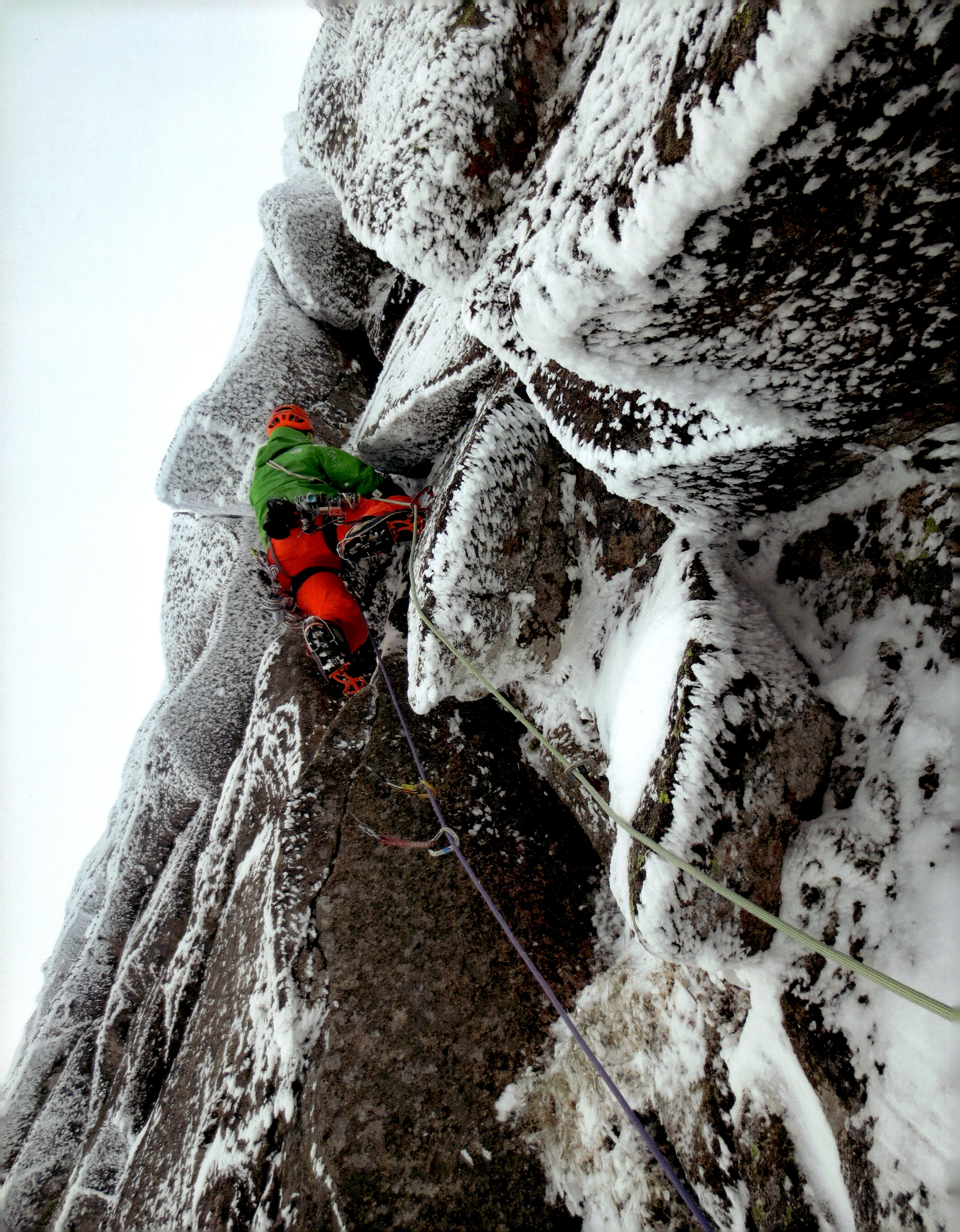

Tough-Brown Face, Lochnagar – *by Brian Davison*

THE PLACE

If Lochnagar is monarch of modern Scottish mixed climbing, the Tough-Brown Face is the jewel in the crown. It would be understandable perhaps to dismiss these 'slabs' as old-school and of little interest to modern climbing, but rise up over the col under Meikle Pap on a midwinter day and notice that the face presents the only visible rock amid a sea of white, and ponder the hours and hours of effort that some of the UK's finest winter climbers have invested in its routes. This is one of those places where any ascent will always be special.

It is only really on making contact with the rock that the steepness, complexity and raw intimidation of the climbing here becomes apparent. The face sits plum centre at the base of one of the most impressive mountain amphitheatres in Scotland, with 800 continuous feet of towering buttress, gully and ridges all around. Aberdonians will tell you that one route on this face in any one winter season is usually enough.

THE CLIFF

For most of the 20th century the face was a forcing ground for winter climbers, particularly Aberdonians, who have pushed further and with ever higher levels of commitment to create climbs of the highest standard. The cliff presents a broad, dome-shaped mass of very steeply inclined slabs and bulges, defined on the left by the vertical fault of *Parallel Gully B* (now a corner following major rock fall in the nineties) and the narrow edge of *Tough-Brown Ridge* overlooking *Raeburn's Gully* to the right.

The face itself has a number of striking crack-lines – first the big corner of *Dirge* (E2), then *Mort* (E2) and *Crazy Sorrow* (E4), from left to right. 30 metres up is a band of overhangs which extends across most of the face, and around a pitch above this the routes merge, becoming intricate and more complex. While in summer this lack of continuous features doesn't pose any undue complications – the lower overhangs constitute the crux of most routes – in winter it prolongs the difficulties substantially. The face proper ends about halfway up the full extent of the cliff, and many people descend by traversing right to an abseil station leading into *Raeburn's Gully*.

THE CLIMBING

This face is always going to offer more to the winter climber than those in search of top quality rock. Although there is some reasonable summer climbing, it is dirty and of relatively poor quality. In winter, however, the cliff offers some of the most testing and 'cerebrally engaging' winter climbing in Scotland. Made up of a series of steep slabs and overlaps, the routes cleave through the very few weaknesses offered in the lower roofs to wind their way tenuously up the steep walls above. Common features are bold traverses and short blind grooves linking incipient cracks to reach the sanctuary of turf-covered ledges. Ice forms, but only occasionally, and in small, dribbling rather than flowing quantities – but every bit will help a lot.

In summer the walls offer steep, delicate moves on spaced protection with spectacular swings through the steep ground. Thankfully, the overlaps often provide deep cracks, unlike the walls in between. So once you've pushed your way through the steep ground, be prepared to search for any hard-won protection in whatever shallow blind crack you can find, bearing in mind in winter these may be iced up, or hidden by snow and rime. Any lead on the face in winter provides a considerable challenge to both mind and body; over-balance or extend too far and those tenuous placements will rip – leading to some considerable air time.

Early developments in the sixties and seventies by Aberdeen climbers took place in summer – it took until the 'Golden Age' of mixed climbing in the eighties before anyone with crampons and axes took on the challenge. The resulting routes, including *Trail of Tears* (VIII,8) and *Diedre of the Sorrows* (VIII,8), all required several attempts before success, and compared to other routes of a similar standard elsewhere, are still only very rarely climbed today. Ironically, it was *Mort*, one of the first summer routes established on the face, which was to be one of the last to receive its winter ascent, and one of Scotland's first grade IX climbs. At the time of writing, *Mort* has only had one repeat ascent.

◀ Pete Benson on an early winter attempt on *Nevermore* (IX,10).
Photo: *Guy Robertson*.

THE ROUTES

Tough-Brown Ridge Direct (VS, V,6)
The right-bounding edge of the face. Although not strictly a 'Tough-Brown tick' the ridge provides superb climbing and a fantastic feel for the face brooding to its left. This is undoubtedly one of the most satisfying ways to climb Lochnagar.

Mort (E2, IX,9)
The central crack-line, running through a large roof at around half height, provides the technical crux in summer and winter. Strenuous climbing through the roof leads to a small ledge. In summer, delicate wall climbing up the right side of a rib leads to a good resting place atop the rib on the left. In winter the route climbs thin ice on the left side of the rib to the ledge, a small haven on top of the rib. An exposed and delicate piece of climbing after the strenuous technical crux of the roof below.

Trail of Tears (VIII,8)
A stunning and cunning route that is probably the most climbed line on the face in winter. It starts up the big corner of *Dirge* on the bottom left, then trends away right before an intricate descent and traverse allow upward progress to be regained. A bit of ice will help a lot, but will never make the climbing easy and will make the first pitch very bold.

Approaching the Tough-Brown Face in winter.
Photo: *Adrian Crofton*.

THE CAIRNGORMS & CENTRAL HIGHLANDS | **TOUGH-BROWN FACE, LOCHNAGAR**

▲ Pete Macpherson attempting an as yet unfinished first winter ascent on the Tough-Brown Face. Photo: *Guy Robertson*.

THE STORY

It was early one morning in January 1985. Andy Nisbet, Colin Maclean and I were heading to Lochnagar's increasingly notorious Tough-Brown Face for an attempt on the striking summer line of *Mort* (E2). Colin's phenomenal strength was our not-so-secret weapon. I had watched in awe earlier that morning as he completed a series of one-arm pull-ups hanging from an ice axe wearing all his winter climbing regalia and a rucksack containing a full winter rack. Anticipation ran high – only recently Graeme Livingston and Doug Hawthorn had succeeded in making the first successful winter ascent of an existing summer Extreme. The weather report from Dyce Airport was good, the only concern being that another party had already asked for a weather report for Lochnagar! New routing was a highly competitive business in Aberdeen during the eighties.

We'd done the first pitch the previous week to a large block on a turfy ledge, so Andy made short work of this. Time to unleash Colin. I, meanwhile, took pictures and climbed routes nearby in an attempt to keep myself warm. Colin's progress up to the roof went smoothly but even his strength waned here. He battled desperately to surmount it, and eventually, with his axes in an icy flared crack just over the lip, he clipped into his leashes. With hindsight it was probably a blessing that he conserved his strength for the horrors that lay above.

About a metre above the roof a rib ascends for several metres to a small flat ledge. In summer the route teeters up the wall to the right to reach this ledge. On this occasion, however, ice had formed to the left. With little else on offer Colin moved very slowly up this. Leaving the last protection near the lip of the roof he made extremely careful progress to attain a precarious kneeling position on top of the rib. After an hour of fruitless clearing he shouted down a request for a blade peg to Andy, who was patiently freezing on the belay below.

290   THE GREAT MOUNTAIN CRAGS OF SCOTLAND

▲ Tim Rankin on *Diedre of the Sorrows* (VIII,8). Photo: *Guy Robertson*.

'It's in the belay!'

'It doesn't matter, send it up!'

Andy passed up the only blade peg, and with it the comfort of at least some protection.

As the two of them started up the final pitch, Colin leading again, I jumared up icy ropes only to reach the ledge just as he came down. With failing light and strength his efforts had ground to a halt. I was very reluctant to give up the hard-earned ground that Colin had gained and even volunteered to go down to fetch bivouac gear, but with energy and spirits low I conceded to retreat. Colin and Andy went on to a have a brilliant winter that year, with seminal ascents of *The Needle* and *Unicorn* in Glen Coe. *Mort*, it seemed, would have to wait.

Andy moved to Aviemore, and Colin drifted away from climbing, but the challenge of *Mort* remained. After several years I mentioned to Andy I was still thinking about the route. Eventually the perfect weather forecast came, so I bought a car and drove to Lochnagar. On reaching the cliff we were met by the rescue team lowering the body of a friend. *Mort* had already struck. The swirl of snow driven by helicopter blades soon left us alone in the coire. As before, Andy belayed by the large flake and soon I was placing runners under the roof. Lacking Colin's one-arm pull-up power, I managed to back and foot my way strenuously up over the lip to find a tiny foot ledge just above. No sooner had I attempted to stand up on this than I was suddenly dangling literally only inches above Andy's head, back at the belay 50 feet below. A second attempt got me on to the little ledge, but this time I stopped there.

Looking left I could see there was no ice left of the rib, so I tried straight up. My teetering progress was stopped tantalisingly close to the ledge at the rib's top; if only I'd had a long alpenstock I'm sure I could have hooked it! I down-climbed and tried to the left of the rib but couldn't get high enough to gain the thin ribbon of shallow turf above. After hours of searching I reluctantly admitted defeat, retreating from a poor nut at the base of the rib. I'd succeeded to climb the roof, but without the prospect of more protection above I didn't have the mental stamina needed to continue.

Another five years elapsed before *Mort* came back to mind, but it was a further year before I was able to arrange a visit to the cliff to coincide with good conditions. It was January 2000. Younger climbers had since tried the route, but it remained unclimbed. I was soon starting up again toward the roof, rehearsing the sequence once again in my mind – reach the roof, back and foot, over the roof, foot ledge, round left of the rib, and up to the ledge on top. Above the roof I scratch around for gear but not for long – I can't let doubt creep in. Once again the ice hadn't formed left of the rib so again I climbed up its right side. Halfway up I make a precarious high step left, leaning across the rib, to find shallow ice that takes the slightest of axe placements. The other axe follows, gentle placements now, the ice is very temporary. Soon I'm staring longingly at the ledge on top of the rib. First a knee, then a foot, and slowly I stand up. I can't find Colin's peg. Poor runners, relax, chip holds gently in the thin ice covering the rock wall above. A few more hard moves and the belay is reached.

Dave and Andy soon join me. There's still plenty of daylight for Andy to climb the top pitch. Despite a lack of ice he soon reaches a hex from a failed attempt a few weeks earlier, but no sign of the peg placed by Colin 15 years before. Andy grinds to a halt at a bulge above – the summer crux, protected by an in-situ peg. A prolonged search however fails to reveal the peg, and any reliable protection is seemingly impossible to find under the thick winter snow. A poor peg is placed before Andy attacks the bulge, but it quickly spits him out. Then he's back up to his high point, but this time when he comes off, the peg rips and he falls further still.

Suddenly it's my turn. I'm much less confident about the outcome than I had been an hour earlier. I reach the bulge and look for the peg placement but can't find it – I've moved up too high. So I stretch up for a bottomless placement but my axe rips, I'm too low to use it. A move up and I can just torque an axe blade in the placement and pull further to reach some turf. Here a crack offers placements for a Friend and axes but as I move up it becomes wider. Suddenly everything happens at once. I look down as the Friend pops out and slides down past the shitty peg and onto the hex five metres below that, then my top axe pops from its hole leaving me arcing backwards as the axe by my chest slides tooth by tooth out of its placement. I pull in and down on the lower axe to stop its exit, and punch a fist desperately at the offwidth in front of me. It works. I'm still in place. I swap my fist for a wobbly nut and move up. Ice re-appears to my right and I move up onto this, arms tiring rapidly. Steep snow now, but where's the belay? An hour of searching and daylight is replaced by moonlight before I finally slump onto a useable flake.

Walking out of the deserted coire, we're each wrapped in our own thoughts of the last few hours, the last 15 years. There's no doubt winter is a waiting game. But the waiting, for now, is over. *Mort* is complete.

Top: Guy Robertson on the first winter ascent of *Crazy Sorrow* (IX,10). Photo: *Pete Benson*. **Bottom**: The Tough-Brown Face in full winter conditions. Photo: *Andy Nisbet*.

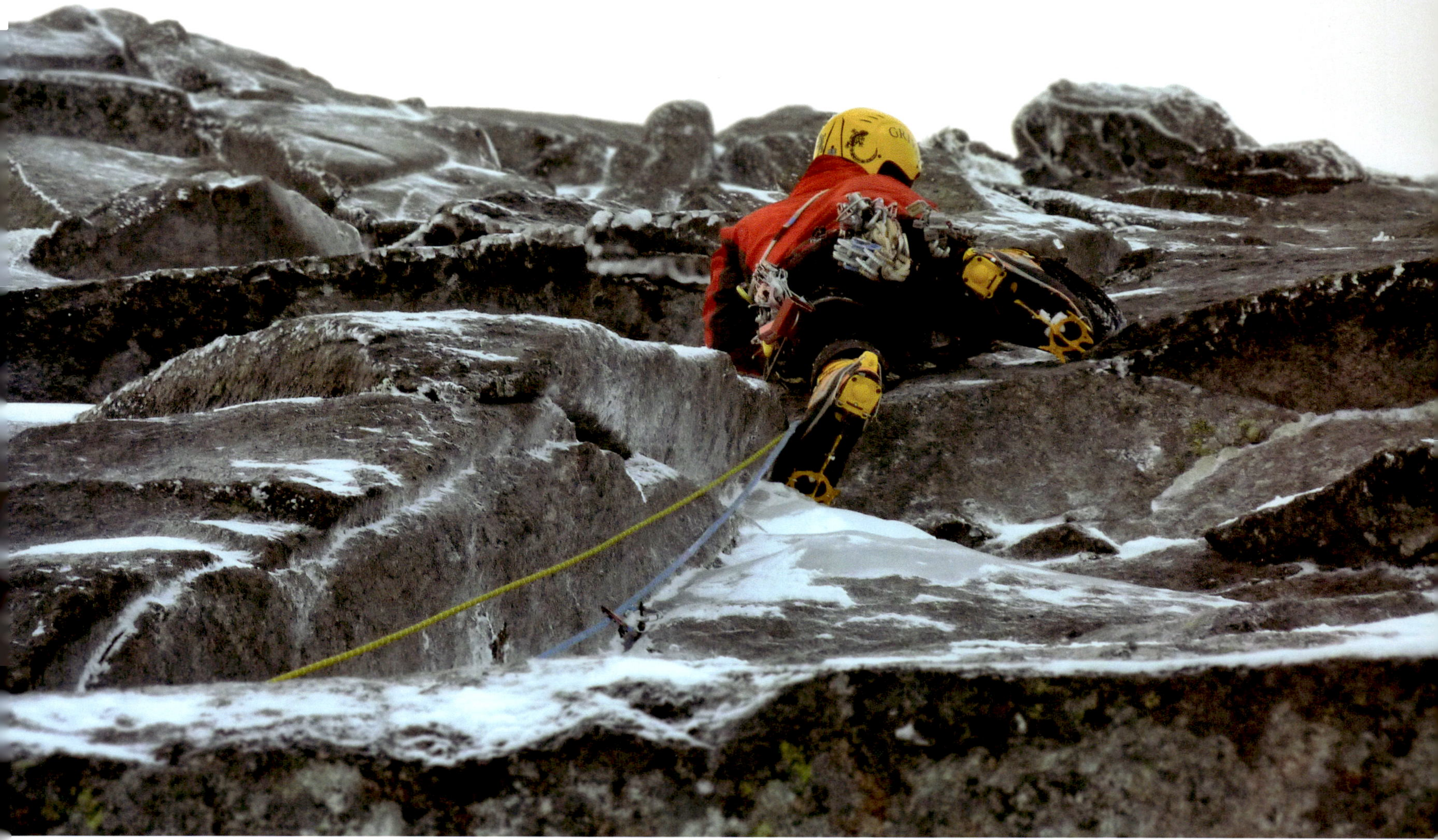

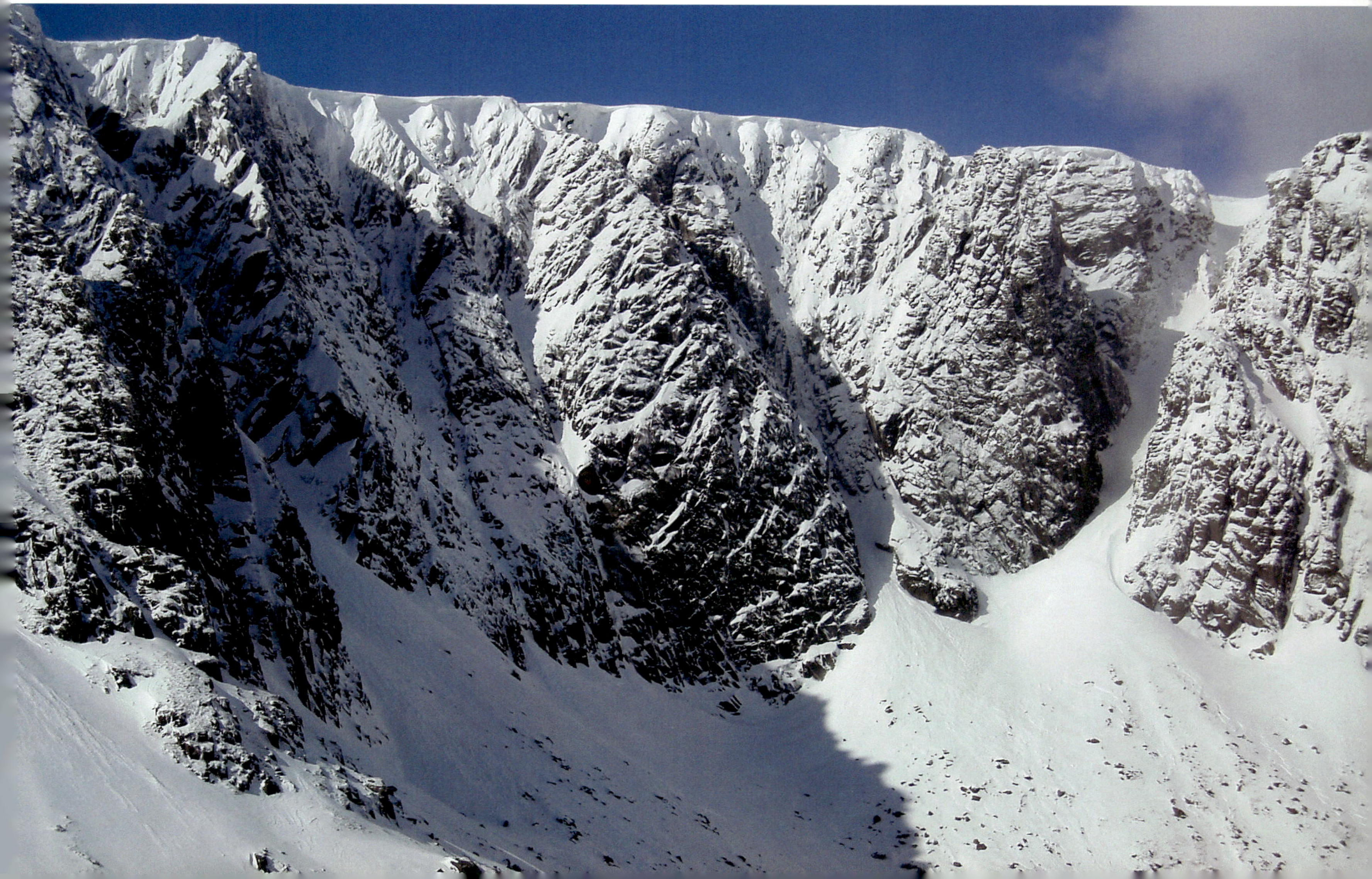

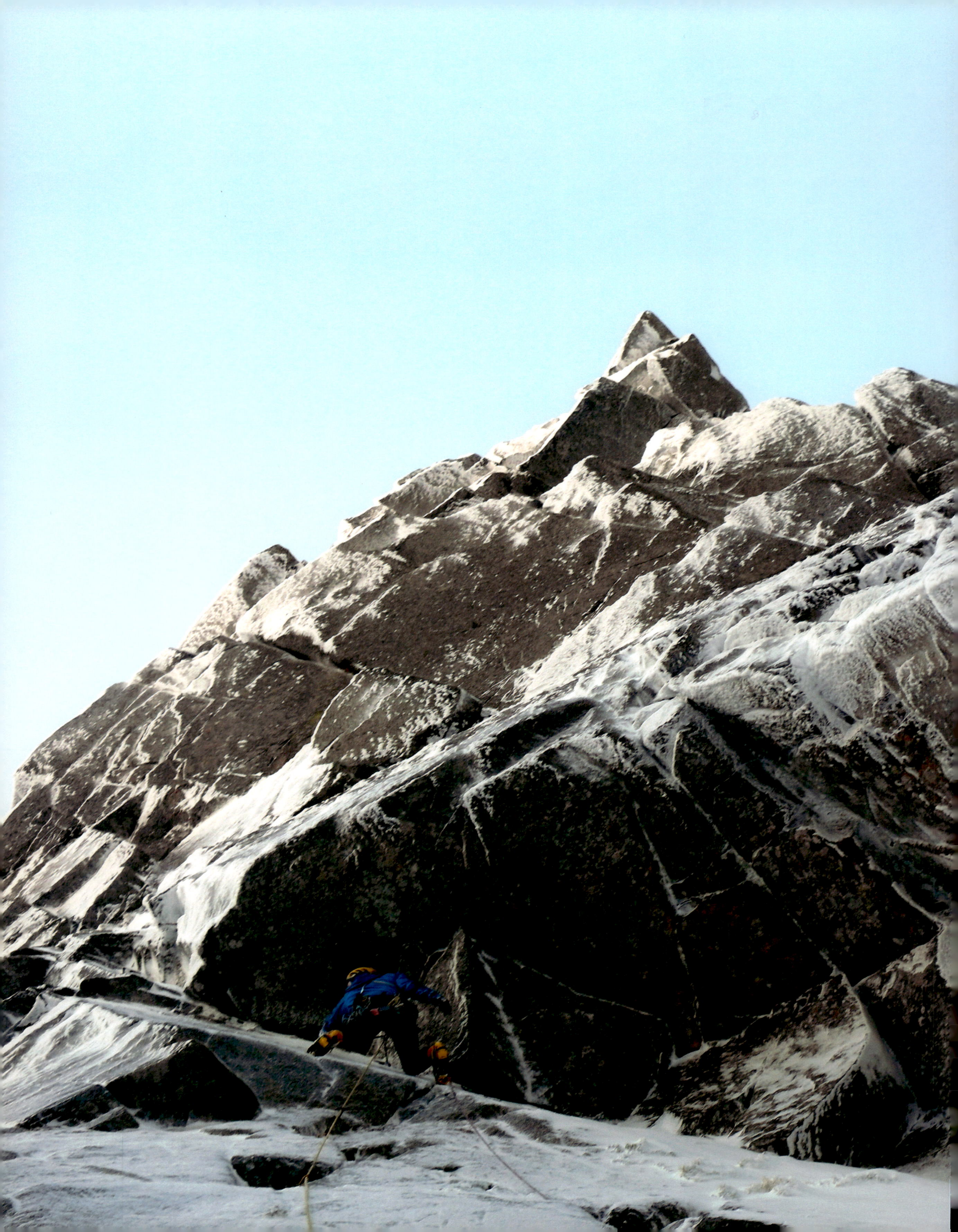

Black Spout Pinnacle, Lochnagar –
by Guy Robertson & Nick Bullock

THE PLACE

Tucked away in the far right-hand corner of Lochnagar's north-east coire, on first impression you may hardly even know the Black Spout Pinnacle is there, its sharp summit neatly camouflaged by the higher rim of the coire behind. But on entering the mouth of the eponymous gully one is immediately impressed by the brooding overhangs dominating the skyline to the left – the formidable Black Spout Wall.

Further up, as the great left wall diminishes in height, it becomes apparent that the whole mass is in fact a separate body, defined on both sides by hidden gullies, and joined to the back wall at a lofty col. These micro towers and nano ridges are Scotland's Alps in miniature, and form the classic end to many a Cairngorm day – Patey's 'Aiguilles des Cairngorms'. After a route on the pinnacle they provide the perfect context to reflect on a great climb, perched airily among some of the finest rock architecture in the Cairngorms.

THE CLIFF

Black Spout Pinnacle describes the large tapering mass of rock that forms the left flank of Black Spout Gully. It only really becomes a pinnacle towards the top where Pinnacle Gullies 1 and 2 curve from the left and right respectively to form a narrow neck ten metres below its summit. The gully itself is deep and impressive, but generally easy in all conditions, providing the best opportunity for anyone new to the place to really get inside the heart of this wonderful mountain.

Towards the lower left aspect of the pinnacle a number of earlier routes climb short steep pitches up to a large platform – The Springboard – from where the angle progressively eases on the upper frontal face. Moving right into the gully, however, the atmosphere is transformed; a sharp crest is turned from whence a long and slender trunk of clean and relatively unbroken granite soars skywards for over 150 metres. The crest itself sports a complex array of shallow corners and steep grooves, while the left side of the great gully wall is split by a scintillating crack-line, the key to the route *Black Spout Wall*. Step right below this crack-line and one is dwarfed by a truly monstrous recess capped by great overhangs of several metres depth. The upper part of the gully wall tapers to a fine crescendo in the form of a well defined, smooth triangular sheet of weathered rock, broken only occasionally by rounded 'offwidth' cracks. It's a complex crag with an array of possibilities – certainly big enough for some secrets to remain.

THE CLIMBING

There's something for everyone on Black Spout Pinnacle. For the traditionalist there is abundant vegetation, and a healthy dose of guile and cunning will outflank the most oppressive sections of rock. For the modern rock climber however there is more than first meets the eye, and this is undoubtedly where to head if higher E-numbers are what you're after. Although route choices are limited, the *Black Spout Wall* is a must for any Cairngorm rock-climbing connoisseur.

For winter climbers the pinnacle is a jewel, although it has to be said there are no easy routes. Yet if you can deal with a couple of hard pitches low down you'll enjoy easier romping higher up on the frontal face. If you are made of sterner stuff, the steep section from the crest rightwards into the gully has some of the finest winter routes on offer anywhere in Scotland.

On the whole, the climbing here is well protected; certainly much more reliably so than on the neighbouring Tough-Brown Face. If there's a crack it will generally be good. Like most of the climbing on Lochnagar, vegetation is in abundance, though there are a couple of glorious exceptions, not least of which is the stunning *Black Spout Wall* (E3) inside the mouth of the gully. The well-defined edge formed where the slabby frontal face turns right into the gully is the line of *The Link Direct* (VS, VII,7) and provides a superb, sustained and very exposed route in either season. The various routes on the frontal face left of this tend to pick out tenuous lines through a complex tapestry of shallow grooves and ribs. The routes to the right, immediately below and then inside the gully, are much more direct and uncompromising with a concomitant increase in the general level of difficulty.

◁ Guy Robertson on the first winter ascent of *Black Spout Wall* (IX,9).
Photo: *Nick Bullock*.

THE GREAT MOUNTAIN CRAGS OF SCOTLAND

Like most of the great Cairngorm walls, development proper began in the fifties, the earlier climbers having more than their hands full on the many surrounding gullies and ridges. Aberdeen climbers were to the fore, and back then the cliff was an important forcing ground for technical standards on summer rock – the first ascent of *Pinnacle Face* (VS) in 1955 was a good example of this. In winter too the cliff played an important part in the development of cutting edge routes, and Andy Nisbet and John Anderson's ascent of *The Link* gave us one of the first grade VII routes in the country. Dougie Dinwoodie and Bob Smith cracked a truly first class nut with their ascent of *Black Spout Wall* (E3) in 1976, and Wilson Moir introduced high standard rock climbing to the steep lower walls in the nineties, with *The Existentialist* (E6) and *Steep Frowning Glories* (E6). The 2012 winter ascent of *Black Spout Wall* (IX,9), linking pitches from various summer Extremes, clearly demonstrated that the future of climbing here is very bright.

THE ROUTES

Route II (Severe, VI,6)
Starts high up inside the gully and swaggers out left onto the upper frontal face. Although the difficulties are concentrated, the climbing is very sustained and the exposure dramatic, ensuring that any ascent will linger long in the memory.

The Link Direct (VS, VII,7)
A tremendous, long and quite complex journey up the crest formed where the frontal face bends right into the steep left wall of the gully. The winter ascent is among the finest routes of its grade anywhere.

Black Spout Wall (E3, IX,9)
An outstanding adventure and one of the best mid-Extremes in the country, based on the searing crack-line up the slender pillar forming the lower left side of the gully wall. The winter ascent is a composite utilising the start of *Steep Frowning Glories* to the right and finishes up the aptly-named *Inhospitable Crack*. Cairngorm climbing at its finest.

◀ The Black Spout Pinnacle of Lochnagar, with the Tough-Brown Face in the shade to the left.
Photo: *Adrian Crofton*.

▲ Black Spout Pinnacle from high up in the Black Spout.
Photo: *Adrian Crofton*.

▲ Two views of Pete Benson on *Black Spout Wall* (E3). Photos: *Adrian Crofton*. ▶

THE STORY — *by Nick & Guy*

The drive from Roy Bridge to Lochnagar is becoming a regular occurrence. A slow, twisting, mesmerising battle with fatigue and hare-avoidance. Arriving at the Glen Muick car park at 7 p.m., I shuffle, re-arrange, plug-in the stove, wrap myself up in my sleeping bag, settle down and wait. At some point the bundle of built-up angry energy called Guy Robertson will arrive.

Waking at 4.15 a.m., breakfasting, coffee x 2, and walking … and walking. The col overlooking the crag is never a disappointment, and now that the weekend is over the weather has once again turned drop dead gorgeous. It is mornings like this that make my frugal, roving existence worth more than any wage slip.

Steep Frowning Glories

Three false starts, the clock ticks but eventually Robertson is cautiously creeping up the technical opening groove of an E6 called **Steep Frowning Glories***. He continues on to beneath a huge roof, which, it seems, is to be passed on the left. 40 metres of rope out behind him and he creeps up, then back down, up again, and then down. The process is repeated until non-existent crampon smears are gradually familiarised. Two hours and more pass as I shiver at the base of the route.*

Faint contours in the granite provide the only source of adhesion for a monopoint out left. After the reassuring grasp of such deep positive cracks below, for a good eight feet of sideways movement the only hold is a wobbling axe placement, reached at a stretch and stuffed horizontally in the underside of the great roof. With this located, both feet come up high on smears at waist height, first the left … hold it, lean back hard on the tool for tension … then swap to the right foot and flag the left. Then a tense, slow, steady swap of hands on the torqued axe, and swap the feet and body weight back left again. It's a strange and marginal repetitive dance. The other axe, held tight in biting jaws,

298   THE GREAT MOUNTAIN CRAGS OF SCOTLAND

is transferred to the left hand to reach away out to the left, probing blindly, desperately round the left end of the roof. But whatever's there is not enough, and I can't see by how much. It sticks, yes, but it has only that slight, tenuous and unreliable grip which I've come to know means a seam, not a crack. The whole process is reversed, repeated, reversed and repeated. One, two, three, four and more times, on each occasion the sticks flaring ever so slightly, and the only crease for a foot threatening to lose its meagre depth.

After what seems an eternity, a switch is flicked. Protection is good, so stop dawdling and commit. The wobbly horizontal, the foot swaps, the probing reach, the marginal seam, and then ... the seam holds, the feet are released left, scuttling higher still to maintain the tension as the footholds disappear. Left arm is locked deep now, first at chest height but then lower still. As the right axe comes out from under the roof and reaches up, higher and higher ... the body elongates up, threatening to dislodge smearing feet. And both feet blow simultaneously — once, then twice — but the miracle seam stays super-glued to the tip of my pick. This time the feet are brought to chest height, and the right axe thrown dynamically up high in the seam. More glue it seems — miraculously, it sticks. In a steam-powered heave, hydraulic triceps lever everything out left onto a grossly sloping rock shelf. Both feet gain the shelf, but the glue suddenly runs out. There are no cracks, no more seam — only rounded, bulging granite. A few feet left along the shelf some belay tat drips with ice. Almost within reach! The feet have to stay or it's all over, and straight up the seam is the only hope, so with right shoulder pressed on frost the lower axe comes out, gingerly, reaches up, drags down gently ... and sticks.

*Now he's perched belaying on the sloping ledge at the top of the first pitch of the E3 **Black Spout Wall**. Somehow — with an equally vivid imagination perhaps — I manage to join him there a while later.*

THE CAIRNGORMS & CENTRAL HIGHLANDS | **BLACK SPOUT PINNACLE, LOCHNAGAR** 299

Black Spout Wall

I start to climb. Guy informs me that once I'm on my way it will be fine, but getting going is the second summer 5c pitch of **Black Spout Wall** *and starting is technical and scary. 'Jesus, these sloping ledges give nothing.' Laybacking from a poor hook I reach … 'Wonders' … a perfect pick slot and I'm away for a further 25 metres, burling on torques, passing roofs with imaginary feet. Superlative.*

Time is passing and Guy joins me in the early red of another sunset on Lochnagar. He frantically passes and climbs the summer line of **The Link** *up to an airy crest beneath the headwall split by several offwidth cracks. Arriving next to him I look hesitantly up – this doesn't look like winter climbing territory. After spending over six hours on the first two pitches, however, the movement is welcomed.*

The Inhospitable Crack

Overtaken now by darkness I pull into a steep offwidth on the left of the wall. My head torch beam fails to illuminate any footholds aside from a rounded, leg-gobbling crack. Having climbed **The Link Direct** *a few days before I can tell this crack leads to just beneath the final overhanging crux of that route, I refuse to be stopped now. Stuffing my right leg into the offwidth, the left scrabbles and flags. Shoulders burn, up is the only way; failure is not allowed. Then suddenly I recognise my surroundings – I'm halfway up the final crux pitch of* **The Link Direct**. *I consider belaying knowing how steep the final section waiting above me is, but I know Guy will crucify me and call me a southern pansy.*

'It will go to the left,' I shout, but I can hear the gnashing of teeth and the cursing of my southern weakness.

'The left? The left?! What?! Traverse off the line? Never, Bullock – the line is up the crack!'

It's been barely 45 minutes since Nick left the belay – launching with conviction into the gnashing teeth of an unknown E2 granite offwidth. When he'd stepped left off our perch, I'd given him up as night-fodder. There are some things well suited to night climbing and this impending rounded granite horror most certainly wasn't one of them. But miraculously he was up. No swearing, no dangling on ropes, no falling and no fuss. Just business as usual – another cold day at the office. As the rope came tight the arms are whirled about frantically, desperately try to flush some blood into frozen, numbed fingers. Can it really be as easy as Nick just made it look?

Unfortunately not. There are perhaps two or three good hooks in ten or more metres of climbing. In between is flared crack. There is little offering purchase for skating crampons, and, with arms buried in the crack, in any case it's impossible to look down. It's a grovelling, unwieldy and exhausting process that spits a tired body into the final niche on **The Link Direct**.

Reaching my van at 10.20 p.m., we shake hands before I head out among the hares once more across the moonlit moors. Then, finally, 22 hours since waking, I lie in my van outside the hut and wrap my sleeping bag around me. The moon shines just the same in Roy Bridge as it does on Lochnagar – bright and full. But the memories I have in my head shine brighter still.

Andy Inglis on *Black Spout Wall* (E3).
Photo: *Adrian Crofton.*

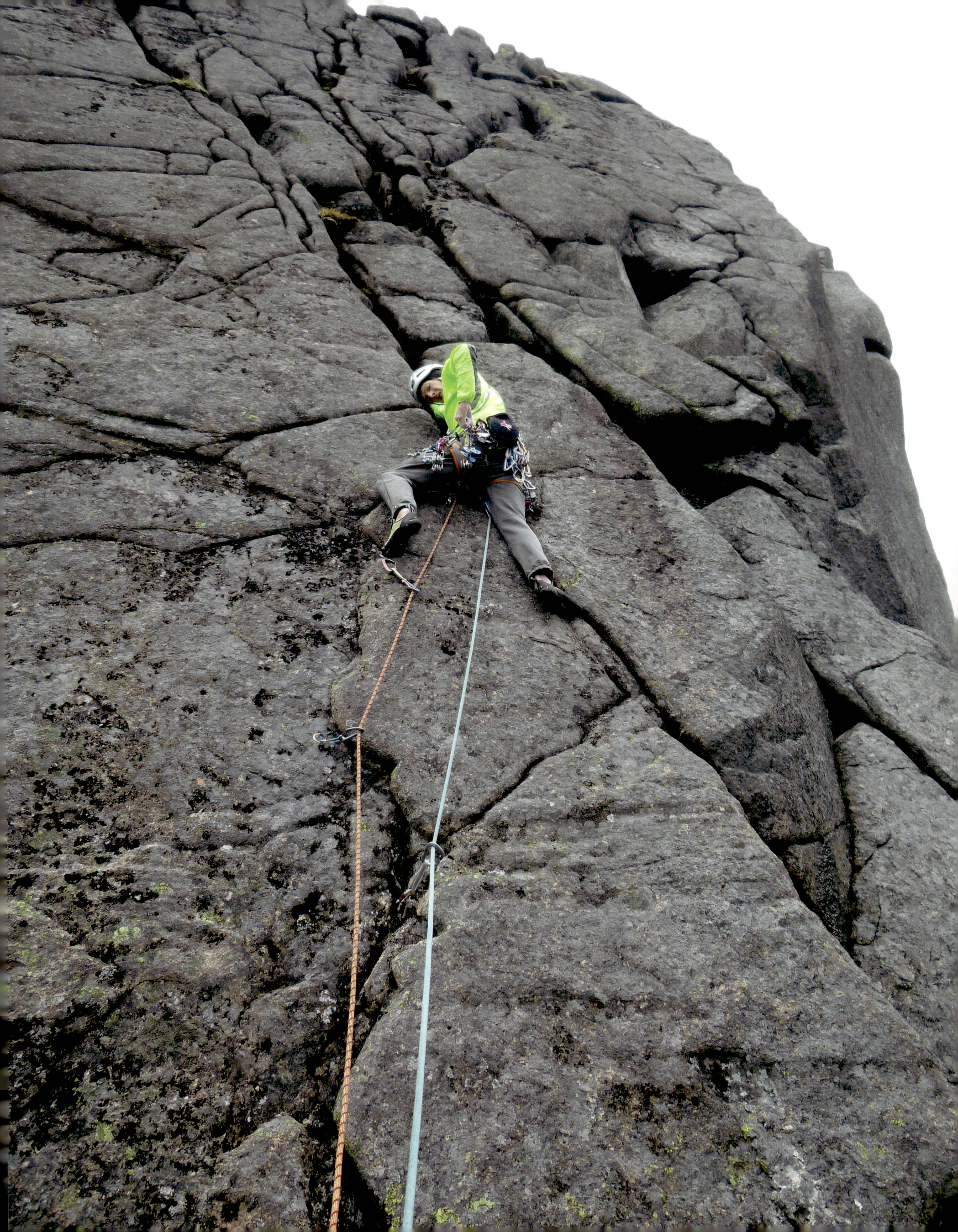

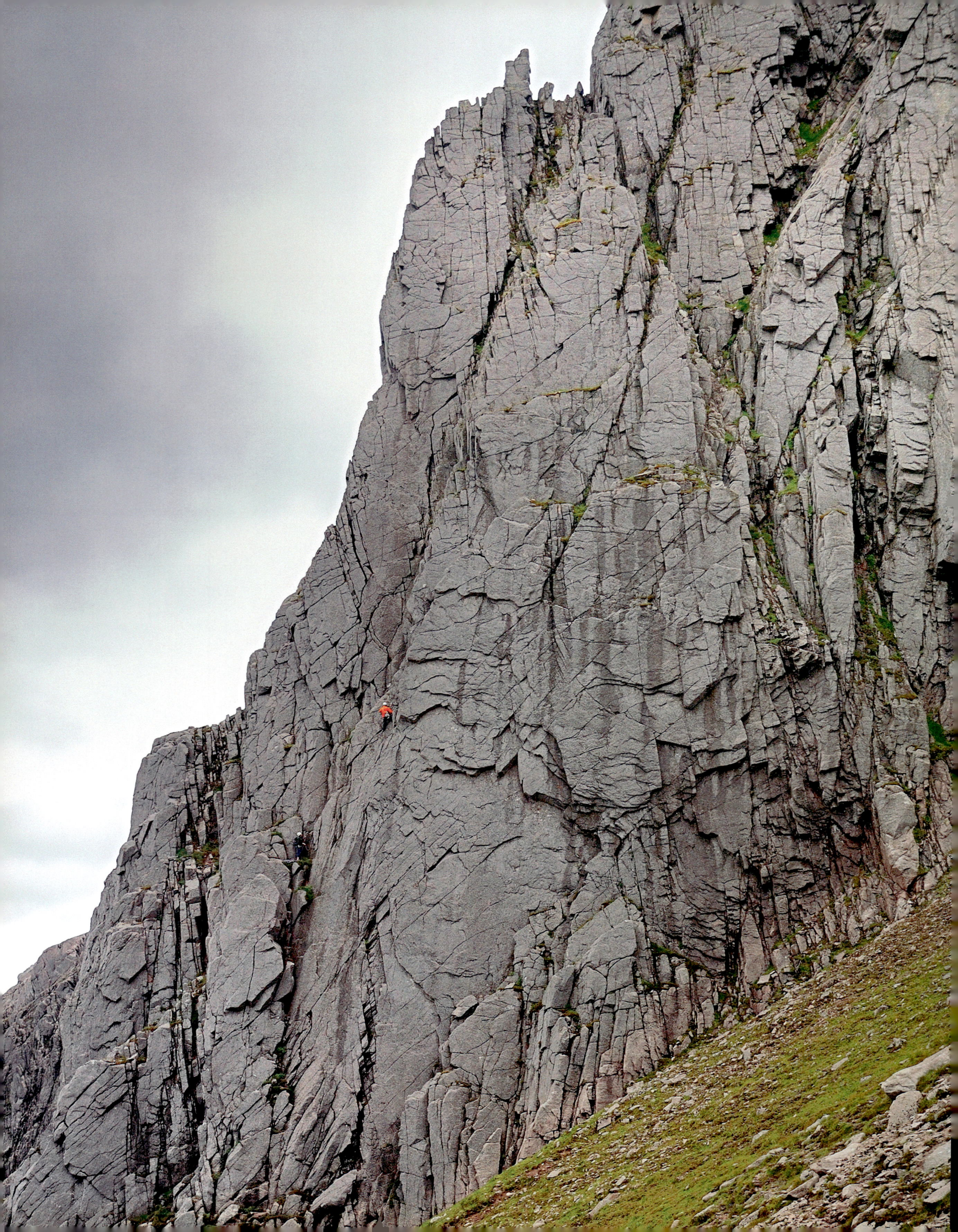

Mitre Ridge West Face, Beinn a' Bhùird – *by Adrian Crofton*

THE PLACE

Garbh Choire has always been a byword for solitude, the epitome of the Cairngormer's Long Walk-In. Beinn a' Bhùird, the great Table Mountain, is part of a vast high plateau above Upper Deeside, and carved into its eastern and northern sides are some beautiful coires. Coire an Dubh Lochain with the elegant Dividing Buttress and its eponymous black lochain is perhaps the loveliest, but Garbh Choire is the grandest and has the most spectacular rock scenery. To approach from the north up the Slochd from the River Avon is to experience an unfolding geological drama.

The glen becomes steadily more narrow and steep-walled as it curves round the northern haunches of the mountain to reveal the Mitre Ridge, the grand finale tucked away in a deep recess of the mountain. I have been accompanied here at different times by snow buntings, dotterel, and, of course, ptarmigan and eagles as well as arctic hares. I have stayed under boulders here, bivied out on the bare plateau, camped in the 'Fairy Glen' and dossed in the many howffs. To ski across this plateau in midwinter under a vast blue sky is to be transported to somewhere ethereal and timeless. Yet, whether on foot or ski or bike, you always return tired, and the last few miles along the track through Invercauld or back to Cock Bridge always feel very, very long.

THE CLIFF

Warmed by the evening sun the clean lines of the west face suggest the architecture of medieval cathedrals with their flying buttresses, towers, arches and deep recesses. An arc of snow lies at its foot till late in the season most years, sometimes there is a small bergschrund to be crossed. There is something for everyone here, with classic routes from Severe to E5, and in winter, from grades II to IX. Even so, I have always been fortunate enough never to have shared the crag with another party.

The standard winter ridge route starts round on the nose of the cliff, but the first climb we come to on the west face is the long *Fundamentalist* starting up the hand crack left of the *Cumming-Crofton* and continuing by a number of exciting exposed pitches up the left arête of the face. The *Cumming-Crofton* takes the big right-slanting corner fault all the way to the col between the first and second towers. Right again is a large wall topped by an obvious ledge — where a convenient abseil can be arranged from a thread on the left — sporting four long quality pitches from E1 to E5.

The dirty great fault of *Ghurka* is an obvious winter challenge, and marks a change in aspect as the cliff tucks in closer to the coire wall. This section is steeper and full of roofs and overlaps, a number of strong lines sprouting out from a common access route at a tapering base — *Chindit, Slochd Wall, Freebird* and *The Primate*. *Northwest Gully* bounds the face on the right — a good easy winter line through tremendous scenery.

THE CLIMBING

The routes follow strong lines, often with good cracks. The climbing is quite different to the granite on Creag an Dubh Loch. Here is a rougher, grey rock with more frequent positive face holds than you would normally expect on granite. The hard routes are concentrated in the centre of the wall while the flanks hold longer, often very varied routes at more amenable grades. The angle is generally just less than vertical, so the climbing, while less on the feet than Creag an Dubh Loch, is not overly strenuous. That said, all routes have steeper sections where a degree of power is required.

Most of the routes here remain undeservedly little known, however, the *Cumming-Crofton* quickly became a great summer classic, and, in 1977, courtesy of Greg Strange and Dick Renshaw, a winter testpiece also. With its size and striking appearance and the quality of the climbing, outsiders have come to climb the classic routes of Mitre Ridge, but the long drive and walk-in has ensured that pioneering has remained in the hands of the locals. There are still good lines to be climbed.

◄ Henning Wackerhage and Adam Henly on *The Cumming-Crofton* (Severe). Photo: *Henning Wackerhage Collection*.

▲ Pete Benson on the first winter ascent of *Slochd Wall* (IX,9). Photo: *Guy Robertson*.

THE ROUTES

The Cumming-Crofton (Severe, VI,6)
Whatever the time of year this gives a fine, satisfying and sustained climb of at least five pitches. The ramp is usually the crux, though the chimney at the start can give pause for thought.

Spear of Destiny (E5)
Bold, intricate, steep slab climbing and then a haven before the spear point and the final pumping head wall – a very big pitch.

Slochd Wall (HVS, IX,9)
Three clean pitches that will test the leader at the grade, with some technical and some run-out sections.

Freebird (E4)
A good pitch is followed by a great pitch – a clean hanging arête with just enough cracks and face holds. Best climbed in the glow of the evening sun.

THE STORY
What is the draw of this place, all grit and ice and heather? Why do I keep coming back?

Beinn a' Bhuird is near enough on my doorstep. Before we owned cars we used to hitch there, or get the bus from Union Street, bristling with ice axes, clumping through town in our plastic boots. Sometimes Guy's mother, Kathleen, would fetch and drop us, waiting with a flask of broth at Keiloch for us to return safely from the hill. The mountain was a wilderness, an arena of freedom and adventure. We never saw anyone else there, it was our secret, the fruit of our explorations. Dawns would break over the eastern skyline beyond Lochnagar, beautiful and furious, and darkness would return after a day spent climbing in the coires, often enough with snow borne on a rampaging gale across the blasted plateau. Very soon it seemed impossible to resist its draw.

I dubbed it The Coming Often Route. I have been into the coire many times, often succeeding, but almost as often not. Rain, unseasonal snow, loss of nerve, fatigue, lack of time; all of these things have at various times thwarted plans. Steadily, however, I climbed most of the routes on this face, but always in the back of my mind was the winter ascent of the *Cumming-Crofton*. I no longer climb many routes in winter, having drifted off into ski touring and cycling:

▲ Mitre Ridge of Beinn a' Bhùird with the West Face catching the sun. Photo: *Colin Threlfall.*

hard winter mountaineering requires a certain singularity of purpose that can be difficult to attain in an otherwise busy life. But this year I was nonetheless fit, and had kept an eye on conditions. Snow had been blowing round the hills for weeks, then there had been a dramatic brief thaw to above the summits, before stable high pressure had brought in cold, calmer weather. I knew that the approach would be on hard snow, there would be plenty of material on the cliff, and the overheads would be reasonable. It was time to do the route. The expedition as a whole I knew would be fairly testing for me, but I felt I had to try now. I had a free day midweek, I just needed a partner. As is often the case, the eternal wheel of off-shore rotas — four on/four off — delivered a partner just at the right moment, but for Richard Biggar too this expedition would be 'off the couch'. He chewed over the proposition on the other end of the line, laughed and said 'why not?' If a grand adventure was what we sought, then he'd be hard pressed to think of a better one.

Moonlight melted into the predawn as we passed the Clachan. At the granite teeth where the Sneck falls into Garbh Choire we donned crampons. The sun lit up the snows of Ben Rinnes beyond. We descended the steep coire wall on perfect neve, crossing old avalanche tracks, and traversed towards the base of the ridge, where a double crescent of snow curved round to the west face. The usual business ensued — tighten boots, rearrange clothing, eat, drink, sort the rack, uncoil ropes. And the route? A white line through grey rock — mostly the cracks were clear. Encouraged, I set off.

The first pitch is all about the chimney. A boulder the height of a man is embedded in it and protrudes outwards. I pondered and looked and looked and pondered; tried this and that. It was clear that the only option was the left-hand crack. This had formed a ribbon of ice only a few inches wide and I needed to get round the bulging arête with my feet in under me to reach it. I placed a pick, weighted it — carefully, smoothly. I wedged my shoulder against the smooth wall of the gully in an attempt to reduce the weight on the picks, stubbing my left front-point into the vertical smear of ice below the crack. Transferring my weight out of the groove I was committed: everything depended on the state of the ice in that crack. Locking off on the bottom pick, the foot now scrabbling unsuccessfully to punch its front-point into the narrrow ribbon, right foot high on the right wall, still trying to minimise the weight on the pick. I reached high and — *thungk*. Solid. At the belay I was a happy man. Joining me, Richard eyed the ramp ahead nervously.

▲ A view of Mitre Ridge in profile. Photo: *Colin Threlfall*.

There's gear I reassured him, pointing out the cracks – here to there, to there, to there, voila! He hadn't led anything in winter for years, but he looked like he knew what he was doing, moving up and right and then making that committing rockover back left on to the slab above, picks in fairy dust, his entire weight on the left foot on a sloping ledge. All done – just like that.

My turn again, starting up the long sustained groove. Just four metres up, reaching high to a crack, and, just as the axe tip hooked it, my feet came away from their poor ice smears. But the hook was a sinker – the only one on the pitch – and I held it. The rest was pure Cairngorm mixed joy; the left foot moving from ripple to crack, the left pick clearing and torquing cracks, the right pick making the most of the snow and ice in the groove, the right foot likewise smearing and front-pointing. Up, steadily up. At a big snowy ledge I contrived an adequate belay and brought Richard up. I was delighted with the climbing and at having done the pitch, but was starting to feel it. I ate and donned the belay jacket, but it was still very cold. The quality of the snow and ice had changed noticeably and there now seemed to be lots more loose sugary stuff and none of the good chewy ice about. The rope inched out slowly, very slowly. More and more snow poured down the route in Richard's wake as he cleared and looked and looked and cleared. I began to shiver. After a very long time I shouted up:

'How's it looking Big Fella?'

'You'll see. We're making steady progress.'

Still I got colder. I made a mental note to make some changes to my wardrobe next time I came out. Best put that in the diary for 2016 then. The torrent of snow continued as the rope occasionally inched out. I had thought this section would be just some tricky steps with easier solid snow between. That's what I had told him anyway.

Eventually the rope started to feed out more quickly and the call came down – 'safe!' When I began to move again it was like wakening after an anaesthetic. Groggy. Stiff. This is starting to feel hard, too hard, I thought, as I saw the reason for the delay. Good usable snow was in short supply and the way forward had to be cleared from under deep snow. There was a lot of technical climbing on this pitch without real respite – not what we had reckoned on. When I reached the belay we were both knackered. Head torches were donned for it was now heading towards dark.

Frankly, I hadn't thought too much about the second tower. On previous occasions I had finished by each of two routes – *Bell's Variation*, and a shorter but brutal central crack. I had planned to take the former this time, but I'd also planned to be here in daylight. I quickly climbed the final 15 metres to the col, where I switched on the head torch. I stood up on the gendarme and inspected the slab before me.

The entire second tower seemed to be encased in verglas then frosted in hoar. The wind had got up, mist and light snow blew about. I hesitated. I had pictured this pitch much like the rest of the route, but it was clearly going to be much more work. I placed my picks in the snow on the slab, hoping they would bite in the verglas beneath, took a deep breath and pulled my weight quickly over the impending wall and rocked over onto the slab. I had no protection at this point, but figured that once up to the foot of the crack I would get something. I stepped up and began to scrape and clear. The entire crack was glued with translucent ice. So I spent some time looking patiently to the left and to the right. Time was pressing, I knew friends were expecting me for dinner in Inverurie, but by now we'd not be home before midnight. I looked and looked.

It is daft to talk about fairness in these situations, but I was certainly disappointed. I now had to think what to do. My mind felt overloaded – I started to find it difficult to think clearly. I was aware enough though to recognise that I was hypoglycaemic. I suddenly felt the situation we were in, and realised that a long way from the road I could not afford to let things get serious. I needed a plan and I needed sugar. What was the safest way off this cliff? Turn back so close to the top? Perhaps fitter and with more mileage under our belts we would have battled on, but really we were chancing our arm as it was. I managed back down to Richard, and two 60-metre abseils later we were able to climb down to the foot of the route again.

Re-climbing the slope to the Sneck we looked behind. Moonlight filled the coire, and the cloud blowing off the plateau billowed and dissolved in brilliant luminescence, its shadow stark as monochrome, Mitre Ridge a flashing blade, stars punctuating the indigo night. We watched for a while, resting our burning calf muscles, more than satisfied in spite of our failure. All this beauty, this solitude: that was why we had risen early to walk through the cold and dark. Our bodies felt hard used, but our senses were preternaturally alive to the world.

The howff eventually welcomed us back. We crawled through the low door and revived ourselves with strong coffee in the candlelight, glad of its shelter, glad to have come full circle, empty-handed recipients of a precious gift. ●

Top: Robbie Miller at the top of Mitre Ridge. Photo: *Henning Wackerhage.*
Bottom: Graeme Tyldesley at the first belay on *Freebird* (E4).
Photo: *Adrian Crofton.*

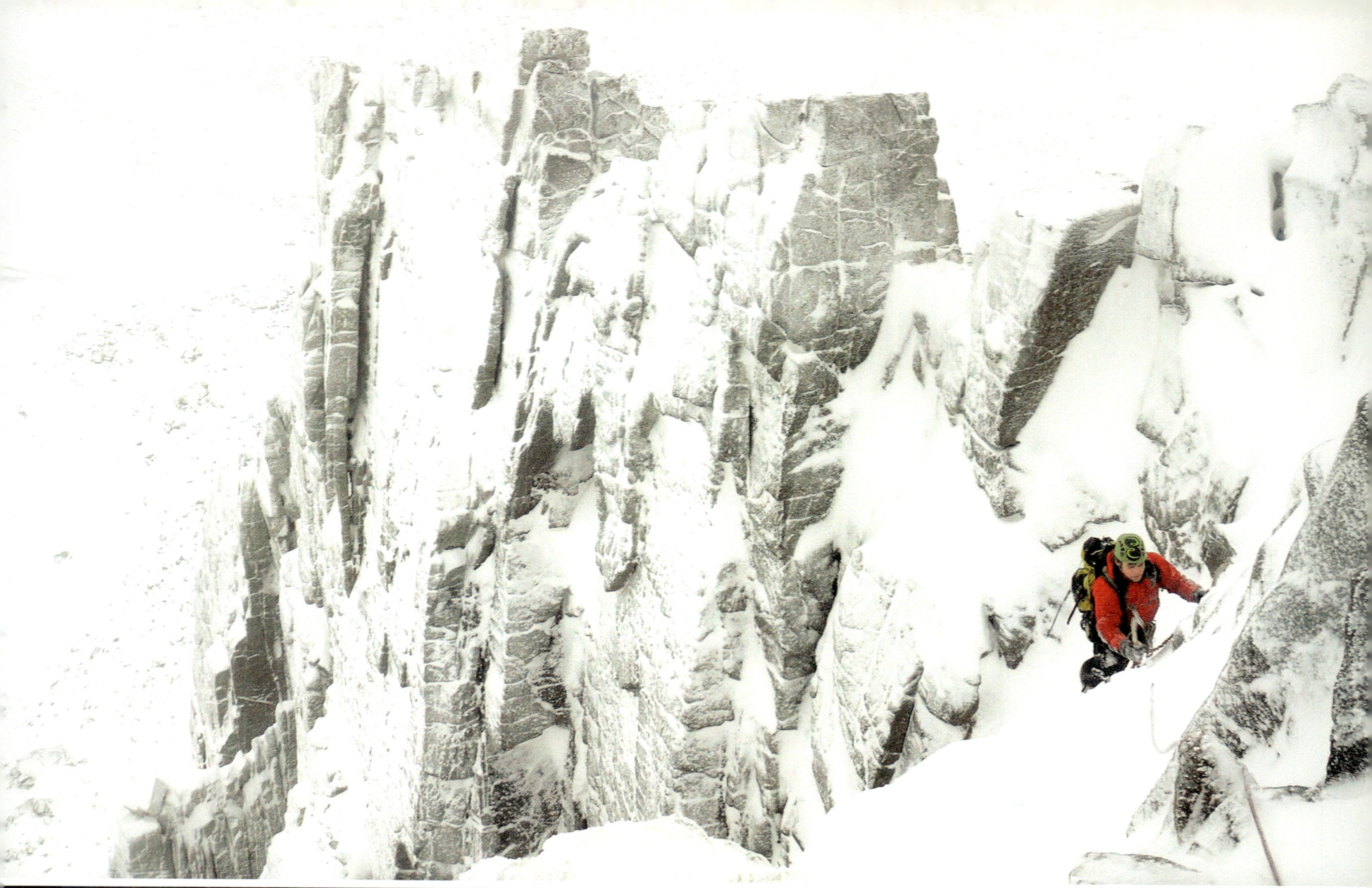

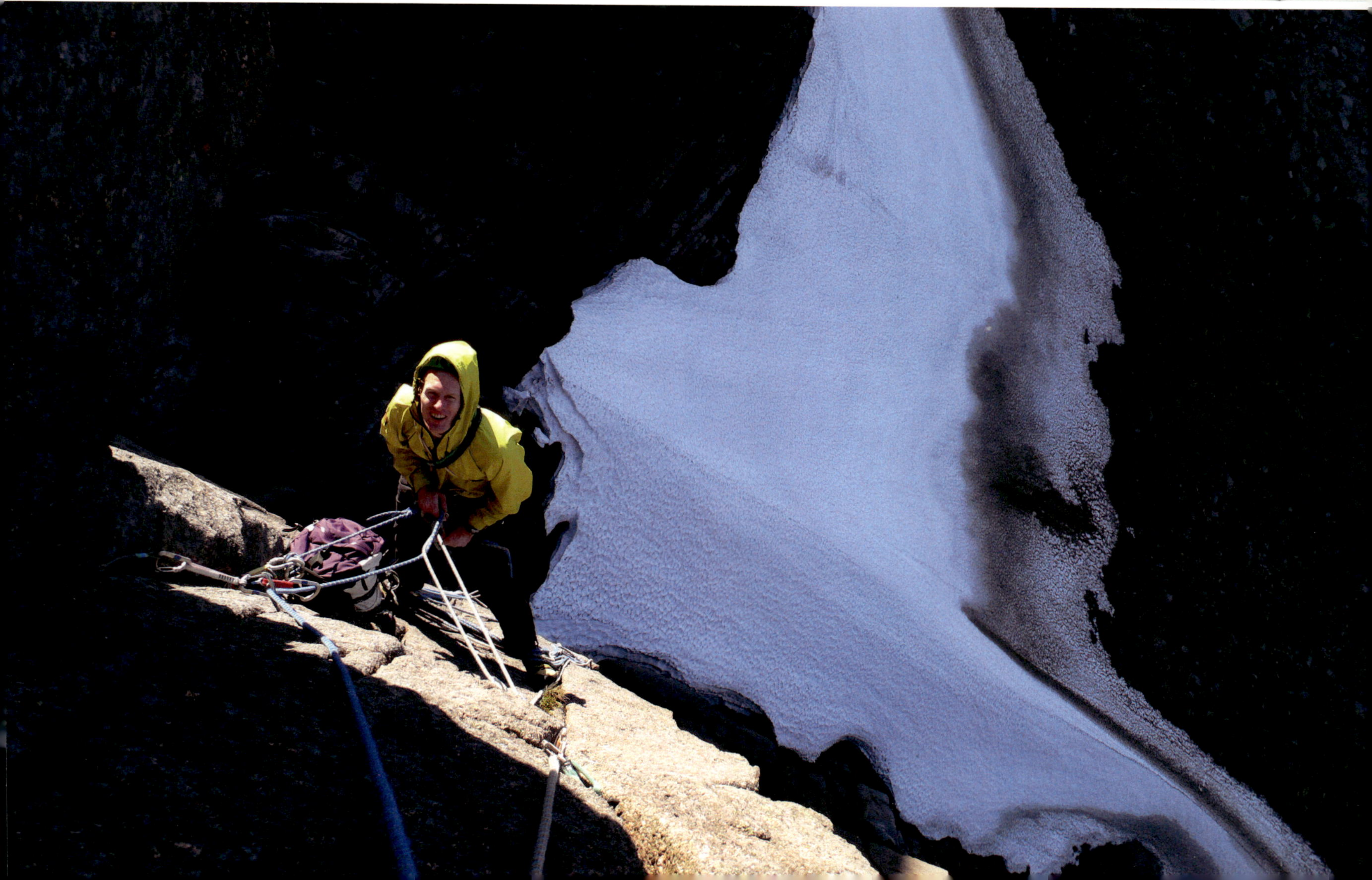

Henning Wackerhage on *The Cumming-Crofton* (VI,6) in winter.
Photo: *Henning Wackerhage Collection*.

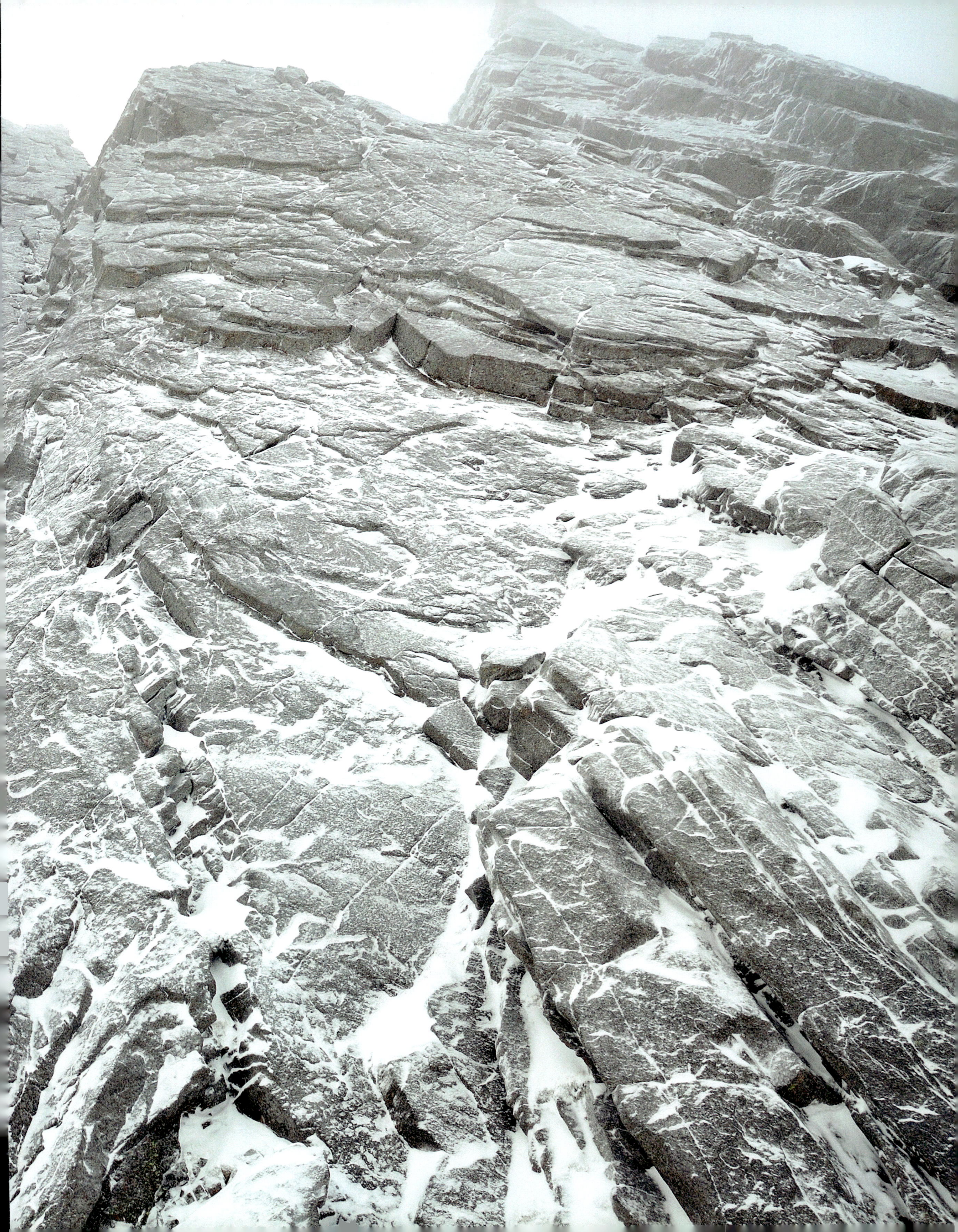

FURTHER READING

Climbing Guidebooks

Scottish Rock Climbs, Compiled by Andy Nisbet
(Scottish Mountaineering Council, 2005).
ISBN: 9780907521860.

Scottish Winter Climbs, Compiled by Andy Nisbet,
Rab Anderson & Simon Richardson
(Scottish Mountaineering Council, 2008).
ISBN: 9780907521983.

Scottish Rock Volume One – South, Gary Latter
(Pesda Press, 2008).
ISBN: 9781906095062.

Scottish Rock Volume Two – North, Gary Latter
(Pesda Press, 2009).
ISBN: 9781906095079.

Highland Outcrops, Kevin Howett
(Scottish Mountaineering Council, 2001).
ISBN: 9780907521549.

Glen Coe, Rab Anderson, Ken Crocket & Dave Cuthbertson
(Scottish Mountaineering Council, 2001).
ISBN: 9780907521709.

Ben Nevis, Simon Richardson
(Scottish Mountaineering Council, 2002).
ISBN: 9780907521730.

Northern Highlands South, Edited by Andy Nisbet
(Scottish Mountaineering Council, 2007).
ISBN: 9780907521976.

Northern Highlands Central, Edited by Andy Nisbet
(Scottish Mountaineering Council, 2006).
ISBN: 9780907521891.

Northern Highlands North, Edited by Andy Nisbet
(Scottish Mountaineering Council, 2006).
ISBN: 9780907521808.

Skye – The Cuillin, Mike Lates
(Scottish Mountaineering Council, 2011).
ISBN: 9781907233135.

Inner Hebrides & Arran, Colin Moody & Graham Little
(Scottish Mountaineering Council, 2014).
ISBN: 9781907233173.

Outer Hebrides, Rab Anderson & Kev Howett
(Scottish Mountaineering Council, in production at time of writing).
ISBN: 9781907233180.

The Cairngorms, Andy Nisbet, Allen Fyffe, John Lyall,
Simon Richardson & Wilson Moir.
(Scottish Mountaineering Council, 2007).
ISBN: 9780907521969.

Scrambling Guidebooks

Skye Scrambles, Noel Williams
(Scottish Mountaineering Council, 2011).
ISBN: 9780907521990.

Highland Scrambles North, Iain Thow
(Scottish Mountaineering Council, 2006).
ISBN: 9780907521884.

Other Titles

Cold Climbs, Compiled by Ken Wilson, Dave Alcock & John Barry.
(Bâton Wicks Publications, 1995).
ISBN: 9780906371169.

Classic Rock, Compiled by Ken Wilson.
(Bâton Wicks Publications, 2007).
ISBN: 9781898573708.